Russian and Eurasian Politics

A Comparative Approach

Mark A. Cichock

University of Texas at Arlington

Longman

New York   San Francisco   Boston
London   Toronto   Sydney   Tokyo   Singapore   Madrid
Mexico City   Munich   Paris   Cape Town   Hong Kong   Montreal

For Tracey, Lauren, Caroline, and Rebecca
with all my love.

Vice President/Publisher: Priscilla McGeehon
Executive Editor: Eric Stano
Senior Marketing Manager: Megan Galvin-Fak
Production Manager: Denise Phillip
Project Coordination, Text Design, and Page Makeup: WestWords, Inc.
Cover Designer/Manager: Wendy Ann Fredericks
Cover Illustration: Dream Maker Software
Photo Researcher: Photosearch, Inc.
Manufacturing Buyer: Lucy Hebard
Printer and Binder: Courier Corporation
Cover Printer: Coral Graphics

Library of Congress Cataloging-in-Publication Data

Cichock, Mark A.
    Russian and Eurasian politics : a comparative approach / Mark A. Cichock
        p. cm.
    Includes bibliographical references and index.
    ISBN 0-205-18945-8
        1. Russia (Federation)—Politics and government—1991–2. Former Soviet
    republics—Politics and government. 3. Russia (Federation—Relations—Former
    Soviet republics. 4. Former Soviet republics—Relations—Russian (Federation) I. Title.

    DK510.763 .C53 2002
    320.3'0947–dc21

                                                                        2002034013

Please visit our website at *http://www.ablongman.com*

ISBN 0-205-18945-8

1 2 3 4 5 6 7 8 9 10—CRS—05   04   03   02

Brief Contents

Detailed Contents

Chapter 3

The Communist Party and its Legacy 39

Part 2 The Russian System in Transition

Chapter 4

Emerging Pluralism 60

Chapter 13

Conclusions   273

Preface

The name of this book implies something of a controversy, that is, Russia and the Eurasian states remain closely connected to each other more than a decade past the Soviet period. Political, cultural, and economic independence has not set aside the reality that within the former Soviet space, the Russian Federation still plays a dominant role. A point of some concern for the Baltic states, Georgia, or Ukraine, it is for other lands such as Belarus, Armenia, or Kazakstan a warm embrace that seems to promise a measure of deliverance from their own developmental troubles. In all respects the Russian connection emboldens us to compare the similar as well as the disparate. Logic might dictate that Azerbaijan, Uzbekistan, and Turkmenistan are economically and politically much more akin today to Turkey or Iran than to the Russian Federation, or that the Baltic states more accurately (as they themselves claim) belong to west European traditions. But the Russian connection is a real one, and for the political future the connection must be recognized. It is the major conditioning factor for post-Soviet studies which supercedes differences in race, ethnicity, culture, and economic development.

Today many analysts of Russia and Eurasia take the analytical approach of evaluating these states according to their transitions to democracy, that is, how far and how fast are state structures and actors going to move from totalitarian political and economic organization toward democracy and political pluralism. On the surface this seems a reasonable, evaluative approach. But beneath the outward appearances of the political system lie a host of factors which threaten to derail these simplistic world views. The political and economic processes that characterized the former Soviet space have given way to a complicated series of calculations and categorizations which may leave you scratching your head and wondering how to make sense out of such a mess. As chaotic and seemingly improbable as this may be, it makes the challenge of Russian and Eurasian politics that much more interesting.

There are a number of enduring questions concerning the political futures of these states, most often defined in terms of ideologies such as communism, democracy, or nationalism; or the economic and political structuring of institutions. How political actors formulate their identities when they move from one form of governance to another is also of particular importance. We must ask ourselves whether it still makes sense to consider Russia and the other fourteen Eurasian states within the context of a single analytical, or even geographic scheme. If we do, is there, then, a rational, uniform, and simple method by which we may proceed?

This text takes a comparative approach to the study of these "successor" systems. The comparative assumption holds that institutions, personalities, and cultures bear traits that may be cross-nationally analyzed. Historic origins and elements of structure are integrated with theories which try to explain participation and political organization. The essence of the book lies in the similarities, dissimilarities, and points in between that characterize Russia and the Eurasian states. Five countries draw our attention: the Russian Federation, both the point of continuity and of departure from all that was Soviet; and Latvia, Ukraine, Georgia, and Uzbekistan, each chosen as the most typical or common examples of the "regions" they occupy in the post-Soviet space. All maintain specific relationships with Russia, their own immediate neighbors, and distinct national pasts. These countries and their peoples are all fascinating in their own rights and virtually unstudied outside of specialty texts. Just as important, they demonstrate what became of an important element of the Soviet legacy, and what has taken shape within that context.

Layout of the Text

The text is organized as follows: The first segment presents the method of analysis (Chapter One), some of the major factors affecting Russian and Eurasian politics, including historic and social environments (Chapter Two), and the rise and fall of communism and the Communist Party of the Soviet Union (Chapter Three). From this point the text goes on to analyze more specifically the Russian political experience especially the institutions, actors, and movements of current Russian politics. Chapter Four presents the case for an evolving process of pluralism as measured through developing political parties and the media. Chapter Five focuses on institutionalized decision making and the conflict between the presidency and the parliament, while Chapter Six details the workings of the government, police, military, and the courts. Chapter Seven then takes the discussion beyond the confines of Moscow to examine the federal structure of Russian power and the issues before Russia's regions. Chapter Eight provides a summation of the economy including the dominant role of the state that still maintains a presence, the planning mechanisms, budgetary procedures and constraints, and the direction of reform.

Chapters Nine through Twelve evaluate the new states of Eurasia, what used to be referred to as the former Soviet republics. Individual case studies of the four "regions" contiguous to Russia are drawn upon: the Baltic states, the western states, the states of the Caucasus, and the Central Asian states. Explicit comparisons to the Russian experience are exhibited throughout these chapters to determine just how far each state has traveled on the road of transitionalism.

As this book is primarily directed at the student, I have tried to keep the material as accessible as possible. With this in mind I have relied heavily on sources in English which are readily available for the student to discover. It seems to me that there is little point in directing students who are not conversant in another language to use material in that language. This is not an argument against our students studying Russian, Latvian, or Georgian, but simply a recognition that many schools (such as my own) have few resources available in foreign languages so we make do with what we have. Increasingly the Internet has made accessible Russian-language newspapers which are not translated into English. Hopefully, this will serve as an enticement for us to learn more from these sources, and generally broaden our comparative understanding of the world.

Each chapter also concludes with a brief selection of books dealing with that subject. These are, I believe, all very good examples of scholarship or personal observances relating to politics in Russia and the Eurasian states, and may serve as sound bases for the student's entry into this field. Specific "Questions for Consideration" and "Useful Websites" are also provided for each chapter. Although the Internet has yet to prove itself equal to the depth that is found in most printed volumes, it is much more up-to-date than almost any book. The "Net" excites our students' interests in ways that monochromatic textbooks with stale discussions of specifics often cannot.

For all the "recovering Sovietologists" (a term used by a reviewer of this text) who have been looking for insight and direction I hope that this text provides some relief. It is an effort to go beyond bridging the gap between what was and what is, and instead focus on what has emerged. It's not been an easy task to become so immersed in areas that were long-neglected within Soviet studies, but it's been more fun and illuminating than any intellectual experience I've ever had. If the information gathered here sheds any new light or at least provides for some solid argumentation I will be happy with the achievement.

For the financial and institutional support that I received from the University of Texas at Austin's Center for Russian, East European, and Eurasian Studies, and especially its directors Michael Katz and Joan Neuberger, and staff members Glenn Mack, Brett Westbrook, and Faedah Totah my sincere thanks. I would also like to thank the editorial staff at Longman especially Eric Stano and Brian Van Buren, and Jami Darby at WestWords for their professionalism and kind support. To my students Trinette Robichaux and Mary Durio and especially Rebecca Kane who all provided much appreciated help and brought to light many of my mistakes. For all of my students at the University of Texas at Arlington, thank you for the inspiration. Special thanks go to the reviewers of this manuscript who helped guide its shape: William Crowther, University of North Carolina, Greensboro; Walter D. Connor, Boston University; Dale Herspring, Kansas State University; Patrice McMahon, University of Nebraska—Lincoln; Darrell Slider, University of South Florida; B. Thomas Trout, University of New Hampshire; Chris Van Aller, Winthrop University; and Sharon Wolchik, The George Washington University. And finally, for my wife Tracey (who helped with many of the graphics) and lovely children Lauren, Caroline, and Rebecca—once again you have my attention. Thank you for the love and understanding.

Mark A. Cichock
Arlington, TX

Chapter 1

Russia and Eurasia: The Path of Comparison

In late 1991 a political revolution took place in the Soviet Union that amazed and confounded the world: a superpower, a state of immense proportions and military might disintegrated. The world at large was not prepared for this, nor were the citizens of one of the most dominating and influential state systems ever known to humankind. Over the course of the next decade political analysts, journalists, statesmen, and ordinary citizens struggled to grasp the concept of successor states and the best means to analyze them. The results have been uneven and our understandings, if not our actual knowledge of what transpired, remains incomplete.

Since 1991 a striking number of new leaders and political elites have appeared on the political scene, institutions have come and gone, military conflicts have threatened to tear apart the social fabric, and sweeping economic changes have pushed populations in directions many of them had no wish to experience. Even after all of this turbulence the balance sheet of positive and negative changes has yet to be added up, but the uncertainty of Russian and Eurasian politics remains a topic of great excitement and interest. Still, a thread of constancy does runs through the confusion, and that is the peoples of the post-Soviet successor states. The historical and cultural patterns of these populations predate both the years of Soviet power and the instability of postindependence politics. Whatever Russia and the Eurasian states become they will be greatly indebted to all that the people are, and have been through.

Today no one, definitive model guides the successors of the Soviet state. In the place of the Soviet system now stand fifteen diverse political systems, some having chosen western-style parliamentary and free market economic systems, others more vaguely defined, quasi-authoritarian concepts of governance, and still others struggle for their very identity and survival in the midst of intense civil strife. The dizzying pace of political, social, and economic change have also caused us as analysts to question the assumptions upon which much of our inquiry had formerly been based. The task of analysis goes beyond the prediction of events to the search for a method that makes sense of a constantly changing world. The point of this

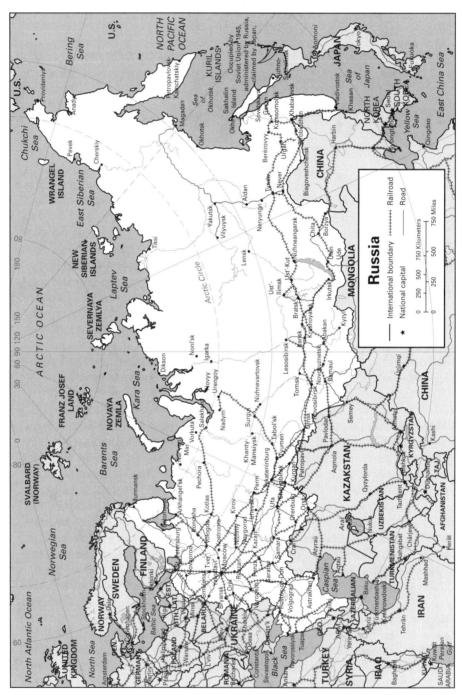

Map 1.1 Russia

book is, in fact, to plant Russian and Eurasian studies solidly within a comparative mode of inquiry that can be used in relation to other regions of the world.

The Environment of Post-Soviet Studies

For the new student of Russian and Eurasian studies, the perceptions of the past, the ideological battles of policy makers and analysts, and the limitations of information that characterized what used to be called *Soviet studies* may seem only vaguely relevant. If you took the time to survey the massive amount of analysis of just the past forty years you might be excused for concluding that analysts of the Soviet Union spent more time arguing than they did trying to reach consensus on such big issues as the "nature" of Soviet politics, economics, or society. The methodology—the means of inquiry that govern a scholarly pursuit—was as diverse as the Soviet Union itself, and just as difficult to characterize.

In comparison to other areas of inquiry, Soviet studies was filled with strong subjective and ideological biases. Almost from its point of origin it was heavily influenced by political concerns and especially throughout the Cold War. In the forum of Soviet analysts were an assortment of emigre scholars (fleeing or expelled from communist states), behavioral-oriented social scientists, ideologues of all shades (liberals, moderates, conservatives), journalists, and policymakers. Detached, objective analysis may have been the goal of many but the realities of politics frequently intruded upon, and often distorted, viewpoints.

In the waning years of the Soviet era however, a new political revolution took place which changed the direction of analysis. This revolution, precipitated by the dramatic changes occurring within the Soviet state, provided Soviet studies with vast quantities of information, access to sources, and insights long thought impossible to achieve. Beginning in 1985 with the reform initiatives of **Mikhail Gorbachev** the effects of the new Soviet revolution reverberated well beyond the borders of the Soviet state. Grudgingly at first, and then with a rapidity and frequency that was startling, the Soviet system began to change. With these changes came an unparalleled excitement and renewed interest in Soviet politics, economics, and society, and later in similar studies concerning Russia and Eurasia.

Keeping pace with the changes has proved to be an immense methodological challenge. Soviet studies was always accorded its own unique place within comparative politics, and for years (and to some extent even now) the study of Russia was thought of as *sui generis* (Latin for "of its own kind"), that is, a field not bound by the same rigorous techniques of the parent field of inquiry, although still claiming to be related to the general discipline. From the 1940s to the 1960s studying the Soviet Union was not generally taken to mean empirical inquiry, the checking and rechecking of sources, or controlling data for intrusive, subjective biases such as political or personal motivations. Notable exceptions were to be found in the works of scholars such as Merle Fainsod[1] and Alex Inkeles,[2] but by the late 1960s Soviet studies as an organized field of inquiry had lagged considerably behind other subfields of political science. Subjective assessments of the

Soviet Union wielded a much greater influence than most analysts were willing to admit.

By the last two decades of the Soviet Union a firm analytical foundation had taken shape focusing on theories, systematic analysis, and case studies.[3] Studies of the Soviet economy were the most sophisticated of these with some based on historical development,[4] and others on system theory and maintenance.[5] The discipline of sociology also produced extensive theories on the specifics of Soviet society.[6] All of this was fueled by the virtual flood of information made available by the Soviet Union's own internal dynamics. The values and principles of the communist system were drastically altered including the desire of many of the peoples of the Soviet system to remain part of a supranational state. What had begun as an elite effort to reform the practice of Soviet politics increasingly included larger elements of the entire Soviet society.

One of the most significant political changes involved the Communist Party of the Soviet Union's (CPSU) decision to allow competition, first within itself and later from other social forces. On 7 February 1990 Soviet politics were irreversibly altered when the CPSU relinquished its monopoly on political life. While the party did not explicitly reject Lenin's organizational code of democratic centralism which prohibited factions or alternative political groupings (more on this in Chapter Three) this code could not coexist with Gorbachev's own concept of *demokratizatsia* (democratization).

In the last year of the Soviet Union's existence the party-dominated system was no longer capable or desirous of setting the needed agenda for change. New political dynamics including the creation of citizen-action groups and elections were increasingly characteristic of the system. With little more than a curt nod to the concept of pluralism which was already underway the Soviet leaders unchained a latent participatory impulse within their peoples. For the communist system it proved to be a fatal error.

Mikhail Gorbachev and his program of *perestroika* riveted world attention upon the Soviet Union in ways that were entirely at odds with the old, Cold War adversarial perspective. British political scientist Stephen White succinctly summed up the Gorbachev phenomenon in this way: "The Soviet Union was suddenly under the control of a youthful and imaginative General Secretary with a personable wife by his side."[7] Political analysts of the Soviet system struggled to get the definitive word in on Gorbachev by either extolling his virtues or condemning him as a wolf in sheep's clothing. In all contexts there was little said about Gorbachev that was neutral.

Gorbachev's distinctiveness within his own political environment stimulated the intellectual appetites of those who had hoped so long for change. This new breed of *Soviet* leader (as compared to **Boris Yeltsin** who must be counted as the first new *Russian* leader) represented more than just a breath of fresh air for his country. To many, Gorbachev extolled not only the virtues of reform, but the long-suppressed undercurrents of Soviet society. The resultant enthusiasm amongst American and European academics (as compared to a very guarded response by American policy makers) led some of these to sidestep disciplinary rigor and to see trends developing where none had yet taken shape (still a dilemma as we will see with regard to electoral studies). Short-term successes in predicting Soviet events failed to yield long-term explanations concerning how the Soviet system—or its Russian and Eurasian inheritors—functioned. As a result, for analysts of this area a real legacy of the Soviet period has been the inability to unite behind a particular explanatory framework.

Analyzing Post-Soviet Politics

The post-Soviet period has brought into focus a new world for Russian politics. The achievements, collapses, fissures, and reconstructions that have characterized Russian and Eurasian politics requires that we as analysts take a broad perspective encompassing many different approaches. For instance, electoral studies have demonstrated methodological advances for explaining this new aspect of modern Russian politics.[8] But the electoral process is only in its infancy in Russia, Ukraine, Moldova, and the Baltics, threatened in Armenia, Belarus, and Georgia, and possibly stillborn in Azerbaijan and Central Asia; thus our expectations from this approach must be guarded. The potential for individual case analysis, nevertheless, gives us the opportunity to construct a solid data base for the future. Consequently, in this text electoral and public opinion data are drawn upon—when available—to indicate valid, systemic change, but are only part of the story.

Since electoral studies have a useful, but limited applicability other approaches such as **elite studies** must supplement our analysis. Early elite studies of the Soviet Union were distinguished by **kremlinology,** or what Darrell Hammer termed "the analysis of protocol evidence."[9] This involved watching for changes in leadership positions or the physical appearances and proximity of leaders to each other at public functions. The underlying assumption of kremlinology was that policy was made only within the upper-most echelons of the Communist Party. This served to justify a near-exclusive focus on the leadership itself. The approach was made necessary by the secretive nature of Soviet politics of which so little was revealed to the world at large. The kremlinology process, described by one critic as a "demonic art",[10] never truly developed a methodology for its consistent application, and although it managed some explanatory successes, particularly during the Soviet power struggles of the 1950s, it rarely adequately addressed changes in Soviet society, culture, or economics.

Over the years studies of Soviet leaders and the communist party elite have consistently added to our body of knowledge. Among those may be included the work of Carl Linden on Khrushchev,[11] Valerie Bunce on leadership change,[12] or George Breslauer's demonstration of consistent patterns of leadership behavior,[13] to name but a few. Despite the limitations of the approach it retained its attraction during the *perestroika* era as observers equated virtually all levels of policy making with the actions of Gorbachev.[14] Simultaneously, a tendency toward historiography and journalistic-style analysis dominated during these years and while some of these proved quite useful,[15] leadership studies generated only marginal insights concerning the last years of Soviet power.

Elite studies also commonly failed to delineate who or what was involved in mid-range decision making. During the Soviet era republican and provincial-level policy choices were largely assumed to be derivative of national-level policy making. As always, exceptions to the rule existed such as in studies by Jerry Hough,[16] Joel C. Moses,[17] Martha Brill Olcott,[18] T. H. Rigby,[19] and Philip Stewart.[20] Citizen-oriented studies received even less attention prior to Gorbachev,[21] but the Soviet leader's rise to power provoked a substantial change, largely attributable again to the emergence of new sources of information thereby setting the stage for a re-orientation of our entire field of inquiry.

In the post-Soviet period studies of leadership in Russia and the Eurasian states have retained their importance as the individuals in power are associated with nation-building. Yeltsin, for instance, exemplified the difficulties of transitionalism and the creation of market-oriented economies. By extension his successor, **Vladimir Putin** has personified the desire within the Russian political culture for a strong authoritarian figure to save the nation from chaos (not an unfamiliar tendency in any political system). Political leaders of all stripes—nationalists, democrats, bureaucrats, or communists—have all laid claims to the political vacuums that developed as the communist party receded in influence.

Our work needs some way of explaining such diverse politicians as Eduard Shevardnadze, Yuri Luzhkov, Gennadii Zyuganov, Islam Karimov, Aleksandr Lebed, or Leonid Kuchma as well as the institutions over which they preside. Still we must be careful of adding too much "color": By focusing on Boris Yeltsin's health problems or Vladimir Putin's secret police background we run the risk of spending too much time on the inputs of politics rather than what comes out of the policy process, that is the outputs and outcomes.

Political Culture: Value and Subjectivity

This book employs a two-track approach for analyzing the Russian and Eurasian states. The first track takes into account the emerging political cultures which shape the frameworks for political action. Every political system has a unique **political culture** contributing to the determination of choices over the allocation and distribution of resources.

One of the best definitions of the concept comes from Sidney Verba who defined it as "the system of empirical beliefs, expressive symbols, and values which define the situation in which political action takes place . . .", or, stated another way, this is our "subjective orientation to politics".[22] This means the analyst's perspective is primarily shaped by being American or Russian, educated or illiterate, rich or poor, or a supporter of a particular political party. Thus, the way we look at Russia or the Eurasian states (even the names by which we designate them such as "Eurasia") is predicated upon both objective and subjective assessments. For instance, anti-Soviet and anticommunist values have served as contours for a wide range of scholars such as the influential Polish-born political scientist Zbigniew Brzezinski (who later became the U.S. National Security Advisor).[23] Similarly, Polish-born, historian Richard Pipes used the study of Russian history and his own conservative world view to develop broad insights about Soviet politics.[24] From a very different perspective the former Soviet dissident, historian, and Marxist scholar Roy Medvedev gave us much of what the outside world initially knew of Stalin's purges in his seminal study *Let History Judge*.[25]

The other side of the analytical coin involves those analysts who err on the side of objectivity and seek to remove all subjective biases. Controlling for ideological orientations while producing bland, almost generic descriptions of how all governments operate results in what British historian Robert Conquest termed "an effort at rationalizing prejudices."[26] Conquest rejected "objective" studies of the former Soviet Union and is critical of analysts who have gone out of their way to avoid contentious issues so they wouldn't have to make judgments. To Conquest, politics itself is an area "where rigor is inapplicable"[27] (definitely not a political scientist's viewpoint). At particular moments of observation this may seem so but taking a longer view allows for assessments such that Conquest himself made on Stalinism and collectivization.[28] Thus, as Alfred Meyer has phrased it, the "pluralism" within the scholarly community "acts as a powerful corrective" to either side trying to control the debate.[29]

The real difficulty, it would seem, lies in trying to integrate subjective cultural elements within the context of objective political facts. Political cultural approaches often seem caught in the middle winding up, as Frederic Fleron puts it, "as a concept that simultaneously captures everything and nothing."[30] Seemingly correcting for this problem some scholars now argue that political change must be analyzed within the context of "a long-term social and cultural process" such as the authoritarian tendencies of Russian and Soviet history.[31]

One useful categorization scheme for evaluating political culture can be found in Archie Brown's four-part typology including the unified political culture, the dominant political culture, the dichotomous political culture, and the fragmented political culture.[32] The last two of these go the greatest distance in characterizing the Russian and Eurasian systems. **A dichotomous political culture,** for instance, indicates a polarization between governing agents/bodies on the one hand, and the general population on the other that leaves virtually no common ground for compromise. In the **fragmented political culture** numerous distinct groups make claims to represent themselves, and no one common voice speaks for society as a whole. To date no post-Soviet state has established a unified political culture, and even dominant political cultures are not readily identifiable (Lithuania is probably the best example of this type). In the post-Soviet period, the problem of fragmented political cultures has become acute, as evidenced in hypercompetitive parliamentary elections and political separatism that have beset many of these states. In some of these systems divided cultures are becoming more harmonious despite the birth pangs of independence. For instance, in Russia, the Baltic states, and Ukraine parliaments and presidents may be in conflict with one another, or the parliament is divided within itself but the outlines of the political system seem apparent for the moment. In more conflictual systems—notably Tajikistan, Georgia, Azerbaijan, and Moldova—fragmented political cultures are compounded by incomplete governmental control over state territory. For these states the short-term result is political paralysis.

Economics and Politics

The second track of analysis employed here involves the interrelationship between economic and political development. Such factors as gross national product, per capita income, distribution of wealth within the population, and proportion of the economy devoted to agricultural, industrial or service production are fundamental to the behavior of political elites, the formation of parties and movements, and the structuring of political institutions. It is not a single factor we examine but instead the entire political system, or what Robert Dahl concluded to be "any persistent pattern of human relationships that involves, to a significant extent, control, influence, power, or authority."[33] By accounting for macroeconomic factors the scope of our study is dramatically improved taking us beyond the Soviet experience, and into the key relationships between Russia and its Eurasian neighbors. This more comprehensive approach allows us to coax Russian and Eurasian studies even deeper into the mainstream of comparative political analysis.

TABLE 1.1   How the Russian and Eurasian States Place in the United Nations' Human Development Index 2001 (ranking in parentheses*)

1.	Estonia (44th)	9.	Georgia (76th)
2.	Lithuania (47th)	10.	Azerbaijan (79th)
3.	Latvia (50th)	11.	Turkmenistan (83rd)
4.	Belarus (53rd)	12.	Kyrgyzstan (92nd)
5.	Russian Federation (55th)	13.	Moldova (98th)
6.	Armenia (72nd)	14.	Uzbekistan (99th)
7.	Ukraine (74th)	15.	Tajikistan (103rd)
8.	Kazakstan (75th)		

*Total number ranked = 162.

Source: United Nations Human Development Report 2001, "Human Development Index", United Nations website [http://www.undp.org/hdr2001/indicator/ indic_18_1_1.html]

Table 1.1 illustrates one dimension of the economic variable. Utilizing the United Nations Human Development Index rank orderings, the Russian and Eurasian states are compared on the bases of gross domestic product (GDP) per capita, life expectancy, health care, and educational level.

In 2001 Estonia ranked the highest of all former Soviet republics at forty-fourth overall, and was followed by the two other Baltic states. While the Russian Federation was not far behind, at fifty-fifth it showed itself to be well below the standards of the world's wealthiest and most-developed societies. Ukraine (seventy-fourth) and Georgia (seventy-sixth) were much further down the list, and Uzbekistan (the last of the countries examined in our case studies) barely cracked the top 100 countries (ninety-nine). The one-dimensional character of this classification urges caution upon us at this point. And yet, these numbers headline a story that this book seeks to explain: the complexities and obstacles of independence of a broad array of formerly associated states and peoples.

Participation in Political Systems

The student of Russian and Eurasian politics must also be aware of the political choices that conflict with analysis.

During the Soviet period the most basic of these was the dichotomy between the values and goals of communism and those of western, liberal democracy. The western analyst, influenced by his/her own perspective, often looked at Soviet political society from a defensive posture culminating in the bias that Meyer described as "celebrating one's own system."[34] Meyer summed up the relationship of politics and political analysis this way: "Politics and methodology inevitably are intertwined. Whatever the negative effects of that relationship, they can be mitigated by uncovering the political implications of any methodology, both in those with whom we disagree and also in our own work."[35] In other words, we must be aware of our own biases and work to isolate them.

Given the roadblocks and detours one can readily imagine the sort of impacts that events such as Yeltsin's crackdown on his domestic political opponents in 1993, the 1994 and 1999 decisions to invade Chechyna, or the collapse of the Russian market in 1998 have had on our opinions. For instance, what is to be inferred from the comment of President of Uzbekistan **Islam Karimov** that "we will build democratic institutions—but keeping in mind our own special circumstances"?[36] If Russian citizens respond electorally to either numerous party appeals or demagogery from particular leaders, or react impulsively to terrorist attacks which kill hundreds of people what will this mean to us who merely watch their fates? How well will we try to comprehend what is occurring within these states?

One of the most poignant examples of values coloring our analysis is the nationalities question. Western analysts and human rights advocates frequently decry the lack of tolerance shown toward minorities or nonconformist opinions and thought in the post-Soviet states. Especially problematic in this regard have been ethno-centric citizenship and language laws. The intolerance which has appeared in these states, it has been said, is due to a lack of experience with democratic values and structures, and the prospects for achieving tolerance are minimized in the prevailing political climates. Again, Karimov makes a pointed observation:

> "Do you (the West) think it was possible to create other political parties in a state long dominated by the Communist Party? We aligned ourselves by the stars atop the Kremlin, and you suddenly expect us to have a democratic state in only two years? Why should this issue become a stumbling block in relations with Uzbekistan?"[37]

As ethnic tensions escalated into open warfare in many parts of the Soviet Union, and carried over into the successor states, the difficulties of making the transition to western-style democracy became apparent. The question, though, is whether western democratic values are a proper framework for assessing the post-Soviet states' performances? Given the democratic value standard so popular in the West (and used in this book as well), were Boris Yeltsin's actions in dissolving the Russian parliament in 1993 any more or less legitimate than the parliament's armed rebellion? A question such as this has no easy answer and poses a major challenge to our evaluation of the new Russian and Eurasian politics.

For this analysis we look to the boundaries of participation including the terminology that describe it. Though the methods may vary, political participation essentially underscores citizen involvement as a primary measure for differentiating between political systems. By focusing on this variable a comparison may be made based on the extent of freedom possessed by the average citizen for making independent political choices. This involves the use of descriptive labels such as "totalitarian", "authoritarian", and "democratic" which represent a unilinear effort to explain systemic change. These terms indicate the degrees to which citizens are involved in a governing process. The terms themselves are frequently subjectively burdened by values that western publics and politicians equate with development. Despite the superficiality of projecting our values onto others this participatory approach helps establish a foundation for comparison that is difficult to arrive at otherwise.

A brief description of each term might be helpful. As commonly used **totalitarianism** implies that political decisions are either entirely in the hands of one person or a very small group of elites resulting in the condition of *dictatorship*. In such a system those who are governed have no political input and only the vaguest hopes that some of the rewards of the political process will be directed toward them. Information is monopolized by the government and especially media outlets which either are run for the purposes of the state, or are curtailed by it. Independence of thought and open political expression of thoughts is not tolerated, and in these capacities the public is **manipulated.** The results of this are: 1) the government determines for the public an exclusive version of political, social, and economic reality; and 2) distortion of truth becomes the norm for society since there are no checks upon governmental authority. The citizen is essentially a captive of the state.

The totalitarian belief structure holds humankind's nature to be irrational and incapable of making sound or correct policy choices. The individual must be led by a strong leader or leadership in whom the public blindly places its trust. The state structure becomes the arbiter of all life and may claim legitimacy from some form of spiritual authority, or even a biological necessity. Thus, if the citizen questions or refutes the decisions of the state he or she would be rejecting the natural order of things, possibly a scientific truth or a mandate of heaven. Under these circumstances a protester is much more than a dissenter: he or she may be termed a heretic who the regime feels must be harshly dealt with in order to prevent the spread of doubt to the rest of the population. In such a system there is no room for alternative interpretations of reality.

Authoritarianism is also threatened by the citizen's independence of political action. Political decisions are monopolized by a relatively small inner-circle of officials, anywhere from several hundred to thousands, while symbolic amounts of authority are vested in the people. Institutions are adopted to accommodate mass participation so as to satisfy citizen's political desires; this may include setting aside seats in the legislature for opposition forces or establishing state-run labor or trade federations. An official ideology may also exist, which (generally) claims that all power originates with the people; in this sense the authoritarian system parrots the philosophical bases of democratic societies. In these circumstances, however, political participation is only marginally meaningful and may best be termed **mobilized,** that is, exhibiting a low degree of independent action, and organized along lines decided upon by the government or elites.

Authoritarianism is a paternalistic belief system involving the assumption that the population does not know what is in its own best interests. Authoritarian leaders often claim that they are gradually raising the population to a level of self-development where it will be capable of self-government, but until that point the government must act on the public's behalf. This may seem cynical by democratic standards, but authoritarian leaders justify these actions by recurrent conflicts within society such as tribal or ethnic animosities, or gross disparities between the rich and the poor. Without centralized control, they argue, these conflicts will explode into extreme violence. The authoritarian system may also be rationalized as the best means to direct the limited economic resources of society, so as not to waste time on the path of modernization. Finally, authoritarianism is often a reaction to real or imagined threats to society, such as predatory neighbors or a problematic economic environment.

Finally, there is **democracy** which represents a polar extreme of participation from totalitarianism. Two principles generally define the democratic system. The first principle involves the masses exercising their abilities to select elites as their leaders. The polity votes to approve or disapprove government actions by changing leaders as well as taking part in full, uncensored debate concerning the merits of various policy proposals. In this is met the classical standard of democracy as described by Joseph Schumpeter, that is, the political society provides meaningful input, and thereby refines the boundaries of that same system which controls it.[38] The second principle concerns those who actually govern. The people choose either to retain power for themselves or to delegate it to others. Both options imply a sense of responsibility to watch over the political process, to insure that power does not flow into the hands of small cliques or factions operating exclusively in their own selfish interests. Participation in this sense is considered **autonomous,** or independent from government controls, but still subject to the political system. Keeping this power in the hands of those who are governed is surely the most difficult task confronting democracy.

Moreover, one has to recognize that the sophistication of political institutions is not the primary characteristic equating this condition with democracy. Rather, the differentiation of institutions, the increasing pluralism of political society, coupled to the development of autonomous sources of power, allows for the categorization of a state according to Robert A. Dahl's distinction of the democratic polyarchy.[39] Distinctions such as these appear constantly throughout the Russian and Eurasian political spheres, but Dahl's scheme is stingy in its acceptance of new polyarchies and leaves aside those states which cannot demonstrate performance instead of just style.

As attractive as all of this may seem, however, it has been consistently noted by comparativists that democracy is not an automatic response to the end of authoritarian rule. And even when it does occur there are any number of forms of democracy which may result due to historic, societal, and economic factors which condition the political system.[40] Further, a transition from authoritarianism involves both "the process of breaking down the preexisting structures" and "the task of creating new structures."[41] In the chapters ahead we will look at both of these conditions to determine whether democracy is the actual goal of Russian and Eurasian political systems and to what extent it has been achieved. Thus, democracy is not treated here as a deterministic goal in and of itself but instead as a possible outcome of the changes that have transpired.

Typing Eurasian Systems

For the convenience of illustration this book employs a typology modified from the model put forth by Almond and Powell.[42] This typology emphasizes the interrelationship between political culture and institutional development (see Figure 1.1). On the one hand it allows us to compare governments that rule by decree to those that employ formalized law making within an established civil society. On the other hand the typology places these institutions against the backdrop of **cultural secularization,** that is, the conditions of isolation or involvement of society in the political process. This is referred to as **penetration** and demonstrates in relative terms how well the governing process is in touch with society's concerns.

The first dimension of the typology involves the degree of penetration, in particular, how much differentiation and specialization characterize political institutions. As society becomes more complex so, too, its political units will become more specific in their tasks and develop distinct boundaries separating

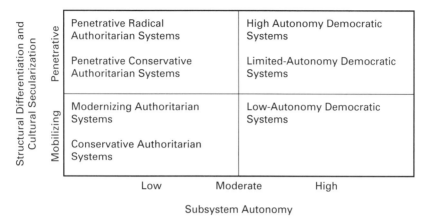

Figure 1.1 Political Organization and Cultural Development

Source: Adopted from Gabriel A. Almond and G. Bingham Powell, *Comparative Politics: System, Process, and Policy,* 2nd ed. (Boston: Little, Brown, 1978),72.

each other in pursuit of these tasks. The citizen is required to follow the numerous, and often unfamiliar rules and regulations of political society even if he or she does not truly respect the organization or style of government. What must be clear from this is that formal institutionalism means little without development of commensurate cultures of legalism. The Soviet Union had more than its share of laws concerning rights and liberties, but little intention of practically implementing them. Much the same can be said about many of the Eurasian states today which again demonstrates the attractiveness of studying political culture.

The second dimension of this typology designates **subsystem autonomy,** or the degree to which citizens are genuinely involved in political decision making. A "low" rate of participation evidences little citizen involvement while a "high" rate indicates the citizen has some meaningful control over the governing process. Any number of indicators can be used to establish degree or intensity of autonomy. A "low" degree of autonomy means elections are manipulated, for instance, the government approving only a single slate of candidates. In contrast multiparty elections represent a substantial amount of autonomy. Another example might be government restrictions on demonstrations and protests (low), versus guaranteed freedom of assembly (high). And a final indicator of autonomy might be governmental censorship and monopoly of mass communication (low), versus freedom of speech, expression, and few restrictions on the media (high). Briefly what we may conclude is that some of the Eurasian states have continued in an authoritarian/mobilizational mode, while others have moved further toward democratic/penetrative principles. All of these points will be revisited in the final chapter of this book.

Knowing more about how politicians or political systems rationalize political action furthers our abilities to successfully analyze. Now more than at any time in the past we have the means—again, in the forms of social attitudes, public opinions, and economic data—to probe deep within the context of these states' politics and their institutions as they develop. The key may well be citizen involvement, but one has to keep in mind that this indicator also includes elite participation. To adequately evaluate which way the issue turns requires an understanding of the historical and social elements of the environment. That is the task to which we turn in Chapter Two.

Key Terms

political culture
autonomous political action
elite studies
dichotomous political culture

systems approach
mobilized political action
kremlinology
fragmented political culture

Questions for Consideration

1. Why should we expect that modern social science techniques are appropriate for analyzing Russia and the Eurasian states?
2. If pluralism is necessary for democracy, which of the states under consideration are making progress toward democracy?
3. How does the political culture approach lend itself to the analysis of Russia and the successor states of the Soviet Union?
4. With the fall of communism as a state ideology, what has become of analytical methods such as *kremlinology*?
5. Are authoritarian style governments "natural" to the Eurasian states?

Suggested Readings

Archie Brown, ed., *Political Culture and Communist Studies* (Armonk, NY: M. E. Sharpe, 1984).

Frederic J. Fleron, Jr., and Erik P. Hoffman, eds., *Post-Communist Studies and Political Science: Methodology and Empirical Theory in Sovietology* (Boulder, CO: Westview Press, 1993).

Ruth Lane, *The Art of Comparative Politics* (Boston: Allyn & Bacon, 1997).

Zhores A. Medvedev, *Gorbachev* (New York: W. W. Norton, 1986).

Richard Sakwa, *Gorbachev and His Reforms, 1985–1990* (New York: Prentice-Hall, 1990).

Nikolai N. Petro, *The Rebirth of Russian Democracy: An Interpretation of Political Culture* (Cambridge, MA: Harvard University Press, 1995).

Useful Websites

Adminet—Russian Federation
   http://www.admi.net/world/ru/#gov

Links to Russian and Former Soviet Union Web Resources
   http://users.aimnet.com/~ksyrah/ekskurs/russlink.html

OFFSTATS: Official Statistics on the Web
   http://www2.auckland.ac.nz/lbr//stats/offstats/

University of British Columbia websites on Russia and Eurasia
http://www.library.ubc.ca/hss/poli/compartee.htm#Soviet

Endnotes

1. See Fainsod's *Smolensk Under Soviet Rule* (Cambridge, MA: Harvard University Press, 1958).
2. Alex Inkeles, *Public Opinion in Soviet Russia, A Study in Mass Persuasion* (Cambridge, MA: Harvard University Press, 1958).
3. See, for example, Jerry F. Hough, *The Soviet Union and Social Science Theory* (Cambridge, MA: Harvard University Press, 1977).
4. For instance, Alec Nove's *An Economic History of the USSR* (Middlesex, England: Penguin Books, 1982).
5. Paul R. Gregory and Robert C. Stuart, *Soviet Economic Structure and Performance,* 3rd ed. (New York: Harper & Row, 1986).
6. See Basile Kerblay's *Modern Soviet Society* (New York: Pantheon, 1983). An example of what is termed "ethnosociology" is found in Rasma Karklin's *Ethnic Relations in the USSR* (Boston: Unwin and Hymin, 1987).
7. Stephen White, *Gorbachev and After* (Cambridge: Cambridge University Press, 1991), p. vii.
8. For instance, see Timothy J. Colton, "The Moscow Elections of 1990," *Soviet Economy,* 6 (1990): pp. 285–344; Thomas F. Remington and Steven S. Smith, "The Development of Parliamentary Parties in Russia", *Legislative Studies Quarterly,* 20 (November 1995): pp. 457–489; and Stephen White, Richard Rose, and Ian Mcallister, *How Russia Votes* (Chatham, NJ: Chatham House Publishers, 1996).
9. Darrell P. Hammer, *USSR: The Politics of Oligarchy* (Hinsdale, IL: Dryden Press, 1974), p. 8.
10. David Lane, *State and Politics in the USSR* (New York: New York University Press, 1985), p. 113.
11. Carl Linden, *Khrushchev and the Soviet Leadership, 1957–1964* (Baltimore: Johns Hopkins University Press, 1966).
12. Valerie Bunce, *Do New Leaders Make A Difference?* (Princeton: Princeton University Press, 1981).
13. George W. Breslauer, *Khrushchev and Brezhnev as Leaders: Building Authority in Soviet Politics* (London: George Allen & Unwin, 1982).
14. The journal *Problems of Communism* was a frequent publisher of articles utilizing elite theory and especially kremlinology. Between 1985 and 1991 by this author's count at least thirteen articles appeared using this method. Typical of these were Archie Brown's "Gorbachev: New Man in the Kremlin", 34 (May-June 1985): pp. 1–23; and Michel Tatu's "19th CPSU Conference", 37 (May-August 1988): pp. 1–15.
15. For instance, see Richard Sakwa, *Gorbachev and His Reforms, 1985–1990* (New York: Prentice-Hall, 1990).
16. Jerry F. Hough, *The Soviet Prefects: The Local Party Organs in Industrial Decision-Making* (Cambridge, MA: Harvard University Press, 1969).
17. Joel C. Moses, *Regional Party Leadership and Policy-Making in the USSR* (New York: Praeger, 1974).
18. Martha Brill Olcott, "Perestroyka in Kazakhstan," *Problems of Communism,* 39 (July-August 1990): pp. 69–77.
19. T. H. Rigby, "The Soviet Regional Leadership: The Brezhnev Generation," *Slavic Review,* (March 1978): pp. 1–24.

20. Philip Stewart, *Political Power in the Soviet Union* (New York: Bobbs-Merrill, 1968).
21. One exception is that by Jeffrey W. Hahn, *Soviet Grassroots: Citizen Participation in Local Soviet Government* (Princeton, NJ: Princeton University Press, 1988).
22. Lucian Pye and Sidney Verba, eds., *Political Culture and Political Development* (Princeton: Princeton University Press, 1965), p. 513.
23. For instance, see Brzezinski's *The Grand Failure: The Birth and Death of Communism in the Twentieth Century* (New York: Scribners, 1989). Even more telling are the titles of his earlier works such as *The Permanent Purge: Politics in Soviet Totalitarianism* (Cambridge: Harvard University Press, 1956).
24. See Pipes' *The Formation of the Soviet Union: Communism and Nationalism, 1917–1923,* revised edition (New York: Atheneum, 1968), or *The Russian Revolution* (New York: Knopf, 1990).
25. Roy Medvedev, *Let History Judge: The Origins and Consequences of Stalinism,* revised edition (New York: Columbia University Press, 1989).
26. Robert Conquest, "How to Avoid Thought on Soviet History" in eds. Uri Ra'anan and Charles M. Perry, *The USSR Today and Tomorrow: Problems and Challenges* (Lexington, MA: Lexington Books, 1987), p. 19.
27. Ibid.
28. Some of Conquest's better-known studies include *The Great Terror* (New York: Macmillan, 1969), and *The Harvest of Sorrow* (New York: Oxford University Press, 1986).
29. Alfred G. Meyer, "Observations on the Travails of Sovietology", *Post-Soviet Affairs,* 10 (1994): p. 193.
30. Frederic J. Fleron, Jr., "Post-Soviet Political Culture in Russia: An Assessment of Recent Empirical Investigations", *Europe-Asia Studies,* 48 (1996): p. 226.
31. Nicolai N. Petro, *The Rebirth of Russian Democracy: An Interpretation of Political Culture* (Cambridge, MA: Harvard University Press, 1995), pp. 20, 16; also see Vladimir Tismaneanu and Michael Turner, "Understanding Post- Sovietism: Between Residual Leninism and Uncertain Pluralism" in ed. Vladimir Tismaneanu, *Political Culture and Civil Society in Russia and the New States of Eurasia* (Armonk, NY: M. E. Sharpe, 1995), p. 7.
32. Archie Brown, "Conclusions" in ed. Archie Brown, *Political Culture and Communist Studies* (Armonk, NY: M. E. Sharpe, 1984), p. 176.
33. Robert A. Dahl, *Modern Political Analysis,* 5th ed. Englewood Cliffs, NJ: Prentice-Hall, (1991), p. 12.
34. Alfred G. Meyer, "Politics and Methodology in Soviet Studies," *Studies in Comparative Communism.* XXIV (June 1991): 127.
35. Ibid., 136.
36. *Time,* 25 July, 1994, 43.
37. Ibid.
38. Joseph A. Schumpeter, *Capitalism, Socialism, and Democracy* (London: Allen & Unwin, 1943).
39. Dahl, pp. 72–74.
40. Terry Lynn Karl, "Dilemmas of Democratization in Latin America" in eds. Dankwart A. Rustow and Kenneth Paul Erickson, *Comparative Political Dynamics: Global Research Perspectives* (New York: HarperCollins, 1991), pp. 163–169.
41. Russell Bova, "Political Dynamics of the Post-Communist Transition", *World Politics,* 44 (October 1991): p. 117.
42. Gabriel Almond and G. Bingham Powell, Jr., *Comparative Politics: System, Process, and Policy,* 2nd ed. (Boston: Little, Brown, 1979), pp. 71–74.

Chapter 2

Historical, Cultural, and Social Perspectives

All political systems are conscious of their origins, regardless of whether they reject their past or stress continuity. In the former case political leaders may reject outright all that characterized the "ancien regime" (literally, the "old regime") as being tainted or corrupted; for these a clean break with the past is necessary. Any association with the past may be considered a negative factor to be avoided at almost all costs. In the latter case, where continuity is considered desirable, the state's past glories and successes are sought to legitimize what is occurring in the present, especially if the current governing system is weak, or carrying out unpopular policies. In either case, the past is integral to the present and political actors cannot escape it.

As well, politics *is* society, or more accurately, a reflection of the demands, pressures, and tensions that make up the everyday lives of citizens. These are the inputs of politics, or the problems that are "loaded" into the policy making process. Among these are social and cultural conditions, which are responded to by governments in either a positive or negative fashion, or ignored, although often at great risk. In a democratic system, for instance, an election gives the citizen the opportunity to express his or her level of satisfaction by means of a vote. For the most part this usually satisfies the citizen, if for no other reason than because the citizen *believes* that he or she may change the system if it is unresponsive. Authoritarian or totalitarian governments, on the other hand, respond by ignoring citizen demands, or by repressing them with force. Even still, these governments *have* responded, although not in a fashion the citizens may find helpful or satisfying.

This chapter focuses, first of all, on the historic patterns of development of the Russian state, how it was subdued by other powers, and in its turn subjugated many of its neighbors. This is important not just for understanding the individual republics surrounding Russia, but also for grasping the depth of the nationality issues that underlie Russia (for instance in Chechnya), the Baltic states, Ukraine, Georgia, and Uzbekistan. Next we concentrate on four specific social variables all of which are vital in drawing the general parameters (boundaries) for exploring the political systems. These factors—race/ethnicity, language, religion, and living standards—are chosen for their broad-ranging impacts on politics, and for the formative influences they exert. They are, as well, highly descriptive and readily lend themselves to assessments of the ongoing process of change in Russia and the Eurasian states.

Of Histories and States' Development

Although Russia and the Eurasian states have been involved for the past decade in the fundamental task of carving out distinct national identities, a common thread forms a bond between them: all have been profoundly affected by the demands, desires, successes and failures of Russian history. First under the tsars, and then Soviet officialdom, the interests of Russia superceded all others, sometimes to the extent that cultures were suppressed, neglected to the point of disappearing, or, in extreme cases, wiped out altogether. Thus, historically Russian control tended to run contrary to either tolerance or understanding of local cultures and populations.

Within the confines of the region we refer to as Eurasia, Russia has traditionally been the primary focus of study because it was the clear winner in the centuries-long struggles on the Eurasian landmass. As a state and culture Russia learned from the conquests visited upon it by its neighbors: first the **Varangians** (or Vikings from Scandinavia), who founded the **Kievan Rus** state and began the unification of the eastern Slavic peoples; this was followed by the Mongols sweeping out of the steppes of Asia, and later by incursions of European peoples such as the Lithuanians, Poles, Swedes, and French. Finally and most destructively, came the dual German invasions of the 20th century. The upshot of continual invasion, and the necessity to prepare for such eventualities has been for the Russians, first of all, a political defensiveness mixed with, secondly, a physical isolation from, and suspicion of the world. These have had striking impacts on the development of the governing process.

The Ebb and Flow of Empires

From earliest times, according to recorded histories of this region, state structures focused on the twin precepts of 1) external growth, and 2) internal assimilation. Whether for reasons of survival, economic development, or sheer rapaciousness the various Russian states—for there were several—began to grow and to incorporate within themselves smaller, and weaker, cultures. Some of the conquered peoples gave no resistance, while others fought doggedly for years, sometimes rolling back Russian gains but most often losing. This millennium-long process might be termed the *ebb and flow of the tides of nations*. As the Russians persevered over other national/ethnic groups this in turn allowed the Russians to dominate the historic discussion. Even more interesting now is the possibility that this historic trend is being reversed as Russians leave the Eurasian states in large numbers and Russian imperial ambitions collapse. With all of this in mind there are definite factors upon which to build our assessments.

The Old and the New: Moscow in the 21st Century

Source: © Maxim Marmu/Getty Images

Fact Number One. The Slavic tribes of what is today Russia gained for themselves vast territories of sparsely populated land (particularly in the north), a sizable proportion of which were of marginal agricultural quality (the exceptions to this were the black-earth districts of Ukraine and southern Russia, which contain some of the richest farmland in the world). And although there would be vast resources of other sorts—particularly timber and furs—which might have excited the interests of other peoples, the Arctic North, the steppeland, and the vastness of Siberia were for the most part unexplored, sparsely inhabited, and isolated lands into which the eastern Slavs spilled.

As the medieval Russian state came together it became increasingly synonymous with external expansion and encroached on other lands almost as a desert moves over fertile ground. Determined opposition to Russia's expansion north, west, or south would not come from Europe until the nineteenth century. Only when Russia threatened the European balance of power by challenging the role of the Ottoman Empire in European politics—first in the Crimean War of 1854–56, and in 1877–78 in the Russo-Turkish War—did Britain and France and later Germany oppose Russian hegemony in eastern Europe. Russia had become by this point one of the poles of influence in the European system of competing national powers.

Fact Number Two. With few exceptions centralism and control of what generally made up the state's structure was a dominant characteristic of the emerging Russian state. The centralizing principle was not necessarily inevitable, but clearly a useful means toward advancing personalistic rule. At an early stage the state became intertwined with the will of the ruler. He or she were considered the embodiment of the state, sometimes legitimized in terms of having a "mandate of heaven" and thereby being unquestionable by the average citizen.

With the end of tsarism and the creation of the communist system in 1917 the centralizing tendency again took precedence. First there was the need to defend the revolution in the face of a civil war; and second, there was a compelling need for an organizational precept to make the revolution succeed. Consequently, centralism has been an enduring feature of the Russian political landscape for well over a thousand years and one which can be abandoned only with difficulty as Russia and its neighbors turn to face new political horizons.

Fact Number Three. While not necessarily better than other forms of political organization, centralism did allow the Russians to mobilize their resources effectively and often ruthlessly. The peoples of Russia and Eurasia have experienced regionalism, local autonomy, and/or democratic control. The historian George Vernadsky, for instance, recounts that the ancient Alans, precursors to the Slavs in southern Russia, "lived originally in a political democracy in which all public affairs were discussed in clan or tribal assemblies".[1] Nicholas Chirovsky depicted the Middle Ages city-state of **Novgorod (the Great)** as an "aristocratic" and "commercialized" democracy, but a democracy nonetheless.[2] But while none of these concepts are alien to the Russian/Eurasian experience (as Figure 2.1 illustrates) they have been most pronounced on the periphery of the Russian lands far from the control of the authorities in Muscovy (Moscow). As proven by the modern example of Chechnya, centralism has not precluded these elements from the Russian political culture, but it clearly has overshadowed their development.

These three points explain only part of the picture. To get a firmer grasp of the historic backdrop we need to look briefly at the individual historic states of Russia and Eurasia as they developed.

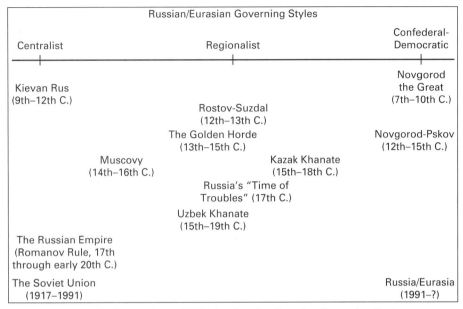

Figure 2.1 A Historic Comparison of Differing Russian/Eurasian Governing Styles

Kievan Rus, Muscovy, and the Russian Empire

The eastern Slavs began developing organized city-states and distinct political entities as early as the seventh century. Some of these cities distinguished themselves by very sophisticated forms of political and social organization, such as the commerce-oriented republic of Novgorod (the Great) in the eighth and ninth centuries. Others attained their positions primarily through force of arms, as unifiers of disparate tribes. This in fact, is the story of the development of most states, including that of Kievan Rus (ninth through the thirteenth centuries), which became the forebearer of the later medieval Russian state located at Moscow and known in its early years as **Muscovy.**

In the early stages of the Kievan state **Eastern Orthodox Christianity,** imported from Constantinople by the Kievan prince Vladimir (Volodymyr in Ukrainian) in 988, came to be accepted by most of the local Slavic tribes.[3] In accepting this version of Christianity, which has substantial differences from western versions, the state fostered the beginnings of a national character which would distinguish it from its western (Roman Catholic, and later Protestant) neighbors and from the nomadic peoples of the east and south (many of whom became followers of Islam). As well, the Russian Orthodox Church developed a relationship with, a heavy reliance upon, and a stake in the governing system; this element of the Russian political character—the intertwining of church and state with the former usually subordinated to the latter—has continued to the present day.

The rise of Muscovy represented the second great epoch in the development of the Russian state; as Michael Florinsky has described it, Muscovy "grew to maturity under a different political sky in the northeast of the country."[4] In Muscovy, and its eventual result, the Russian empire under the **Romanov dynasty** (1613–1917), can be found the full development of the Russian state and the Russian national character. Under the tsars (the term is derived from Roman title *Caesar*) Russia in its turn conquered the Tatars and laid the foundation for autocratic governance (Ivan IV, "the Terrible"), established a stable dynastic tradition (Michael I), modernized itself in the face of a changing world (Peter I, "the Great"), became a major European power (Catherine II, also "the Great"), liberated the majority of its population from serfdom (Alexander II, the tsar-liberator), and plunged itself headlong into the most destructive war the world had ever known, World War I (Nicholas II). Most important, however, was the solidification of autocratic governance at the same time that political cultures were being liberalized in western Europe. Under its latter rulers the Russian imperial state precluded change at the very historic instance it was most needed and demanded by the populace. The end result was revolution and the destruction of much for which Tsarist Russia had come to be known.

That which succeeded it was even more complex than the old governing system. The Bolshevik Revolution of 1917 brought communism to power on the foundation where the old Russian state had stood, and with it came a new sort of absolutism. This part of the story will be treated in the next chapter; it is enough to say at this point that communism left its own historic legacy on the emerging states of Russia and Eurasia inasmuch as tsarism had a dramatic impact on the development of communism.

The Mongol and Turkic States

Unlike the gradual introduction of the Slavs to the lands of medieval Rus, the Mongol sweep across Eurasia in the early thirteenth century was rapid and violent, overwhelming all who had come before, and along the way recasting the governing process. Traditionally, Mongol, or more commonly Tatar, rule has been credited with providing, some of the essential elements of the Russian political culture. Vernadsky phrased it as follows: "The Mongolian state was built upon the principle of unquestioning submission of the individual to the group, first to the clan and through the clan to the whole state. This principle was in the course of time impressed thoroughly upon the Russian people."[5] The long period of Mongol rule—from the 1230s through 1480—and the state structure known as the **Golden Horde** saw the creation of both new rivals to the Russian principalities (the Khanates of Kazan and Crimea) and the establishment, or revitalization of Central Asian states (Bukhara, Khiva).

Even as the Tatars were conquering traditional Russian lands they were also occupying lands of other peoples, or pushing before them tribes long situated in what is today Central Asia. It could be argued that the Tatars' deliberate shifting of populations throughout Eurasia was every bit as important as their impacts on political organization. The origins of the Uzbek nation, for instance, have been traced to Tatar peoples who followed the ruler Uzbek Khan in the early fourteenth century.[6] The Kazaks, of the same Turkic grouping as the Uzbeks themselves, coalesced into a distinct union (eventually a *nation*) to defend newly acquired territories in the fifteenth century.[7]

As already mentioned one of the primary results of the Mongol occupation of Russia and Eurasia was the furthering of the autocratic tradition especially in placing overwhelming authority in the hands of a single leader. The Russian monarchy embraced the Mongol concept of absolutism and refined it to be understood as a matter of divine enlightenment ultimately causing the regime to be blinded to its problems. Another result of the Mongol conquest can be found in the prominence of religion as a key ingredient in formulating the Russian national identity. While the Tatar tribes did seek to spread the faith of Islam this was not an overriding goal or a necessity of successful conquest. The Orthodox faith was allowed to operate relatively unhindered, and, in fact, even to expand its activities within the Tatar-controlled lands. In this sense a form of religious tolerance prevailed, while at the same time fostering the intertwining of state and religion as various rulers relied heavily on the Church for their authority.

And last we must consider the visible legacy of Tatar populations which continue to reside in Russia, Ukraine, and Central Asia. Direct descendants of the remnants of the Golden Horde, they were steadily swallowed up by Russian expansion beginning with Ivan IV's conquest of Kazan (1552). The modern-day struggles of these peoples for political autonomy (in the case of Tatarstan) or self-determination (as with the Crimean Tatars in Ukraine) represent some of the more intractable problems that multiethnic states like Russia and Ukraine encounter in establishing their political agendas.

Dependent States and Absorption

Dependent states are those which must rely heavily on a more powerful neighbor or ally—a patron—to maintain their independence or to foster growth in their economies. In its earliest days Muscovy was such a dependent state, first in relation to Kievan Rus, then to the successor principalities of Vladimir and Suzdal, and finally to the Golden Horde. As the Muscovite state grew in power and eclipsed its rivals, other states such as Kievan Rus and the Crimean Khanate, came to view Moscow as their protector and provider. More currently, since independence a number of the Eurasian states find themselves still heavily reliant upon Russian raw materials (oil and natural gas for Ukraine and the Baltic states), protection or military assistance (Armenia, Tajikistan), or Russian neutrality (Georgia, Azerbaijan). Perhaps with the exceptions of Armenia, Belarus, and Tajikistan there is no great appreciation within these states of the role that Russia now plays as a patron.

It seems, however, that the issue of dependency is a historic condition caused by demographic factors (large vs. small populations), coupled with economics (size and health of the dependent economies), factors over which most of these states have had little or no practical control. The three Baltic republics, for instance, were absorbed into the Tsarist empire in the early 1700s, did not reemerge until World War I altered the regional political landscape, and were swallowed again in 1940. Armenia's period of independence was even more brief, lasting from 1918–21 (having been under Turkish control since the eleventh century) and only resurfacing in 1991.[8] Georgia, a country sandwiched between much larger neighbors, retained its independence until the nineteenth century when Russian dominance became too much for it to resist; it, too, temporarily regained its independence in 1918–21 but was then submerged within the Soviet giant.[9]

For all of these states and peoples, and the numerous ones unmentioned, the historic factor has left deep impressions—in some cases scars—on the development of the political framework. For each state analyzed herein, the historic factor has to be carefully assessed, and will prove to be crucial in unlocking the political stories of modern politics in the post-Soviet space. If applied carefully along with other inputs a clearer perspective of politics in Russia and the Eurasian states will emerge.

Race, Ethnicity, and Language in Russia and the Eurasian States

With few exceptions the Russian and Eurasian states are multicultural mosaics of peoples, languages, and customs (Armenia is the closest to being a homogenous system). The best description of these traits is the term *ethnic group* which describes "a social group which, within a larger cultural and social system, claims or is accorded a special status in terms of a complex of traits."[10] Such traits typically include a collective name, a sense of common descent, shared history and culture, association with a specific territory, and a sense of solidarity.[11] As an example, the Belarussians are part of the Eastern Slavic group of peoples which include both the Russians and Ukrainians, but over a period of centuries the Belarussians have established a separate identity complete with unique language and cultural traits.

The Russian and Eurasian states' vast assortments of more than one hundred languages and dialects, and a myriad of peoples to go along with them, were more often hindrances rather than aids in the process of state building. Typical of multiethnic/multicultural states, one group did dominate, that known as the "Great Russians" or more commonly, just Russians. In the last Soviet census (1989) the Slavic peoples made up approximately 69.7 percent of the total population of the USSR.[12] This figure represented a net decline from 72 percent of this group's share of the population in 1979. Taken alone, the Russians' proportion of the total population also declined in this ten-year period from approximately 52.4 percent of the population (137,397,000 people) to the barest of majorities, 50.8 percent (145,155,000 people). The Ukrainians and Belarussians alike saw their overall numbers increase from the former census to the latter, but their proportional totals fall, in the Ukrainian case from 16.2 percent (42,347,000) to 15.5 percent (44,186,000), and for the Belarussians from 3.6 percent (9,463,000) to 3.5 percent (10,036,000).

In a multiethnic and ethnically conscious state of which the Soviet Union was a prime example, issues such as nationality or ethnicity are often found to be concerns of the highest order, both for policy makers and the public in general. When the size of a population group begins to decrease, this results in a perceived or actual loss of control by the dominant group in society over its destiny. For hundreds of years the Russians extended political, social, and economic power over their neighbors, expanding into a massive empire that knew no rivals. And along with this expansion came the restrictions of local languages, cultures, and religious practices that most nations fear. Even in the case of the relationship between the Russians and the Ukrainians, the latter being a people of cultural development and political organization predating the Russians, the Ukrainians were treated as "Little Russians" by their more numerous and powerful neighbors. Such condescension by one group toward another rarely builds strong, friendly relations, as the Estonians, Latvians, and Ukrainians have all impressed upon the Russians since 1990–1991.

Changes in population growth rates take on a new dimension when extremely different cultural elements are part of the same political system. In the last several decades of the Soviet Union the most important demographic shifts involved the growth of the peoples of Central Asia, particularly those of Turkic and Iranian ethnicity. While these various peoples taken together comprised only about twenty-five percent of the USSR's total, they also represented the fastest growing segments of the collective population with birthrates considerably in excess of the Slavic peoples (see Figure 2.2). Ethnicity alone, however, is not the problem confronting the state, but rather whether all ethnic groups are accorded equal treatment as the state pursues its economic and cultural goals.

But in the multiethnic state equal treatment is hardly ever the norm. Most often, a phenomenon referred to here as **favored nation status,** or **FNS,** occurs (not to be confused with **most favored nation** status) whereby one group gains

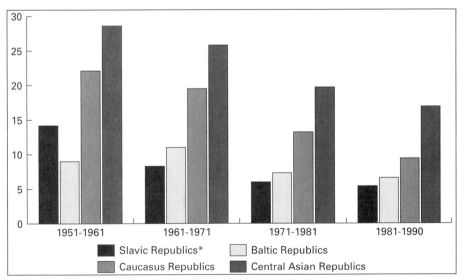

Figure 2.2 Population Increase in the Soviet Union, 1951–90 (in percentages)

*Includes Russian Federation, Ukraine, Byelorussia, and Moldavia

Source: The First Book of Demographics for the Republics of the Former Soviet Union, 1951–1990 (Shadyside, MD: New World Demographics, L.C., 1992), B–3, B–9, B–15,C–13

for itself specific privileges denied to others by virtue of being the politically dominant group in society. The FNS group considers itself to be the norm by which all other elements of society are judged. When FNS conditions prevail, less-favored groups may be shut out of political representation, economic development, or cultural expression (such as using their native languages or customs), or they can expect only limited rewards granted them by the favored nation. This condition may occur in both a benign fashion (the privileged group does not see itself as doing wrong, and in fact considers itself to be acting justly), or deliberately exclusionary (other groups are considered inferior). The FNS group may also act in a missionary capacity to enlighten those not of the favored nation's background.

Primarily because of its size, the Russian population has long filled the FNS role. Under the tsarist, Soviet, and now the Russian state systems the Russians have viewed their mission as that of dominating and civilizing their neighbors. In addition, the Russians have frequently seen themselves as protecting their neighbors from the encroachments of western values or economic and political dominance. Some of the nationalist literature which emerged beginning in the late 1980s played up this idea that Russia has a unique and possibly even divine mission.[13] It is not a new concept; in the 1800s this idea was fostered by the Slavophiles, the proponents of a Russia-first ideology which, at that time, was intricately related to the tsarist governing philosophy of "orthodoxy, autocracy, and nationality."[14] The idea may seem archaic, but at the dawn of the twenty-first century nationalist conflicts seem as prevalent and destructive as ever.

Today favored-nation status may be applied to virtually every one of the fifteen successor states. In fact titular nationalities had been in control of local and regional decision making during much of the latter years of Soviet power, though within the constraints of the Soviet system. With the breakup in 1991 only in Kazakstan did the FNS become the prerogative of a nonmajority population at the state level (ethnic Kazaks made up approximately forty-six percent compared to thirty-four percent of ethnic Russians[15]). In some regions of individual countries groups have actively fought to gain FNS, as shown in the bitter protracted dispute in the principally Armenian-populated Nagorno-Karabakh region of Azerbaijan, thus evidencing the extreme dangers of nationalism.

The high rates of population growth among the Central Asian peoples foreshadowed an uneasy future for the central authorities of the USSR. The various Central Asian peoples exhibited few inclinations to move to those areas where labor shortages were acute. Between 1979–89, Central Asian populations consistently increased unlike those of the various Slavic peoples (see Table 2.1). Most notable were the Tajiks, whose population increased by a remarkable 31.25 percent from 1979 to 1989. Although it is difficult to say exactly why this group increased so dramatically, part of the reason may have been the war in neighboring Afghanistan during this period. This conflict stimulated an exodus of ethnic Tajiks from Afghanistan who sought refuge amongst their ethnic kin across the border in the Soviet Union. By themselves, the Tajiks certainly posed no realistic challenge to the Russians since even in 1989 they represented only 1.5 percent of the total Soviet population. But coupled with the increases of the other Central Asian/Turkic

TABLE 2.1   Population Changes of Central Asian/Turkic Peoples in the Former USSR, 1979–89 (in thousands)

	1979	1989	% change of group, 1979–89	% change w/ whole population 1979–89
Uzbeks	12,456	16,698	+25.5	+1
Kazaks	6,556	8,136	+19.5	+0.3
Azeris	5,477	6,770	+19.1	+0.3
Tatars	6,317	6,649	+5	−0.1
Tajiks	2,898	4,215	+31.25	+0.4
Turkmen	2,028	2,729	+25.7	+0.2
Kyrgyz	1,906	2,529	+24.7	+0.2

Source: Data from *USA/USSR: Facts and Figures,* United States Bureau of the Census and the State Committee on Statistics of the USSR, United States Government Printing Office, Washington, DC, 1–4/1–5.

groups, which, on the average, increased 21.5 percent over this period, some cause for alarm amongst the Russians may be understood. Consequently, the Soviet leadership paid close attention to the expansion of the population in Central Asia as a potential long-term threat to Russian dominance.

Nationalism has been defined and redefined probably as much as any other political concept. The term implies a common sense of identity of a people based on shared characteristics such as language, ethnicity, culture, or religion; thus the ideology is an expression of this unity which may take the form of a nation-state. It is "a theory of political legitimacy, which requires that ethnic boundaries should not cut across political ones, and, in particular, that ethnic boundaries within a given state . . . should not separate the power-holders from the rest."[16] Put another way, nationalism is about how national groupings find common expression in the form of autonomy or state-building.[17] Some nations may never seek these specific purposes or goals, as is true of numerous smaller ethnic/national groups living throughout Russia and Eurasia. The tendency amongst larger national groups, and now even within some of the smaller ones such as the Chechens or the Abkhaz, however, is to try to establish a nation-state in which they may control their own fate.

As one might expect, the breakup of the Soviet system heightened already tense relations between different ethnic groups. The Soviet system had proven effective in keeping the lid on such tensions, but the problem could only be suppressed for so long. In some cases Russians have lived for generations in states such as Ukraine, Kazakstan, and in the Baltics with little assimilation or efforts at learning local languages and customs. Non-Russians among the local population however, often see the ethnic Russians among them as both outsiders and interlopers bent on russifying lands taken by force. From a Russian nationalist's perspective, these are lands belonging to the Russian nation by right of conquest, by the economic development Russians have fostered, or in terms of Russians having been born, lived, or died in a given region.

Almost inevitably actions taken by one group result in responses by another, or what is termed an action-reaction scenario, indicating the interrelationships of differing elements of public policy. Thus in the 1940s under a policy instigated by Soviet leader Joseph Stalin, groups such as the Volga Germans, the Crimean Tatars, numerous peoples of the Caucasus (see Chapter Seven on the Chechens), and elements of the Estonian, Latvian, and Lithuanian populations (see Chapter Nine) were expelled from their homelands. Considered disloyal or potentially so during World War II (or the Great Patriotic War as the Soviets termed it), or unwilling to accept Soviet control upon incorporation of their countries into the Soviet Union, hundreds of thousands and possibly millions were exiled to Central Asia or Siberia, thrown in concentration camps, or executed for their resistance. This left the way open for thousands of Russians to be settled in their places. After the 1991 declarations of independence a backlash occurred against the Russians which is still ongoing. This reaction has taken the form of narrowly defined citizenship and language laws, or long-term residency requirements that restrict Russian political participation. The reaction seems to have been strongest in those states where Russian oppression was harshest and where the titular nationalities themselves are in decline. Latvians, for instance, saw a steady rise in the number of Russian immigrants to their republic in the post-World War II years; subsequently, ethnic Russians comprised thirty-four percent of Latvia's population in 1991. Conversely, ethnic Latvians' numbers dropped steadily until, by the time of the last Soviet census in 1989, they made up barely more than a majority within Latvia itself (51.7 percent).[18] Faced with considerable hostility toward their presence many Russians responded with the formation of their own interest groups to protect their rights. Whether the cycle of retribution continues or reaches some form of accommodation must today depend on whether the value of multiethnic inclusion develops within these individual societies; otherwise these systems will continue to experience political instability accompanied by less-than-desirable economic development.

Religion and National Identity

Religious affiliation is often cited as one of the strongest factors shaping national identity. It is, as well, probably the most frequently misinterpreted. For starters, religious affiliation is never uniform within a population, and typically it serves only as a modifier of national identity, that is, one major condition among many. But religion involves emotional and deeply seated value structures beyond which citizens often cannot or will not look, thereby making it more difficult to deal with than most other factors.

The use of religion as a descriptive tool is complicated by the desire for quick and simple portraits of the peoples we study even though the religious factor is a multidimensional characteristic. Descriptions in the western media of Armenians as Christians or Azerbaijanis as Muslims add only marginal depth to our understanding of the political culture. Moreover, after seventy-four years of Soviet hostility toward religion, many of the peoples of the Eurasian states are only now finding new associations with religion (see Table 2.2). These religious descriptions, then, are most often nominal and need to be explained for their cultural impacts as much as their religious beliefs. To demonstrate the importance and appeal of religion in Russia and Eurasia today it helps to take a brief look at the makeup of the two largest religious groupings—Orthodox Christianity and Islam—and what their relationships have been, and are, to their governing systems.

Orthodoxy and the Slavic Identity

Traditionally, the majority of the Russian, Ukrainian, and Belarussian peoples were Eastern Orthodox, a branch of Christianity that came to the Slavic peoples through missionaries from Constantinople, the capital and spiritual center of the ancient Byzantine Empire. By means of direct state intervention Orthodoxy became the primary religion of the eastern Slavs. From the fourteenth century when the **patriarchate,** or governing body, was located in Moscow the Russian Orthodox Church became a bulwark of autocratic state power. By the nineteenth century the church-state relationship was embodied as one of the key elements of the state's official ideology. The Russian Orthodox Church bestowed its blessings upon the civil authorities in the person of the tsar and became an essential component of the state's existence. In return for the church sanctioning the tsarist political agenda, the state granted the Orthodox Church extensive privileges and the status of being a state religion. And as the religion filtered down to the people, its values and precepts helped consolidate the formation of national identity.

By the early twentieth century this long standing intermingling of church and state had caused a pervasive moral and intellectual decay within the Church and provided greater license for Russia's revolutionaries to vehemently attack the

TABLE 2.2   Religious Resources in Russia/Eurasia
(approximate figures from 1991 unless otherwise indicated)

Religion	# of Followers	# of Clergy/ Religious leaders	Religious Centers*
Russian Orthodox	50,000,000	19,950**	19,544**
Islam	20,000,000	7,200	2,302
Roman Catholic	+3,000,000	973	2,014
Protestant***	+3,000,000	2,000	+1,000
Georgian Orthodox	+3,000,000	400	322
Armenian Apostolic	+3,000,000	120	77
Greek Catholic (Uniates)	500,000	na	1,920
Judaism	350,000	30	70
Buddhism	300,000	70	16

Source: Igor Troyanovsky, ed., *Religion in the Soviet Republics* (San Francisco: Harper, 1991)
*Includes places of worship, active monasteries, and religious schools
**Figures for 1996, Russian Orthodox Church-Moscow Patriarchate website [http://www.russian-orthodox-church.org.ru/today_en.htm]
***Includes Lutherans, Baptists, Pentecostalists, and other major denominations

Patriarch of Moscow and all Russia, Aleksii II

Source: © TASS/Sovfoto

church structure. In the Soviet era, churches (mosques and temples as well) were closed, some converted into museums (the most notable being St. Basil's in Moscow's Red Square), and others demolished. Priests, clerics, and other religious officials were imprisoned or executed, and religious properties seized in the name of the state.[19] Testifying to the importance of organized religion, however, religion itself was never officially outlawed; instead the Communist Party controlled religion for the purposes of the state. State institutions such as the Council of Religious Affairs within the Council of Ministers, effectively compartmentalized religious groups and ensured their subservience to the goals of the party-state structure.

The ascendency to power of Mikhail Gorbachev in 1985 did not bring an immediate reversal of decades of religious suppression, but change did come. For the same reason that Stalin had eased up on religious believers in the 1940s, Gorbachev and other reformers also created conditions for a religious revival: the state's need for popular support. Beginning in 1986 with a series of amnesties, prisoners who were in Soviet jails due to their religious convictions began to be released. By 1988 on the 1000th anniversary of Orthodox Christianity's formal introduction to Russia the Communist Party authorities gave full recognition to the importance of the Orthodox Church as a pillar of social and political authority.

The relationship between religion and state in the post-Soviet era is far from perfectly defined. Animosities and wrongs that occurred over decades have not been immediately corrected or forgotten. Particularly problematic have been the efforts by the Russian Orthodox Church to reestablish its role as the "official" religion of Russia. In part, this has been accomplished by agreements such as that in 1994 between the Orthodox Church and the Ministries of Defense and Interior permitting church officials to visit garrisons, prisons, labor camps, and provide spiritual conferences. Just as important have been the growth of Protestant and evangelical religious faiths. In many cases foreign-based denominations have looked upon Russian society as an untapped field, and in some respects not even Christianized, despite Orthodoxy's 1000 year presence amongst the Slavic peoples. Having been denied the right to proselytize during the Soviet era, the fall of communism left the Orthodox Church unprepared for a competition over the public's spiritual allegiances. The Orthodox Church has responded to this competition by portraying these groups as foreign to the native values of the population and therefore deserving of being locked out.[20] Having tried unsuccessfully for several years, in 1997 the Orthodox Church's lobbying of the State Duma brought about the "Law on Freedom of Conscience and Religious Organizations" which restricted foreign-based religions from conducting missionary activity in Russia without permission of the government, or in lieu of association with Russian religious organizations.[21] Russia's general religious revival has clearly benefited the Orthodox Church and by 1999 possibly as many as half of all Russians considered themselves to be of that faith compared to thirty-four percent in 1991.[22] For the time being the Orthodox Church has managed to turn back the forces that dominated it throughout much of the 20th century.

Islam and Political Dynamics

Since 1991 the Russian and Eurasian Muslim peoples have experienced a sense of religious freedom and identity unknown for generations. The renewed identifications with Islam have also caused considerable suspicion and fear among many Russian and Eurasian politicians who often associate this phenomenon with fundamentalism such as that which has prevailed in Iran. Central Asian governments, in their efforts to limit the competition for power have also raised the specter of fundamentalism as a means to discredit opposition groups. The governments in Uzbekistan and Tajikistan have used this tactic largely to limit domestic criticism, but the repression that has accompanied it has in some cases radicalized otherwise moderate, but change-oriented groups.

The Muslim populations of the former Soviet Union, whether in the Russian Federation or in Central Asia, are overwhelmingly Sunni Muslims; only in Azerbaijan does the Shi'a practice of Islam—similar to that which prevails in Iran and Iraq—predominate. The Azeri people, however, are Turkic rather than Persian, thereby differentiating them in both social and political terms from Iran. Sunni Islam takes a decidedly secular approach to the relationship of religion and state. In Central Asia it is closely associated with what is known as the **Hannafi** school of Islamic jurisprudence which seeks to balance legal needs to societal concerns. Western perceptions that any Islamic rebirth is equal to fundamentalist politics were fueled by the separatist conflict in Chechnya. But the Chechen revolt was in fact motivated by Wahhabist tendencies, a radical interpretation most closely associated with Saudi Arabia rather than Iran. In most cases, the identification with Islam is primarily about the recapturing of lost or obscured national identities.

As with Orthodoxy, Islam was also heavily repressed under Soviet rule, and many elements of the official Muslim hierarchy compromised their positions in order to retain power and prestige. In the 1920s and 1930s thousands of mosques were closed and clerics imprisoned or exiled. By the 1960s the situation had improved as Soviet leaders sought allies in the Middle East and in other Islamic states; consequently, restrictions on Muslim customs and worship were lifted or eased. The Muslim leadership was co-opted to state purposes by means of the four Muslim Religious Boards which were structured along lines similar to that of the CPSU itself. At the head of these bodies were the local religious establishment who could then be counted on to carry out formalized state policy.[23]

In the post-Soviet era the **Muslim spiritual boards,** or **muftiats,** still exist, but their areas of authority have been altered to conform to new national boundaries. During the Soviet era the Muslim Religious Board of Mavarannahr (Transoxiana) in Tashkent was responsible for the religious concerns of all Muslims in Central Asia; today it deals only with the Muslims of Uzbekistan and Turkmenistan while a separate institution for Muslims in Siberia and the Russian Far East was created in 1997.[24] In all cases Islam has experienced a considerable revival fueled by outside forces such as the Saudi government which has funded the construction of mosques and religious centers throughout Central Asia. The bottom line, however, remains the citizens' own desires to pursue their spiritual development.

Religion, Glasnost, and Beyond

Despite what had gone before, religion has experienced a new openness and a flourishing as political society has changed. Many of the changes are positive and significant. On 26 September 1990 the Supreme Soviet of the new parliament, the Congress of People's Deputies (CPD) passed a law to facilitate the instruction of religion in schools. Going beyond this just several days later (1 October) the Supreme Soviet passed legislation guaranteeing the right of citizens to worship without governmental restraint. Gorbachev's own admission to having been baptized,[25] the burial of Yeltsin's mother according to Orthodox rite in March 1993,[26] the presence of the Russian patriarch at Yeltsin's inauguration in 1996, or that of Yeltsin at the Orthodox reburial of the Romanovs in 1999, are actions that would have been unthinkable for political elites in the Soviet era.

The problems presented in establishing new church-state relationships are, to say the least, daunting. The post-Soviet states have attempted to shake off the more intrusive aspects of communism such as the state forcing its way into the everyday concerns of the family, private relationships, and issues of right and wrong. The Ukrainian constitution, for instance, states that "no person may be released from one's duties before the State or refuse to obey the laws by reason of one's religious beliefs."[27] The state's role appears more directed in Lithuania where that country's 1992 basic law guarantees that the state "at the request of parents . . . shall offer classes in religious instruction."[28] But that constitution and a subsequent law also recognize nine "traditional religious communities . . . which comprise a part of the historical, spiritual and social heritage of Lithuania," and in effect have established religious preferences.[29] Since the Lithuanian population prior to absorbtion into the Soviet Union was overwhelmingly Roman Catholic this type of political action puts the Catholic Church in a privileged position. As religious activity was so heavily proscribed during the Soviet era (for instance, only thirty-two percent of Lithuanian infants were baptized in 1987[30]) the Catholic Church's hold over the public is not as prevalent now as during the Soviet era. Still, the Catholic Church is often portrayed as being native to the Lithuanian culture and part of the Lithuanian identity.

The clash of political and spiritual values will continue to pose vexing problems for the Russian and Eurasian states well into the new century. While religion promises to be an important defining characteristic of Russian and Eurasian societies, we still must look to other factors.

Living Standards and Social Order

Social Foundations

At its inception the Soviet state sought to demolish the economic basis of the old order it had replaced. This meant that the family, considered by Marxists as a tool of exploitation where the male dominated his wife and children for the sake of economic survival,[31] was in for drastic change. Particularly telling were the means by which the developing Soviet state of the 1920s tried to pit family members against one another so as to root out disloyalty and ideological infection. But by the 1930s the Stalinist authorities had come to see the family as a stabilizing force for society and one that had to be maintained; the underlying proviso to the family's existence, however, was that it be loyal to the state, not apart from it.

The post-Soviet political world has presented a drastically different recognition of the family's role and, to a lesser extent, the role of women in society. The family is mentioned as the basic unit of society and/or given explicit protection under law in most of the constitutions of the fifteen republics. But is this the reality of these states' politics or merely legalistic window-dressing for outside observers? The answers are proving to be markedly different from Central Asia to the Baltic and, as one should expect, across the length and breadth of the Russian Federation.

Under Soviet rule the family was conditioned by the dramatic socioeconomic changes of the time, such as the massive industrialization drive of the 1930s. Millions of people left the countryside due to forced relocations, rural impoverishment, famine, or because of the availability of urban jobs, all resulting in havoc for the social fabric. In the decade since the end of the Soviet Union emigration to the cities was again a major feature of social change. In 1993 dramatic differences characterized Russian-Eurasian urbanization: Russia (73.9 percent), Estonia (71.49 percent), and Latvia (71.1 percent) exhibited the highest concentration of city dwellers; in contrast Kyrgyzstan (38.1 percent) and Tajikistan (31.4 percent) remained largely rural societies. This emigration is largely internal, however, as Russians have shown themselves remarkably contented to live within their own society and disinclined to leave the country outright (only six percent expressed a desire to leave permanently in 1997).[32]

Urbanization and Modern Society

In Russia and Eurasia, as in most of the modern world, populations flow into major urban areas primarily for two reasons. First, this occurs due to economic hardships faced in the countryside, or the inability of the land to sustain the population. A second reason for such population shifts is that the city may be viewed as a place of stability in difficult political times. With the economies of Russia and Eurasia in serious decline throughout the 1990s (excepting the Baltic states), and civil strife producing large numbers of refugees (especially in Tajikistan, Azerbaijan, Georgia, and southern Russia), Russian and Eurasian cities have increasingly found it necessary to cope with the burden of immigration. The lifting of the Soviet regime's travel restrictions on the populations meant a freer flow of peoples than at any time since the 1930s (prior to the introduction of the Soviet internal passport system); consequently, the cities, where goods, jobs, security, and modern values seem possible are the most frequent destinations.

The swelling of urban populations has not always meant qualitative improvements in the standards of urban living. Living conditions in Russian and Eurasian cities are crowded, adequate housing is hard to find or too expensive (in spite of some constitutional provisions guaranteeing it), and crime is now a chief characteristic of the urban landscape. Refugees from outside the major metropolitan areas only seem to exacerbate the problem by putting greater strains on already limited city resources such as housing, hospital facilities and medical care, and the capacity of the cities' infrastructures (roads, sewage, water, etc.) to meet their needs. Additionally, cities must also accommodate concerns about the restoration of historic buildings and monuments, and most are hard pressed to find the resources needed to reverse decades of deterioration. The end result for many citizens faced with these conditions is often emigration within the former Soviet space: for instance, Ukrainians, Georgians, and Moldovans have tended to move to Russia; Baltic peoples and Germans to Europe;[33] Ukrainians and Russians to the United States and Canada; or Russians to Israel. In general these populations are seeking economic opportunities, social tolerance, or large emigre communities to support themselves.

Life Expectancy: An Ominous Barometer

While the foregoing factors do not paint a rosy picture, by contrast the issue of life expectancy shows things to be improving, but oftentimes grim. Measured in terms of the number of live births versus deaths for a population, life expectancy rates for Russia and the Eurasian states have held little news that is positive. Deterioration of life expectancy statistics for these populations began to occur prior to the breakup of the Soviet Union. Since 1991 population numbers throughout Russia and Eurasia have generally declined. For instance, in 1994, the Russian population fell by 124,000;[34] in 1995 it dropped by almost 300,000;[35] in 1996 it declined by 430,000;[36] in 1998 by 401,000;[37] and by the new millennium by over 600,000.[38] For the period 1989–1997 the State Statistics Committee of Russia (Goskomstat) reported the birth rate to have dropped by six percent while the country's death rate increased by 3.5 percent.[39] Compare these figures to Tajikistan's projected growth rate of 27.4 per 1,000 for the years 1993–1999, and the Russian data seems even more stark (Tajikistan's infrastructure, too, is dramatically less developed than that of Russia which may have caused the former to be less affected by declining living standards).[40] Most telling, however, is that the average Russian's life expectancy has fallen to the extent that Goskomstat estimated that if conditions continued in this vein only fifty-eight percent of males currently aged sixteen would reach their sixtieth birthday![41] No other major industrial nation has gone through such a drastic decline in life expectancy in a peacetime setting.

The causes of these population changes are largely found in the deterioration of the social, physical, and economic systems of the Soviet era. The social safety nets of the Soviet state have largely been stripped away, and in most cases not yet replaced. Because of this, Russia and the Eurasian states must now dedicate a great deal of their attention and precious fiscal resources to the re-creation of their social structures. The case studies which follow in this text take up many of these issues; for now we need to look to the system that has been replaced: communism. It is in the origins and ideological underpinnings of the Soviet state that much of the successes and failures of political development for Russia and Eurasia may be found today.

Key Terms

Kievan Rus

Eastern Orthodoxy

Golden Horde

diaspora

Muscovy

Romanov Dynasty

Nationalism

favored nation status

Questions for Consideration

1. Does history act as a positive or negative factor in state building in Russia and the Eurasian states?

2. What is meant by the term "the ebb and flow of the tides of nations"?

3. How is Russian ethnicity determined in the modern era?

4. In the postcommunist era can the Russian Orthodox Church withstand the intrusion of so many real and imagined competitors?

5. Can Russia's demographic crisis be overcome? What are the root causes of the population's dramatic decrease?

Suggested Readings

Galina Dutkina, *Moscow Days: Life and Hard Times in the New Russia* (New York: Kodansha International, 1996).

John P. LeDonne, *The Russian Empire and the World, 1700–1917* (New York: Oxford University Press, 1997).

David Mackenzie and Michael W. Curran, *A History of Russia and the Soviet Union,* 3rd ed. (Belmont, CA: Wadsworth Publishing Co., 1987).

———, *Russia and the USSR in the Twentieth Century,* 3rd ed. (Belmont, CA: Wadsworth Publishing Co., 1997).

Mary McAuley, *Soviet Politics, 1917–1991* (Oxford, England: Oxford University Press, 1994).

Lawrence McDonnell, *The October Revolution* (Staplehurst, England: Spellmount Limited, 1994).

Nicolai N. Petro, *The Rebirth of Russian Democracy, An Interpretation of Political Culture* (Cambridge, MA: Harvard University Press, 1995).

Aleksandr Vysokovskii, *Stillborn Environments: The New Soviet Town of the 1960s and Urban Life in Russia Today* (Washington, DC: Kennan Institute for Advanced Russian Studies, 1995).

Useful Websites

Bucknell University Russian History website
    http://www.departments.bucknell.edu/russian/history.html

Islam in Russia
    http://www.islam.ru/

Russian History on the Web (especially section on maps, "Kartii Roosii")
    http://www.russianhistory.org

Russian Orthodox Church-Moscow Patriarchate
http://www.russian-orthodox-church.org.ru/en.htm

Endnotes

1. George Vernadsky, *A History of Russia,* new revised edition (New Haven: Yale University Press, 1944), p. 17.
2. Nicholas L. Fr.-Chirovsky, *A History of the Russian Empire, Volume 1* (New York: Philosophical Library, 1973), p. 48.
3. David Mackenzie and Michael W. Curran, *A History of Russia and the Soviet Union,* 3rd ed. (Belmont, CA: Wadsworth Publishing Co., 1987), pp. 43–45.
4. Michael T. Florinsky, *Russia: A History and Interpretation, Vol. I* (New York: The Macmillan Co., 1953), p. 41. The author also provides a rich account of the successor states to Kievan Rus, particularly that of Rostov-Suzdal.
5. Vernadsky, *A History of Russia,* p. 56.
6. Edward A. Allworth, *The Modern Uzbeks: From the Fourteenth Century to the Present, A Cultural History* (Stanford, CA: Hoover Institution Press, 1990), p. 32.
7. Martha Brill Olcott, *The Kazakhs* (Stanford, CA: Hoover Institution Press, 1987), pp. 8–12.
8. See the essay by Edmund M. Herzig, "Armenians", in ed. Graham Smith, *The Nationalities Question in the Soviet Union* (New York: Longman Publishing, 1990), pp. 146–47.
9. Robert Parsons, "Georgians", in Smith, *The Nationalities Question in the Soviet Union,* pp. 180–82.
10. Melvin M. Tumin in Gould and Kolb, *A Dictionary of the Social Sciences,* p. 243.
11. Anthony D. Smith, *The Ethnic Origins of Nations* (New York: Basil Blackwell, 1986), pp. 22–30.
12. *USA/USSR: Facts and Figures,* U.S. Bureau of the Census and the State Committee on Statistics of the USSR (Washington, DC: United States Government Printing Office, 1991), pp. 4–5.
13. A detailed discussion of this trend in Russian thought can be found in Yitzhak M. Brudny, *Reinventing Russia: Russian Nationalism and the Soviet State, 1953–1991* (Cambridge, MA: Harvard University Press, 1998), especially Chapter Six.
14. Students interested in learning more about this period's intellectual and political development may want to read Nicholas Riasanovsky, *Nicholas I and Official Nationality in Russia, 1825–1855* (Berkeley, CA: University of California Press, 1959).
15. *CIA World Factbook, 2000,* Central Intelligence Agency website [http://www.odci.gov].
16. Ernest Gellner, *Nations and Nationalism* (Ithaca, NY: Cornell University Press, 1983), p. 1.
17. See, for instance, Anthony H. Birch, *Nationalism and National Integration* (London: Unwin Hyman, 1983), p. 4.
18. *CIA World Handbook, 1992.*(Washington, DC: United States Government Printing Office, 1992).
19. For a sampling of English-language translations of Soviet-era documents of the state's conflict with the Orthodox Church see Diane P. Koenker and Ronald D. Bachman, eds., *Revelations from the Russian Archives* (Washington, DC: Library of Congress, 1997), Chapter Five.
20. See the discussion on these points by Wendy Slater and Kjell Engelbrekt, "Eastern Orthodoxy Defends its Position," *RFE/RL Research Report,* 2 (September 3, 1993): pp. 48–58.
21. Interfax, 19 September 1997.

22. Interfax, 7 May 1999. A study conducted in 1997 and 1998 found as many as forty-eight percent of poll respondents calling themselves Russian Orthodox, but a striking forty-four percent identified with no religion or would not comment. See Stephen White, Bill Miller, Ase Grodeland, and Sara Oates, "Religion and Political Action in Postcommunist Europe", *Political Studies,* 48 (2000), Table 2, p. 688.

23. *Muslims in the USSR* (Moscow: Novosti Press Agency, 1989), pp. 7–8.

24. ITAR-TASS, 25 August 1997, cited in *RFE/RL Newsline,* 26 August 1997.

25. Gail Sheehy, *The Man Who Changed the World: The Lives of Mikhail S. Gorbachev* (New York: Harper Collins, 1990), pp. 34–35.

26. *New York Times,* 24 March 1993, p. 1.

27. Article 35, *The Constitution of Independent Ukraine,* Ukrainian Rada website [http://www.rada.kiev.ua/const/conengl.htm#r2].

28. Article 40, Chapter Three, *Constitution of the Republic of Lithuania,* Legal Information Center at the Ministry of Justice of Lithuania website [http://www.tm.lt/Eng/Frames/Laws/Fr_laws2.htm].

29. Article 5, "Law on Religious Communities and Associations of the Republic of Lithuania", 4 October 1995, Legal Information Center at the Ministry of Justice of Lithuania website [http://www.tm.lt/].

30. Saulius Girnius, "The Catholic Church in Post-Soviet Lithuania", *RFE/RL Research Report,* 2 (15 October 1994).

31. Frederick Engels, *The Origin of the Family, Private Property, and the State* (Chicago: Charles H. Kerr & Company, 1902), pp. 88–90.

32. Interfax, 30 January 1997.

33. "Press release", 7 December 2000, Interstate Statistical Committee of the Commonwealth of Independent States website [http://www.cisstat.com/].

34. ITAR-TASS, 7 February 1995.

35. *Izvestiya,* 15 November 1996, reprinted in RIA-Novosti, 15 November 1996.

36. AFP, 2 January 1997 cited in *OMRI Daily Digest,* 3 January 1997.

37. ITAR-TASS, 4 February 1999, cited in *RFE/RL Newsline,* 5 February 1999.

38. Goskomstat figures reported in *RFE/RL Newsline,* 27 December 2000.

39. Interfax, 3 December 1998.

40. Interfax, 17 February 1994.

41. Interfax, 4 January 2001, cited in *RFE/RL Newsline,* 5 January 2001.

Chapter 3

The Communist Party and Its Legacy

Writing from his place of exile in Switzerland in late 1901 to early 1902, **Vladimir Ilyich Ulyanov,** the man known to the world as Lenin, engaged himself in the central task of his life: creating a structure by which the task of revolution could be achieved. His writing that year produced *What Is To Be Done?*, a primer in revolutionary strategy grounded in Marxian principles.[1] It is a convoluted masterpiece, difficult to read, brilliant in its analysis of how to foment a revolution, somewhat boring in describing the infighting prominent amongst Russia's revolutionary cadres, but never lacking in its abilities to stimulate passionate argument. Lenin's foremost political work revolutionized revolution and laid the groundwork for what would become the most important structure of Russia for most of the twentieth century, the communist party.

From 1917 when Lenin's party captured power in St. Petersburg, until 1991 when the communist governing structure crumbled of its own weight in the chaotic, sloppy drama of the August coup, the communist party governed the largest country on the face of the earth. It challenged the world with its ideology, as well as with its ability to mobilize the masses for revolution, propelling a collection of backward nations into the forefront of modernization. The organized expression of communism thus became one of the twentieth century's defining characteristics, and although dramatically weakened by events it remains an ideology that cannot be readily dismissed for the new century. As Lenin paraphrased **Karl Marx,** the intellectual progenitor of modern communism, the communist society was one "which has just emerged into the light of day out of the womb of capitalism and which is in every respect stamped with the birthmarks of the old society."[2] By extension, Russia and Eurasia in the last decade of the twentieth century also bear the hereditary markings of the communist state. The extent of these markings requires an examination of what Russian/Soviet communism was and how it evolved in the twentieth century.

Communism vs. Commercialism

Source: © Sel Ahmet/Sipa

The Past as Prologue

Marxism and Political Power

Marxism as a political doctrine is a call to action, to radically transform the capitalist society into socialism, and eventually communism which is defined by the classless society. Communism is the goal to be achieved although not necessarily the end result since man continues to progress. Thus communist *parties* are those which seek the attainment of the communist ideal; the goal and its realization are two separate parts of the overall process. Even at the height of Soviet power, Soviet authorities were careful to distinguish between the socialism they felt they had achieved and the end result of communism.

Probably the most succinct definition of communism one can find is that belonging to **Friedrich Engels,** Karl Marx's longtime collaborator. Engels put it this way: "Communism is the doctrine of the conditions of the liberation of the proletariat."[3] More to the point, communism is a body of theories which seek to explain political and social organization in terms of economic cycles. The best known of the many variants of communist thought, Marxism has been the foundation from which virtually every modern communist theorist has begun.

Marx himself was not interested so much in the specifics of seizing political power as in the question of why power would inevitably shift from one group to another. Marx's foremost contributions instead involve his **critique of the capitalist system** and his efforts to find its unique historic role. And while Marx and Engels were far from totally effective in establishing scientific procedures for analysis, they created a unique world view, a philosophy, that would pit much of the world against itself throughout the course of the twentieth century.

Marxism and Russia

Marx and Engels did not have Russia in mind as a test case of how revolution could or should be achieved. To them Russia was something of the poster child for malformed capitalism, certainly not in the forefront of development; virtually all other capitalist states seemed to be better prepared for the leap to socialism. Not that there weren't Marxist adherents amongst the Russian intelligentsia: Georgi Plekhanov, for instance, was often referred to as the father of Russian Marxism.[4] But Marx's opinions on Russia were few, and his assessments generally negative. To Marx, Russia was a peasant-based economy ill suited to proletarian

---

BOX 3.1   The Essential Marx

Marx' and Engel's writings are voluminous, to say the least, so knowing what aspects of the theory are to be found where should be of some help.

What	Where
Historical Materialism	*The German Ideology* (1845–46); *Socialism: Utopian and Scientific* (1892)
The direction and form of the communist revolution	*The Communist Manifesto* (1848)
A general outline of Marx's theory of economics	*Grundrisse* (1857–58)
Critique of capitalist society	*Capital* (1867)
A model for the proletarian revolution	*The Civil War in France* (1871)
What communism will involve	*Critique of the Gotha Programme* (1875)

revolution. Moreover, the path of capitalism upon which Russia was traveling could only defeat Russia's chances for a genuine transformation.[5] There was a saving grace for Russia, however: the village commune, or *mir*. This institution could serve as a means for backward Russia to bypass the capitalist stage of development in favor of moving directly to communism. But it could only be done in conjunction with proletarian revolution taking place in the advanced industrial states.[6]

Revolution can occur almost anywhere; but a proletarian revolution leading to a socialist society is a particular matter. Before it occurs Marxists have theorized, class antagonisms must come more sharply into conflict, that is, the proletariat must fight amongst itself in the competition for wages. Gradually, however, the working class will develop a sense of consciousness and, realizing its downtrodden position, assert itself in the struggle for power. This struggle is centered on the concept of private property, which is the divisive factor of capitalist society. Property as such is not to be eliminated, but rather the approach to property undergoes dramatic change; property for the purpose of exploiting the labor of others is done away with, as are attempts to expropriate the products of common or social labor.[7]

The revolution takes form as antagonisms become sharpest and the conflict in society grows unbearable. The seizure of political power occurs first. As the Polish scholar of Marxism Leszek Kolakowski phrased it, "political action is a means to economic emancipation after the revolution."[8] Fighting for its very existence, the bourgeoisie resists being dispossessed with all the forces at its disposal. When the proletariat and its guiding force, the revolutionary party, do seize political power, they consolidate their gains over the long-term, for the evils of the system of private property cannot be abolished overnight.[9]

Political power, then, is the key to the revolutionary transformation of capitalist society. It was upon this point that Lenin would base his revolutionary writings, mold the modern revolutionary party, and found the Soviet state. It was also upon this point that **Joseph Stalin** would subordinate both party and state to the will and needs of his personality. And finally it was upon this point that each of Stalin's successors would fixate on placing power above all concerns of economic theory. Thus, as mentioned in Chapter One we turn to evaluations of the Soviet elites, particularly the leaders of what was the communist party, and how they employed mobilizational politics, to illustrate the party's historical development.

Five Eras of the Communist Party

The Party Under Lenin

Although founded in 1898 at a clandestine meeting in Minsk, the Russian Social Democratic Labor Party (RSDLP, the earliest version of what became the CPSU) began to take form only with its second congress held in Brussels and London in 1902. At this decisive meeting, Lenin temporarily engineered a majority and subsequently took for his group the name **Bolsheviks** (*bolsheviki*, those in the majority),[10] and relegated his opponents to the psychologically disadvantageous position of being called **Mensheviks** (mensheviki, those in the minority). For the next fifteen years, more often in the minority himself, Lenin continued to compete with emigres and other revolutionaries back in Russia for the mantle of being the "true" Marxist party. As well, he fought doggedly with virtually everyone over his core principle of centralism which was to be the revolutionary organization's operational standard.[11] By the time his party actually seized power in October 1917 the Bolsheviks were far and away the best organized of the revolutionary parties, although having only an estimated 200,000 members by then.[12]

The Leninist period (1902–1924) is notable for several reasons: first, for the crucial achievement of creating a successful clandestine organization of dedicated, full-time revolutionaries. Between 1902 and 1917, Lenin built from scratch a force with the single-minded goal of bringing about the socialist revolution. Toward this end Lenin formulated the doctrine of *democratic centralism*, which would be a governing principle of the party until 1990. In Lenin's estimation, the party had to be composed of professional revolutionaries who could not be easily discovered by the regime, and must be committed to the task of the revolution.[13] The party would be governed by a strict regimen designed to guarantee the centrality of decision making and the subservience of minority groups to the majority, particularly lower party bodies to higher authorities. The somewhat logical outcome of this was the party's banning of internal groupings or fractions in 1921 as Lenin and those around him sought to consolidate power. Thus strict centralism and secrecy became core features of the party's culture.

BOX 3.2   The Essential Lenin

Lenin, too, was a prolific writer. Since there are 45 volumes of writings to his credit here are some of the essentials as matter of quick reference.

What	Where
The purpose of the party; organization of the party the party newspaper	*What Is To Be Done?* (1902)
The value of colonies to capitalism	*Imperialism, The Highest Stage of Capitalism* (1916)
The state as a repressive tool; The stages of socialism and communism	*The State and Revolution* (1917)
The new economic policy	*The Tax in Kind* (1921)
Lenin's assessment of his successors	*Letter to the Congress* (1922)

These characteristics have been especially difficult to supplant in present-day Russian, and Eurasian (excepting Baltic) politics.

A second characteristic of the Leninist period was the party's achievement and retention of power. For this purpose the party needed a special organizational acumen, which was largely found in the personality of Lev Davidovich Bronstein, more familiarly known as **Leon Trotsky.** A brilliant speaker and theoretician, and probably the most insightful Marxist chronicler of the Russian revolutions of 1905 and 1917,[14] Trotsky provided the architectural design for seizing power. In service to the new socialist state first as Commissar for Foreign Affairs, and then War, Trotsky created the Red Army and was one of those most responsible for the physical survival of the new state during the Civil War (1918–21). But both his ideas (for instance, the militarization of the factories) and his aloof, personal style created for Trotsky many more enemies than loyal followers, foremost among these being Stalin. Despite Trotsky's failings his contributions were essential to the early survival of the revolution.[15]

Finally, the Leninist period initiated the process of state building and vigilantly guarding the revolution. As much as any other element of Leninism this proved to be controversial especially in terms of the mechanisms and policies needed for this purpose. In December 1917, the new regime organized its police powers with the creation of the All-Russian Extraordinary Commission for Combatting Counter-Revolution, Sabotage, and Speculation (*Vhcheka* or more commonly, **Cheka**). Under the direction of Feliks Dzerzhinskii, the Cheka became synonymous with terror, its mission to sniff out and neutralize those who were disloyal to the party/state, or had no practical allegiances to it. From its inception this nucleus of the police state was a power unto itself, free of many of the party restraints but cautiously controlled due to the implicit dangers to the revolutionary regime itself.

More so than any other feature, the police state came to be associated with the Soviet system. This was primarily because the Vhcheka and its successors, the State Political Directorate (GPU, 1922–23), the Unified State Political Directorate (OGPU, 1923–34), the Peoples' Commissariat of Internal Affairs (NKVD, 1934–46), the People's Commissariat for State Security (NKGB, 1946–54), and finally the **Committee for State Security** (KGB, 1954–91) were effectively states-within-a-state. The secret police were responsible for mass executions, arrests, and management of the system of forced-labor camps, all of which served as pillars of regime support.[16] But in ensuring the regime's survival the system of state-sponsored terror and control also de-legitimized the Soviet system in the eyes of much of the citizenry who ultimately in 1991 offered the Soviet system at best passivity, but at critical junctures active opposition.

Stalin and Personal Power

While Lenin's contribution to Marxist thought is principally that of developing a revolutionary vanguard, Stalin's place in the party's annals is more abrupt: the realization of uncontested personal power with, or in spite of, the party. Stalin accumulated power slowly, competing with rivals throughout the 1920s, pitting one against another, all the while building a base of support within the party organization. Stalin's actions were a clear reflection of his personality of which the outside world knew or believed so little until so late in the game.[17] Born Josip Vissarionovich Djugashvili in Tsarist Georgia, he took the name Stalin ("man of steel") while working in the revolutionary underground. As Theodore von Laue points out,

> "While Lenin had lived abroad in relative ease, Stalin had worked and suffered for the cause inside Russia. The exiles' mastery of Marxist theory and their cultural refinement were out of his reach. But he possessed an advantage over them by representing the organizers and agitators without whom they were impotent."[18]

The Stalinist period (1924–53) was one of unceasing hardship, struggle, and conflict for both the Soviet people and the party. Outmaneuvering his political rivals after Lenin's death in 1924, Stalin moved to the commanding heights of the Russian Communist Party (bolshevik), initiating along the way what came to be known as his **cult of personality.** In the 1930s he consolidated his power by eliminating those he considered enemies—real or imagined—within the party, including the Old Bolsheviks (Kamenev, Zinoviev, Bukharin, Tomsky, Radek, and others; Trotsky was murdered in exile in 1940) who were all members of the party prior to the revolution. With the assassination of the popular Sergei Kirov in 1934,[19] a series of massive purges were initiated by Stalin that decimated the party ranks, weeding out those Stalin suspected of disloyalty or as being potential rivals, and many who were just in the way. Hundreds of thousands of party members, literally millions of peasants, workers, and intellectuals were murdered, millions more exiled or sent into forced labor detention from which they often never returned.[20] The best elements of both the party and the army were destroyed, leaving only those of unquestionable loyalty and sycophancy and an uncertain ability to defend the country in the face of fascism's and especially Hitler's rising threats.

Robert C. Tucker has argued that Stalinism was not a direct linear descendant of Leninism but rather conditioned by it, and all the same "an integral phase of the Russian revolutionary process as a whole."[21] Coming from a historically pragmatic standpoint Sheila Fitzpatrick contends that, "the Stalin era was the outcome of the Russian Revolution—not the intended, inevitable or desirable outcome, no doubt, but the actual outcome, the only one that exists."[22] Thus the party of Lenin became the party of Stalin; all those within and without the party had to swear their fealty to Stalin, even those to be executed. And through the massive changes which swept the Soviet state in the 1920s and the 1930s, the party took on a decidedly different character. The revolution, civil war, the decimation of the industrial proletariat, and intense recruitment of new party cadres in the 1920s changed the party from a small clandestine organization dedicated to underground work to a mass organization bent on achieving the goals of socialism.[23]

The machinery of control in the Stalin era was also altered to produce a new structural emphasis involving a clear-cut, top-to-bottom line of authority. After the removal of Stalin's opponents in the party, the military, and even the police, any potential rank-and-file opposition would find itself without leadership, an amorphous bunch that could not prevail against the Stalinist state.[24] In particular, emphasis was placed on the development of the bureaucracy in both the party and society. Beginning with the first **Five-Year Plan** in 1928, bureaucratization became almost an inevitable outcome since virtually every aspect of the economy had to be reconciled to government planning.[25] As new policies such as the gathering together of the peasantry and the consolidation of their resources—what came to be known as **collectivization**—were hammered out, the state met its ever-growing challenges with increasing centralization (in fact, the collective or communal farm was not new to Russian agriculture and made up much of the small landholder segment of the economy).

By the end of the 1930s the party was thoroughly cowed and the military a weak shadow of its former self; Stalin now felt it possible to devote his attention to international affairs. The menace of fascist Germany was already recognizable, but Stalin had hampered his own ability to determine where the threat really lay by destroying so much that could have helped him. As some contend, the German invasion in June 1941 came as a surprise to Stalin,[26] and resulted in near catastrophic losses in the early part of the war. For its part, the party was unable and unwilling to speak out, to debate the impending invasion without fear of reprisals. The party would not be the country's saving grace during the long, bloody years of war; instead the war was won by the tenacity and heroic instincts for survival of the Soviet peoples. The party, however, had galvanized the nation in the resistance, and being in authority was credited, as the leaders of victors usually are, as the vanguard of all that went well. Being in control of the resources of a heavily centralized state the party could, and did, quash any competing myths that may have threatened its laurels.

With the end of the Great Patriotic War (World War II), the fascist menace defeated, and the party recast in his own image, Stalin fully turned his attention to waging the international class struggle. Assisted by foreign communist parties, like the Russian Communist Party (b), which had been purged of any possibility of independent thought or action, Stalin focused on the post-war order. The remaining years of Stalin's life (he died in 1953) were spent playing out the drama of the Cold War and confronting a hostile world-capitalist camp surrounding the Soviet Union. It was a confrontation of Stalin's own making as it provided the opportunity to expand the socialist revolution into a global crusade with Stalin at the head.

Khrushchev Demystifies Stalin

For a brief period after Stalin's death an uneasy collective leadership prevailed much as it had after Lenin's demise. But in a system where primacy had become the rule, the collective system was not to last. Named First Secretary of the party (the title had been changed from General Secretary in 1952) six months after the dictator's death, **Nikita Khrushchev** remained in this position until being deposed in October 1964. It was not an easy tenure for him, nor one of unbridled control and power such that Stalin held; the system never again allowed for someone of such undiminished strength.

Khrushchev's period as party leader is most frequently characterized by his efforts to de-Stalinize the Soviet system, first by eliminating Stalin's henchmen (NKVD head Lavrenty Beria for instance[27]); and second, by showing Stalin to be responsible for not just "party errors", but mass murder as well. In what came to be known as the **Secret Speech** delivered to a closed Twentieth Party Congress in 1956 Khrushchev denounced the excesses of Stalin and branded him an enemy of the party, the building of socialism, and of the Soviet people.[28] Not really a spontaneous effort by Khrushchev, this campaign was planned in advance by the First Secretary as he and his opponents grappled for power.[29] The speech served two crucial purposes: 1) legitimizing the post-Stalin leadership and its policies; and 2) allowing Khrushchev to gain an advantage over his enemies, all of whom, like himself, were in some way culpable for the crimes of Stalin.

The Khrushchev period was also notable for its efforts to rehabilitate the party. Crucial to this effort, the repression of the Stalin years was greatly reduced. Millions of citizens were freed from the prison camps that had been the backbone of Stalinist governance. Opposition to the leadership was no longer automatically met with torture or death, although these approaches were still used; admittedly, opposition was still barely tolerated, but a new accommodation had to be reached. And, unlike his predecessor, Khrushchev dealt with his enemies with what amounts to a sense of black humor, demoting one to managing a cement factory, another to a power station, and a third to being ambassador to Mongolia.[30]

The Khrushchev era saw the most significant growth in party membership since the early Stalin years. Statistics on party growth show dramatic gains in both full and candidate members of the communist party from 1953—when a drop of 32,000 occurred—until 1964 by which time there had been a net growth of 879,000.[31] This growth trend was carried on throughout the Brezhnev years and represented at least a partial continuity of party policy. Less well-received within the party was the 1962 plan to split the party hierarchy into industrial and agricultural management components so as to more fully integrate the party with social development. An interesting idea for the purposes of production, it proved instead to be a threat to the centralized bureaucratic system and its proponents in Moscow.[32] Threatening the party's base of power, as well as failed agriculture programs (the "Virgin Lands" campaign), and foreign policy "adventurism" (the split with China; the Cuban Missile crisis) eroded Khrushchev's party support and led to his ouster in 1964.

Brezhnev: Personal Rule and Stagnation

It was a coalition of leaders that ejected Khrushchev from power in October 1964. The principal instigators of this action (technically it wasn't a coup, since party rules were followed) included Mikhail Suslov, the chief party ideologist, Nikolai Podgorny, named the chairman of the Presidium of the Supreme Soviet, or titular head of state, Alexei Kosygin, chairman of the Council of Ministers, or premier, and **Leonid Brezhnev,** First Secretary (the title was changed back to General Secretary in 1966) of the Central Committee of the CPSU. For the next eighteen years the party worked under what proved to be a highly stable leadership committed to making the Soviet Union a true military and economic superpower. Along the way the CPSU also continued its growth until it had nearly nineteen million members by the early 1980s.

After the political and social thaw of the Khrushchev years, the Brezhnev era was characterized by much less tolerance of autonomous behavior amongst the population, party members, or allied communist parties. Anti-Soviet activities were brutally repressed with dissenters confined to "harsh regime" labor camps or mental institutions; in a few prominent cases such as that of novelist Aleksandr Solzhenitsyn individuals were exiled from the country after serving long prison terms.[33] Although the class struggle had been declared over by Stalin in 1936, the party continued to view itself as the vanguard of society fighting against those who resisted the progress of socialism. Because the party was certain that scientific Marxism-Leninism was best represented by itself it had to retain a monopoly on political participation and the masses' best interests.

Unwilling to defend the Khrushchev thesis that the Soviet Union was in the stage of building communism, Brezhnev and his supporters retreated into what Mary McAuley has aptly phrased "a more conservative, bland, style."[34] Party theoreticians postulated that the country had reached a new intermediate stage on the path to communism that they termed **developed socialism.** In particular, they promoted the concept of the **scientific-technological revolution** (or STR) which became formal policy at the Twenty-Fourth Party Congress in 1971. This policy sought to link scientific advancements to production and economic planning so as to offset shortfalls in production.[35] But in the 1970s the slowing of economic growth and a widening developmental gap with the capitalist world revealed a dangerous shortsightedness by the party elite as to how to direct the country. By the end of that decade the economy was stagnant, the standard of living deteriorating, and income disparities between the party elite and the bulk of society were becoming more blatant.

The perennial problem of leadership succession also remained unaddressed, much less unresolved. At no point had a formal mechanism for replacing leaders been developed; under Brezhnev's rule a **gerontocracy** had emerged, that is, a leadership group much older than the rank-and-file party members. Between 1950 and 1962 the average age of members of the CPSU Presidium increased from fifty-five years to fifty-nine, then dropped due to the infusion of a new leadership group in 1964. But from 1966 until 1980 the median age within the renamed Politburo increased from fifty-seven to sixty-nine,[36] while the average age of Central Committee members increased from fifty-two in 1966 to sixty-four in 1980. The rapid aging of upper- and mid-level party personnel was a direct consequence of a policy termed **trust-in-cadres** initiated with the rise to power of Brezhnev. Simply put, this was a trade-off of reassurances to party personnel that their jobs/positions were secure from tampering by the leadership provided the party members supported the leadership (hence, trust). Having removed the threat of arbitrary dismissal the leadership unwittingly fostered complacency toward job performance and systemic reform.[37]

The aging of the leadership coupled to the lack of new blood being introduced to decision-making circles were the most visible aspects of the Brezhnev system. The impetus for reform had been stifled, and corruption among the elite was rife in Brezhnev's last years. Brezhnev's own daughter Galina and her husband, Deputy Minister of Internal Affairs General Yuri Churbanov, were investigated for graft and bribery in 1982,[38] and Churbanov was sentenced to prison. Brezhnev's death in November 1982 capped the rise of **Yuri Andropov,** the former head of the KGB. As head of this body he was fully aware of, and opposed to the depth of corruption that permeated Soviet society during the Brezhnev years. Andropov's real measure of success proved not to be his anticorruption drive but rather his ability to consolidate power as head of party and state in a remarkably brief period of seven months. Also a product of the gerontocracy Andropov died within fifteen months of taking office (February 1984). He was succeeded by **Konstantin Chernenko,** in whom the conservative, reactionary proponents among the elite placed their fleeting hopes for holding onto power. Within thirteen months Chernenko, too, was dead, an indication of how desperate the leadership crisis had become. The way had been paved for a reformer in whom the system had to place its trust.

Gorbachev Opens the Pandora Box

In retrospect, Andropov's most significant contribution may have been the promotion of his (relatively) young protege, Mikhail Gorbachev. When elevated to candidate status on the Politburo in 1979 at age forty-eight Gorbachev was the youngest member of that body. When he became General Secretary at the age of fifty-four, he was still younger than anyone else on the Politburo. Having earned both a law degree and a degree in agronomy-economy, Gorbachev was better prepared intellectually for his job than any of Lenin's successors. Moreover, he was well-versed in Marxist theory, a claim which neither Khrushchev nor Brezhnev could make.

Having witnessed the failures of the Khrushchev reforms, and later the stiff orthodoxy of the Brezhnev years, Gorbachev came to the leadership determined to correct the mistakes of the past and reinvigorate socialism. This was undertaken through a series of policies collectively termed *perestroika,* or "restructuring" the economic system. In the space of the next several years it evolved into a four-point program: perestroika; *glasnost,* or "openness" in Soviet society; *demokratizatsia,* or "democratization" of decision making; and *novoe myshlenie,* or "new thinking", primarily in foreign policy. These policies clearly invigorated a dynamic that Gorbachev and other reformers were confident of controlling. The conditions of modern Soviet society, however, had been substantially underestimated by the leadership.[39] The CPSU had done everything in its power for several generations to define society according to the rhetoric of Soviet-style socialism. But, as Timothy Colton described the problem, "the main reason that familiar formulas misfire is that the conditions under which they were first defined evolve more quickly than the formula itself."[40]

Gorbachev's first efforts at reform were announced at the April 1985 Central Committee Plenum. He drew upon the ideas of long-frustrated party officials such as Alexandr Yakovlev and nontraditional academics including sociologist Tatiana Zaslavskaya and economist Abel Aganbegyan. Yakovlev and Aganbegyan in particular have often been referred to as the architects of *perestroika*, their input giving substance to the general political and economic assessments arrived at by Gorbachev.[41] Economic reform was essential, they knew, but in order to effect even minor changes the party itself had to be cleared of its corrupt elements and dead wood; principal figures from the Brezhnev era had to be retired, moved aside, or demoted. A constant shuffling of the players in lieu of concrete reforms was to be a hallmark of this period, perhaps a herald of how Yeltsin himself would lead after 1991 (see Chapter Six).

Initially heralded for his reform efforts, resistance to Gorbachev's programs began to build from critics on both the left and right. Defying the democratic centralism principle a loosely defined left opposition emerged within the party headed by such figures as Yeltsin, St. Petersburg party leader (mayor) Anatolii Sobchak, and his Moscow counterpart Gavril Popov. This group's demands for even broader reform were countered by the conservative party bureaucracy which was increasingly alarmed that their hold on power was slipping, and consequently began marshaling their forces.[42] By 1989 intraparty resistance to *perestroika* had grown and Gorbachev attempted to transfer power from the party to the state structure through his own election as the legislature's (the **Congress of Peoples' Deputies**) president.[43] The new form of governance taking shape seemed to be based on "the old model of commune democracy, with its emphasis on fusing executive and legislative functions."[44] But Gorbachev's innovations were largely drawn from west European experiences and alien to much of the party leadership and rank-and-file; the party was as yet unprepared for such levels of change.

The biggest blow was still to come. With the warning that *perestroika* now depended upon the party abandoning command-and-control methods toward the state and the economy,[45] Gorbachev convinced party elites in February 1990 to surrender their monopoly on political power. Amending **Article Six** of the Soviet Constitution, which enshrined this principle, was unquestionably the most dramatic development the party had faced since the purges of the 1930s. Whether Gorbachev and others intended it to be so or not, these changes sounded the party's death knell. At the Twenty-Eighth Party Congress in July 1990, the split between party and state was formalized with the removal from the Politburo of all government officials and their replacement with the heads of the various republican party organizations.[46] It was too little, too late, as several republican parties (notably the Baltics) had already formally separated themselves from the CPSU.

The near inevitable result to all of this was the coup of 19–21 August 1991. The conservative element of the party had been pressuring Gorbachev for the better part of the past year with some successes, but Gorbachev's efforts to craft a new federal structure for the Soviet Union's republics—known as the **Union Treaty**—was the breaking point.[47] Due to the gross ineptitude of the coup planners (several admitted to having been drunk during its plotting), especially in not arresting Yeltsin, the coup was a dismal failure that shifted the disintegration of both the CPSU and the Soviet system into high gear. The leaders of the coup had misread the country's mood; support for Gorbachev personally was not the key issue to the public. Rather, people were concerned about the survival of their fledgling experiment with democracy, and especially pluralist expression. Returning from house arrest with Yeltsin's assistance Gorbachev and the other reformers were swift in their reactions to the plotters: the CPSU was suspended the day the coup ended, Gorbachev resigned as General Secretary, party property was confiscated and files seized, statues honoring communist party leaders were torn down around the country, and members fled the party in droves.

Both during the coup and for the next several months the public remained largely indifferent to the events in Moscow and to the party's fate, leaving Gorbachev increasingly reliant on Yeltsin who by now had little use for either Gorbachev or the CPSU. It was an awkward position for Gorbachev; within four months he was out of power completely and the Soviet experiment in building communism begun by Lenin was no more.

How the Party Functioned

Rules of the Game: Party Statutes and Congresses

Despite the changes wrought by Gorbachev's *perestroika* certain patterns of party behavior remained constant over the years, the most important of these being the party statutes (rules) and party congresses. The statutes embodied the principles and rules governing membership and structure of the communist party. Rules were only infrequently changed and then only at party congresses. In 1986, for instance, the minimum age for full membership was raised from twenty-one to twenty-five years.[48] The significance of the rules lay in the formal outline they provided of the party and its essential components, the party congress (articles 31–34), the party conference (article 40), the Central Committee (articles 35–39), the Politburo and Secretariat (article 38), the Central Auditing Commission (article 36), the Party Control Committee (article 39), the Primary Party Organizations (articles 52–59), the Komsomol (articles 63–66), and the party-military relationship (articles 67–69).

Over the years the party congresses represented the seminal events in the CPSU's development. From Khrushchev's time to the end of Gorbachev's tenure the congresses were regularized to meet at least once every five years (exceptions being the Twenty-First and Twenty-Eighth Congresses). From the 1920s congresses were massive gatherings used by the leadership to ratify key decisions. Composed of the elite of the party membership, as many as 5000 delegates representing republican and regional organizations from throughout the Soviet

Union came together in Moscow. Dignitaries from communist parties around the world also attended, largely (although not exclusively so) in recognition of the Soviet Union's place at the forefront of the international socialist movement. Highly formalized affairs, the basic decisions had already been agreed upon by the leadership prior to the actual meeting. The new five-year plans for guiding the economy were typically unveiled at this juncture, and course changes in political and international matters were proclaimed.

Certainly the most interesting events at a congress were the promotion and demotion of the leadership. Revisions to the party rules during the Brezhnev years restricted new appointments to the **Central Committee** (CC) until a congress had met; candidate members—that is, nonvoting members of the CC—could, however, be promoted to full membership at the CC plenary (twice-yearly) meetings. The Central Committee also maintained the prerogative of demoting those who had fallen out of favor, or those who might obstruct the Politburo's or General Secretary's policies. At the Twenty-Eighth Party Congress in 1990 the premier, the defense minister, the head of the KGB, and the foreign minister were all dropped from the Politburo and all republican First Secretaries were included for the first time. As well, the Politburo agreed to meet only once a month as compared to its former weekly schedule. Regular decision making was to have been the province of a refurbished sixteen-member Secretariat.[49]

Making Policy: the Politburo and Secretariat

The **Politburo,** or Political Bureau, first formed in 1919, was not the original primary governing institution for the communist party: that role was played by the Central Committee until the early 1920s. By the middle of the 1920s power had gravitated to the Politburo as an executive body for an enlarged Central Committee. Until 1990 the Politburo consistently had between ten and fourteen full, or voting members with four to eight candidates, or nonvoting members (changes in 1952 were the exceptions). The odd thing about the Politburo was that its decision-making powers were not formally spelled out in the party rules. Records of Politburo meetings were not provided to its legitimating body, the Central Committee, and voting on issues which came before it was done by consensus rather than by majority rule. Until Andropov's time in office what was known of Politburo meetings came largely from anecdotal sources; more recently party archives have been opened giving us fuller accounts of the decision-making process.[50]

Clearly, the Politburo was the most important institution in the party hierarchy, although the Secretariat was technically of equal importance (see Figure 3.1). Party rules dictated that the Central Committee elect Politburo members, but the reverse was actually true: the Politburo decided who was to be appointed to the CC and "suggested" who was to be promoted to the Politburo. To serve in the Politburo was to have arrived at the pinnacle of Soviet power. To hold a position simultaneously on the Secretariat was to have moved a notch higher. Decisions made by the Politburo involved national and international affairs, questions relating to the party, the economy, agriculture, and politics (for instance, decisions to exile dissi-

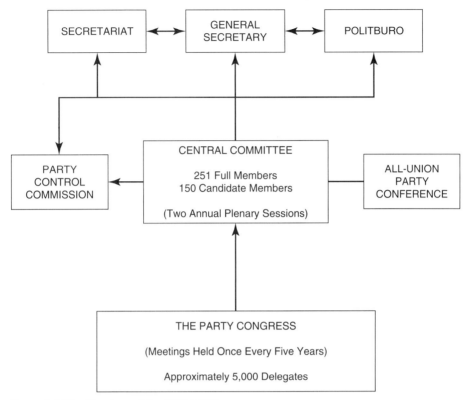

Figure 3.1 The Structure of the CPSU 1989

dents). At its worst, the Politburo micromanaged the economy by setting production quotas for individual factories or by determining who worked where. Its power was broad-ranging and largely without precedent in western democratic systems.

The **Secretariat** was composed of the principal Central Committee figures responsible for day-by-day party, and in some cases state, functions. Until 1990 the General Secretary drew his formal power from this institution, not the Politburo. Smaller than the Politburo, the Secretariat had on average eight to twelve members who were charged with running the various departments of the Central Committee (see below). Secretariat members were responsible for party functions such as personnel, inter-communist relations, agriculture, and organizational party work. Like the Politburo, its activities were obscured to the extent that even those who closely observed higher party organs could not fully determine its operational procedures.[51]

Influencing Policy: The Central Committee

Whereas once the Central Committee had only a handful of members and acted as the guiding force for the Bolshevik Party by its end in 1991 it consisted of 412 full and candidate members. Technically, the CC was superior to the Politburo or the Secretariat, having derived its authority from the Congress. Article 35 of the CPSU rules dictated a series of functions: 1) guiding the "entire activity of the Party and the local Party bodies"; 2) selecting and appointing leading functionaries (until 1990 the Central Committee was responsible for electing the General Secretary; at the Twenty-Eighth Party Congress this authority was transferred to the congress itself[52]); 3) directing "the work of central government bodies and public organizations of working people"; 4) setting up new party bodies, institutions, and enterprises, and guiding their activities; 5) appointing editors of party papers and journals; and 6) distributing and controlling party funds.[53] In short, the CC carried out functionary activities including control of the party bureaucracy. For this purpose approximately several thousand professional and technical workers were employed to carry out day-by-day operations for the party. The CC could therefore exercise influence over, but avoid directly governing the Soviet system.

Implementing Policy: The Rank and File

With approximately 19.4 million due paying members as of 1989 (the high-water mark for membership) the CPSU was a mass-mobilization organization (see Figure 3.1). Membership was treated as an earned privilege, and candidates had to be nominated by three party members (each of whom had to have been a member for five years and had worked with the applicant for one year, both professionally and socially (article 4 [a]), and be twenty-five years old; the exception to the rule involved **Komsomol** (the party youth organization) members. It should come as no surprise that getting kicked out of the party was not a desirable option.

The tumult of the *perestroika* years precipitated a general decline in party membership. The loss of the party's political monopoly opened the door for alternative forms of participation, although competing parties were not immediately legalized. Figures on the decline in party membership are sketchy, but between January and July 1990 alone approximately 130,000 party members resigned, and prior to the August 1991 coup total membership dropped to an estimated 6.8 million, setting the stage for a calamitous failure of the system.[54] The rebirth of the CPSU organization as the **Communist Party of the Russian Federation (KPRF)** in 1992 demonstrated that a much smaller, but nevertheless solid core of support for the ideals of socialism remained. Even still the KPRF has not come even close to matching the CPSU's party membership numbers as the KPRF has counted only a half-million in its ranks,[55] a far cry from the glory days of the party of Lenin and Stalin (more on this in Chapter Four).

The basic organizational unit of the party was, and is, the **Primary Party Organization** (PPO). During the Soviet period PPOs were organized in all work places (industrial, agricultural, military, etc.), and consisted of from three to 1000 members. The PPOs required self-criticism by party members, and called to task those who were not fulfilling their duties. The organization of the PPO in the work place allowed the party to see that its directives were being carried out and ensured that party members would actually attend meetings.

So why would the typical party member join? With party support the individual was assured some level of professional advancement that was generally denied to nonparty members. It was a two-way street with party members getting access (the Russians use the word *blat*, or "influence") to goods and services denied to the average citizen, and the party gained acquiescence to its way of doing things. As a mass mobilization organization not everyone was going to be privy to the ultimate "perks". Still, for those who aspired to travel, who wanted the best education, prime placement in government and academic jobs, or simply knowledge of when, where, and how things were to be obtained, party membership provided the edge.

The problem of **careerism** was recognized by Lenin and virtually every other Soviet leader, and periodic purges were conducted to weed out careerists. Once the system lost its ability to deliver on the goods, or to monopolize political decision-making (as was the case by 1990), however, the institution was doomed. Only those who had ideological commitments to communism would now be willing to make it their home.

The Party and the Republics

Finally, there were the republican party organizations. Each of the republics of the Soviet Union—except the Russian Federation—had its own party hierarchy, although in actuality these were integral parts of the CPSU. Leadership selection in the republics was largely a function of Moscow with the local party organizations accepting whomever the center chose to send to the republic. Politburo and Secretariat members often first served in the republican party organizations before being advanced to Moscow. Khrushchev, for instance, was First Secretary in Ukraine while Brezhnev held the same post in Moldavia. Under Brezhnev, this principle of giving the top job in the republic to an ethnic native was strengthened, but the deputy position now became reserved for an ethnic Russian.

When Gorbachev challenged this policy in 1986 by deposing the corrupt Kazakhstan First Secretary Dinmukhamed Kunaev, in favor of a Russian, Gennadi Kolbin, it led to riots by ethnic Kazaks who saw Moscow's move as an attack on a native son. The republics' subsequent movements toward autonomy were dramatically altered when the Lithuanian Communist Party declared itself independent from the CPSU in December 1989.[56] And with the republics' emergence as free states many of the republican First Secretaries discovered the utility of governing as formal state leaders. For them, leaving the party behind meant little as power was their real goal, and the communist party's dismantling was made easy by the loss of revolutionary elan.

Key Terms

class struggle
trust in cadres
democratic centralism
Politburo

Secret Speech
Bolshevik Party
perestroika
Central Committee

Questions for Consideration

1. How can you explain communism's success in Russia given the lack of conditions suitable to the Marxist model?

2. What impact did Stalin's brand of totalitarian rule have on the development of the Russian political culture overall?

3. Why did the CPSU's governing abilities stagnate in the 1970s at the very time that the Soviet Union had reached its greatest expanse of power?

4. Was Mikhail Gorbachev's reform platform of *perestroika* too little, too late, or could it have saved socialism given other circumstances?

5. Should the failure of Soviet power be attributed to the strict centralism of the CPSU's governing structure? Where in the structure of the party can support be found for this thesis?

Suggested Readings

Robert V. Daniels, ed., *Soviet Communism from Reform to Collapse* (Lexington, MA: D.C. Heath, 1995).

Robert Freedman, *The Marxist System: Economic, Political, and Social Perspectives* (Chatham, NJ: Chatham House, 1990).

Mikhail Gorbachev, *Perestroika, New Thinking for Our Country and the World* (New York: Harper and Row, 1987).

Ronald J. Hill and Peter Frank, *The Soviet Communist Party*, 3rd ed. (Boston, MA: Allen & Unwin, 1986).

Warren Lerner, *A History of Socialism and Communism in Modern Times*, 2nd ed. (Englewood Cliffs, NJ: Prentice Hall, 1994).

Karl Marx, *The Communist Manifesto*, ed. by Frederic L. Bender (New York: W. W. Norton, 1988).

Roy Medvedev, *All Stalin's Men* (Garden City, NY: Anchor Books, 1985).

Useful Websites

Communist Party of the Russian Federation
http://www.kprf.ru

Communist Party of the Soviet Union
http://www.kpss.ru

Marxist Labour Party
http://www.geocities.com/marxparty

Marxists' Internet Archive
http://csf.colorado.edu/mirrors/marxists.org/

Pravda (in Russian)
http://pravda.ru

Pravda (in English)
http://english.pravda.ru

Social Democrats of Russia
http://www.sd.org/ru/

Endnotes

1. On the writing of *What Is To Be Done?* see Bertram D. Wolfe, *Three Who Made a Revolution* (New York: Dell Publishing, 1964), pp. 156–66.
2. V. I. Lenin, *Collected Works*, vol. 25, 5th ed. (Moscow: Progress Publishers, 1980), p. 470.
3. Friedrich Engels, "The Principles of Communism" in Karl Marx and Friedrich Engels, *The Communist Manifesto* (New York: Modern Reader Paperbacks, 1968), p. 67.
4. Plekhanov's contributions are frequently overshadowed by Lenin, but are still worthy of attention. Notable among these is *The Development of the Monist View of History* (1885); *The Role of the Individual in History* (1898); and *Fundamental Problems of Marxism* (1908).
5. Karl Marx and Friedrich Engels, "Russia's Pattern of Development", in Feuer, ed. Lewis S. Feuer, Marx and Engels: Basic Writings on Politics and Philosophy (Garden City, N.J.: Anchor Books, 1959), p. 439.
6. See Marx's introduction to the Russian edition of *The Communist Manifesto* in David McLellan, *Karl Marx: Selected Writings*, (New York: Oxford University Press, 1990), p. 584.
7. See Marx's comments in Robert C. Tucker, ed., *The Marx-Engels Reader* (W. W. Norton, 1978), p. 486.
8. Leszek Kolakowski, *Main Currents of Marxism: Its Origins, Growth, and Dissolution*, vol. 1 (New York: Oxford University Press, 1978), p. 304.
9. Engels, "The Principles of Communism", pp. 75–76.
10. Among the better accounts of this tumultuous meeting see Leonard Schapiro, *The Communist Party of the Soviet Union*, 2nd ed. (New York: Vintage Books, 1971), chapter two; and Wolfe, *Three Who Made a Revolution,* Chapter Fourteen.
11. For a concise discussion of why Lenin succeeded in gaining control of the party organization, see Harold Shukman, *Lenin and the Russian Revolution* (New York: Longman, Inc., 1977), especially chapter five.
12. Ibid., p. 173. The actual size of the party is a subject of some debate, but for all intents and purposes it was of only middling strength.
13. V. I. Lenin, *What is to be Done?*, in *Lenin: Collected Works*, Vol. 5 (Moscow: Progress Publishers, 1977), p. 464.
14. See Trotsky's *1905* (New York: Vintage Books, 1971), and *The History of the Russian Revolution* (Ann Arbor, MI: University of Michigan Press, 1932).
15. The exceptional biography of Trotsky by Isaac Deutscher remains a work worth reading. See *The Prophet Armed, The Prophet Unarmed,* and *The Prophet Outcast* (New York: Vintage Books, 1963).
16. V. I. Lenin, "How to Organize Competition", in *Lenin, Collected Works*, vol. 26, 5th ed. (Moscow: Progress Publishers, 1977), pp. 404–15; and "Note to F. E. Dzerzhinskii with a Draft of a Decree on Fighting Counter-Revolutionaries and Saboteurs", vol. 26, pp. 374–6.
17. For an interesting psychological profile of the man, see Robert C. Tucker, *Stalin as Revolutionary, 1879–1929: A Study in History and Personality* (New York: W. W. Norton, 1973).
18. Theodore H. Von Laue, *Why Lenin? Why Stalin?: A Reappraisal of the Russian Revolution*, 2nd ed. (New York: J. B. Lippincott Co., 1971), p. 187.
19. A thorough account of this issue may be found in Amy Knight, *Who Killed Kirov?* (New York, NY: Hill and Wang, 1999).
20. In the post-Stalinist era the purges stimulated numerous eyewitness and literary accounts including Aleksandr Solzhenitsyn's *One Day in the Life of Ivan Denisovich* (New York: Farrer, Straus, Giroux, 1991), Anatoli Rybakov's *Children of the Arbat* (Boston: Little, Brown, 1988) and *Fear* (Boston: Little, Brown, 1992), and Vasilly Aksyonov's *Generations of Winter* (New York: Random House, 1994).

21. Robert C. Tucker, "Stalinism as Revolution From Above", in Tucker, ed. *Stalinism: Essays in Historical Interpretation* (New York: W. W. Norton, 1977), p. 78.

22. Sheila Fitzpatrick, *The Russian Revolution, 1917–1932* (Oxford: Oxford University Press, 1982), p. 154.

23. Helene Carrere d'Encausse, *Stalin: Order Through Terror* (London: Longman Group Limited, 1984), pp. 1–5.

24. Robert C. Tucker, *Stalin in Power: The Revolution From Above, 1928–1941* (New York: W. W. Norton, 1992), p. 378.

25. d'Encausse, *Stalin: Order Through Terror*, pp. 15–16.

26. Adam B. Ulam, *Stalin: The Man and his Era* (Boston: Beacon Press, 1989), pp. 536–8.

27. Khrushchev, *Khrushchev Remembers*, pp. 321–41.

28. The Secret Speech may be found in Ibid, pp. 559–618.

29. Edward Crankshaw, *Khrushchev: A Career* (New York: Viking Press, 1966), pp. 227–28.

30. Appendix 3, "Khrushchev's Kremlin Colleagues" in Khrushchev, *Khrushchev Remembers*.

31. T. H. Rigby, *Communist Party Membership in the USSR, 1917–1967* (Princeton, NJ: Princeton University Press, 1968), pp. 298–300.

32. Carl Linden, *Khrushchev and the Soviet Leadership: 1957–1964* (Baltimore: The Johns Hopkins Press, 1966), pp. 149–52.

33. The decision on Solzhenitsyn's exile by the CPSU Politburo can be found in "Kak oni gotovili raspravu" ("How They Prepared Reprisals"), "Literaturnaia gazeta" 15 December 1993, translated in *Russian Politics and Law*, 33 (March–April 1995): pp. 89–93.

34. Mary McAuley, *Soviet Politics, 1917–1991* (New York: Oxford University Press, 1992), p. 75.

35. Paul Cocks, "Science Policy and Soviet Development Strategy", in Alexander Dallin, ed., *The Twenty-Fifth Congress of the CPSU: Assessment and Context* (Stanford, CA: Hoover Institution Press, 1977), pp. 41–42.

36. Jerry F. Hough, *Soviet Leadership in Transition* (Washington, DC: The Brookings Institution, 1980), p. 70.

37. Donald R. Kelley, "The Communist Party" in Donald R. Kelley, ed., *Soviet Politics in The Brezhnev Era* (New York: Praeger Publishers, 1980), pp. 30–35.

38. Zhores A. Medvedev, *Andropov* (Middlesex, England: Penguin Publishers, 1983), pp. 93–98.

39. On this viewpoint, see Marshall I. Goldman, *What Went Wrong with Perestroika*, (New York: W. W. Norton, 1992), especially Chapter Three.

40. Timothy J. Colton, *The Dilemma of Reform in the Soviet Union*, revised and expanded ed., (New York: Council on Foreign Relations, 1986), p. 39.

41. Mikhail Gorbachev, *Political Report of the CPSU Central Committee to the 27th Party Congress* (Moscow: Novosti Press Agency, 1986).

42. Michel Tatu, "19th Party Conference", *Problems of Communism*, 37 (May-August 1988): pp. 1–3. Also, see Goldman, *What Went Wrong with Perestroika*, pp. 172–75.

43. Elizabeth Teague and Dawn Mann, "Gorbachev's Dual Role", *Problems of Communism*, 39 (January–February 1990): p. 9.

44. Richard Sakwa, *Gorbachev and His Reforms, 1985–1990* (Englewood Cliffs, NJ: Prentice-Hall, 1990), p. 148.

45. *New York Times*, 6 February 1990; also, FBIS-SOV, 8 February, 1990, p. 42.

46. *New York Times,* 15 July, 1990. Also, Mikhail Gorbachev, *Towards a Humane and Democratic Socialist Society* (draft platform for the 28th Party Congress) (Moscow: Novosti Press Agency, 1990), pp. 45–46.

47. For the formal statement announcing Gorbachev's replacement by the coup plotters see the "Statement of the Soviet Leadership", 19 August 1991, "News and Views from the USSR" press release, Soviet Embassy, Washington, DC.

48. *Rules of the Communist Party of the Soviet Union* (Moscow: Novosti Press Agency, 1986), p. 8.

49. *New York Times,* 15 July 1990.

50. An example of this decision making process may be found in the 15 December 1993 *Literaturnaia Gazeta* article "How They Prepared Reprisals", reprinted in *Russian Politics and Law,* 33 (March–April 1995): pp. 89–93.

51. See, for instance, Jerry F. Hough and Merle Fainsod, *How the Soviet Union is Governed* (Cambridge, MA: Harvard University Press, 1979), pp. 409–19.

52. Sakwa, *Gorbachev and His Reforms,* pp. 174–75; also see news reports on the Congress for the challenge to Gorbachev and the vote tallies.

53. *Rules,* p. 16.

54. "Communist Membership Falls from 6.8 Million to 600,000", Interfax, 21 April 1997, World News Connection [http://wnc.fedworld.gov].

55. In 1997 the KPRF contended it had as many as 540,000 in its ranks. See Gennadii Zyuganov, "Russia Will be Great and Socialist", *Sovetskaya Rossiya,* 22 April 1997, World News Connection [http://wnc.fedworld.gov].

56. Alfred Erich Senn, "Toward Lithuanian Independence: Algirdas Brazauskas and the CPL", *Problems of Communism,* 39 (March–April 1990): pp. 21–28.

Chapter 4

Emerging Pluralism

I f any condition marks the passage of a political system from one form to another it is that of participation. It is the condition both sought after by adherents of democracy, and feared by authoritarian leaders. Participation comes in numerous forms ranging from the use of mass parades and rallies in totalitarian systems to massive voter solicitation in democratic polities. The presence of multiple levels of participation does not ensure that democracy is the logical outcome but instead that it is a possibility. Nor does extensive participation guarantee that a democratic system will prevail. Participation in and of itself is no more than a condition of involvement measured by degrees between political systems.

The diversity of the Russian political scene can be illustrated by the startling range of involvement by citizens and groups in Russian public life. Already at the time of the 1991 coup there were in excess of 500 political parties and 1200 political formations in the USSR.[1] In 1998 the government of the Russian Federation recorded 18,895 public amalgamations—including parties, movements, trade unions, cultural organizations, and public funds—nationwide.[2] New competitive political organizations have continued to surface at a rapid-fire pace: for instance, over fifty blocs and 15,000 candidates registered with the Central Election Commission (TsIK) for the December 1995 elections,[3] and in the 1999 State Duma elections thirty-one parties and movements were listed for the voters' choices.[4] Just as important, segments of the public have been actively involved in demonstrations, strikes, and other political activities in a manner virtually impossible in the days of the USSR. Although much of the most visible activity is still confined to Russia's largest cities, these changes are historically dramatic and culturally significant.

For Russia and the Eurasian states none of this necessarily means that democracy has either arrived, or is going to. But it is hard to deny that Russia and many of its Eurasian neighbors are increasingly pluralist, and pluralism foments the development of both rule of law states and the democratic condition. *Pluralism,* as defined by one of its foremost proponents, Robert Dahl, implies that numerous groups (or actors) exhibit autonomy of action within the state, which in turn has an impact on the character of governance.[5] In other words, a political system where diversity of participation is the norm is one that is pluralist.

As political parties, movements, interest groups, and individual actors—both legal and illegal—expand, pluralism is increasingly the defining characteristic of political life in Russia today.

Russia in a Transitional Stage

Building Democratic Values

Writing in 1993 prior to the siege of the Russian parliament and the elections of December, Bruce L. R. Smith remarked that "the institutional features that constitute democratic government (in Russia) are beginning to be present in more than embryo, if less than fully developed, form."[6] Supporting this assessment, one Russian observer has noted that "democratic ideals . . . are becoming part of the mass consciousness and psychology" but that "these beliefs are still essentially abstract: not everyone thinks freedom and democratic self-organization are right for Russia today . . ."[7] Not exactly a ringing endorsement of Russian progress, you might conclude, but certainly not a searing condemnation either. The truth of the matter is that the prospect of Russian democracy is severely hampered by institutional constraints, a lack of a clear direction, and hyper-competition over who shall set priorities. In some respects Russia's present condition is better described as a competitive oligarchy, or a system that is "transitional to democracy but not democratic as such."[8]

A more apt description of what is occurring in Russia is to term it a transitional system. **Transitionalism** represents an intermediary stage, one which is not restricted in how long it may exist, but still distinct. Russell Bova has suggested that transitions from authoritarianism involve both the breakdown of the old structures (such as the system of soviets) and the development of new governing institutions.[9] For his part Dankwart Rustow stipulated that to enhance the outcome of democracy some conditions must be in place including national unity which he concludes occurs where "the vast majority of citizens . . . have no doubt or mental reservations as to which political community they belong to."[10]

Other preconditions are also important such as a growing diversity of representational parties, variegation of political viewpoints, the expansion of media sources, and a growing recognition and acceptance of the political game's new rules. As some Russian analysts have observed, the Russian public generally supports democracy in principle but has yet to come to terms with how it will be worked out.[11] Moreover, citizens' opinions and the social networks they maintain have become "extremely politicized", if not politically active.[12]

The political debate has also focused on whether Russia has appropriately borrowed values from western democracies. Russian nationalists regularly denounce western intrusion into Russian affairs, especially demands made by western governments or lending institutions that Russia bring itself into conformity with democratic norms or free market economics.[13] Parties of both the left and right, however, see a dominant theme in the breakdown of Russia's moral values, fueled by the "Americanization" of Russian culture and its economy.[14] As one way out of this dilemma Russia's various communist parties frequently espouse the goal of reviving the Soviet Union within its former boundaries.[15]

A second downside to Russia's democratic development is an intense hostility by many groups to what the country may become. A striking illustration of this was the so-called "red-brown" alliance. Taking form in 1992–93 this loose association included far-left forces such as the communists ("reds") and far-right—both fascist and nationalist forces ("browns"). An unthinkable combination during the decades of communist rule, the cooperation of red-brown forces demonstrated the hostility of extremist elements to the new political system. This tentative alliance also pointed to how explosive the political arena had become as two polar opposites discovered that cooperation between themselves suited each group's radical political agendas.

A third element contributing to the slow growth of democracy is the extent of political fragmentation. During the first decade of the Russian Federation's existence political parties and movements have formed, reformed, and disintegrated at a dizzying pace. Actual multiparty systems are, in fact, a condition of the political scene in many of the Eurasian states (the exceptions are in Central Asia and Belarus). If, as one Soviet analyst writing in 1990 put it, political parties serve a useful purpose in organizing demands made of the political system and acting as "the objective mouthpiece" of these demands,[16] then Russia is well served in its pluralist orientations. But the Russian party system is only conditionally representative. Parties are infrequently formed in response to citizen demands despite a growing sense of party identification amongst the voting public.[17] Instead, political elites have tended to take their cues from within their own small circles and only after the fact made efforts to bring the public in.

The most obvious manifestation of this problem, however, is the elite-driven party system. Russian elites have certainly formed parties across the political spectrum, but most tellingly according to individual or small group manifestoes. Yeltsin's use of force to disband the parliament in 1993 (see Chapter Five) forced upon the voters an excess of marginally-differentiated choices representing momentary, and therefore, micro policy approaches to macro policy issues, as well as the vanities of the political moment. Thirty-five parties or blocs were organized to compete in very short order for the December 1993 elections; only twenty-one acquired the necessary 100,000 signatures for registration purposes. Of these only thirteen parties were certified by the Central Electoral Commission to compete on the party list ballot (voters cast ballots for both a single-member list and the already mentioned party list), and only eleven eventually won representation in the State Duma. In 1995 sixty parties, blocs, or movements initially registered and the TsIK certified a total of forty-three.[18] Of these, sixteen blocs or parties won some form of representation in the Duma, although only four parties cleared the five percent threshold required to gain deputies from the party list.[19] In 1999 the pattern was repeated as twenty-nine parties, blocs and movements found TsIK approval, and six achieved the five percent threshold.

Reflecting the elite's desire to control the policy agenda, the Russian presidency has responded by restricting, or attempting to restrict, party formation.

Boris Yeltsin attempted in 1994–1995 to craft a bipolar party system of pro-presidential and loyal opposition forces. This blatant effort to exclude or simply ignore the largest and most-organized party in Russia—the KPRF—was doomed before it got to the polls.[20] Voters simply did not have the same vision of participation as did the president.[21] Yeltsin's party blocs barely gained voter recognition in the 1995 State Duma elections and the next concerted effort at consolidation did not occur until Vladimir Putin tried his hand at it in 2000–2001 with the passage of a new electoral law which stiffened requirements for party registration.

Creating a Culture of Participation

Succinctly stated, Russia's version of the democratic game is characterized by the following: 1) minimal control by the public over the political process ("checks", as Americans might call them); 2) an underdeveloped political culture of participation; and 3) a merging of democratic and patriotic ideals. The first of these factors is part of the long-standing governing culture mentioned in Chapter Three. Although today rapidly decreasing in numbers, political elites during the 1990s were largely products of the old Soviet system (even counting those who were dissidents within that system). One obvious example is the fact that of the fifteen Russian and Eurasian presidents holding office a decade beyond the USSR's collapse, *eight* had either been leaders of Soviet-era republican communist party organizations, or high-level functionaries of the Soviet state (see Table 4.1). Further, the prevalence of former communist party functionaries at all levels of the Russian and Eurasian governments indicates that the old political culture has yet to be shaken off by the new.

A third feature of the Russian transitional process is the merger of democratic values and nationalism. Observing the new Russian scene in 1995 Carl Linden concluded that "the civil democracy movement cannot prosper without engaging patriotism as its motive force."[22] What Linden was implying was that for democracy to gain the appeal it needs to survive in Russia it must take account of Russian patriotism. Nationalism is deeply embedded in the Russian political culture and is thus a matter of some value to the average citizen. The issue has even become crucial to parties of the Russian left which are dismayed by the loss of international prestige that Russia has suffered, the difficulties Russia now encounters in trying to keep its domestic obligations, and even the need to support the Orthodox Church against competing foreign religions.[23] In such circumstances patriotism serves as a panacea for the turbulent political and economic environments in which Russia finds itself.

Political Parties in Russia

Since 1993 a broad array of new parties have emerged in Russia, but not a true **multiparty system** if we measure it as Richard Sakwa does, as "one in which parties are crucial to the operation of the political system."[24] Competition has

TABLE 4.1   Political Backgrounds of the Russian/Eurasian Presidents, 2002

Country	President	Party Affiliation
Armenia	Robert Kocharian	no affiliation, former member CPSU
Azerbaijan	Geidar Aliev	New Azerbaijan Party, former member CPSU Politburo
Belarus	Alyaksandr Lukashenka	procommunist, no party affiliation
Estonia	Arnold Ruutel	no affiliation, former First Sec.,CP Estonia
Georgia	Eduard Shevardnadze	Union of Citizens of Georgia, former member CPSU Politburo
Kazakstan	Nursultan Nazarbayev	Kazak Socialist Party, former First Sec., CP Kazakstan
Kyrgyzstan	Askar Akaev	no affiliation, former member CPSU
Latvia	Vaira Vike-Freiberga	People's Party, returned emigre and ex-Canadian citizen
Lithuania	Valdas Adamkus	no affiliation, returned emigre and ex-US citizen
Moldova	Vladimir Voronin	General Secretary, Communist Party of the Republic of Moldova
Russia	Vladimir Putin	no affiliation, former CPSU member
Tajikistan	Imomali Rakhmonov	Tajik People's Democratic Party, (procommunist)
Turkmenistan	Saparmurad Niyazov	former First Sec. CP Turkmenistan
Ukraine	Leonid Kuchma	no affiliation, former member CPSU
Uzbekistan	Islam Karimov	no affiliation, former First Sec. CP Uzbekistan

rapidly become the hallmark of the Russian party process, and along the way created a false sense of a democratic group dynamic as ideologies seem unconnected to policy positions. In their formative stages Russian political parties are often "vehicles for political leaders' or would-be leaders' ambitions."[25] These ambitions may include personal gain, ideological fulfillment, or expressing group or social interests. As a result, it is not entirely clear if political parties are shaping public opinion, or society is expressing itself through the party mechanism—sort of the "chicken or the egg" puzzle. There are at least some indications that the latter condition has been strengthened since the October 1993 showdown,[26] and as Robert G. Moser concludes democratic consolidation won't occur "if the social context never produces a relatively institutionalized system."[27] But the question remains, where do all those parties, movements, and blocs spring from in the first place? If, as one might assume, the answer lies in "the existence of deep social cleavages" in Russian society,[28] then we need look to the ideological distinctions that make up the Russian political landscape. These are examined in the sections that follow.

Parties of the Left

What is referred to as the Russian left is anything but a unified mass. Instead, it includes a composite grouping of communists, socialists, and social-democratic parties. For the most part these are groups which call for a reorientation of society back to the socialist past with preference given to state direction in economic planning, state ownership of land and production capabilities, and unified decision making on political and social issues, all for the purpose of eliminating social and economic class differences. Within this context the more radical parties prefer the strict, ironhanded control of Stalinism, and the return to a one-party dominated system. Socialist and social-democratic parties, on the other hand, extol a quasi-pluralist, competitive system where the left challenges both the right and moderate center. In this latter scenario changes occur within the system rather than by rejecting the system outright.

The Russian left is most often identified with communism, and consequently with the numerous communist parties which have proliferated since the CPSU was banned in the wake of the 1991 coup. Several communist factions have laid claim to the mantle of successor of the old CPSU structure, ideology, and resources. The largest of these in terms of membership is the Communist Party of the Russian Federation (KPRF) led by **Gennadii Zyuganov.** Zyuganov, who at the end of the Soviet era had risen to the position of vice-chairman of the CPSU Central Committee's Ideology Department, has been given much of the credit for resurrecting a moribund party organization and making it electorally viable.[29] Despite its past and the institutionalized prejudices of the Yeltsin administration against it, by the mid-1990s the KPRF could claim 550,000 members primarily drawn from white-collar professions and with relatively few members coming from the working class (which could be a matter of paying dues). As the party's main source of power now lies in the Duma the KPRF has largely abandoned revolutionary politics in favor of parliamentary politics. Its willingness to participate in electoral institutions evidences a "negotiated settlement" with the regime that is avoided by other components of the left.[30]

The KPRF has stressed the need for organizational reinforcement and youth recruitment. Toward this end the party lowered its minimum membership age in 1995 from eighteen to sixteen, and provided for a shorter probationary period for candidates of one year as compared to the previous three years.[31] Zyuganov also rejected on behalf of his party the concept of revolutionary leaps and forceful solutions to problems, and instead embraced a policy of "popular state patriotism."[32] The KPRF's concept of governing has focused on gaining greater power for the legislative branch at the expense of the powerful executive.[33] Moreover, the KPRF has variously argued that the presidency should be elected by the parliament rather than directly by the people, or be eliminated altogether. These views, nevertheless, did not deter Zyuganov from running for the presidency himself in both 1996 and 2000.

For various reasons other communist-oriented parties or movements have not proven themselves to be electorally significant. The extreme left-wing parties

Gennadii Zyuganov, Head of the KPRF

Source: © Oleg Nikishin/Liaison/Newsmakers/Online USA /Getty Images

have tended to be opposed to the 1993 constitutional system and desirous of a restoration of the Soviet Union. Uniquely, the more hard-line communist groups such as the **Russian Communist Worker's Party, Working Russia,** and the **Stalinist Bloc for the Soviet Union** are also highly critical of the KPRF, which they consider social-democratic rather than Marxist-Leninist. Several of these groups formed an electoral bloc called **Communists, Working Russia—for the Soviet Union** to compete in both the 1995 and 1999 Duma elections separate from the KPRF.[34] Unable to break the five percent threshold in 1995 the bloc did poll 4.53 percent of the vote, indicating that all was not well within the ranks of the left. The 1999 elections told a different story as voters found other, more moderate political voices including Unity and Fatherland All-Russia (OVR, see below). As such the electoral strength of the communist-oriented left waned, although the KPRF remained the single largest Duma faction (113 deputies).

The noncommunist, but allied **Agrarian Party** has also experienced some electoral successes, although minor when compared to the KPRF. The Agrarian bloc, which is composed of several small agriculture-oriented parties, favors the development of farmers' associations and the agro-industrial complex (that is, industry servicing the agricultural sector). The Agrarians have been vehemently resistant to the idea of privatized agriculture (the overwhelming majority of agricultural land is still held by collectivized farms) and have supported reinstitution of state agricultural subsidies. With many of its members coming from the ranks of collective farm management (the agricultural nomenklatura of the Soviet era) the party has consistently supported the KPRF and generally been hostile toward market-oriented reforms. But the Agrarians, who had fifty-three deputies after the 1993 elections, failed to retain the allegiances of their voters, and by 1999 had literally fallen off the electoral radar altogether. Attributable to many factors, one that must be closely considered is that Russia is increasingly an urbanized society and the electoral base for an agriculture-oriented party has steadily constricted in recent decades.

The Russian left also encompasses a social-democratic wing. Better known for the personalism of their leaders than their organizational skills, the social-democratic parties have thus far experienced identity crises and the public has not responded to their electoral messages. One reason for this may be the association that many make between the social-democratic groups and the painful transitions begun in the *perestroika* era. Among these groups the more notable include the **Social-Democratic Party** of former *perestroika* architect Alexandr Yakovlev, and the **Russian Unified Social Democratic Party** which counts among its members Mikhail Gorbachev. This and other organizations such as former Moscow mayor Gavril Popov's **Russian Movement for Democratic Reform,**[35] and the **Young Social Democrats Movement**[36] reject Soviet-style political and economic structuring and borrow heavily from the western European traditions of social democracy within pluralist contexts. What they have not discovered is how to make themselves attractive to voters and thereby implement their agendas.

Fragmentation on the left has in at least one instance produced a renewed effort at coalition-building: the **Popular-Patriotic Union of Russia (NPSR)** headed by Zyuganov. Founded in 1996 to promote patriotism and social justice,[37] the NPSR was not an electoral coalition but rather an opportunity for the left to set aside partisan wrangling and instead develop a national base of support while pressuring the administration. A marginal success, the NPSR did not cause the differences of the left to melt away; in the 1999 Duma elections seven left-oriented parties, blocs, or movements stood for election. The lack of a clear, unifying consensus seemed to escape the voters, however, and most proved electorally insignificant. Especially in divisive polities elections are won on the basis of group solidarity, a lesson which has been consistently lost on partisans of both the left and the center of the Russian political system.

Parties of the Center

In the Russian context the term "centrist" implies efforts to transform the political and economic systems away from the Soviet legacy toward western-style democracies and market-economies. Centrist—often referred to as "reformist"—parties argue vigorously for the rapid privatization of the economic system, the development of a strong multiparty system, the distinct trifurcation of the branches of government, and permitting private individuals and businesses a freer hand in determining production and the direction of the economy. In the American system these parties would be portrayed as moderately conservative, liberal, or mildly populist, although some describe them less accurately as "rightist." This distinction is not used here due to the confusion it causes with regard to the far-right wing.

As much as with the left the centrist-democratic parties have been deeply divided over both the personal ambitions of their leaders, and party goals regarding Russia's transformation. The irony confronting the centrists has been their very adherence to pluralism which seems to prevent them from setting aside their differences in favor of electoral unity. As such, no centrist party has been successful in seizing the initiative in policy making and most have come to rely instead on the presidency's direction and pacing of reform. Even though it has been centrist parties which have been accorded the title *party of power,* indicating their preeminence in government, none of these (Russia's Choice, Our Home is Russia, Unity) have been able to control the public agenda. It is to these parties, nevertheless, that Russia has looked for support of the current system.

As the centrist category may also be said to include populist organizations it bears mentioning that such groups differ from reform-oriented parties/ movements in that the former bear the indelible stamp of personalism, and as such are less likely to be operationally democratic. The most notable case is the **Fatherland** movement of Moscow mayor **Yurii Luzhkov.** One of Russia's most outspoken politicians, Luzhkov promoted himself as a presidential candidate and formed Fatherland prior to the 1999 Duma elections as a vehicle to attain his ends. To offset the influence of other democratic/reformist parties such as the Union of Rightist Forces, Luzhkov formed a strategic alliance with **Yevgenii Primakov,** who was at that time heading the regions-oriented **All Russia** movement; together they scored sixty-six seats in the State Duma, but Luzhkov was not to take a seat since he already served in the Federation Council by right of his position as Moscow's mayor. The alliance with Primakov proved an uneasy one, however, due to the personal ambitions of both men, and by 2001 Luzhkov had abandoned it to link up with the propresidential **Unity** movement of **Sergei Shoigu,** a more promising venture.

The surprise second-place finisher in the 1999 Duma elections (23.3 percent), Unity has since been cast as a party of power. Committed to a state-centric reform process involving market reforms, and to the consolidation of state institutions, especially the presidency,[38] Unity staked out a place for itself at the very center of Russian politics. The degree of input to the party's formation or organization by Putin, while uncertain, gives the party a strength and clarity of purpose which cannot be matched by other parties of the center-right. Unlike its competitors Unity does not boast of a prominent, national-level leader as Shoigu's claim to fame is that of having the longest tenure within the cabinet, but in a relatively innocuous position (Minister of Emergency Situations). The party is, nonetheless, a statement of the obvious: proximity to the president is equal to power. Perhaps it was this factor which lead Luzhkov to throw his lot in with Unity in October 2001 in a highly publicized merger. Either way, the party's success may lead to the assessment that there is now underway Yeltsin's and Putin's long sought-after consolidation of the party system.

While reform-oriented organizations such as **Russia's Choice** and **Our Home is Russia** have come and gone, the **Yabloko Bloc** (Russian for "apple" but also an acronym for the original leaders' names) has been the most successful to date. Originally a joining of small, proreform parties (the Republican Party, the Social Democratic Party, and the Christian Democratic Union-New Democracy) under the joint leadership of **Grigorii Yavlinski, Yuri Boldyrev** (who left in September 1995 and formed his own bloc in 1999), and **Vladimir Lukin,** Yabloko achieved a high profile as an uncompromising outsider group. Its electoral showings have not been overly impressive (7.83 percent in 1993; 6.93 percent in 1995; 5.9 percent in 1999) but it has made a place for itself in both the Duma and the public's mind. Consistently critical of both Yeltsin and Putin, Yabloko has kept its distance from government policies and frequently sided with the opposition including the KPRF.

Much of Yabloko's success may be attributed to the personality and energies of the economist Yavlinski. Consistently one of the most popular political figures in post-Soviet Russia, Yavlinski has also been quite influential. Yabloko's decision in 1995 to transform itself into a party with national appeal and scope has also caused its leadership to reject appeals to consolidate forces with other democratic-minded parties.[39] Yavlinski especially has been subjected to frequent criticism for this stance and it has undoubtedly hurt the party's prospects at the regional, as well as national, levels. Yavlinski's nomination as his party's presidential candidate in 1996 and 2000 similarly demonstrated the marginal basis of Yabloko's support as Yavlinski placed fourth (7.34 percent) in the former campaign, and third (5.8 percent) in the latter. Nor has Yabloko been very successful in regional elections; as of 1999 no candidate had won a gubernatorial election as a Yabloko candidate, although several had won seats with Yabloko support.

The center also provides an interesting mix of issue-oriented parties including the **Women of Russia** (ZhR) bloc which has posed Russian political issues in a format unique to the Russian political scene. While trying to avoid the stereotype of being a "women's issues" party, Women of Russia has contested the elections from the standpoint that Russian women were shut out of politics during the Soviet era and needed new voices to represent them.[40] Since 1993 only about ten percent of Duma deputies have been female, a reality which the sociologist Galina Sillaste has attributed to the distance between "female elite formations" and women in general, and the former group's lack of connection to "day-to-day problems."[41] Between 1993 and 1999 Women of Russia dropped from twenty-three deputies in the Duma and being a major political actor to having no representation. Despite this decline in August 1998 yet another "women's issues" group was formed: the Russian Party for the Protection of Women. Much remains to be accomplished by these groups on their issues even if they have trouble generating electoral support.

The centrist parties have yet to develop a lasting, positive relationship with an ambivalent Russian public who as often as not hold the reformers to blame for both the economic and social dislocations of the past decade. To overcome this perception the centrists need to convince the public that the goal of normalizing society is fully worth the sacrifices made along the way. A difficult proposition, normalization lies victim to powerful forces on both left and right which have simple, clear messages to sell to a weary public. This has not dissuaded democratic/reform forces from trying, nevertheless, as evidenced by the formation of the **Union of Right Forces** (SPS), an electoral compendium of fifteen small parties and movements from the center-right. Formed by several of the most influential government officials of the later Yeltsin years including the reform-minded former governor of Nizhny Novgorod **Boris Nemtsov,** the controversial (see Chapter Six) head of the state-run **Unified Energy Systems** (EES) **Anatolii Chubais, Irina Khakamada,** and former Prime Minister **Sergei Kirienko** (who left to join the Putin administration), the SPS experienced modest electoral success in 1999 (8.9 percent of the national vote) by promoting a balanced state-private sector economic relationship, freedom, and human rights all within a constitutional framework.[42]

The dilemma for the centrist parties is they seem interchangeable from one election to the next. Parties of power come and go and few of the voters' concerns seem resolved. These parties portray themselves as distinct from one another,[43]

Anatolii Chubais, Co-leader of the SPS

Source: © TASS/Sovfoto

Boris Nemtsov, Co-leader of the SPS

Source: © TASS/Sovfoto

and thereby resist key opportunities to consolidate their efforts. At other moments they attempt to set aside their disputes and form cooperative blocs. As illogical as their behavior may seem, it warrants closer examination considering that in 1999 those groups which are clearly, or even nominally, centrist captured approximately 55.7 percent of all votes cast.[44] Although there is no certainty of the duration of this prize the growth of the Russian center is a significant phenomenon for ensuring political stability and may be of much greater value than analysts have been willing to admit.

Parties of the Right

Like left-wing parties, parties of the right exhibit antireformist stances but also hold strongly conservative attitudes toward change. As with their ideological opposites, right-wing parties champion a strengthened state structure, a greater measure of state control over the economy, the enhancement of police powers to deal with social and economic problems, the promotion of a strong Russia in relation to the outside world, and an intense, strident sense of nationalism. Politically, economically, and socially deterministic these parties are generally revisionist, that is, seeking a return to a past which is heavily idealized, and especially noncommunist. To them the past is also mythic, extolling real or imagined traits of the Russian people, its leaders, and its origins. The mythic element for monarchists, for instance, is idealized in the former autocracy, particularly the Romanov dynasty; for Christian Democrats it is the return of Russia to a Christian society replete with its values and norms.[45] For extreme nationalists or fascists the mythic element is served through their portrayal of the Russian people as culturally and ethnically pure, superior to other ethnic groups, and independent of outside forces. The fact that the myth or ideal may not mesh with reality is of little importance to these groups, but it does make a difference to the voters who have consistently rejected these visions.

Nationalism is an issue of varying importance for all elements of the Russian right, but it is the defining issue of the far right. Some groups such as **Vladimir Zhirinovskii's Liberal Democratic Party of Russia** (LDPR) or the National Republican Party of Russia identify wholly with nationalist values in both political and economic form. This can be contrasted to parties of the left such as the KPRF which also use nationalist values, but more as rallying points for the masses or as a means to gain legitimacy (what Linden terms "civic patriotism"[46]). The most extreme nationalist forces have raised alarms both inside and outside Russia by proposing the expulsion of non-Russian peoples from the Russian Federation and/or the reinclusion of ethnic Russians from neighboring states into the Russian Federation, by either reabsorbing them, or seizing control of those lands occupied by ethnic Russians. As already noted, these are positions which not infrequently are accepted by the left as well as by the right.[47]

The LDPR has proved itself as both the best organized and most electorally successful party of the right. The personalism of the social-democratic parties, as well as many of the reformist parties is most obvious in this organization. Under the direction of the conflict-prone Zhirinovskii this party largely became a star vehicle for him with little attachment to the centrist-liberal philosophy spelled out in its program of 1990 which called for a freely operating market system, a law-government state, and equal treatment of all types of property.[48] Instead the LDPR has more recently presented itself as a defender of the disaffected, of those who have been victimized or forgotten by the new political system.[49] The party effectively claimed that all of this could be cured by Zhirinovskii's election to the Russian presidency where he would have the power to deal with Russia's former dependent republics (especially the Baltics) and then lead a strong and peaceful Russia into the new millennium.[50]

The success of Zhirinovskii's, and subsequently the LDPR's, appeal can again be measured by comparing electoral results. In the first Duma elections the LDPR tallied 22.8 percent of the vote, putting it ahead of all other parties and permitting it to lay claim to the leadership of the right-wing. This was as much due to Zhirinovskii's capacity for entertaining the masses as for any particular sense of empathy the public may have had for LDPR ideals. Looking harder at the evidence the LDPR's claiming of only sixty-two deputies in the first State Duma can be primarily attributed to the LDPR's limited appeal to a core constituency. Apparently neither Zhirinovskii nor his party managed to sway many voters who identified themselves with other parties.[51] By 1995 voter choices had shifted away from the antiestablishment stance of the right wing, the LDPR's deputy totals declined to fifty-one, and its share of the popular vote was cut in half to 11.06 percent. In 2000 Zhirinovskii's personal appeal also seemed to have worn thin when he gained only 2.7 percent of the presidential vote, much lower than what he had received in the 1991 presidential election when he was virtually unknown. In 1999 the party failed to achieve TsIK registration at all and had to settle for a last minute listing on the ballot as the "Zhirinovskii Bloc" and its lowest vote tally (six percent) to date. This does not spell the end of the LDPR or Zhirinovskii's influence, but it does seem likely that it will remain marginalized.

The more moderate elements of the right wing have also produced their share of national figures such as former Vice-President **Alexandr Rutskoi** who headed a movement called **Derzhava** ("Power") and won the governorship in Kursk oblast in 1996, and former General **Aleksandr Lebed,** who formed his own political movement, the **Russian People's Republican Party** in 1997,[52] and also won a governorship in Krasnoyarsk Krai in 1998. These leaders' electoral appeals have generally been too narrow or exclusionary to interest more than a small segment of the public, and their uncompromising rhetoric now faces the challenges of office-holding and problem-solving. For Rutskoi there is always the possibility that he will return to the national stage as an icon of national salvation, but for Lebed the end came tragically in 2002 in a helicopter crash that closed a colorful career.

The extremist elements of the right wing have been represented by several openly fascistic parties such as **Russian National Unity** (RNE), or its successor **Russian Revival,** or the Russian National Union. Nothing could at first glance seem more anathema to a country that suffered more than twenty million deaths in World War II than the political participation, let alone the mere existence, of a fascist movement. And yet, not only do they exist, they have thrived, if not electorally, at least organizationally.

Beyond the wildly exaggerated estimates of their membership (anywhere from 20,000 to 200,000 members[53]), the fascist parties oppose in vitriolic form anything that does not look, sound, or smell Russian. This broad sweep includes foreigners, military conscientious objectors, homosexuals, alcoholics, drug addicts, and representatives of non-traditional religions (i.e, Jews and Roman Catholics).[54] The extreme right's is a draconian vision of the Russian future with little sympathy for popular involvement, and a willingness to use the harshest means available to achieve the reordering of society. Surprisingly, governmental efforts to quell the growth of fascism were dormant until March 1995 when Yeltsin issued a decree banning fascistic groups and the Duma took up a law restricting them in July 1996.[55] These actions have not eliminated an element which already considers itself outside the system; however, some of its impact has been countered by the election of a president (Putin) with a background in the security services.

All of this underscores that the Russian parties, whether left, center, or right, operate within a political framework where to date they exercise minimal influence.

Russian Skinheads at a Russian National Union Rally

Source: AP/Wide World Photos

The legislature does not control the political agenda but more properly responds to it (more on this in Chapter Five); thus, the competition for seats in the Duma has had little practical impact on the distribution of power. Other factors are at work in Russia's pluralist development, however, most notably the media which plays an equally critical role shaping policy and process.

The New Russian Media

Controlling the Media: the State and Private Sectors

The key to the success of pluralism in any modern state may well be the develop-ment of the media since the media controls the flow of information regarding poli-tics. A broadly-based media permits the public to select that information which it wants to hear or read; this, in turn, offsets some of the intrusion that occurs with the selective presentation of information. The pluralist-oriented society stakes much of its prospects on the development of a pluralistic media. Competing sources of infor-mation, whether controlled by individuals, parties, the government, or private busi-ness guarantee a varied presentation of the news, and to some extent its veracity. The state-run media of the Soviet years presented information in a formulaic and sani-tized format. The primary reason for this was three-fold: 1) it allowed the CPSU to control what the public knew; 2) it allowed the party to develop its own historical in-terpretation; and 3) it prevented information from being used to assist opposition po-litical forces. Total media control was both the desired and actual result of this policy.

Two factors led to the breakdown of this situation after 1985. First, the increas-ingly sophisticated nature of the Soviet public—due to the Soviet state's provision of wide-scale education—produced a people capable of differentiating between fact and fiction in government pronouncements. A second factor involved the technological revolution occurring in the world around the Soviet Union. This made it very nearly impossible for Soviet authorities to filter out everything that challenged their basic precepts. Despite massive efforts to jam foreign radio and television transmissions, restrict access to foreign newspapers and foreigners in gen-eral, prohibit foreign travel except for the elite few, and make it illegal to privately possess any device for copying information, such gestures were ultimately futile.

Russia's media is today characterized by a continuing struggle between the state, which seeks to retain some measure of control over information, an information-hungry populace, and expansive media conglomerates which try to influence the policy agenda through their media outlets. The serious nature of this strug-gle became apparent in 2000–2001 as state-controlled energy corporation Gazprom successfully fought to acquire a controlling interest in independent **Nezavisimoe Televidenie (NTV).** Since coming to power Vladimir Putin has staged a strong and sustained assault on the independent media, especially those elements controlled by the so-called *oligarchs* (wealthy entrepreneurs who found favor in the Yeltsin administration). The most visible of these, including **Vladimir Gusinskii** of Media-MOST and **Boris Berezovskii** of Logovaz, have been both forced into exile, and threatened with divestiture of their holdings to government-approved sources. Thus the development of a diversified media could very well be in decline with commensurate results for an informed public.

The Sources of Information

The Russian and Eurasian media are characterized by an extensive mix of pri-vate and publicly held news services (see Table 4.2). In Russia's case the most

TABLE 4.2	Primary News Agencies in the Eurasian States	
Country	Government-Owned	Private/SemiPrivate
Armenia	Armenpress	Aragil News, Noyan Tappan, Snark
Azerbaijan	AzerTAj,	Assa-Irada, Asbar News Agency (Turan Nagorno-Karabakh) Sharg
Belarus	BelTA (Belarussian Telegraph News Agency)	
Estonia	ETA	BNS (Baltic News Service)
Georgia	Sakinform	PNA (Prime News Agency) Iprinda, Iberia
Kazakstan	Kazak News Agency	
Kyrgyzstan	KABAR National News Agency	AKIPress
Latvia		LETA (Latvian Telegraph Agency)
Lithuania		ELTA (Lithuanian Telegram Agency)
Moldova	Infotag, MOLDPRESS	BASA-press
Tajikistan	Khovar	Asia-Plus
Turkmenistan	Turkmen Press	
Ukraine	Ukrinform (Ukrainian National Press Agency) UNIAR	UpresA (Ukraina Press Agency), UNIAN
Uzbekistan	UzTAG	

notable of these are: the **Information-Telegraph Agency of Russia-Telegraph Agency of the Soviet Union** (ITAR-TASS); and **Rossiiskoe informatsionnoe agentstvo-Novosti** (RIA-Novosti). As the successor agency to the Soviet era's TASS, ITAR-TASS is both a news gathering source, and information provider to media outlets. Since 1998 RIA-Novosti has been part of a federal media system, or holding company, called **RIA-Vesti,** which operates numerous television and radio stations across the Russian Federation.[56] As such it is the agency of record for the government. Competing against the state-run agencies are numerous private news organizations including **Interfax,** Postfactum, and Globus Press Syndicate, providing alternative, and in the case of Interfax, authoritative, sources of information for domestic and foreign markets. None of the private agencies have found competition to be easy and obstacles—especially governmental—have been common.[57]

Regulation of the media has been a government response right from the beginning with first the Supreme Soviet in 1991, and then its successor the State Duma, passing at least ten laws applicable to various aspects of the mass media.[58] Foreign-based news organizations such as Reuters and the Associated Press feed the Russian market information not otherwise obtainable and thereby broaden the political debate. But in both the government and amongst the opposition there exist strong beliefs that the foreign media represents values sometimes at odds with those of the Russian political culture.[59] Such attitudes have provoked reactions such as in 1997 when the Russian government's deputy prime minister for the media publicly stated that one of his priorities was to "legally limit" western news agencies in Russia,[60] a statement echoed by his successor Mikhail Lesin in 2000,[61] and one which became a reality with the Duma's passage of foreign ownership restrictions the next year. More telling, however, was the development of a doctrine of information security produced by the Security Council in 2000 which listed numerous threats to Russia's information sphere and established the government's responsibility for coordinating responses to these threats.[62] In general a legitimate concern of any state, Russia's government could well use security issues as a pretext for reining in a recalcitrant and opposition-minded media, actions which clearly pose their own threats to pluralist thought.

The Print Media

Russia's *print media* consists of a broad array of newspapers, news weeklies, periodicals, professional, scholarly, and increasingly sensationalist publications. Soviet-era newspapers such as *Izvestiya, Sovetskaya Rossiya, Krasnaya zvezda, Komsomolskaya pravda, Ogonek,* and *Moscow News* have been joined by less formulaic publications including *Nezavisimaya gazeta, Kuranty,* and hundreds of other regional, local, and specialty topic newspapers. Governmental organs such as the newspaper *Rossiyskaya gazeta*—since 1993 the official organ of the Russian government[63]—are important in that laws and decrees are considered formally adopted once they are published in its pages. The parliament began publishing its own journal, *Parlamentskaya gazeta,* only in May 1998. Today governmental viewpoints compete with the multiplicity of ideas in the general society, although it is an uneasy relationship. For instance, *Izvestiya,* formerly the paper of record of the Soviet Union's Council of Ministers (the government) and now controlled by a banking conglomerate (Oneksimbank-Rosbank), tends to support the reform process and frequently, but not uncritically, the government. In contrast, there has been the unique case of *Pravda,* the most visible and important paper of the Soviet era. After 1991 *Pravda* saw its circulation plummet from eleven million to the point where its management sought out foreign capital to continue operating. After a lengthy battle over editorial and name control, the paper today continues to publish as an organ of the KPRF, as does its sister publication, *Sovetskaya Rossiya.*

Privately-held newspapers have consistently faced considerable limitations on their operations especially from the government sector. The Russian government has maintained nearly a total monopoly on newsprint and paper supplies giving it considerable leverage in dealing with views contrary to official policy.[64] Papers that are independent and critical of the government like *Nezavisimaya gazeta,* have occasionally been forced to shut down operations due to the rising cost of newsprint and advertising problems.[65] Other critical voices such as *Kuranty* and *Moskovskiye Novosti* have similarly experienced cutbacks or suspensions; both *Segodnya* and *Itogi* which were part of Vladimir Gusinskii's Media-MOST group were closed completely in the Kremlin-orchestrated assault on certain financial oligarchs (and some say press freedom in general) in 2001.

The lack of appropriate resources available to the independent media has led to a number of high-profile buyouts by banking and commercial concerns. In an economy where privatization has come to mean not a relative distribution of state resources but instead a concentration of state assets in the hands of a tiny entrepreneurial elite, ownership of media outlets translates to both power and success. Beginning in 1996 many of the major newspapers including *Izvestiya, Komsomolskaya pravda,* and *Nezavisimaya gazeta* came under the influence of the oligarchs and financial conglomerates. The most obvious of these, such as Berezovskii and Gusinskii, have used these resources to fight their own partisan political battles. Hardly unusual in an open society where competition is essential, it is a startling change from the way the media worked during Soviet times,[66] and for that matter a reflection of a growing, but still dramatically diminished state authority.

The Electronic Media

The electronic media, or all variations of electronically transmitted communication, including television, radio, and computer sources, offers another variation in the political struggle. The privatization of state-run television produced a scramble by many of the same banks, state-run companies, and commercial interests who were vying for dominance of the print media. The jockeying for rewards has been even more frenetic in that the opportunities were more limited and potentially more profitable. Hardly stepping out of the media arena, however, the government has kept its share of ownership close to, or greater than fifty percent in many cases. In this sense privatization of the electronic media has been less pronounced than in other sectors of the economy, and arguably more strategic. Control of editorial policy, and blunting of independent criticism of the Kremlin's agenda appear to be the goals of government policy toward the electronic media. During 2001 and into 2002 the government utilized its consortium VGTRK and its extensive holdings of radio and television stations to squeeze out privately-held competition.[67] The 2001 buyout of NTV by Gazprom-Media, and the 2002 closing of independent **TV-6** supposedly for reasons of indebtedness again raises the question of how far the state will go in servicing its interests at the expense of the private sector.

Obstacles aside, the private or independent side of broadcasting has grown dramatically since the end of the Soviet state. In 1999 there were an estimated 500 privately-held television stations, the most prominent of these was NTV, which has commanded one of the largest of viewing market shares.[68] The aforementioned concentration of media sources in the hands of a relatively few oligarchs has nonetheless raised the question of whether the media is really free, or simply bringing new bosses to prominence often at the expense of reformers and informative journalism. Citizens, on the other hand, may appreciate or dislike the transformation of the media, but it is hardly their position to demand changes since they have virtually no economic leverage in the process. The policy debate is set for the near future: whoever controls the media will determine what can be discussed about policy issues, and whether the public will be able to make autonomous decisions concerning these debates.

The electronic media remains today very much a product of its political environment. But as much as political interference occurs there is increasingly the option of the **Internet.** As of 2001 it was estimated that only about 0.8 percent of Russians had access to the Internet.[69] This extremely low figure among industrialized states is due to the lack of home computers and the under-developed conditions of Russia's telecommunications infrastructure. Even this small percentage nevertheless holds immense prospects for Russians to discover the world around them. Government propaganda about the war in Chechnya, for instance, may be countered by Chechen- or foreign-supported web sites. Just as important is what the outside world and policy analysts can learn of Russia through the Internet (this book, for instance, owes a great debt to on-line sources which otherwise would not have been accessible). The closed society is still a possibility, but no longer a reality in Russia. Access is now the key, and as the Russian media matures in its new role the Fourth Estate is assured of gaining crucial support for the concept of civic society.

Key Terms

pluralism

competitive oligarchy

Popular Patriotic Union of Russia

NTV

transitionalism

Yabloko

party of power

ITAR-TASS

Questions for Consideration

1. Can the Russian Federation be considered a pluralist democracy today? How do you justify your conclusion?

2. Does Russia seem to be headed in the direction of a consolidated party system, or are multiparty elections suited to the Russian political culture?

3. Are so-called reformist forces prepared to lead Russia in the new millenium? Why has no single party or movement emerged to lead Russia?

4. Do the risks of extremism seem all that great for Russia? What mitigates the possibility of greater extremism, if anything?

5. Can media sources be counted on to support reform in Russia? What factors limit the media in acquiring a greater say in setting the Russian public agenda?

Suggested Readings

Robert A. Dahl, *Dilemmas of Pluralist Democracy* (New Haven: Yale University Press, 1982).

Judith Devlin, *The Rise of the Russian Democrats* (Brookfield, VT: Edward Elgar, 1995).

Christopher Marsh, *Russia at the Polls: Voters, Elections, and Democratization* (Washington, DC: CQ Press, 2002).

Michael McFaul and Sergei Markov, *The Troubled Birth of Russian Democracy: Parties, Personalities, and Programs* (Stanford, CA: Hoover Institution Press, 1993).

Stephen D. Shenfield, *Russian Fascism: Traditions, Tendencies, Movements* (Armonk, NY: M. E. Sharpe, 2000).

Gennady Zyuganov, *My Russia* (Armonk, NY: M. E. Sharpe, 1997).

Joan Barth Urban and Valerii D. Solovei, *Russia's Communists at the Crossroads* (Boulder, CO: Westview, 1997).

Useful Websites

Centre for the Study of Public Policy (University of Strathclyde)/Russian Center for Public Opinion and Market Research (VCIOM)
http://www.russiavotes.org

Central Electoral Commission (TsIK)
http://www.fci.ru.

Communist Party of the Russian Federation
http://www.kprf.ru

Political Resources on the Net
http://www.politicalresources.net/

Pravda
http://www.pravda.ru/

Russian National Information Service
http://www.strana.ru/

Unity
http://www.edin.ru/

Yabloko
http://www.yabloko.ru

Union of Right Forces
http://www.pravdelo.ru/index.htm

Endnotes

1. *Russia: Parties, Associations, Unions, Clubs,* vol. 1 (Moscow: RAU-Press, 1991).
2. "Number of Registered Public Amalgamations in 1998", State Statistical Committee of the Russian Federation website [http://www.gks.ru].
3. TASS, 21 September 1995.
4. A complete listing of parties can be found at the "Elections Around the World" website [http://www.agora.stm.it/elections/].
5. See Robert A. Dahl, *Dilemmas of Pluralist Democracy* (New Haven: Yale University Press, 1982), p. 5.
6. Bruce L. R. Smith, "Constitutionalism in the New Russia" in eds. Bruce L. R. Smith and Gennady M. Danilenko, *Law and Democracy in the New Russia* (Washington, DC: Brookings Institution, 1993), p. 4.

7. Leonid Gordon, "Russia at the Crossroads", *Government and Opposition*, 30 (Winter 1995): p. 11.
8. Grigorii V. Golosov, "New Russian Political Parties and the Transition to Democracy: The Case of Western Siberia", *Government and Opposition*, 30 (Winter 1995): p. 111.
9. Russell Bova, "Political Dynamics of the Post-Communist Transition: A Comparative Perspective", *World Politics*, 44 (October 1991): p. 117.
10. Dankwart A. Rustow, "Transitions to Democracy: Toward a Dynamic Model", *Comparative Politics*, 12 (April 1970): p. 350.
11. L. M. Vorontsova and S. B. Filatov, "'The Russian Way' and Civil Society", *Svobodnaia Mysl*, no. 1 (1995) reprinted in *Russian Social Science Review*, 38 (May-June 1997): p. 25.
12. James L. Gibson, "Social Networks, Civil Society, and the Prospects for Consolidating Russia's Democratic Transition", *American Journal of Political Science*, 45 (January 2001), especially p. 58.
13. See the 1991 interview with the leader of the group *Pamyat'*, "Interview with Dmitrii Vasiliev", in eds. Michael McFaul and Sergei Markov, *The Troubled Birth of Russian Democracy: Parties, Personalities, and Programs* (Stanford, CA: Hoover Institution Press, 1993), chapter 3.
14. *L'Espresso*, 18 March 1995.
15. Gennadii Zyuganov, "'Junior Partner'?—No Way." *New York Times*, 1 February 1996.
16. A. Ivanchenko, "The Multi-Party System in the Soviet System: Problems of Creation", in ed. M. A. Babkina, *New Political Parties and Movements in the Soviet Union* (Commack, NY: Nova Science Publishers, 1991), p. 3.
17. Ted Brader and Joshua A. Tucker, "The Emergence of Mass Partisanship in Russia, 1993–1996," *American Journal of Political Science*, 45 (January 2001): pp. 69–83.
18. ITAR-TASS, 28 September 1995.
19. Complete lists of parties and their members in the Duma are to be found in *Panorama*, 10 January 1996, reprinted at the Open Media Research Institute (OMRI) website [http://www.omri.cz/].
20. Robert W. Orttung, "Rybkin Fails to Create a Viable Left-Center Bloc", *Transition*, 1 (25 August 1995): p. 28. Also, TASS, 13 September 1995.
21. *Panorama*, 10 January 1996, reprinted at the OMRI website.
22. Carl Linden, "The Dialectic of Russian Politics", *Problems of Post-Communism*, (January–February 1995): p. 11.
23. For instance, see the platform of the Russian Socialist Party in *Trud*, 30 April 1996.
24. Richard Sakwa, "Parties and the Multiparty System in Russia", *RFE/RL Research Report*, 2 (30 July 1993): p. 8.
25. M. Steven Fish, "The Advent of Multipartism in Russia, 1993–95", *Post-Soviet Affairs*, 11 (1995): p. 342.
26. Thomas F. Remington and Steven S. Smith, "The Development of Parliamentary Parties in Russia", *Legislative Studies Quarterly*, 20 (November 1995): p. 457.
27. Robert G. Moser, "Electoral Systems and the Number of Parties in Postcommunist States," *World Politics*, 51, 3 (1999): p. 383.
28. John Barber, "Opposition in Russia", *Government and Opposition*, 32 (Autumn 1997): p. 613.
29. On Zyuganov and the KPRF see Aleksey Kiva, "Portrait of a Contender. Zyuganov is Not as Simple as He is Painted", *Rossiyskaya gazeta*, 11 April 1996, translated in FBIS-SOV, 11 April 1996, World News Connection website [http://wnc.fedworld.gov].

30. This concept comes from Jeffrey J. Ryan's continuum of revolutionary movement behavior. See "The Impact of Democratization on Revolutionary Movements", *Comparative Politics*, 27 (October 1994): pp. 27–28.
31. *Kommersant-Daily*, 21 January 1995.
32. ITAR-TASS, 1 April 1994.
33. "Russian Presidential Candidate Gennadiy Zyuganov's Appeal to the People", *Rossiyskaya gazeta*, 14 March 2000, translated in FBIS-SOV, 14 March 2000, World News Connection website [http://wnc.fedworld.gov].
34. TASS, 6 September 1995.
35. On the goals of the Social Democrats see "Programma", Social Democrats of Russia website [http://www.sd.org.ru/programma/programma.htm].
36. TASS, 13 September 1995.
37. *OMRI Daily Digest*, 8 August 1996.
38. "Programma obshcherossiiskoe politicheskoe obshchestvennoe organizatsii partii '"Edinstvo'", Party of Unity website [http://www.edin.ru/user/index.cfm? open=658% 2C167&tpc_id=167&msg_id=2546].
39. *Obshchaya gazeta*, no. 48, in RIA-Novosti, 6 December 1996; also Interfax, 1 December 1996.
40. Wendy Slater, "Female Representation in Russian Politics", *RFE/RL Research Report*, 3 (3 June 1994): pp. 27–28.
41. Galina Salliste, "Female Elites in Russia and Their Distinctive Features", *Obshchestvennye nauki i sovremennost* (1994), reprinted in *Russian Politics and Law*, 33 (May–June 1995): p. 78.
42. "Soyuz pravikh sil pravii manifest", Ideologiya, Union of Right Forces website [http://www.pravdelo.ru/sps4_manifest.htm].
43. "Interview with Vladimir Ryzhkov of 'Our Home is Russia'", 21 September 1999, Polit.Ru website [http://www.polit.ru/].
44. Electoral results available at "Elections in Russia", Elections Around the World website [http://www.agora.stm.it/elections/russia.htm].
45. See "Dukhovnoye Vozrozhdenie Otechestva" (Spiritual Rebirth of the Fatherland), Programma partii Russiiskoi Christiansko-Demokraticheskoi partii website [http://www.aha.ru/~rcdp/1m_aims.htm].
46. Linden, pp. 11–12.
47. See, for instance, ITAR-TASS, 21 December 1995, translated in FBIS-SOV, 21 December 1995.
48. V. F. Levichev and A. A. Nelyubin, "A Survey of New Political Organizations, Parties, and Movements" in M. A. Babkina, *New Political Parties and Movements in the Soviet Union*, p. 127.
49. See Zhirinovskii's 2000 presidential election manifest "Why I Am a Candidate for the Presidency of Russia", *Rossiyskaya gazeta*, 18 March 2000, translated in FBIS-SOV, 18 March 2000, World News Connection website [http://wnc.fedworld.gov].
50. Mark Yoffe, "Vladimir Zhirinovsky, the Unholy Fool" in *Current History*, 93 (October 1994): pp. 324–326; also see the interview with Zhirinovskii in the *Evening Standard*, 3 June 1996.
51. This argument is made by Matthew Wyman, Stephen White, Bill Miller, and Paul Heywood, "Public Opinion, Parties, and Voters in the December 1993 Russian Elections", *Europe-Asia Studies*, 47 (Winter 1994): p. 598.
52. Interfax, 1 March 1997.
53. *Izvestiya*, 24 September, 1994; also *Moscow News*, 9–15 July 1998.

54. "Questions of personal, family, and social morality," *Bases of the social conception of Russian National Unity (RNU)*, Russian National Unity website [http://www.rne.org/vopd/english/concept.shtml#1].

55. ITAR-TASS, 5 July 1996.

56. *RFE/RL Newsline*, 22 May 1998; for a commentary on the government's reorganization of the media see "Premier Reanimates Sovinformburo", *Nezavisimaya gazeta*, 19 May 1998, RIA-Novosti Daily Review, 19 May 1998.

57. Terhi Rantanen and Elena Vartanova, "News Agencies in Post-Communist Russia", *European Journal of Communication*, 10 (June 1995): pp. 207–220.

58. For a discussion of these laws see "Russia" in *Media in the CIS*, European Institute for the Media, February 1999, Internews Russia website [http://www.internews.ras.ru/books/media1999/55.html].

59. For instance, Gennadii Zyuganov, "Political Report of the Central Committee of the Communist Party of the Russian Federation", 19 April 1997, translated in FBIS-SOV, 22 April 1997, World News Connection website [http://wnc.fedworld.gov/].

60. *Obshchaya gazeta*, 8–14 June, 1995.

61. *RFE/RL Newsline*, 7 July 2000.

62. "Doctrina informatsionnoye bezopasnosti Rossiiskoye Federatsii", 9 September 2000, especially parts Two and Ten, Security Council of the Russian Federation website [http://www.scrf.gov.ru/Documents/Decree/2000/09-09.html].

63. *Kommersant-Daily*, 21 December 1996, cited in *OMRI Daily Digest*, 31 December 1996.

64. On how the government privatized some of these resources see "Law on the State Support of Mass Media and Book-Publishing in the Russian Federation", 1 December 1995, Internews Russia website [http://www.internews.ras.ru/law/support_eng/support_eng.html].

65. ITAR-TASS, 25 May 1995.

66. For a breakdown of who owns what see the special report "Russian Media Empires", 26 September 1997, Radio Free Europe/Radio Liberty website [http://www.rferl.org/].

67. Several of these including RTR and Radio Mayak may be accessed at the allnews.ru website [http://www.strana.ru/].

68. "Russia" in *Media in the CIS*, [http://www.internews.ras.ru/books/media1999/57.html].

69. Rafal Rohozinski, "How the Internet Did Not Transform Russia", *Current History*, 99 (October 2000): pp. 334–338.

Chapter 5

The Struggle for Power: The Presidency and the Parliament

The 26 March 2000 presidential elections in Russia marked several milestones in the democratic transition of the Russian state. First, Vladimir Putin was elected the Russian Federation's second president. Putin's rapid ascendancy from virtual obscurity only months before effectively brought to an end the Yeltsin era which had spanned an entire decade. Second, for the second time since 1996 the candidate of the Communist Party of the Russian Federation (KPRF) Gennadii Zyuganov was both the primary challenger to the incumbent and the subsequent loser in the election (see Table 5.1). Third, the issue of presidential succession, long one of the most vexing questions facing Soviet and Russian politics, was resolved with Yeltsin's passing of the reins of power according to constitutional dictate (article 92) on 31 December 1999 to Putin.[1]

Fourth, the 2000 poll and Putin's election ensured the state's development along the path of a strong executive system. By extension this also eliminated, or at least postponed, efforts to more equitably balance power between the executive and legislative branches. How the particular distribution of power has occurred is much of the story of this chapter. It cannot be complete, however, without first a description of the powers of governing bodies and their prospects for change within the confines of the political process.

Conflict rather than compromise has traditionally been the dominant tendency in Russian politics and remains so today. A relatively normal condition of politics in most nonauthoritarian states is that power is split between several competing centers. These centers usually attempt to expand their power by exploiting the weaknesses of rivals, sometimes in blatant disregard of constitutional or legal boundaries. Even today after a decade of change since the disintegration of the Soviet Union the principle power relationships have not completely jelled. This means that the capacity of either an individual or an institution to shape power in its own image is immense. Both

TABLE 5.1   Results of the 2000 Russian Presidential Election

Candidate	%
Vladimir V. Putin	52.94
Gennadii A. Zyuganov	29.21
Grigorii A. Yavlinskii	5.8
Amangel'di M. Tuleev	2.95
Vladimir V. Zhirinovskii	2.7
Konstantin A. Titov	1.47
Ella A. Pamfilova	1.01
Stanislav S. Govorukhin	0.44
Yurii I. Skuratov	0.43
Aleksei I. Pod'beryozkin	0.13
Umar A. Dzhabrailov	0.1
Against all	1.88
Total eligible voters	109,372,046
Valid votes	74,369,773
Turnout	68.63

Source: "Vybori 2000", Federalnoye Informatsionnii Tsentr website [http://www.izbircom.ru/2217/preres/index.shtml]

the executive and legislative branches of Russian government have sought to shape the political process whether through the drafting of the constitution or in structuring and restructuring its institutions. Toward this our analysis must now turn.

In constitutional form Russia today is a **strong presidential system** with a weak, although not powerless, parliamentary/legislative branch. Among western political systems it most closely approximates the French Republic especially in that Yeltsin controlled the development of the constitutional process much as French President Charles de Gaulle had done in bringing about his country's Fifth Republic. Politics in such a context are heavily reliant upon political elites defining the policy agenda and legalistic norms according to their particular interests. In contrast, in strong legislative systems politics is dominated by a collective decision-making process and a culture of give-and-take leading to political compromise. No one leader dominates the process and it is heavily weighted toward elite groups. Thus as Gerald Easter argues, through a strong presidency the Russian transition has guaranteed economic and political protections for "old regime elites . . . against the encroachments of democracy, liberalization, and the market."[2] At times these new-found priorities may also dovetail with those of the new governing elite but this is not always constant.

Boris Yeltsin, President, 1990-1999

Source: AP/Wide World Photos

Presidential Leadership

Establishing the Office

Leaders frequently see themselves in the light of history and Russian leaders are no exception to this tendency. This means more than just considering what their places will be in the annals of their people, however; it also means they measure their individual rule against the accomplishments of their predecessors. In this sense Boris Nikolaevich Yeltsin's years in office (1990–1999) did not represent a deviation from the patterns of Russian history. Russia's political culture has both been shaped by strong rulers as well as accepting of their eagerness to dominate the political process. The implications of these cultural conditions upon a system in transition to democracy are considerable especially in terms of the often-used western evaluation of power-sharing between branches of government.

Yeltsin's time in office was most visibly marked by the emergence of a strong, politically viable presidency, a condition denied to the ceremonial heads-of-state of the Soviet era. Yeltsin's primary contribution to the new Russian system was the revolutionizing of the presidency, and possibly the very practice of politics. He was directly responsible for infusing the presidential institution with significant powers and restructuring the government into a strong presidential system. President Yeltsin developed his own signature-style, a distinctly personalistic rule which served to differentiate him from his predecessors.[3] Nevertheless, the con-

Vladimir Putin, President of Russia since 2000

Source: AP/Wide World Photos

centration of decision-making power in a presidential oligarchy rather than amongst a myriad of representative or accountable institutions is typical of Russia's historical development.

Given Yeltsin's lack of experience with electoral politics prior to 1990 his attachment to it may seem a rather odd development. After being initially elected by the **Russian Federation Supreme Soviet** as its chairman in 1990 Yeltsin fought an uphill battle to become the republic's first directly elected president. This, he calculated, was the best means to counterbalance the influence of the CPSU apparatus.[4] Direct election gave him an unassailable position in that his term of office was set by law and could not be altered by either an anti-Yeltsin majority within the Russian legislature, or by the communist party. Yeltsin's June 1991 election victory over several foes provided him with a mantle of legitimacy; his authority to govern thus lay with the people instead of the CPSU (which Yeltsin had quit in 1990).[5] Even Gorbachev had only been elected President of the Soviet Union from within the Congress of People's Deputies!

To Yeltsin, democracy's foremost importance lay in its potential for rescuing the country from the chaos and catastrophe that he saw as surrounding the crumbling Soviet Union. "Half measures and timid steps", as he termed them, were insufficient for the purpose of preventing the system from crashing in upon itself.[6] Democracy was the goal toward which Russia would head but as a governing concept it was much more elusive and complex. For Yeltsin the paradox of democracy revolved around the struggle to attain and hold power. In his own words:

> "How will our Russian democracy appear to historians if the first time (1991), the Communist putsch was afraid to shoot at democracy, but the second time (1993), democracy itself was not afraid to shoot its enemies? Is there not a malicious irony of fate in this?"[7]

Thus, the political reality of controlling and shaping the Russian political system laid bare the facade of democratic political theory.

Yeltsin's bravado in the face of armed force during the August 1991 coup attempt allowed democratically minded forces throughout the Soviet Union to rally around a strong, symbolic leader. Literally standing on a tank that was aimed at the Russian White House Yeltsin brought himself into sharp contrast with not only the reactionary coup leaders, but Gorbachev as well.[8] In fact, the Soviet President had been fighting a losing battle of public perceptions with Yeltsin throughout 1991 such that as Yeltsin saw it, "even the very word *Soviet* (Yeltsin's italics) was no longer possible to pronounce; it had exhausted its resources."[9] Gorbachev's return to power after the coup was in a greatly weakened capacity; within days it became apparent that the balance of power had shifted dramatically toward Yeltsin. The Soviet president could no longer prevent the secession of virtually all of the Soviet republics, nor stop the Russian republic from siphoning off much of the central government's authority. For his part Yeltsin drew upon the ambitions of autonomy-minded republican leaders and forged not so much an anti-Gorbachev coalition, but instead a group determined to ignore the Soviet leader. The decisive blow came on 8 December 1991 when Yeltsin and the presidents of the other two Slavic republics (Ukraine and Belarus) met in a barely-secret conclave in Belarus and committed themselves to founding an expedient replacement to the moribund Soviet state system. This move effectively cast off the remnants of Soviet power and heralded the beginning of a new system of Eurasian states.

With the Soviet Union gone the most immediate political problem which confronted Yeltsin was the distribution of power between the presidency and the Soviet legislature, the **Congress of People's Deputies,** or CPD. Within the Kremlin government offices and positions changed at seemingly breakneck speed as political participation was no longer reliant upon the strict operational codes of the CPSU. Making matters more unpredictable Yeltsin "did not replace people; he collected them, inventing new sections and duties for them, creating one advisory group after another."[10] This was a characteristic he retained throughout his tenure in office. As the Russian public saw it, politics of this sort was nothing more than changing names on the doors of offices while the plight of the people went unheeded. Even still, Yeltsin maintained a high level of support well into 1993, a factor which proved crucial to his survival.

Showdown with the Parliament: 1993

The year 1993 began with a political stalemate. The president was able to appoint those cabinet ministers he wanted, but unable to gain approval for his candidate for prime minister, **Yegor Gaidar.** Neither parliament nor president could put the other in checkmate; however, in March the Russian CPD rescinded the emergency powers it had granted Yeltsin the year before, and canceled a referendum on his economic reforms. Yeltsin parried with a declaration of emergency powers—including a suspension of the Congress' ability to overturn presidential orders—and a rescheduling of the referendum. After legislators barely failed in an effort to impeach the president the national referendum was held in April: fifty-nine percent of voters expressed support for Yeltsin personally, and fifty-four percent positively viewed his economic reform strategy.[11] The political conflict had advanced to a new stage.

In the next several months the lines of battle shifted to the drafting of a new constitution.[12] Yeltsin's version focused on establishing strong presidential powers while the CPD actively pursued the abolition of the presidency altogether, a theme closely associated with the communist faction. The unresolved nature of the dispute came to a head on 21 September when Yeltsin suspended the parliament and a blockade of the Russian White House, where legislators were defying the presidential order, ensued. On 4 October, after procommunist supporters instigated a riot in Moscow Russian army and Interior Ministry troops stormed the parliament building and in a bloody show of force put an end to the CPD. Yeltsin, it seemed, was now firmly in control and simultaneously scheduled elections for a new parliament (the current State Duma) as well as the constitution that would legitimate it.

The next two years were anything but an easy time for Yeltsin. Even after merging his authority with so-called "coercive elites"[13] the president found governance to be as much about public perceptions as who was holding it. As noted in Chapter Four, Yeltsin's allies did not fare well in the 1995 parliamentary elections, to some extent due to the president's own declining popularity. But the 1996 presidential elections provided a textbook study of how to successfully manipulate public opinion while skirting the edges of democratic procedure. With his public approval ratings at a dismal five percent in early 1996,[14] Yeltsin managed to rally democratic and reform-oriented supporters by promising to end the war in Chechnya (which he had begun), doling out financial support along the campaign trail,[15] and playing upon a fear of a return to communism.[16]

Considering Yeltsin's health it was a risky strategy. The president won the first round of the election on 16 June 1996 with 35.28 percent of the vote to communist rival Zyuganov's 32.03 percent.[17] Faced with a second round Yeltsin reached out to the third-place finisher, Aleksandr Lebed, who had polled 14.52 percent, and offered him the position of chairman of the Security Council and a promise of broader powers.[18] The Yeltsin-Lebed alliance, combined with the KPRF's lack of campaign funds ensured an easy victory for Yeltsin in the 3 July runoff (Yeltsin won fifty-three percent of the vote). While there remained crucial doubts about Yeltsin's health and the issue of succession, the process itself had been strengthened and legitimated. Making the system work remained an even greater challenge.

Constitutional Authority and the Limits of Action

Political scientist Robert Sharlet has aptly described the Russian political process as one in which "the constitution serves as the scaffolding for an ambitious state-building process."[19] The 1993 constitution stipulates that the president is at once the "guarantor of the Constitution . . . and of human and civil rights and freedoms" (article 80). The president is granted extraordinary authority and powers to protect citizens and their rights. In contrast, no specific mention is made of the legislature's duty to the people; the principal focus of that body instead involves its relationships with other governing institutions (article 94). Yeltsin had structured constitutional power to enhance the president's role at the expense of the legislature. Moreover, the constitution empowers the president to be an arbitrator between the central government and the regions, and in case of disputes between Russia's territorial units (article 85).

Many of the executive powers of the president are to be found in article 83 of the constitution including the abilities to appoint and dismiss the Chairman of the Government of the Russian Federation (the prime minister) and his cabinet, the chairman of the Central Bank, the general prosecutor of the state, members of the federal court system, and the "high command of the Armed Forces."[20] Beyond this, the president has even more authority, most notably that of issuing decrees which allow him to shape the contours of the governing process with virtually no input from the legislative branch (although it has to be noted that the Constitutional Court may challenge his actions).

Other appointive powers have since been added: The president heads the **Security Council,** appoints its secretary, and may alter that body's composition as in March 1998 when Yeltsin merged its staff with that of the State Military Inspectorate. At the same time Yeltsin also used his ability to dissolve a state body (the Defense Council) and transfer its personnel within the governing apparatus;[21] none of this is subject to legislative confirmation. Similarly, the president heads the Political Consultative Council, a body created in July 1996 by the Duma, formulates the military doctrine of the Russian Federation, creates an executive administration separate from the government bureaucracy, appoints and recalls ambassadors of the Russian Federation, and appoints and recalls representatives to the territorial regions. Articles 86 and 87 provide the president with the leadership role in foreign policy including that of supreme commander in chief of the Armed Forces, a power which has served both Yeltsin and Putin well in their conflicts in Chechnya. Finally, the Russian president may declare martial law, although the upper chamber of the legislature must confirm this (article 102).

All constitutions are shaped in response to a country's specific political, social, and economic conditions which provide for notable differences with its neighbors. Table 5.2 presents a comparison of selected presidential powers in the respective Russian and Eurasian states. Most important for the Russian president are the powers laid down in articles 84 and 90. In the former the president is called upon to schedule elections to the State Duma and to dissolve it should this prove necessary in his opinion. But the office is further enhanced by the capacity to schedule referendums (as in the French case) and to submit draft laws for the State Duma's consideration. The Duma may ignore these proposals, but it is still an important policy lever denied to presidents in mixed or strong legislature systems (for instance, Latvia and Estonia).

Presidential involvement in the legislative process extends beyond proposing draft laws; he also issues edicts and directives, an ability that to a degree allows him to circumvent the legislature. Using this power gives the president the opportunity to involve himself in both minor and major issues, to both fine-tune the system (for instance Yeltsin's January 1995 and Putin's 2000 decrees to increase pensioners' monthly stipends),[22] and to shape its general parameters (Yeltsin's October 1995 directive for the holding of elections for governor in several regions,[23] or Putin's August 2000 creation of the State Council, see below). In all of these cases can readily be seen a tremendous potential for creating and directing policy.

Crucial to the success of the president is his authority to form or influence the formation of the government of the Russian Federation (article 83, section e). The president chairs its meetings and is responsible for the state's vast bureaucracy. While the State Duma must confirm the prime minister and thus serves as a check on presidential power (as demonstrated in 1998 when Yeltsin failed to gain the reappointment of the unpopular, but pliant, **Viktor Chernomyrdin**), the deputy chairmen of the government and the federal ministers are also chosen by the president and are not subject to legislative approval (more on this in Chapter Six). The president therefore exercises considerable control over the government but without an effective check upon the quality or skills of these officials. Crises, emergency conditions, and intergovernmental battles may be sound reasons for such bureaucratic impulses but as will be considered in Chapter Six the cultural choice of familiarity—that is, the president choosing those he knows—is key to understanding "politics as usual."[24]

The president also may hire or fire ministers at his discretion, often for nothing more than political reasons. The sacking of longtime Foreign Minister Andrei Kozyrev in January 1996 came about due to parliamentary pressure.[25] And Yeltsin's decision to replace key security officials came on the heels of the first round of the 1996 presidential elections.[26] Yeltsin also dismissed his defense minister, Pavel Grachev, in June 1996 when the president found himself in need of challenger General Aleksandr Lebed's support.[27] Both Yeltsin and Putin have readily fired top members of the military when it became clear that they did not favor presidential policy initiatives.[28] But the best illustration of how the president may use this power is found in the numbers themselves. By the end of Yeltsin's time in office in 1999 six prime ministers (one was "acting") had served under him, as well as forty-five deputy prime ministers, and a staggering 185 ministers![29]

Beyond politics there are some second-rank limitations on presidential powers. In some instances presidential powers overlap with legislative prerogatives as in February 1994 when the opposition-dominated State Duma voted to grant amnesty to those imprisoned for taking part in the October 1993 uprising.[30] Rather than complementing presidential power (article 89, section c) this provoked a challenge to unchecked presidential authority (article 103, section f) leaving the president with no legal remedy to the release of some of his most bitter foes.[31] The constitutional system also requires the president to cooperate with the parliament in formulating a budget, although presidential input in this area is dominant.

A final constraint upon the presidency is the legislature's impeachment power (articles 93 and 102, section f). Unlike the American case, no trial of the president

TABLE 5.2 Constitutional Powers of the Presidencies (Constitutional Articles in Parentheses)

Country/ Date of Constitution	Term	Call Referendum	Submit Draft Laws	Issue Edicts/ Decrees	Dismiss the Legislature	Appoint/Recall Government	Name Cabinet Members
Armenia 1995	5 Yrs./2 Terms (50)	No	No (62)	Yes (56)	Yes (55.3)	Yes (55.4)	Yes (55.4)
Azerbaijan 1995	5 Yrs./2 Terms (81)	Yes (109.8)	Yes (96)	Yes (113)	No	Yes (109.5.6)	Yes (109.5)
Belarus 1996	5 Yrs./2 Terms (101)	Yes (84.1)	Yes (99)	Yes (85)	Yes (84.3)	Yes (84.7)	Yes (84.7)
Estonia 1992	5 Yrs./2 Terms (80)	No	No	Yes (78.7, 109, 110)	Yes (89)	Yes (78.10, 89, 90, 92)	Yes (78.10, 89)
Georgia 1995	5 Yrs./2 Terms (70.1)	Yes (74.1)	Yes (67.1)	Yes (73.1, i)	No	Yes (80.3)	Yes (73.1, b, c, d)
Kazakstan 1995	7 Yrs./No limit (41.1)*	Yes (44.10)	No	Yes (45.1)	Yes (63.1)	Yes (65.1)	Yes (44.3)
Kyrgyzstan 1996	5 Yrs./2 Terms (43.1, 43.2)	Yes (46.VI.2)	Yes (64)	Yes (47.1)	Yes (46.VI.3)	Yes (46.I.3, 4)	Yes (46.I.3)
Latvia 1922	4 Yrs./2 Terms (35, 39)**	No	Yes (47, 65)	No	Yes (48–50)***	Yes (56)+	No

(continued)

TABLE 5.2 Constitutional Powers of the Presidencies (Constitutional Articles in Parentheses)

Country/ Date of Constitution	Term	Call Referendum	Submit Draft Laws	Issue Edicts/ Decrees	Dismiss the Legislature	Appoint/Recall Government	Name Cabinet Members
Lithuania 1992	5 Yrs./2 Terms (78)	No	Yes (68)	Yes (85)	Yes (58.1, 58.2)	Yes (84.4)	Yes (84.9)
Moldova 1994	4 Yrs./No Limit (80)	Yes (88.f)	Yes (73)	Yes (94.1)	Yes (85)	No (100, 101)	No
Russia 1993	4 Yrs./2 Terms (81)	Yes (84.c)	Yes (84.d)	Yes (90)	Yes (84.b)	Yes (83.c)+	No (112)
Tajikistan 1994	5 Yrs./2 Terms (66)	No	Yes (61, 70.8)	Yes (71)	No	Yes (70.3)	Yes (70.3)
Turkmenistan (1992)	5 Yrs./2 Terms (56, 55)	Yes (57.7)	Yes (68)	Yes (58)	Yes (64)	Yes (76)	Yes (76)
Ukraine (1996)	5 Yrs./2 Terms (103)	Yes (106.6)	Yes (93)	Yes (106.31)	Yes (90)	Yes (106.10)	Yes (106.10)
Uzbekistan 1992	5 Yrs./2 Terms (90)	No	Yes (82)	Yes (94)	Yes (95)	Yes (93.9)	Yes (93.9)

*Amended by the parliament 7 October 1998;

**Amended by the Saeima, 4 December 1997

***Requires popular approval through referendum; if the referendum fails, the president must resign;

+The president chooses someone to create the cabinet

is required by law, but instead a special commission must first recommend impeachment, followed by one-third of the State Duma forwarding this recommendation for a vote, two-thirds of each chamber approving it, and finally the Federation Council voting to remove the president. As Yeltsin's opposition discovered it's difficult to gather such a large number of votes; consequently the Duma has been limited to debating impeachment rather than taking action on it.[32] A **vote of no-confidence** in presidential actions is also an option, as illustrated by several communist/opposition attempts,[33] although it is always a difficult process.[34]

The Presidential Apparatus

The structure of the presidential administration—as distinct from the government/cabinet—is easier to determine than its actual size. Under Yeltsin the administration was reorganized several times[35] and underwent continual expansion until 1998 when its total personnel was reduced to less than 2,000. Its most important components include the **Presidential Administration,** the Security Council, the Presidential Security Service, the Foreign Intelligence Service, and the Federal Security Service; the latter two are actually part of the cabinet/government (see Chapter Six) but report directly to the president instead of the prime minister. Aside from these the most important units are those which cover such issues as administration, foreign policy, personnel, citizenship, interactions of citizens with the president, pardons, and state awards.

The leading officials of the presidential administration have typically been among the most powerful individuals in the executive branch. Presidential aides reflect presidential emphases toward policies and are delegated extensive authority for problem solving in select areas of the economy or politics. For instance, Anatolii Chubais was put in charge of the so-called "war ministries" in 1996 while he was Yeltsin's chief-of-staff.[36] As a rule these administrators have possessed presidential access based on their unwavering loyalty to the president. Both the access and loyalty were vital to the Kremlin's functioning throughout Yeltsin's protracted illnesses and in Putin's appointment and consolidation of power.

The head of the presidential apparatus is the **chief of staff** whose job combines the functions of chief administrator and personnel director (he heads the Council for Cadre Policy). It is also a physical gateway to the president as the chief-of-staff's office is typically next to the president's on the third floor of the Kremlin Senate building. Unlike other administration officials the chief of staff can build a base of power independent of the president by fostering his own patron-client relationships, usually with trusted advisers from his home region or city. Certainly not unique to Russia (for instance, in Mexico this is termed a *camarilla* system) this kind of factionalism can be greatly destabilizing for policy making. Chubais' appointment to this position in mid-1996 allowed him to bring trusted advisors from his home city of St. Petersburg to the capital. His successor, the less influential Valentin Yumashev, was notable not for his administrative expertise but rather his close friendships with Yeltsin's daughter, **Tatyana Dyachenko,** and wealthy entrepreneur Boris Berezovskii. As the president's principal aide the chief-of-staff must be sensitive to, and supportive of, presidential policies.

The chief of staff and other insiders are often the focal points for Kremlin intrigues as political actors jockey for power. One of the most notable of these in the Yeltsin years was the head of the **Presidential Security Service** (SBP), the shadowy **Aleksandr Korzhakov.** Instrumental in the early survival of the Yeltsin presidency and later one of the most powerful and feared men in Yeltsin's entourage (he headed the Main Directorate for the Protection of the President, and the Analytic Center for Presidential Information Administration[37]) Korzhakov typified the loyalty valued so highly by Yeltsin. At the height of his power Korzhakov was reported to exercise authority over a full air force squadron, all Kremlin special services, and management of the president's wartime bunker.[38] Eventually, however, even Yeltsin himself came to feel uncomfortable with his subordinate's influence and dismissed him in June 1996 after the first round of the presidential elections.

In many respects the presidential apparatus had become a kremlin within a kremlin, a fortress isolated against the rest of society. Yeltsin considered Russian politics—and especially presidential-legislative relations—as a conflictual arena and insulated himself against its worst aspects.[39] It was not so much the institution of the legislature that Yeltsin distrusted, but rather the remnants of the old communist party bureaucracy, or *apparat* within it. Despite concerns about how undemocratic the system has become both Yeltsin and Putin have seen themselves with few options: They could either control the direction and pace of change or allow the legislature to accumulate power at their expense. In either case both presidents have forged the tools necessary to fulfill their goals and have not been shy in the application of these instruments of power.

The Legislature

Establishing an Independent Character

If the story of the Russian executive's development is steeped in centuries of Russian history, the legislative branch of the Russian government is a newcomer still trying to make its way. In historic terms assemblies (or *vetches*) were part of the political makeup of ancient Rus, and *soviets* or councils became significant in the last years of tsarist rule. But the impact of these institutions on political development was always muted in the face of executive power. In the Soviet era an autonomous, representative legislative system was not permitted as this would have meant a base of power independent from the control of the Communist Party. Consequently, legislative power in the Russian Federation has been proscribed by a political culture which placed considerable emphasis on executive authority.

Compared to other Eurasian states' legislatures the Russian **Federal Assembly** exercises less influence than the Baltic states' parliaments, yet considerably more than similar bodies in the Central Asian states (see Table 5.3). The Federal Assembly could well be described as an institution which, without a definite direction, stumbles slowly toward where it will be comfortable. The obstacles to effective legislative governance have been both of its own making (divisiveness within and between its component parts) and external to it (the siege of the parliament, hotly

TABLE 5.3 Constitutional Powers of the Legislatures (Constitutional Articles in Parentheses)

Country/ Date of Constitution	Term Lower house/ Upper house	Right to Initiate Legislation	Creates/ Approves Budget	Elect/ Impeach President	Approves Cabinet	Vote No- Confidence in Gov't?
Armenia 1995	4 Years (63)	Yes (75)	Approves (76)	No/Yes (50/57)	Yes (74)	Yes (74)
Azerbaijan 1995	5 Years (84)	Yes (96)	Approves (95.5)	No/Yes (101/107)	No (109.5)	Yes (95/14)
Belarus 1996	4 Years (93)	Yes (99)	Approves (97.2)	No/Yes (81/88)	No (84.7)	Yes (97.7)
Estonia 1992	Not mentioned in the Constitution	Yes (103)	Approves (115)	Yes/No (79)	Yes (89)	Yes (97)
Georgia 1995	4 Years/ (49.1)*	Yes (67.1)	Approves (73.e)	No/Yes (70.1/63, 75.2)	Yes (77.1)	No
Kazakstan 1995	5/6 Years (50.2)**	Yes (61.1)	Approves (53.2)	No/Yes (47)	No (44.7)	Yes (53.7)
Kyrgyzstan 1996	5 Years (54.3)	Yes (64)	Approves (73.2)	No/Yes (44.2/51.1)	No (46.1)	Yes (58.18)

(continued)

TABLE 5.3 Constitutional Powers of the Legislatures (Constitutional Articles in Parentheses)

Country/ Date of Constitution	Term Lower house/ Upper house	Right to Initiate Legislation	Creates/ Approves Budget	Elect/ Impeach President	Approves Cabinet	Vote No-Confidence in Gov't?
Latvia 1922	4 Years (10)+	Yes (65)	Approves (66)	Yes/Yes (35/54)	Yes (59)	Yes (59)
Lithuania 1992	4 Years (55)	Yes (68)	Approves (67.14)	No/Yes (78/74)	Yes (92)	Yes (61)
Moldova 1994	4 Years (63)	Yes (73)	Approves (66.h)	No/Yes (78.1/81.3, 89)++	Yes (98.2)	Yes (106)
Russia 1993	4 Years (96)	Yes (104)	Approves (114.a)	No/Yes (81/103.g)	No (112)	Yes (103.b, 117)
Tajikistan 1994	5 Years (49)	Yes (61)	Approves (50.11)	No/Yes (66/73)	Yes (74)	No (75)
Turkmenistan 992	5 Years (63)	Yes (68)	Approves (67.6, 57.5)	No/Yes (56/60)***	No (76)	Yes (67.4)
Ukraine 1996	4 Years (77)	Yes (93)	Approves (85.4)	No/Yes (103/111)	No (114)	Yes (87)
Uzbekistan 1992	5 Years (77)	Yes (82)	Approves (78.8)	No/No (90)	Yes (93.9)	No

*Georgia's upper house, or Senate, has never met;
**Amended 7 October 1998;
***Only in cases of medical disability;
+Amended by the Saeima, 4 December 1997;
++Parliament votes to suspend the president subject to confirmation in popular referendum; +++only in the Prime Minister

contested elections, and presidential restructuring of its powers). It has survived, however, as an accepted and necessary ingredient of transitional Russian politics and a key element in the pursuit of democracy.

Whereas the Russian presidency's particular development owes much to one man's determination, the legislature developed almost by default. No one person stands out as the father of the Russian legislative process, no single group of theorists or reformers saw legislative representation as the best possible means of realizing the ideal of democracy. Until the middle of the Gorbachev period the Soviet legislature (the Supreme Soviet) had been only symbolically representative; its Russian descendent, the CPD, achieved a measure of real authority in a brief period, but even its speaker **Ruslan Khasbulatov** could only see the parliament's role in terms of it being able to "prevent the government from taking extreme measures."[40] As it turned out, the distinction between the CPD and the Supreme Soviet was only a matter of degree.

The Russian Federation parliament that first elected Yeltsin in 1990 was not a radical body bent on overturning the Soviet system, nor could it as it represented only a small part of that system. Under Yeltsin's leadership this legislature concerned itself with acquiring authority for the Russian Republic within the diminishing context of the Soviet state; as such it was governed more by nationalist aspirations than democratic inclinations.[41] When the Soviet state dissolved, the Russian parliament alongside the Russian presidency, partially filled the vacuum of national power. Russian legislative and presidential leaders alike found that the legislative institution was not easily controlled. Parliamentary governance requires a deft hand, an ability to keep one's own party and allies in line while preventing the opposition from capturing the policy initiative. While neither Yeltsin, nor his parliamentary rivals, were able to utilize the parliament entirely to their advantage, Putin has been able to quickly impose his standards and sense of direction.

As already indicated throughout 1992 and much of 1993 Yeltsin continually came into conflict with communist and nationalist forces in the Russian parliament. By 1993 the struggle for control of the political process had evolved into a no-compromise, winner-take-all scenario. The April 1993 national referendum and the siege of the parliament later that year proved to be the highwater marks of conflict within the governing process.[42] Since that point politics has continued in a confrontational vein, but actualized by electoral cycles and delineation of authority. The extent of presidential influence and the role of the Russian legislature will be laid out in the remainder of this chapter.

The Struggle for Rule-Making Authority

Two features in particular differentiate the post-1993 Russian legislature from the Russian CPD. First, the Federal Assembly—that is, the parliament as a whole—served an initial term of only two years (1993–1995).[43] Electoral cycles thereafter have been for four years (article 96); the shorter initial term made it possible for both parties and the president to assess successes or failures and try to correct mistakes before they became institutionalized. Second, the promise of regularized elections to the State Duma was made to assure stable governing institutions. The president was empowered to suspend the Duma or call for early elections (article 84, sections a and b), which many in the Duma feared Yeltsin might do to preserve his powers (prior to the 1995 elections and again in

KPRF Deputies singing in the State Duma
Source: © TASS/Sovfoto

April 1998). However, dissolving the legislature also requires that new elections be held within four months (article 109) so as to guarantee a law-based political state *(pravovoe gosudarstvo)* and culture.

The constitution provides little guidance on how each chamber's membership is to be selected (articles 95 and 96). This dilemma was partly resolved in June 1995 when the Duma reached a compromise with Yeltsin to ensure that the procedures utilized in 1993 would remain in effect: 225 deputies elected from single-member districts (each consisting of approximately 466,000 voters[44]), and the other 225 deputies elected from party lists, that is, proportional representation where parties share in a proportional total of all votes cast in the election. Not considered optimal by either the Duma or the presidential administration both sides have continued to try to expand their powers at the expense of their opposing number.[45] On the other hand, the upper chamber of the legislature—the Federation Council—has not provoked as much attention, and no serious effort to alter its composition developed until Putin proposed major changes in 2000. What might be concluded from this is that changes in the constitutional structure of power are still possible. Constitutional manipulation of this sort would seem out-of-place in the American context but it is not that unusual in parliamentary systems. The danger lies in the confusion it promotes among Russian voters and the prospect that it will sever the bond that exists between voters and their representatives (see Figure 5.1).

In national-level elections Russian voters are given two ballots to cast: one representing a party list, and the other for an individual candidate. This divided nature has become the formative principle of the lower chamber and secured in law as it is,[46] will undoubtedly persist for years to come. The minimum voter turnout necessary for a legislative election to be valid is twenty-five percent, a low, but still practicable threshold.[47] While the 1995 electoral law specifically required that party lists contain no more than twelve names from each party's leadership (thus shifting power away from Moscow and St. Petersburg to the regions) this was removed in the 1999 version of the law.[48] Electoral associations (parties) and blocs are now also free to determine who will best be able to represent the party although a problem arises in that there are no guarantees that elected officials will take their seats.[49] One of the more visible examples of this situation occurred with the 1999 Duma elections when the Fatherland/All Russia bloc presented Yevgenii Primakov, Yurii Luzhkov, and Vladimir Yakovlev as its top three candidates; of the three only Primakov accepted his Duma mandate, as both Yakovlev and Luzhkov already held positions in the Federation Council.

The State Duma

Unlike the Soviet state, but typical of most parliamentary systems, the Russian Federation's legislature is dominated by the lower chamber, the State Duma. Since the constitution states that laws are adopted by the Duma and only in some cases are these then examined by the Federation Council the center of legislative power is apparent. President Putin's legislative reforms in 2000 further placed

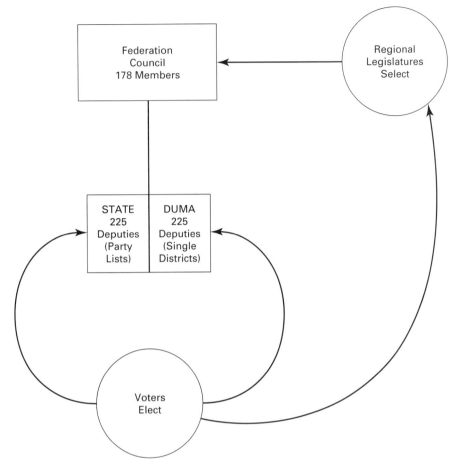

Figure 5.1 The Federal Assembly

the onus of legislative responsibility on the Duma but at the same time did little to clarify the Duma's relationship to the president.

The right of legislative initiative (article 104) states that all draft laws must first be submitted to the State Duma. Once a draft law is approved by the Duma it is submitted to the Federation Council within five days for "examination" and subsequent approval or rejection.[50] If a bill is rejected, the Duma can override the upper chamber by a two-thirds majority vote. This provision gives the Duma an important authority denied to the Federation Council (fairly typical amongst the other former Soviet republics' legislatures, see Table 5.3). On the most important of federal concerns such as deciding the budget, raising taxes, and declaring war, the Duma must cooperate with the Federation Council (article 106). In all cases laws must be submitted to the president within five days of passage and signed by him within fourteen days (article 107). If the president vetoes a bill, as happened when the Duma and Yeltsin clashed over a law regarding the return of valuables seized by Soviet forces during World War II ("trophy art"),[51] the president must then sign the bill into law, or appeal to the constitutional court.

The president maintains other controls over the State Duma. For instance, the Duma is funded through the presidential administration rather than the Finance Ministry, a condition which has allowed the president to manipulate the Duma on occasion by threatening to cut off perks for deputies such as housing in Moscow. The president may also dissolve the Duma and call for new elections, except in cases where he is under the threat of impeachment (article 109). In the event of dissolution the constitution demands that a new Duma be sitting within four months of an act of dissolution. However, the president is prevented from dissolving the parliament at those times when it has filed charges against the president, during states of emergency and declarations of martial law throughout Russia, and for the last six months of the president's term. This last point is important in that it could prevent the president from arbitrarily extending his term of office.

One constitutional measure—the privilege of immunity from prosecution (article 98)—has caused as much controversy as most of the others combined. The provision was designed to protect deputies from political harassment; instead, it has been used by unscrupulous politicians to hide behind the letter of the law and by outright criminals who want protection from their illegal activities. The collapse of a nation-wide pyramid investment scheme run by **Sergei Mavrodi** in 1994 led him to seek a Duma seat the next year so as to avoid prosecution. While the Duma eventually denied him his seat, this type of refuge proved attractive to other lawbreakers.

By October of 1995 the issue of criminals running for parliament had become a scandal attracting international attention when the Russian Interior Minister claimed to have provided the Central Electoral Commission with a list of eighty-five candidates who were under investigation.[52] Despite other legislators adding their voices in alarm,[53] several convicted felons were seated in the Duma as a result of the 1995 elections.[54] But Duma reluctance to take action may have been attributable to that body's desire to keep deputies' immunity intact as a hedge against presidential ambitions.

The constitution gives both chambers the leeway to determine their internal structures. Like many other parliaments the Duma has organized itself primarily according to committees dealing with important and broad-ranging topics such as Labor and Social Protection, Budget and Taxes, Agrarian Issues, Defense, Security, and others.[55] The First (Convocation) Duma began work with seventeen committees (later increased to twenty-three), and both the Second (1995) and Third (1999) Dumas have had twenty-eight. Nominally based on proportional representation committee chair positions have been doled out based on political alliances which include some parties or blocs and exclude others. In 2000 in the Third Duma the KPRF was given eight committee chairs, the pro-Putin faction Unity seven, the People's Deputy faction five, and the remainder were parceled out to smaller groups.[56] As not all parties which had won seats were included in this division of spoils (i.e., Yabloko, SPS, Otechestvo), as had been the case in previous years, there was a considerable outcry which threatened Duma working relations. Eventually a compromise was reached but in April 2002 the Kremlin engineered a reordering of committee controls that left the KPRF in charge of only two committees and with a bitter taste in opposition.

The selection of the Duma's speaker is also significant. The First Duma's speaker, **Ivan Rybkin,** failed to win reelection to this post in 1995 after his bid to create a center-left coalition failed (see Chapter Four) and the various pro-reform factions proved unwilling to unify behind his candidacy. Rybkin's successor, KPRF member Gennadii Seleznev who had served as deputy speaker in the First Duma has served continuously as speaker since 1995 although he very nearly fell victim to the same Kremlin intrigues that successfully pushed the KPRF into opposition in April 2002 and left Seleznev expelled from his own party. As complicated as the politics have been the speaker must also direct the work of the Duma by coordinating relations between the various parties/factions. His power is less formal than it is based on the strength of his leadership in forming coalitions among the multitude of groups represented in the parliament. As well, he needs to know how to coordinate activities with the Federation Council and, as events have shown, the presidency.

The Federation Council

The upper chamber of the Russian parliament contrasts sharply with the State Duma. In its first term it was selected by presidential appointment or presidential approval to hold elections. Since the upper chamber operated in such close proximity to presidential desires it did not develop a clear vision or sense of purpose. Its limited powers do not permit it to act as a counterweight to the State Duma, but it does have its role to play and must be deferred to at the appropriate junctures.

Nor does the **Federation Council** have the certainty of existence of the State Duma. Yeltsin saw to it that the chamber reflected his views by early on appointing thirty-six of the eighty-nine regional heads of government;[57] all were subsequently required to stand for election to the Federation Council in 1993. But from 1994 to 1995 an increasing number of governors appealed to the president to be allowed to stand for elections in their respective regions so as to gain greater legitimacy.[58] The electoral law governing the Federation Council was debated throughout 1995 and finally reached a conclusion when the Federation Council vetoed the bill dealing with its own formation, the State Duma overrode that veto, and Yeltsin agreed to sign it into law. This law determined that the composition of the Council was to include the heads of administrations and the heads of the various legislatures in the eighty-nine regions of the Russian Federation for a total of 178 members (including Chechnya). Election to this body was not to be required for one year after the law's passage (December 1996) but after that time all members were to stand for election in their respective regions and the president would no longer have the ability to make appointments (the president does, however, retain a representative in each chamber of the Federal Assembly).

Not all of those elected from that point were automatically supportive of the administration. A number of Yeltsin's candidates for governor or heads of administration were defeated in elections beginning in December 1995. By 1999 left-oriented (largely NPSR, but also KPRF) governors held positions in several dozen republics and regions which inevitably made it more difficult for Yeltsin's agenda to be well-received by the Council.[59] Moreover, the composition of the Federation Council ensured it a part-time character since members were first of all responsible as governors or heads of legislatures in their home regions. Whereas the constitution says the State Duma works "on a full-time professional basis" (article 97) no similar provision exists concerning the upper chamber.

At first glance the powers of the Federation Council might seem peripheral compared to those of the State Duma. Of the ten powers specifically mentioned in the constitution none are initiating or primary elements in the legislative process; more accurately these powers help to fine-tune the relationship between the legislative and executive branches. Article 102, which lists most of the Council's powers, primarily limits the Council to confirming actions taken or officials chosen by others. The most important of these relate to the presidency: The Council is charged both with scheduling presidential elections, and deciding whether or not to remove the president after an impeachment conducted by the Duma.

But despite the restricted number of duties the Federation Council does have other legislative functions. Article 106 requires laws concerning the budget, taxes and levies, financial matters, ratification and denunciation of international treaties, questions of border demarcation, and war and peace to be scrutinized by the Federation Council before gaining the force of law. The "compulsory examination" of laws accorded the Federation Council gives it a veto power over this type of legislation which then requires a Duma override. But this still represents only a portion of the principal laws defining the business of the state. Left out are laws concerning legal affairs, society, the military, and foreign policy all of which minimize the role played by the Federation Council. As such, the Russian president has not yet had to be concerned with two potentially combative legislative components at the same time.

The Federation Council has fewer committees within which to conduct its work than does the State Duma. There are eleven committees which meet on a permanent or semipermanent basis dealing with both major issues (Security and Defense; Budget, Tax Policy, Finance, Currency and Customs Regulations, Banking Activities) and those of lesser importance (Northern and Small Peoples). The selection of committee chairs is not based on party affiliation since the Council's operational makeup is not determined by the party principle.

The most powerful individual in the Federation Council is the **speaker.** The convening of a new Council always brings about a new election for this position from within the chamber, a matter of some importance as the president relies heavily on his services to guarantee passage of legislation. The most recent of these—**Sergei Mironov,** the former deputy speaker of the St. Petersburg legislature—was not a major actor in national politics prior to his December 2001 selection but his connection to Putin's home town reiterates the importance of regional connections.

The Federation Council leadership also consists of a number of deputy chairmen (four in 2000) whose tasks are to substitute for the chairman when necessary, and assist in the organization of the Federation Council.[60] The Council meets much more irregularly than the Duma at intervals of every third week and then only for three days of the week. This reflects the weakest element of the Council's character: its part-time membership. In October 1995, for instance, the Council had to appeal to the Duma to enact legislation guaranteeing that the Federation Council's term would extend through to the seating of the next Council in January 1996.[61]

The direct election of governors did seem to hold some prospect that the Federation Council would become a key actor in the legislative process. But Putin's election in 2000 gave the new president the opportunity to again alter the balance of power. On 19 July 2000 the State Duma voted overwhelmingly to approve a law amending the Federation Council. Within days (26 July) the Council itself succumbed to pressure to reorganize; the Council agreed that future members would be appointed by the regional legislatures and executives. Thus governors (heads of administration, presidents) and chairmen of legislative assemblies were no longer to automatically serve in the upper chamber, although they would retain control over those selections. In August Putin crafted a new quasi-representative body known as the **State Council** and formally appointed its members on 2 September. These included governors from each of the seven new federal districts (more on these in Chapter Seven) who would be rotated every six months within each district. The State Council is scheduled to meet four times a year; when not in session a presidium is established to tend to the State Council's business and can meet as often as once a month with a set agenda of two issues.

A clear reflection of the Russian/Soviet political culture whereby nominally representative institutions delegate power to more compact executive bodies, the State Council's presidium could prove to be a power broker between the president and the legislature, although not independent in its own right. Just as important, however, is the fact that members of this body regain some of their lost national exposure by serving on this advisory—not legislative—body. Everything, though, is reliant upon Putin's desire to truly utilize the State Council and not simply placate the hurt feelings of significant political actors.

All of this leads to the conclusion that parliamentary governance is still being developed in Russia, and that the struggle for political power is not over. The formal option for expanding legislative power by means of the rule of law (again, a precursor to democracy but not equivalent to it) is that of amending the constitution. But another option might be simply stepping into the breach of power when the president is weak. An uphill battle given the opportunities that have been missed (again, during Yeltsin's illnesses, and Putin's fumbling response to the 2000 sinking of the submarine "Kursk"), and the lack of leadership, it seems obvious that the legislature's role remains at best secondary to the executive: outmaneuvered and outfoxed at most every turn. There are no guarantees, however, that a stronger legislature would promote the goal of parliamentary democracy. In fact, events have shown that there is reason to believe just the opposite. But the character of Russian politics has changed dramatically in the space of a decade and become highly institutionalized. As one analyst has observed, "today political conflict is more likely to be waged with no-confidence votes, vetoes, and rival public relations campaigns."[62]

Key Terms

presidential administration
vote of no-confidence
State Council
Federation Council

Security Council
presidential administration
State Duma
Gennadii Seleznev

Questions for Consideration

1. Does Russia's super-presidential system preclude the effective participation of the legislative branch?
2. What in the Russian political culture ensures the retention of the strong presidential system formed in the constitution?
3. Does the reorganization of the Federation Council indicate that the presidency has gained control over part of the legislative branch?
4. If the constitution is indeed the scaffolding for the political process, what does this say about the system's legitimacy?
5. What are the most effective tools at the State Duma's disposal for overcoming the constraints placed upon it?

Suggested Readings

Robert B. Ahdieh. *Russia's Constitutional Revolution: Legal Consciousness and the Transition to Democracy, 1985–1996* (University Park, PA: Pennsylvania State University Press, 1997).

Laura Belin and Robert W. Orttung. *The Russian Parliamentary Elections of 1995: The Battle for the Duma* (Prague: Open Media Research Institute, 1997).

Jerry Hough, Evelyn Davidheiser, and Susan Goodrich Lehmann. *The 1996 Russian Presidential Election* (Washington, DC: Brookings Institution, 1996)

Peter Rutland, ed. *The Russian Presidential Elections of 1996* (Prague: Open Media Research Institute, 1998).

Boris Yeltsin. *The Struggle For Russia* (New York: Times Books, 1994).

Gennady Zyuganov. *My Russia: The Political Autobiography of Gennady Zyuganov* (Armonk, NY: M. E. Sharpe, 1997).

Useful Websites

Federation Council of the Russian Federation
http://www.council.gov.ru/index_e.html

State Duma of the Russian Federation
http://www.duma.gov.ru/

Russian Informational Center
http://www.infocentre.ru

President of the Russian Federation
http://president.kremlin.ru/

Endnotes

1. Yeltsin's health had deteriorated steadily through his first term, most noticeably with his need for open heart surgery following the 1996 presidential election. Yeltsin's decision to step down meant that Putin as chairman of the government assumed responsibility and an election would have to take place within three months.
2. See Gerald M. Easter. "Preference for Presidentialism: Postcommunist Regime Change in Russia and the NIS", *World Politics,* 49 (1997), p. 189.
3. See George W. Breslauer's discussion of Yeltsin's six presidential "types" in "Boris Yel'tsin as Patriarch", *Post-Soviet Affairs,* 15 (2): pp. 186–200.
4. John Morrison, *Boris Yeltsin* (New York: Dutton, 1991), p. 259.
5. Michael E. Urban, "Boris El'tsin, Democratic Russia and the Campaign for the Russian Presidency", *Soviet Studies,* 44 (1992): p. 199.
6. Boris Yeltsin, *Against the Grain,* (New York: Summit Books, 1990), p. 249.
7. Boris Yeltsin, *The Struggle for Russia* (New York: Times Books, 1994), p. 21.
8. A good brief account of the events of the coup can be found in Morrison, pp. 281–87.
9. Ibid., p. 35.
10. Vladimir Solovyov and Elena Klepikova, *Boris Yeltsin: A Political Biography* (New York: G. P. Putnam's Sons, 1992), p. 279.
11. Data from "Russia: Regional Voting Patterns in the April 1993 Referendum", National Technical Information Service, Springfield, VA, 1993.
12. See Vera Tolz, "Drafting the New Russian Constitution", *RFE/RL Research Report,* 2 (16 July 1993): pp. 1–12.
13. Easter, "Preference for Presidentialism", p. 197.
14. All-Russian Institute of Public Opinion Research (VCIOM), 28 January 1996; also, CNN/Moscow Times, 22 April 1996.
15. See, for instance, *Moscow News,* 2 May 1996.
16. *Russia Today-Central European Online Navigator* [http://www.ceo.cz/rtoday/rthome.html], 17 June 1996.
17. National News Service, 21 June 1996.
18. CNN Interactive World News, 18 June 1996.
19. Robert Sharlet, "The New Russian Constitution and its Political Impact", *Problems of Post-Communism,* 42 (January-February 1995), p. 5.
20. As when Yeltsin dismissed the commander of the Russian land forces, General Vladimir Semyonov, in 1996; see Interfax, 2 December 1996.
21. "Decree of the President of the Russian Federation on Measures to Streamline State Administration in the Field of Defence and Security," *Rossiiskaya gazeta,* 4 March 1998, reprinted in RIA-Novosti, 4 March 1998 [http://www.ria-novosti. com/].
22. See ITAR-TASS, 30 January 1995 and *RFE/RL Newsline,* 18 October 2000.
23. ITAR-TASS, 17 October 1995.

24. See the argument of Eugene Huskey, "Yeltsin as State Builder", *Soviet and Post Soviet Review,* 21 (1994), pp. 56–62.
25. *RFE/RL Newsline,* 10 January 1996.
26. CNN Interactive World News, 20 June 1996.
27. "Yeltsin Picks Lebed's Choice to Lead Defense Ministry", *OMRI Analytical Brief,* 1 (18 July 1996).
28. Yeltsin's actions came in June 1996; see CNN Interactive World News, 25 June 1996, and National News Service, 26 June 1996. Putin replaced other key officials in July 2000; see Interfax, 31 July 2000, translated in FBIS-SOV, 31 July 2000; and RIA, 31 July 2000, FBIS-SOV, 31 July 2000.
29. *RFE/RL Newsline,* 7 March 2001.
30. *New York Times,* 24. February 1994.
31. *New York Times,* 27 February 1994.
32. Interfax, 22 January 1997.
33. ITAR-TASS, 21 September 1995.
34. For instance, see *Kommersant-Daily,* 26 November 1996.
35. See *OMRI Daily Digest,* 14 November 1995; ITAR-TASS, 30 January 1996 cited in *OMRI Daily Digest,* 31 January 1996; also *Izvestiya,* 14 February, RIA-Novosti Daily Review, 16 February 1998 [http://www.russia.net/ria/ria_main.html].
36. *Izvestiya,* 5 November 1996.
37. *Izvestiya,* 29 January 1995.
38. *Komsomolskaya pravda,* 10 February 1995.
39. See, for instance "This Country Must be Ruled by Authority, Not Circumstances," President Boris Yeltsin's annual address to the Federal Assembly, RIA-Novosti, 8 March 1997 [http://www.russia.net/ria/dr/db07030.htm].
40. Ruslan Khasbulatov, *The Struggle for Russia* (London: Routledge, 1993), p. 241.
41. See, for instance, Aurel Braun, "All Quiet on the Russian Front? Russia, Its Neighbors, and the Russian Diaspora" in ed. Michael Mandelbaum, *The New European Diasporas* (New York: Council on Foreign Relations Press, 2000), pp. 89–90.
42. For public reaction to the referendum see "Regional Voting Patterns in the April 1993 Elections," Central Intelligence Agency (Springfield, VA: National Technical Information Service, 1993).
43. *Constitution of the Russian Federation,* Section Two, Concluding and Transitional Provisions, part 7.
44. *Rossiyskaya gazeta,* 6 July 1995.
45. For instance, see Interfax, 10 January 1997.
46. Article 3, "Federal Law on the Election of Deputies of the State Duma of the Federal Assembly of the Russian Federation" (Law #121-F3), 24 June 1999, *Rossiyskaya gazeta,* 1 and 3 July 1999, translated by International Foundation for Electoral Systems (Moscow) [http://www.ifes.ru].
47. Article 79.2(a), "Federal Law on the Election of Deputies."
48. Article 39.8, "Federal Law on the Election of Deputies."
49. Article 82.10, "Federal Law on the Election of Deputies."
50. For example, in December 1996 when the Federation Council voted down the Duma's draft bill on organizing the government. See Interfax, 4 December 1996.
51. Interfax, 7 April 1997.
52. "85 Alleged Criminals to Run for Russian Parliament-Minister", ITAR-TASS, 3 October 1995.
53. "Lawmakers Fear Next Parliament Might Shelter Criminals," ITAR-TASS, 4 October 1995.

54. *Izvestiya,* 31 January, 1996.
55. See "Komitetii GD", State Duma of the Federal Assembly of the Russian Federation website [http://www.duma.gov.ru/deputats/committe.htm].
56. *RFE/RL Newsline,* 20 January 2000.
57. Vera Tolz, "Russia's New Parliament and Yeltsin: Cooperation Prospects," *RFE/RL Research Report,* 3 (4 February 1994): p. 6.
58. See ITAR-TASS, 17 October 1995.
59. A complete listing of governors and leaders of regional legislatures may be found at the Norwegian Institute of International Affairs website [http://www.nupi.no/russland/russland.htm].
60. Article 11, "Iz Reglamenta Soveta Federatsii Federalnovo Sobraniya Rossiiskoye Federatsii", Federation Council of the Russian Federation website [http://www.council.gov.ru/ruk/zam_pol.htm].
61. ITAR-TASS, 5 October 1995.
62. M. Steven Fish, "Democracy Begins to Emerge", *Current History,* 94 (October 1995): p. 317.

Chapter 6

The Administration of Power

The stability of every governing system is simultaneously, although not equally, conditioned by a number of key factors. We have seen in the previous two chapters the importance of the representative institutions and governing practices, and the public's ability to participate in politics. Whether the system is democratic, transitional, or authoritarian these factors are all present to some degree. Democratic systems rely heavily on electoral procedures for their legitimacy but like their authoritarian counterparts they also require some nonparticipatory decision making (the role of the bureaucracy) and force (the military, the police) to stay in power. Implementing and interpreting political decisions has come to be accepted as the logical—but not exclusive—purview of the courts. Transitional systems are by definition in the process of finding a balance for these conditions; flexibility and alteration are values that constantly come into conflict with those groups which are resistant to change. And authoritarian systems usually adopt some pretense about responding to the public will but more commonly value the means used to protect elites' power.

Determining the distribution of governmental power allows some insight into the amount of force that is necessary to sustain the status quo. For example, power concentrated in the government (cabinet) may restrict the autonomy of the bureaucracy but a bureaucracy that is not constrained is just as apt to limit the government's capacity for political action. And if institutional development is still in a state of rapid change it will be difficult to reach sustainable conclusions about the political systems's mid- or long-term prospects for survival. But from a political culture perspective studying the instruments of Russian policy implementation tells us much about what both elites and publics expect out of politics and the lengths to which each group will go to achieve their goals. These are the rationales for this chapter: to develop a detailed examination of the governmental apparatus so as to enhance our clarity of the entire political picture.

The Central Government

The Ministries

A specific interpretation of what constitutes a state's government is the **cabinet.** As in other countries the Russian cabinet consists of representatives of the ministries, agencies, and other formal bodies who report directly to the chairman—referred to as the **premier** or **prime minister**—of the Government of the Russian Federation, and in all cases is answerable to the president. In accordance with the constitution (article 113) this person is responsible for defining "the basic guidelines for the activity of the Government of the Russian Federation and federal ministers" and organizing its work. Since so much power is vested in the Russian cabinet—whether by constitutional mandate, parliamentary action, or presidential decree—outlining the cabinet tells us a great deal about the direction of policy and power. Power does not originate in the Russian cabinet/government; this body is instead a repository where power is collected for the purpose of realizing presidential aspirations.

The physical structure of the Russian Federation's government/cabinet is not limited to Russia itself and can be found in other Eurasian systems as well. The constitution mentions only the positions of Chairman of the Russian Federation and deputy chairmen by name, but does provide that other ministries necessary to carry out governmental work may be created (article 110). Forming a cabinet is largely the domain of the president although Yeltsin conceded authority to his prime minister-designates as a result of the 1998 economic crisis which had caused the fall of the previous government (see Figure 6.1). The need for individual ministries and ministers is made apparent by the constitution's directives that the government deal with such issues as implementing budgetary and fiscal policies, carrying through on science, culture, education, health, defense and other forms of policy (article 114).

The Russian president's power to reorganize the cabinet when he is dissatisfied with its performance has proven to be a key feature of Russian governmental procedure. Throughout Yeltsin's tenure he frequently dismissed his cabinets, sometimes with little warning to the legislature, the public, or financial markets. The year 1998 stands out as particularly volatile in this regard as Yeltsin first dismissed his long-serving (1992–1998) prime minister Viktor Chernomyrdin in favor of the young (thirty-five-year-old) technocrat Sergei Kirienko. Only five months later at the height of an economic crisis Kirienko was sacrificed and Chernomyrdin reintroduced, but this move failed to win Duma support and the president charged his foreign minister, Yevgeny Primakov, with forming a government. In the process Yeltsin also had to promise the Duma that the new government would represent other political parties but no confirmation powers were formally transferred to the Duma. Still, presidential changes within the cabinet represent more than just erratic mood swings on the president's part; they can also reflect new directions in policy. Thus Yeltsin's March 1997 reorganizing of the cabinet so as to reinvigorate reform

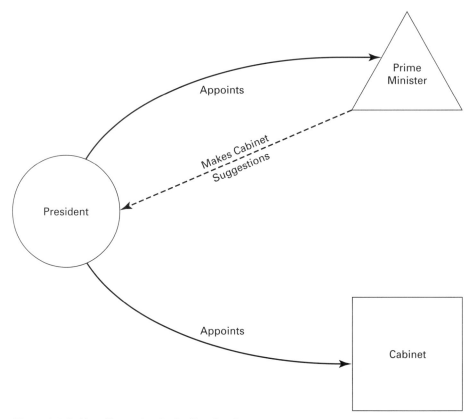

Figure 6.1 Cabinet Formation in the Russian Government

was particularly notable in that he again hired on his favorite reformer, Anatolii Chubais as both First Deputy Prime Minister and Finance Minister.[1] This constant shuffling of political figures allows valued members of the government to be used again and again and in different capacities. The downside to all of this is that by continually using the same individuals new voices are not heard and innovation may be neglected.

The Russian government makes use of both first deputy prime minister and deputy prime minister designations for key policy figures. These individuals are assistants to the prime minister responsible for specialized areas of the economy, politics, or social issues. A 1997 presidential decree prohibited ministers from simultaneously holding other portfolios but the enforcement of this provision has been lax. Cabinet positions are filled by individuals who are directly connected to either the president or the prime minister and closely reflect presidential policy choices. Yeltsin, for instance, erratically eliminated, and then reinstated, all first deputy prime minister positions in 1998, and Putin fired his scandal-plagued Railways Minister (a holdover from the Yeltsin years) in January 2002. Thus the cabinet member serves at the president's pleasure, effectively prohibiting the creation of independent power bases.

Significant also is the expression of party affiliation within the cabinet. Despite calls from various opposition parties, notably the KPRF, to develop broad-based governments of "national unity" Yeltsin made only token efforts to represent other parties in his cabinets. Among these have been Deputy Prime Minister Aleksandr Zaveryukha (1996–1997) and Agriculture Minister Gennady Kulik (1998, both of the Agrarian Party); KPRF members Aman Tuleev (Minister for CIS Affairs until 1997), First Deputy Prime Ministers Yuri Maslyukov and Vadim Gustov, and Minister for Antitrust Policies and Support for Entrepreneurship Gennadii Khodyrev (all in Primakov's cabinet); former Yabloko MP Mikhail Zadornov (Finance Minister, 1997–1998); and LDPR member Sergei Kalashnikov (Labor Minister in 1998). This resistance to greater inclusion remains today a sign of the president's power, especially over the government.

The ministries themselves vary considerably in size and importance based on both presidential and governmental policy priorities. Among these are the so-called **power ministries,** that is the organs of police and military power which report directly to the president. Specifically these include the ministries of Foreign Affairs, Defense, Internal Affairs, the Federal Security Service, the Foreign Intelligence Service, the Federal Border Service, and the Federal Agency for Government Communication and Information. Other ministries of national interest include Agriculture and Food, Finance, Labor, Justice, Nationalities Affairs and Regional Policy, and Land Policy, all of which report directly to the prime minister. Finally there are the specific issue-oriented ministries including Fuel and Power Engineering, Railways, and the Media, among others. In the 1980s the central-planning Soviet system had as many as sixty-two ministries, but with the Russian government's withdrawal from the economy a consolidation of ministries took place. For instance Chernomyrdin reorganized his cabinet in 1994 causing a net decrease of twenty percent of the size of the government.[2] In August 1996 the government was further scaled back from eighty-nine ministries and state committees to sixty-six of which twenty-four were ministries.[3] In late 2000 under Putin's and Prime Minister **Mikhail Kasyanov's** direction there remained twenty-four ministries, but restructuring ensured the emergence of six state committees, two federal agencies, thirteen federal services, eight "Russian" agencies, two supervisory offices, and three "organs of executive power."[4] One can imagine the difficulty of trying to bring together even just the heads of the two dozen ministries for twice-weekly meetings as Chernomyrdin attempted to do in 1994![5]

To both citizens and legislators the ministries are a potent force with which to be dealt. They represent institutionalized forces which, though shaken up by the collapse of the Soviet Union, are still considered necessary in the development of the state system. Prime Minister Chernomyrdin, for example, found it necessary to occasionally warn his ministers to follow through on policy implementation, and support government programs.[6] The downsizing of government bodies since 1991[7] resulted in a substantial turnover of trained personnel at the highest levels.[8]

Marat Baglai, Chairman of the Constitutional Court
Source: © TASS/Sovfoto

Initially in 1992 most of the government's top administrators were trained as part of the Soviet culture and carried the problems of that culture to the new government. But in another sense Soviet-trained administrators brought with them considerable experience needed during the transition. Ministers such as Sergei Kirienko and Boris Nemtsov came into the government with broad fields of expertise and a willingness to use nongovernmental perspectives in the exercise of their duties. Given time the Russian cabinet may become like its British counterpart with positions filled by policy generalists rather than narrowly focused specialists.

The ministries are joined in their tasks by the state committees, usually between eight and ten. These bodies are charged with such tasks as gathering statistics, managing resources, or focusing on policy-related issues such as the defense industry, industrial policy, or higher education. With such functional command over the state's vast resources the government is not heavily restricted by parliamentary decisions about the pace or direction of reform, even though it pays attention to prevailing political winds.

The work of the government occurs under the direct supervision of the prime minister, and he is responsible for its cohesion, although the president is empowered by the constitution (article 83, section b) to chair its meetings. The government's authority is extensive: it drafts and submits to the Duma a federal budget; implements the country's fiscal and monetary policies; administers state property; puts into effect the country's defense and foreign policy; and "implements measures to ensure the rule of law, civil rights and freedoms, the protection of property and public order, and the struggle against crime" (article 114). Article 115 further grants the government power to issue decrees and directives based on previously declared presidential, legislative, and constitutional actions. Nevertheless, the bottom line remains crucial: most of these actions (such as determining budget parameters) are overseen by the president who will determine how far or how committed the government is to be.

One final note concerns the governing process and the citizen's access to it. The Yeltsin administration opened and closed cabinet meetings to the media on several occasions in 1994 and 1995. At one point the government attempted to block media observance of cabinet meetings for all media outlets except the government newspaper *Rossiyskaya gazeta*. The political backlash this generated caused the government to back off from this particular effort to manage the news and to instead bring other media sources into the governmental chambers.[9] It would take another year before the media was granted "permanent" observer status at cabinet meetings and access to government officials through regular press briefings.[10] Although the mercurial atmosphere of Russian politics provides no certainty that this will be a permanent condition, the struggle to attain media access was a necessary step in establishing governmental accountability. At the very least it gave the media an incentive to probe the governmental labyrinth and consequently inform the public.

The Bureaucracy

Writing in the 1960s American Soviet affairs specialist Merle Fainsod commented that "the concentration of power in the hands of the tsars and their successors . . . provides an element of continuity in Russian history which transcends the drastic social upheavals of the last decades."[11] Fainsod was noting not just the centralization of power in Russian and later Soviet society but the fact that the central governing *apparatus*—or more commonly, the bureaucracy—remained in place despite the comings and goings of individual leaders. In fact, continuity is the hallmark of bureaucratic governance, its chief distinguishing feature.

Politicians may leave their individual marks on the political process (i.e., Stalin, Gorbachev, or Yeltsin), but something must keep the system operating. That is the role of the bureaucracy.

The constant juggling and rearranging of government bodies that one may read about periodically in the Russian press does not necessarily lead to the conclusion that the government is downsizing, or that it is operating in a more efficient manner. Occurrences at the national level, though, are not necessarily reflected at the regional or local levels. Here in particular, the political culture is slow to change and it seems certain that the local bureaucracy has altered little from Soviet times, except in its funding levels. As the bureaucracy usually appears little interested in disturbing its own status quo, government programs which seek to devolve or otherwise innovate authority from their control have few prospects of success.

Government at the Local Level

Until October 1993 local government (cities, raions) remained *soviet* (council) in form and largely operated by the old communist party apparatus. In some areas local elections had already replaced elements of the old party vanguard, but for the most part local elites had little allegiance to Yeltsin and were often openly obstructionist toward reform policies. Yeltsin's 9 October 1993 decree dissolving the soviets dramatically changed the political equation but not the political culture of the Federation. If a definite program of reform was envisioned for the local level, the center did not clearly explain it,[12] and new institutions or procedures would not be forthcoming from the administration until early 1995.

Some of this could have been remedied by a more specific constitution, but the 1993 document provided little help since it stressed governing principles rather than operational procedures (something that is more common to other Eurasian states). Article 131 states that "the structure of local self-government organs is autonomously determined by the population." Article 132 points to the devolution of authority from the "state" level to the local level; this, in fact, reverses an important definitional character of a federal system: the sharing of powers between levels. If power originates at the center and flows downward or outward, then the local organs of state authority do not exercise their power autonomously. As Alfred B. Evans, Jr. points out, "the local government's chronic need for benevolence from higher levels of authority has a major effect on the relationships between the legislative and executive branches within the local government,"[13] which limits western-style decision making and democratic behavior. In this way local government powers are "delegated" and "monitorable by the state."

From 1993 until Yeltsin signed the law "On general principles of local self-government in Russia" in August 1995 the fate of local government remained in a state of limbo. The suspension of the local legislatures put new power in the hands of local administrators, many of whom owed their positions to Yeltsin. This law sought to formalize the selection process and clarify the extent of independence available to the local level. Even still, there remained a blurring of lines of distinction between federal authority and the local level in such areas as public order, sanitation, and fire safety.[14]

The new law was designed and promoted to incorporate the "historical traditions of the Russian zemstvo" and thereby give local government a sense of attachment and legitimacy to the Russian past.[15] Further, as then Prime Minister Chernomyrdin saw the situation, "organs of state power . . . will be able to adopt their own legal acts that flesh out the organization of local self-government in the light of local traditions and possibilities." The idea seemed to be to allow some latitude to the citizens in shaping their local governing organs. The success of the law required several conditions, though, such as the commitment of central authorities to genuinely resist interfering in local affairs, and a change in the public's attitudes regarding participation. Either of these conditions are potential obstacles to the realization of change, but both also represent learned responses by leaders and the public and may be viewed as potential opportunities as well.

The Instruments of Power

The Police

All governing systems utilize police powers to some degree to ensure that laws or directives are carried out. As bland as this assessment may be, it should be remembered that Russia and the Eurasian states are the successors to not just one, but two strict police state cultures: the tsarist and Soviet systems. Today's Russian Federation still retains extensive police structures reminiscent of its Soviet predecessor including a dual system of internal and external intelligence-gathering services in conjunction with the regular police whose jobs are to combat crime and keep the peace (see Figure 6.2). But there is no reason to expect, as some commentators have put it, that the movement toward democracy somehow precludes the need for the police or intelligence functions.[16] The United States, after all, has at least thirteen separate components to its own intelligence/police community! The difference lies in their functions, that is, what the police and intelligence agencies actually do.

As already noted, the Russian president appoints the head of the **Ministry of Internal Affairs,** or MVD, which commands the police; in addition, in July 2001 the Duma gave the president the formal authority to hire and fire regional MVD chiefs.[17] The MVD has been headed by both career military men as well as by civilians although there is often only a nominal distinction between them. The leadership of the MVD is part of the country's defense structure; while not unusual in parliamentary-style systems, it is overdeveloped in the Russian case. The phenomenon can be traced back to tsarist times when governors often held military rank. In the Soviet Union civilian control over police agencies was required by the CPSU and all security agencies were kept strictly in check. This was justified in terms of making the police responsive to the working class on whose behalf the

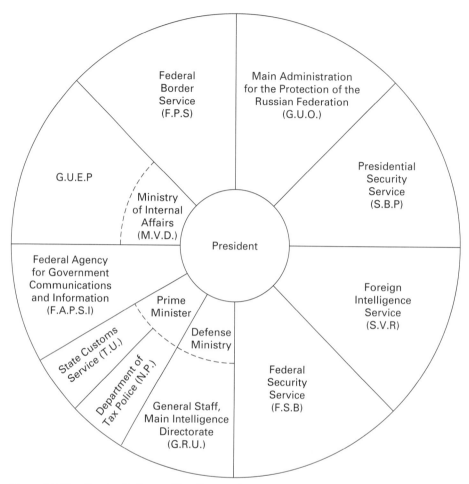

Figure 6.2 The Russian Police and Intelligence Community

party governed, but in reality the party recognized the danger of military or security-instigated coups, as proved to be the case in August 1991. The situation became more poignant after Yeltsin used force against legitimately-elected institutions in 1993. Keeping the instruments of coercion loyal to presidential interests has meant either rewarding them with pay incentives and rank, or by playing one institution off against another.

At the local level the police, or militia, carry out the day-by-day maintenance of public order and the investigation of crime—at least that which is not committed against the state. Traditionally the MVD has also been in charge of the country's penal system, but in October 1997 Yeltsin decreed that this authority be transferred to the Justice Ministry so that Russia would be in compliance with norms set by the Council of Europe.[18] Even still the MVD's role is to *administer* justice or mete it out

CHAPTER 6   The Administration of Power   **119**

as compared to the *ministering* of justice which is the function of the Justice Ministry and the courts (see below).[19] Both police and prison work often appear to involve low-level policy determinations and seemingly menial labor; they are thus accorded a very low status in the pecking order of federal security. Nevertheless, these functions also guarantee funding for the Interior Ministry, and the MVD has been reluctant to give up these prerogatives. The police's work is fundamental to the functioning of whatever system prevails in Russia, but this in no way guarantees that the police or prison systems get the amount of funding or resources they need to do their jobs properly,[20] nor does it prevent the federal security services from involvement in domestic law enforcement, including investigation of economic crimes.[21]

The skyrocketing rate of economically related crimes in Russia since 1991, and the violence associated with these crimes, caught the MVD unprepared.[22] Because of budgetary restrictions the MVD must work closely with the intelligence community, and as such has lost some of its enforcement authority. But it does have several organs available to assist in the fight against crime. There is no direct Russian equivalent to the American Federal Bureau of Investigation, but the MVD investigates crime primarily through the **Main Administration for Combating Economic Crime** (GUEP) whose focus is crime, corruption, and abuse of power. Until 2001 the MVD was assisted by a number of Regional Administrations for Combating Organized Crime (RUBOP), the mission of which was "to reveal, expose, and institute proceedings against organized criminal groups, alliances, leaders and criminal world bosses,"[23] but their efforts failed to satisfy the Interior Minister that organized crime had been countered and they were abolished in August.[24] Increasingly police and security agencies approach the issue of crime as a threat to national security, a position which was used to justify the militarization of state structures and threatened to undermine the development of the rule of law state.[25]

The MVD has its own military units which are used to maintain domestic order. Interior Ministry troops are subject to presidential orders and are separate from the Defense Ministry's organizational command. Their duties (originally laid out in a 1992 law) include "ensuring law and order, social security, and the legal regime of emergency situations," and helping to defend the country in time of war. This mandate has been interpreted to include terrorism, whether crime-related, subversive, or foreign in origin.[26] The Interior Ministry troops are seen as elite "shock" forces whose job the 1993 **Military Doctrine of the Russian Federation** defined as preventing and suppressing internal conflicts and other actions which threaten Russia's territorial integrity.[27]

Although Interior Ministry troops were in the forefront of the first Chechnya war in 1994–1996, their poor performance as well as budgetary constraints led to their being downsized from a 1992 high of 440,000 to a planned level of less than 170,000 by 2005. In addition to the regular troops, the Interior Ministry also employs paramilitary forces including the **Special Purpose Militia Detachments,** or **OMON** (Otryad militsii osobogo naznacheniya), **Special Rapid-Reaction Detachments, or SOBR, and Special Motorized Police Units, or SMChM.** These units are used primarily for crowd control, quelling domestic disturbances, and for strike breaking,[28] tasks which have made the Russian public wary of them.

Despite the importance of the MVD's policing duties the ministry has been consistently underfunded and overworked. The police often find themselves overwhelmed while trying to prevent and investigate crime, especially as the sheer number of illegal activities have expanded. As in the other Eurasian states, the Russian police are poorly paid, suffer from inadequate training, and must utilize outdated equipment including radios, cars, and computers. These conditions are in striking contrast to the gangs of criminals that have spread so rapidly throughout the country.[29] Gone are the days when the police could arbitrarily use force to accomplish policy goals. In addition, the deterioration of border controls and resultant importing of foreign weapons, and black-market purchases, or outright theft of Russian military hardware have provided for well-armed and highly dangerous criminal gangs. At no time in recent memory have the Russian police been as subject to escalating violence and death.[30]

All of this has led to increasing corruption of the police and the diminishing of their legal authority. Probably the worst example of this occurred in the summer of 1995 when at the height of the Chechen conflict (see Chapter Seven) several hundred rebels infiltrated the southern Russian city of **Budennovsk.** The rebels were able to penetrate as far as they did by bribing police at checkpoints along the way. This was a major factor in the firing of the country's top security officials in June 1995 including the head of the MVD, Viktor Yerin. But despite his replacement by Colonel-General Anatolii Kulikov, a man who profiled himself as incorruptible,[31] and a new program to deal with crime and terrorism, this remained a cosmetic approach which did not address the problem of corruption itself.

Several other federal agencies conduct police functions along with the MVD including the **Department of Tax Police,** and the **Federal Customs Service.** Both agencies go beyond simple policing and mix intelligence gathering into their plans of action. Another important agency is the **Federal Border Service** (FPS), which has the difficult task of patrolling and controlling the Russian Federation's 12,486 miles (19,917 square kilometers) of border with fourteen countries.[32] Formerly a component of the KGB, the head of the FPS reports directly to the president and in time of national defense the Service's 210,000 troops are mobilized into the army.[33] All of the aforementioned bodies' leaders hold the rank of general in the military. Among the resources at the FPS's disposal are the Western and Arctic groups of troops, as many as nine operational troop departments, several border detachments, individual border command offices, operational reserves, more then thirty combat and other units, and a Border Troops Academy.[34] Still, this organization's principle utility occurs in normal peacetime operations such as in 1994 when seventy-four million people and 8.5 million vehicles crossed Russia's borders.[35]

The Intelligence Agencies

In contrast to the police functions, the intelligence agencies are responsible for upholding federal laws, decrees, and edicts; and protecting the government and the state against external threats to security. The intelligence agencies are the successors to the Committee for State Security, or KGB, the most vaunted and feared of the coercion bodies of the latter Soviet era. Russia's security demands and illusions have not, however, resulted in the pervasive surveillance of the population characteristic of Soviet goals. The intelligence agency story since 1991 has largely been one of reorganization, splitting, and reorganizing again the various successors to the KGB. The result has been a proliferation of competing agencies and confusion over areas of authority. And while the intelligence community's power is not to be underestimated, collectively and individually these agencies are not equal to their predecessor.

One of Yeltsin's first actions with the fall of the Soviet Union was to dissolve the KGB, seen by the president and others as the principal architect of the coup.[36] Yeltsin had decided that the agency was beyond reform and potentially still dangerous to his own political future. Within less than two years, however, Yeltsin's experiment in creating a new Ministry of Security had failed and the president abolished this organ, too, in favor of a new **Federal Counterintelligence Service,** (or FSK, Federalnaya Sluzhba Kontrrazvedki). Although open resistance to the reorganization was not apparent, many of the career officers in the ministry were offended by Yeltsin's move and protested these changes by resigning their commissions.

The new arrangement likewise did not succeed, whether due to a deeply held suspicion that Yeltsin may have had toward the security organs (his father had been briefly arrested by the secret police in the 1930s but managed to escape being purged),[37] or because as Yeltsin's decree put it "the existing system of ensuring Russia's security (had) outlived itself."[38] At least initially the FSK took up where the Security Ministry left off; throughout 1994 and 1995 the FSK gained authority previously held by the KGB. For instance, in what seemed a flashback to the days of the Soviet police state in January 1995 it was reported that the FSK was requiring various ministries to again keep tabs on foreigners.[39]

But in the intelligence business the proof is in how effectively you do your work, not necessarily how many areas of responsibility you may have. In April 1995 Yeltsin signed a bill renaming the FSK the **Federal Security Service** (FSB, or Federalnaya Sluzhba Bezopasnosti). The purpose of this action was to enable the new body to expand its authority beyond counterintelligence. The FSB was mandated the same tasks as those of the FSK, and then some, including the ability to obtain economic information from both the public and private business sectors.[40] The remaining powers of the FSK were transferred to the Foreign Intelligence Service, although the FSB continued to pursue those it thought to be foreign agents.

For an organization formed out of several parts the FSB got its act together in a very short time. The principal task of the FSB at its outset was counterintelligence, but its leaders and their political supporters wanted more than this. Steadily the FSB expanded its powers to include the following: 1) the investigation and interrogation of criminal suspects; 2) conducting intelligence operations in foreign countries; 3) counterintelligence against or cooperation with "special services" of other CIS countries; 4) the operation of special armed detachments; 5) maintaining detention centers throughout the Russian Federation;[41] and 6) the ability to maintain "special units", that is extra legal groups for activities such as assassinations.[42]

In the areas of domestic surveillance and crime fighting the FSB provokes the strongest images of a reborn KGB. The enormous growth of crime in the Russian Federation since 1992 has provided a reason for the security services' existence. Recognizing the popular reaction against crime in Russian society, Yeltsin, Putin, and the Duma have all taken strong law-and-order stances. In 1995, for instance, FSB head Sergei Stepashin stated that his agency was not required to inform the **Procuracy** (the state prosecutor's office) of "our ways and methods of obtaining this or that information on this or that criminal group,"[43] an interesting position considering that in 1997 Stepashin was named Justice Minister! The FSB was allowed to coordinate all intelligence gathering requiring the use of surveillance equipment for purposes such as phone tapping; one source placed the number of illegal phone taps in 1995 at 7,500,000![44] The service also collected information on white collar crime including violations of the tax laws.[45] At one point in 1996 the head of the FSB stated somewhat cryptically that his agency was also "making a certain contribution to stabilizing the economy and developing market relations."[46] Such conditions are reflective of attitudes within the security services which generally remain opposed to the liberalization of Russian society and the deterioration of centralized control. Without some placating of these groups the prospects for political stabilization remain thin at best.

While the FSB may be the strongest element of the security services, others with similar powers or agendas have also carved out their own areas of authority. As already noted the Presidential Security Service (SBP) accumulated considerable power under Korzhakov. Another agency, the Main Protection Directorate (GUO, Glavnoye Upravleniye Okhrany) has been tasked to guard members of the Security Council, the government, regional and provincial leaders, and important foreign dignitaries. In addition, since 1992 the GUO has been the principal repository of information on telephone conversations that take place on government lines,[47] is charged with securing state weapon's exports, and maintains the network of government underground bunkers, tunnels, and communications that would be used in time of war.[48] Significant also is the **Federal Agency for Government Communication and Information** (FAPSI, Federal'noe Agenstvo Pravitel'stvennoi Svyazi I Informatsii) which is charged with protecting the country's communications system as well as the functions of coding and decoding.[49] Some overlap occurs between these organs but how much is not certain.[50]

The **Foreign Intelligence Service** (SVR) is the final KGB successor. Its purpose is the gathering of information in foreign countries relating to Russia's national security; toward this end it employs the traditional methods of spying and is responsible for advising the president and the national security apparatus on potential threats to Russian security.[51]

Formed in December 1991, the agency's longevity may be attributable to the lack of competition it has from other bodies in carrying out its duties. It could also be due to the influence of its first director, Yevgenii Primakov who served in this capacity from 1991 until his appointment as Foreign Minister in January 1996. Primakov's previous career in intelligence structures and his conservative approaches to foreign policy gained him much needed support in the Duma from both communists and nationalists and was instrumental in his confirmation as prime minister in 1998.

Given the conditions limiting the growth of Russia's democratic institutions and values, it is not reasonable to expect that the security/intelligence agencies will remain content to be simply equal—albeit powerful—players in the game. The control that the CPSU exerted over these groups in the past, and the direction that the party and its ideology provided them is crucial to understanding the current political scene. Loyalty to a particular leader tends to be a more transitory concept than loyalty to an ideology such as communism, or to a particular governing system. It is less realistic to expect that a taming influence will be exercised over the intelligence agencies in the near future.

The Military

Both above the political fray and at the same time enmeshed in it is the military. Despite decades of CPSU control to keep the military out of politics the military has been utilized at key political junctures in recent history such as the August 1991 coup, the September–October 1993 parliamentary siege, and the war in Chechnya. As already noted, the relationship the military has with the security/intelligence services is a close one and they share a kinship with these other politicized bodies. Thus, the control mechanism the political sector has over the military requires examination.

The minister of defense, like his American counterpart, is chosen by the president and serves at his behest. This largely removes him from the chain-of-command headed by the prime minister. Typically the Russian Defense Minister has been a career military officer, not a civilian. This is a pattern traceable to the period of the Civil War (1918–1921) when the first Soviet defense minister (originally called People's Commissar for War), Leon Trotsky, held this position. The issue has occasionally resurfaced but not until 2001 was a nonmilitary man assigned the position of Defense Minister (former Security Council Secretary **Sergei Ivanov**).[52] Putin's efforts to put his own supporters in the most important positions thereby provided the Russian Federation with actual civilian control over the defense sector comparable to western standards. In contrast, among the other former Soviet republics only the Baltic states and Armenia have had civilian defense ministers.

In November 1993 after two years of preparation, a new Military Doctrine of the Russian Federation was approved; among other things this important document called for "the improvement of a military policy-making mechanism ensuring state control over the adoption and fulfillment of military-political decisions." Further, it stated that the "Russian Federation Armed Forces . . . are utilized in accordance with the Constitution and existing legislation of the Russian Federation."[53] But as already pointed out, the doctrine says nothing about when or if a civilian will hold the office of Minister of Defense, nor whether the military should be accountable to the Federal Assembly as well as the president.[54]

The military's budgetary competition and its symbolic role in defending Russia's national survival are compelling reasons for studying the military's role in domestic politics. The first of these may be the root cause of much of the turmoil surrounding the military today. The demise of the Soviet state brought about a need to reexamine the military's share of national resources, and consequently the scope of its operations. The military has thus found itself in the unfamiliar situation of open competition for its share of the budgetary pie. Most striking about this competition has been the fact that the military has experienced few victories in the post-Soviet budgetary battles and a good number of sharp setbacks.[55] For instance in the 1995 budget debates the government proposed a military budget of R45.2 trillion (at a ruble exchange rate of 3500 to the dollar), down 40–45 percent from the previous year.[56] By September of 1995 the Defense Ministry had received only half of the total amount necessary to cover defense costs for the year.[57] In 1996 the Defense Ministry requested R71 trillion but the government's allocation amounted to only fifty-seven percent of this, or R41 trillion,[58] and by October the Finance Ministry had to come up with R9.5 trillion more just to break even.[59]

Russia's defense ministers have all decried the lack of federal and local support the military has received.[60] Mounting Defense Ministry debts are made worse by a flood of crises: local officials cutting power supplies to bases and garrisons;[61] military wages going unpaid due to the cost of the Chechen conflict;[62] only one-third to one-half of servicemen being paid at any given time; the Finance Ministry allocating only half of expected outlays; and crucial support elements such as food procurement shutting down.[63] Conditions had deteriorated so sharply by 1996 that Defense Council Secretary Yuri Baturin found it necessary to deny that these problems were leading the army toward mutiny.[64]

Coupled to the problems of military spending have been those of the defense industry. The change in military priorities of the Russian Federation—particularly the downsizing of the Russian armed forces—has had the direct effect of reducing orders from the state for procurement of military hardware and weapons systems, and research and development. Formerly a sector of the highest prioritization in the budgetary process the defense industry has had to search for new markets, convert itself to civilian-oriented production, and in some cases closed down altogether. In the first post-Soviet years western investors with help from their governments scoured the Russian economy for defense sector bargains, even as the government became delinquent on contracts (such as not paying for production of TU-160 bombers in 1994[65]) or canceled them outright. All of this has added fuel to the fire of communist, nationalist, and anti-Western forces in the debate over the direction the Russian political system is to take.

The Courts

Building a Legal System

Underlying the foundation of the rule-of-law society and especially the establishment of democracy is the need for a stable and authoritative judicial process.

This requires a codified set of laws and norms (civil and criminal codes of law), a nonpolitical court system, a strong federal procuracy, and general conformity to the rule of law by politicians and political parties of all backgrounds. This asks a lot from any political system much less a transitional one experiencing the wrenching social, political, and economic change of Russia. By all appearances the process is underway but still occurring after a painfully slow start.

As noted earlier in this chapter the ministering of justice in any modern society is the responsibility of the courts while the administering of justice rests with law enforcement agencies. The Russian judicial system is a complicated series of courts and judicial advocates. Twelve constitutional amendments address the judicial system's structuring and operating principles, and these are supplemented by individual federal laws giving substance to the organizational framework. While the constitution only mentions three component parts of the judicial system—the Constitutional Court, the Supreme Court, and the Supeme Court of Arbitration—several other types of courts do exist.

At the apex of the judicial system is the **Constitutional Court.** A reformulated institution—that is, it existed prior to the 1993 constitution—it deals exclusively with matters of constitutionality. Justices of the court are granted immunity (article 122), may not be removed during their single fifteen-year term, and are paid out of the federal budget separate from other branches (article 124).[66] The Constitutional Court is responsible for most federal matters of constitutional significance including interpreting the constitution, determining whether federal laws, regardless of who issues them, are in compliance with the constitution; the regulation of disputes between the Russian Federation and its individual parts (the republics and regions); disputes between the republics and regions themselves; and issues of international concern (article 125). In addition, the court is granted the power to "take(s) legislative initiatives on questions within its own purview."[67]

The Constitutional Court consists of nineteen justices; justices may begin service at forty years of age, and (as of January 2001) have no upper-age limit.[68] Justices are appointed by the president and approved by the Federation Council (article 128); all other federal judges are also appointed by the president. At least half of the Federation Council (ninety members) must vote in favor of a candidate and the voting is done by secret ballot. The selection of justices was clouded in 1994 by Yeltsin's nomination of multiple candidates for single seats, which resulted in several rounds of voting before the appointments were actually made.[69] This meant the court could not take up its duties until all members had been appointed. Justices may neither be members of political parties or movements during their terms and in general are prohibited from taking part in political campaigns or discussions of activities pending before the court. The chairman of the Constitutional Court is elected from within the court's membership.[70]

Presidential control over the courts is furthered by the president's ability to appoint a "representative" to the Constitutional Court, and by the government's constitutional authority to establish a judicial system and "the procedure for their organization and activity" (article 71, sec. c). Yeltsin reinforced this point during the drafting of a law governing the powers of the Constitutional Court by stating that "questions pertaining to the judicial system are under the Russian Federation's exclusive jurisdiction."[71] That law laid out in detailed form the authority, limitations, selection and replacement of justices. Taken in conjunction with the June 1995 law guaranteeing both political and physical security for judges, the judicial system has been granted a sense of security that is desperately needed in Russia's quest for stability and law.

The judicial system has two other ostensibly co-equal areas of judicial action (see Figure 6.3) but their functions are left to be explained by federal law. The **Supreme Court** is described as (article 126) "the highest judicial organ for civil, criminal, administrative, or other cases under the jurisdiction of the courts of general jurisdiction." The Supreme Court also "provides clarification on questions of judicial practice," and guides the activities of the lower courts in both civil and criminal matters. Among the courts mentioned in the constitution it is this one which has the greatest impact upon the citizens as it is effectively the peak of the appeals process. Jurists on this court are, again, selected by the president and confirmed by the Federation Council. The **Supreme Court of Arbitra-**

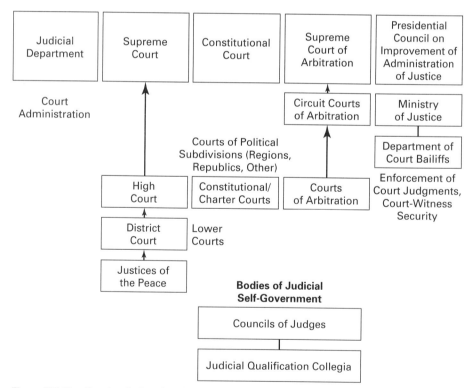

Figure 6.3 The Russian Federation Judiciary

Source: Russian Federation Supreme Court website [http://www.supcourt.ru/]

tion is largely a court for resolving economic conflicts. Under a federal law passed in April 1995 the roles of this court and inferior courts of arbitration were clarified as being "necessary to form a market economy, recognize the equality of all forms of property and protect the rights of all participants in market relations."[72] While not spoken of much in the media these courts' abilities to address enterprise and commercial disputes gives them a potential for growth, if allowed by the state.

Finally, the constitution provides for the development of a highly centralized prosecutor's system to be headed by a **Procurator General** who combines the functions of the American Attorney General, Solicitor General, and sometimes that of an independent counsel. Answerable to the president, the procurator general is the state's chief lawyer and defends its interests. The office is an advocate for the government and much of its work is directly related to political concerns. Presidential control is exercised by the hiring and firing of this individual as Yeltsin did on several occasions. Moreover, since the federal procurator general has appointment authority over all other prosecutors throughout the federation (with the "agreement" of the "Federation components", article 129), the involvement of the president can be assumed at other levels as well.

Defending Citizen's Rights

While citizen's rights are prominently placed in the constitution it's not entirely clear that the judicial system is working in their interests. Articles 17 through 64 present a lengthy list of human and civil rights, and the mandates that the state has to protect them; these cannot be simply amended by the Federal Assembly but instead require a constitutional convention to be convened. The importance of these provisions lies in the efforts being made to dramatically break from the state-centered emphasis of the Soviet period in favor of a focus on the role of the individual ("the individual and his rights and freedoms are the supreme value", article 2), human rights ("each person has the right to life," article 20), and restraining the coercive character of the state ("no one must be subjected to torture, violence, or other brutal or humiliating treatment or punishment," article 21).

Theoretically, at least, these provisions sketch out a political culture of respect, tolerance, and a rule-of-law society where the government is kept a distinct distance from the citizen's existence. In reality, the citizen is at a disadvantage judging by limitations such as the provision in article 22 that citizens not be detained for more than forty-eight hours without a judicial decision. In June 1994 Yeltsin issued an edict giving authorities the right to hold a suspect for up to thirty days before filing charges (this number was reduced to ten days in June 1997). This makes other protections such as the assumption of innocence before the fact (article 49) extremely difficult to uphold. Compounding this situation has been an overworked judicial system as indicated by an MVD report in 1996 claiming a total of 372,000 unpunished "serious" crimes;[73] another report in 2001 stated that the courts had at least eight million cases before them the year before.[74]

The right to trial by jury is mandated by Article 123 of the constitution, which states that "court proceedings are carried out on the basis of the adversarial system and equal rights of the parties," although this only occurs in cases "stipulated in federal law." Nine regions were given permission to experiment with jury trials in 1994,[75] but the expansion of this tool of justice remains only in the most basic stages. Articles 46 through 52 lay out the citizen's rights in relation to the judicial system including making appeals to particular courts (article 46), trial within a proper court's jurisdiction and trial by jury in criminal matters (article 47), the right to an attorney (article 48), protection against double jeopardy and the right of appeal (article 50), protection against self-incrimination (article 51), but also protections for the rights of victims including compensation for damages (article 52). But as with so much already discussed, theory and practice vary greatly. A concerted effort to establish the trial by jury principle only came under serious discussion in the presidential administration in 2001 at which point the costs of implementation were already extremely high.[76]

For all of this to work Russians will not only have to break the mold of their old political culture and traditions but move beyond them as well.[77] The citizen is at a disadvantage when the power of the state is arrayed against him or her. Developing an adversarial legal system and a competitive party process are difficult indeed but may succeed with dedication to the task and agreement on particular restraints on the authorities. In many respects neither the constitution nor the federal laws may prove to be much more than theoretical guidelines for the construction of the new political order. Regardless, all of these are pieces of the puzzle necessary to describe the Russian political process.

Key Terms

power ministries

Federal Security Service

Federal Intelligence Service

Viktor Chernomyrdin

Ministry of Internal Affairs

Constitutional Court

Supreme Court

Yevgenii Primakov

Questions for Consideration

1. How may Russia's governments gain legitimacy if they are not formed by electoral mandates or from within the legislature?

2. What reforms may be necessary to prevent the "power ministries" from taking effective power in Russia?

3. Are Russia's intelligence agencies a shadow of the old KGB or do they pose a threat to the ideas of self-government and reform?

4. What role is the judiciary going to play in Russia's emerging political system? What sort of model is being used to develop the Russian courts?

5. Are constitutional guarantees of civil rights and liberties effective constraints against the revival of a strong one-party system?

Suggested Readings

Amy Knight, *Spies Without Cloaks: The KGB's Successors* (Princeton, NJ: Princeton University Press, 1996).

Peter B. Maggs, ed., *The Civil Code of the Russian Federation* (Armonk, NY: M. E. Sharpe, 1997).

Lilia Shevtsova, *Yeltsin's Russia: Myths and Reality* (Washington, DC: Brookings Institution Press, 1998).

Gordon B. Smith, *Reforming the Russian Legal System* (New York: Cambridge University Press, 1996).

Alexander M. Yakovlev, *Striving for Law in a Lawless Land: Memoirs of a Russian Reformer* (Armonk, NY: M. E. Sharpe, 1995).

Useful Websites

Ministry of Defense
http://rian.ru/mo/mo.htm

Official Russia
http://www.gov.ru/

Rosinformcentre
http://www.infocentre.ru/

Security Council of the Russian Federation
http://www.scrf.gov.ru/

Supreme Court of the Russian Federation
http://www.supcourt.ru/

System of Arbitration Courts of the Russian Federation
http://www.arbitr.ru/

Endnotes

1. *Nezavisimaya gazeta,* 11 March 1997, RIA-Novosti website, 11 March 1997 [http://www.ria-novosti.com]; also *Itogi,* no. 10, 1997, RIA-Novosti website, 13 March 1997.
2. Interfax, 21 January 1994.
3. "Decree of the President of the Russian Federation on the Structure of Federal Executive Bodies," *Privatisation in Russia,* no. 11, November 1996, RIA-Novosti website [http://www.ria-novosti.com].
4. "Federalnye organye ispolnitelnoye vlasti Rossiiskoye Federatsii", "Official Russia" website, [http://www.gov.ru/main/ministry/]
5. Interfax, 21 January 1994; FBIS-SOV, 24 January 1994, p. 22.
6. ITAR-TASS, 8 August 1994; FBIS-SOV, 8 August 1994, p. 19.
7. *Sovetskaya Rossiya,* 29 October 1991.
8. Stephen Fortescue, "Civil Service in the New Russia," *Australian Journal of Politics and History,* 41 (1995): pp. 112–113.
9. Radio Mayak (Moscow), 4 February 1994; FBIS-SOV, 7 February 1994, p. 27.
10. *Rossiyskaya gazeta,* 9 February 1995; FBIS-SOV, 10 February 1995, p. 12.
11. Merle Fainsod, "Bureaucracy and Modernization: The Russian and Soviet Cases," in ed. Joseph La Palombara, *Bureaucracy and Political Development* (Princeton, NJ: Princeton University Press, 1967), p. 239.

12. Liudmila Lapteva, "Problems of Local Self-Government in Russia," *Russian Review*, 55 (April 1996): p. 322.

13. Alfred B. Evans, Jr., "Economic Resources and Political Power at the Local Level in Post-Soviet Russia", *Policy Studies Journal*, 28 (2000): p. 124.

14. *Rossiyskaya gazeta*, 1 September 1995; FBIS-SOV, 8 September 1995, pp. 33–35.

15. *Rossiyskaya gazeta*, 21 February 1995; FBIS-SOV, 22 February 1995, p. 12.

16. See, for instance, Alexander Rahr, "Reform of Russia's State Security Apparatus," *RFE/RL Research Report*, 3 (25 February 1994): p. 19.

17. Interfax, 12 July 2001, cited in *RFE/RL Newsline*, 13 July 2001.

18. Interfax, 5 October 1997 and *Rossiyskaya gazeta*, 15 October 1997, RIA-Novosti website, 16 October 1997. Also see Kulikov's interview in *Vek*, no. 36, RIA-Novosti website, 6 October 1997.

19. This is made clear in the "Statute on the Ministry of Internal Affairs"; see *Rossiyskaya gazeta*, 31 July 1996, World News Connection.

20. *Delovoi mir*, 15 October 1997, RIA-Novosti website, 16 October 1997.

21. On the problems of maintaining the military/police in the capital alone, see the article by Valeri Buldakov, "How Many Men in Uniform Are There in and Around Moscow?", *Argumenty i fakty*, no. 43 (1996), RIA-Novosti website, 25 October 1996.

22. See, for instance, *Ekonomika i zhizn*, (February 1996): p. 34; FBIS-SOV, 20 February 1996, p. 97.

23. *Moscow News*, 2 May 1996.

24. RTR, 8 August 2001, cited in *RFE/RL Newsline*, 9 August 2001.

25. See the interview with GUEP head General Aleksandr Dementyev in *Rossiyskaya gazeta*, 25 January 1996, World News Connection website [http://wnc.fedworld.gov].

26. *Nezavisimoye voennoye obozreniye*, (no. 23), RIA-Novosti website, 5 January 1997.

27. *Rossiyskiye vesti*, 18 November 1993; FBIS-SOV, 19 November 1993, p. 1.

28. An example of this would be the June 1996 OMON intervention at the Gorokhovets shipyard; Radio Rossii cited in *OMRI Daily Digest*, 7 June 1996.

29. See ITAR-TASS, 3 October 1995.

30. Penny Morvant, "Corruption Hampers War on Crime in Russia," *Transition*, 2 (8 March 1996): pp. 23–27.

31. See Kulikov's interview in *Trud*, 12 March 1997, RIA-Novosti website, 12 March 1997.

32. "Russia," *CIA World Factbook, 2000*, Central Intelligence Agency website [http://www.odci.gov/cia/publications/factbook/].

33. See "General Turned Politician," *Moskovsky komsomolets*, 3 February 1998, RIA-Novosti Daily Review, 9 February 1998.

34. *Rossiyskiye vesti*, 11 May 1995; FBIS-SOV, 11 May 1995, p. 21.

35. Ibid. Also see the interview with Nikolaev in *Rossiyskiye vesti*, 10 December 1993, reprinted in *Russian Politics and Law*, 33 (March–April 1995): pp. 85–88.

36. For instance, see Alexander Rahr, "Kryuchkov, the KGB, and the 1991 Putsch", *RFE/RL Research Report*, 2 (30 July 1993), p. 16.

37. ITAR-TASS, 27 September 1993.

38. ITAR-TASS, 21 December 1993.

39. *Moskovskiy komsomolets*, 20 January 1995; FBIS-SOV, 23 January 1995, p. 12.

40. ITAR-TASS, 6 April 1995.

41. Russian National Television (NTV) for 7 April 1995; FBIS-SOV, 12 April 1995, pp. 17–18.

42. *Moscow News*, 21–27 April 1995, p. 3.

43. Russian Public Television First Channel, 13 April 1995; FBIS-SOV, 17 April 1995, p. 24.

44. *Moscow News*, 2 February 1996.

45. Interfax, 17 December 1996; also Interfax, 8 January 1997.

46. *Nezavisimaya gazeta,* 24 October 1996, RIA-Novosti website, 24 October 1996.
47. *Komsomolskaya pravda,* 9–16 June 1995; FBIS-SOV, 13 June 1995, pp. 23–25.
48. See Victor Yasmann, "Security Services Reorganized: All Power to the Russian President?", *RFE/RL Research Report,* 3 (11 February 1994): p. 12.
49. Amy Knight, *Spies Without Cloaks: The KGB's Successors* (Princeton, NJ: Princeton University Press, 1996), p. 36.
50. Ibid. Also see *Nezavisimaya gazeta,* 30 March 1995; FBIS-SOV, 3 April 1995, p. 19; and *Komsomolskaya pravda,* 9–16 June 1995; FBIS-SOV, 13 June 1995, p. 25.
51. ITAR-TASS, 27 April 1994.
52. Former Defense Minister Igor Rodionov briefly held the post as a civilian in 1996 after reaching the then mandatory military retirement age of sixty, and being reappointed. See *Segodnya,* 11 December 1996; Interfax, 11 December 1996; also see Russian Presidential Decree No. 1659, "On Igor N. Rodionov", *Rossiyskaya gazeta,* 14 December 1996, RIA-Novosti website, 14 December 1996.
53. See *Rossiyskiye vesti,* 18 November 1993; FBIS-SOV, 19 November 1993, p. 1.
54. Charles Dick, "The Military Doctrine of the Russian Federation", *Jane's Intelligence Review Special Report,* (January 1994): p. 4.
55. For instance, see Interfax, 12 November 1996 and *Segodnya,* 13 November 1996.
56. *Kommersant-Daily,* 22 December 1994; FBIS-SOV, 22 December 1994, p. 23.
57. *Izvestiya,* 29 September 1995; FBIS-SOV, 29 September 1995, p. 34.
58. Russian Television, 15 February 1996; reported in *OMRI Daily Report,* 16 February 1996.
59. FIA-Interfax, 3 October 1996.
60. See, for instance, OMRI, 13 November 1996 and Reuters, 20 April 1998.
61. See the press releases of both Interfax and ITAR-TASS for 12 July 1995.
62. ITAR-TASS, 2 August 1995.
63. *Krasnaya zvezda,* 31 August 1995; FBIS-SOV, 1 September 1995, p. 28.
64. Interfax, 5 October 1996; also Interfax-Argumenty i fakty, no. 44, RIA-Novosti website, 30 October 1996.
65. Russian Television Network, 17 May 1994; FBIS-SOV, 20 May 1994, p. 32; also *Segodnya,* 9 July 1994, FBIS-SOV, 11 July 1994, p. 27.
66. See the law "On the Russian Federation Constitutional Court", *Rossiyskaya gazeta,* 23 July 1994; FBIS-SOV, supplement for 28 July 1994, p. 1.
67. See the law "On the Russian Federation Constitutional Court," *Rossiyskaya gazeta,* 23 July 1994; FBIS-SOV, 28 July 1994, Supplement, p. 1.
68. ITAR-TASS, 31 January 2001 cited in *RFE/RL Newsline,* 1 February 2001.
69. Interfax, 15 November 1994.
70. Interfax, 20 February 1997; also *Segodnya,* 4 December 1996.
71. *Rossiyskiye vesti,* 9 November 1994; FBIS-SOV, 9 November 1994, p. 8.
72. ITAR-TASS, 12 April 1995.
73. Interfax, 14 August 1996.
74. *Izvestiya,* 26 March 2001, cited in *RFE/RL Newsline,* 27 March 2001.
75. *Kommersant-Daily,* 29 October 1993; reprinted in FBIS-SOV, 1 November 1993, p. 23; also Peter H. Solomon, Jr., "The Limits of Legal Order in Post-Soviet Russia", *Post-Soviet Affairs,* 11 (April–June 1995): pp. 103–104.
76. Presidential aide Dmitrii Kozak cited in *RFE/RL Newsline,* 17 May 2001.
77. This point is made by Pamela Jordan in her article on the court system, "Russian Courts: Enforcing the Rule of Law?", in ed. Valerie Sperling, *Building the Russian State* (Boulder, CO: Westview Press, 2000), pp. 193–209.

Chapter 7

Federated Russia

Over a period of eight years (1994–2002) Russia waged two separate wars within the confines of its own borders. The 1994–1996 conflict in Chechnya ended in the abject failure of Russian power to determine the fate of its constituent units. But the humiliation of Russian military might, coupled to the unresolved status of Chechnya and the chaos of its internal politics festered over the next several years. By 1999 when Chechen militants attempted to export their religious revolt into neighboring Dagestan, Moscow could tolerate this no longer and struck back with a ferocious and much better planned assault giving it again at least nominal control of the republic. Whereas the first Chechen war forced Russia to look long and hard at an unflattering portrayal of itself,[1] the second invasion gave Russians the opportunity to shake off the long, hard night of the slide beyond mediocrity. The end result for policy was a return to the no-nonsense centralism of the country's not-too-distant past.

The wars in Chechnya have not been the only factors damaging the foundations of Russia's federal structure. Throughout the 1990s economic conditions fluctuated radically throughout the country posing the prospects of social and ethnic explosions should the government fail to pay attention to the public's plight. As one Russian source phrased it "life in some regions is comparable to that in Western Europe, and in others, to existence in Tropical Africa."[2] What this chapter attempts to determine is the essence of Russian federalism, or more accurately, center-periphery relations. Unaccustomed to the idea of regional autonomy Russian political actors have increasingly crafted new national-regional relationships. They are literally trying to keep pace with events lest societal developments—particularly the new assertiveness characteristic of many of Russia's peoples—outpace the policy process. Whether it is in the form of power-sharing agreements between Moscow and the regions, or allowing regions to make laws in anticipation of federal actions, the Russian Federation has worked its way out of the strict centralism of the Soviet period, but held at bay designs which would constrict Moscow's power to the advantage of the periphery. Laying out these new relationships should tell us as much about Russian politics as have the preceding discussions of pluralism, or presidential and parliamentary power.

Russian Federalism: Theory and Practice

If you were to try and plan a specific model of governance for a country as large and diverse as Russia, federalism would certainly be a strong option. A country of a wide range of contrasts, Russia consists of large urban centers such as Moscow, St. Petersburg, Nizhny Novgorod, Novosibirsk, Ekaterinburg, Kubyshev, Omsk, and Rostov-on-Don each with populations in excess of one million people. This is counterpoised to the vastness of underpopulated Siberia: roughly two-thirds of the entire land mass of Russia but with less than thirty million people. Overlapping geography with political-administrative boundaries provides equally stark contrasts: the enormity of the Republic of Sakha (Yakutia) in the Far East with its 1,197,760 square miles, for instance, as compared to the Republic of Adygea in southwest Russia and its mere 1,150 square miles. Russian federalism's most immediate concern is how to reconcile eighty-nine disparate political units with one another and still keep Moscow as the focal point of decision making. And while political elites in the capital may agree on this or another course of action there's no guarantee that it will captivate the attention of regional leaders or the general public.

The Soviet Union was a federal system in name but one formulated on a basis of power being highly concentrated at the center and devolving toward specific administrative units for implementation. In many respects Soviet federalism, despite great shortcomings, and partially due to the equalitarian component of the state ideology, functioned well enough to satisfy certain basic needs of citizens as measured in terms of education, housing, and social services. However, it was clearly a *unitary* system rather than one of autonomous or coequal parts; that is, the subnational units such as republics, oblasts, and okrugs received powers from the center and were subject to having their organizational structures and geographic contours changed as the center wanted it. Thus the western understanding of federalism as a sharing of powers between the central government and regional or local authorities has never been an accurate assessment. Pretensions to the contrary such as article 72 of the 1977 Soviet (Brezhnev) constitution guaranteeing the right of secession to the union republics provided only window dressing to the concept of federalism.[3] In fact, this was a criticism leveled by Gorbachev against the Soviet system as he attempted—futilely, as it turned out— to reconcile nationalism and regional demands to the Soviet national interest.[4]

For the federal system in Russia to develop it must be able to reinforce itself. It does this through popular acceptance, stable governing units, the use of force, and the creation of a legitimate legal system. A system of free and fair elections is one means to gain public acceptance, a possibility the Yeltsin administration gambled on in allowing municipal elections in early 1996 which were largely won by Yeltsin supporters.[5] Equally necessary is a clear *delimitation of powers* between the central authority and the regional governments. This means that the governing units cooperate by means of an interlocking process of shared powers and compromise as to the areas of each level's authority. But if the federal government maintains a disproportionate balance of power and resources, then the federal idea cannot succeed. In many respects this is the Russian Federation's principal dilemma in the post-Soviet era.[6]

The last component—building a legitimate legal system—is crucial, especially if the democratic society is the desired goal. Here again examining the constitution is required, as well as the 1992 **Federation Treaty** regulating relations between the center and the regions. Together these represent the basic rules of conduct in relations between the federative structure and the various federal components. What they don't represent is a finalization of the debate on the delimitation of power in either political or economic terms, as can be seen by the prolonged approval of the Federation Treaty which was originally proposed by the Russian Supreme Soviet in March 1992.[7] Eventually, the treaty would be accepted by all but two of the republics: Tatarstan and Chechnya (then, Checheno-Ingushetia).

By 1993 many of the regions were calling for the Federation Treaty to be fully incorporated into the draft of a new constitution. Yeltsin's success in dealing with the revolt of the CPD in late 1993 encouraged him to resist the demands made by the territorial units, although it was clear that there was considerable dissension amongst provincial leaders.[8] Instead, the constitutional draft technically put all republics on an equal footing and restricted their abilities to deal with foreign entities in an autonomous capacity. In its final form the constitution made it clear that federal law and structures were dominant over those of the republics or regions, and that changes in their systems of governance or borders, was not just a question of local concern, but one that might determine whether Russian federalism would survive.[9] For instance, article 78 states that "the federal organs of executive power can create their own territorial organs and appoint the relevant officials"; in this way both Yeltsin and Putin were able to appoint presidential envoys to the republics and regions and gain greater centralized control over them. And while article 67 allowed individual units to change their borders "by their mutual consent," this could only be accomplished under conditions laid out by federal law. Consolidation efforts such as that attempted by five regions (Orenburg, Kurgan, Perm, Sverdlovsk, and Chelyabinsk) in September 1993 to create a Ural Republic were deemed extra-legal.[10] Political elites used the constitution to make it clear that this was a federal system, not a confederation, and that the regions by themselves were not equal to the center.

The constitution also guarantees that the federal government will decide the form of the economic system. Article 71 gives the federal government authority over "federal state property and the management thereof" (section 3), "the establishment of the fundamentals of federal policy and federal programs in the sphere of . . . economic . . . development of the Russian Federation" (section f), and "the establishment of the legal foundations of the single market; financial, currency, credit, and customs regulations, monetary emission, and the foundations of pricing policy, federal economic services, including federal banks" (section g). The regions maintain joint responsibility for "issues relating to the ownership, use, and disposal of land, mineral resources, water, and other natural resources" and "the delimitation of state property" (article 72, sections c and d).

Here, too, constitutionalism is subject to question as the center has yet to fully define the context of land ownership, much less implement it.

On another economic level, various regions have withheld, or threatened to withhold, tax revenues from Moscow unless the government met its obligations of paying wage arrears or money owed to productive facilities.[11] The central government has responded to this situation by threatening sanctions against those regions. In October 1993 the federal government declared itself willing to halt subsidies and subtract tax debts from the individual region's accounts with the federal government.[12] At the same time the federal government was regularly defaulting on its payments to the regions or finding itself unable to fund programs which depended almost entirely on Finance Ministry allocations. This caused some of the regions to form their own economic associations and fill in the gaps left by Moscow's economic pullback. One example involved seven regions of the troubled, and distant, Primorskii Krai (on the Pacific coast), which decided in February 1994 to consolidate their resources and form a "minicommunity" within the territory. With too little funding coming from Moscow these regions stopped payments to those federal programs affecting them (forestry, fur industries, and mining) since little of this was being rerouted to satisfy local needs. Instead, the regions directly invested these revenues into the local economy with the central authorities' permission and with funding from the territorial government. Local administrators were extremely careful to reiterate that the program was purely economic and had no political goals or separatist motives.[13]

In many respects the center has treated the regions—especially those very few (approximately nine) which have been able to pay their taxes—as "cash cows," that is, areas with funds or resources that can be milked with little being returned. The center's narrow-minded views of its own needs clash with those of the republics and regions which desire investments at the local level to ensure healthy economies (more on this trade-off in Chapter Eight). Moreover, the federal approach leads regional governments and populations to the conclusion that they are being exploited (the 2001 federal budget earmarked approximately sixteen percent of total resources to be transferred to the regional budgets[14]), which in turn can result in dangerous separatist tendencies, a possibility the central state cannot ignore.

Federalism, if worked at, can be an effective solution for dealing with separatism, especially in that it allows for policy innovation in the sharing of power.[15] The most obvious illustration can be found in the Yeltsin government's negotiation of a series of new relationships with the regions beginning in 1992. These **power-sharing arrangements,** or treaties, were designed to placate these federal units and yet retain their accountability to Moscow. By the time of the October 1993 crisis many of the regions were acting with impunity toward the federal government. Yeltsin's use of force caused many of them to back off from what was referred to as the "sovereignty parade" and instead turn their attention "to obtain as many privileges and benefits from the federal center as possible."[16] In December 1995 following parallel developments occurring with Russia's republics, the first of the power-sharing arrangements was signed between Moscow and one of its regions (Orenburg Oblast).[17] By June 1998 a total of forty-five such agreements had been completed and signed. These "treaties" were not ratified by the State Duma but instead were expressions of "federal organs of executive power" in relation to Russia's component parts (article 78).

The Putin administration's preference for strong central control has, however, altered the balance. In 2001 Putin created a commission to review the legality of the agreements; this, in turn, lead to a number of them being canceled for being out of step with the federal constitution. In May 2000 Putin made another tactical move against regionalism by issuing a decree creating seven new **federal administrative districts** overlying (but not dissolving or integrating) the country's eighty-nine federal subjects[18] (a constitutional amendment would be required to formally change the present system). In June the Procurator-General's office acting on the Kremlin's orders, demanded that all federal subjects make their laws comply with federal practice.[19] Since then federal courts have increasingly ruled against local governing initiatives, and regions and republics have generally fallen into line with Kremlin policies. This is, however, only part of the picture as the remainder of this chapter shall demonstrate by examining the specific categories of federal administrative units.

The Oblasts

The Slavic Heartland

As much as Moscow is the heart of the Russian character, the Slavic-dominated regions west of the Ural Mountains represent the soul of the Russian nation, that is, the core homeland of the Russian people over the last millenium. Included in this category are those areas from the Federation's western borders, to regions just beyond the Ural Mountains in the east, and from the Caucasus Mountains in the south to the frozen reaches of the White, Barents, and Kara Seas of the north. This comprises roughly thirty-three oblasts (regions), two krais (territories), two autonomous okrugs (districts), and the two cities of federal signficance (Moscow and St. Petersburg). What really sets them apart is that the overwhelming majority of their populations are ethnically Russian. Some exceptions to the rule are apparent in those ethnic homelands (Adygea, Bashkortostan, Chuvashia, Mari-El, Mordovinia, Tatarstan, and Udmurtia) situated more-or-less in the middle of the Russian population. But even within these republics ethnic Russians make up a majority in two of them (Mordvinia, Udmurtia), form pluralities in two more (Bashkortostan, Mari-El), or are almost as numerous as the titular population in one (Tatarstan).

Given the strong geographic and cultural attachments between the Russian regions and the federal government the probability of regional political separatism has proven quite remote.[20] Instead, the regions have focused on establishing economic autonomy (including developing separate international

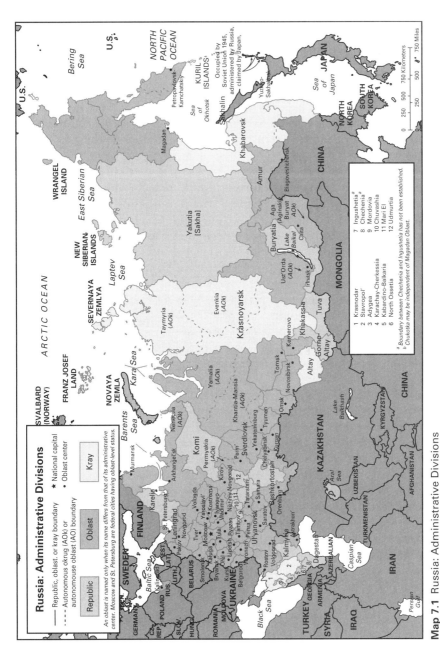

Map 7.1 Russia: Administrative Divisions

commercial and trade relations), and thereby development.[21] The federal government's negotiation of power-sharing arrangements with the regions legitimated this autonomy, and even Yeltsin's home region of Sverdlovsk has pursued this path.[22] Initially what these regions had in common was that they were either a good distance from Moscow, bordering on foreign countries or an exclave (Orenburg and Kaliningrad oblasts, respectively), or they possessed considerable economic resources or potential (such as Krasnodar Krai). In any case the need to work out the details and degrees of these relationships was obvious to the political elites.

Probably the most significant center-periphery relationship to date has been that involving **Nizhny Novgorod** (formalized by a treaty in June 1996). This ancient Russian city—called Gorki in the Soviet period after the writer Maxim Gorki—is a bustling industrial center with the third largest population in the Federation. From 1991 to 1997 Moscow permitted a formerly unheard-of independence of decision making to the then governor, Boris Nemtsov,[23] to draft and carry through on far-reaching economic reforms. In effect since 1989, Nizhny Novgorod's reforms have included modernization, privatization of military-industrial firms, building a rural infrastructure, selling bonds in both the public and private sectors, and instituting tax cuts,[24] all of which have permitted Russian officials opportunities to evaluate the process without making sizeable commitments.[25] As Nizhny Novgorod posed no threat to Russian territorial integrity Moscow's sense of security increased and other regions were encouraged to follow suit.

Thus the federal government's relationship with its core constituency—the Slavic regions—has basically been one of status quo politics and electoral give-and-take. These regions don't always agree with the center, and many of them have been consistently at odds with Moscow. Nowhere is this more obvious than in the so-called **red zone** of central Russia, a swath of regions running from Pskov in the northwest, and variously including Smolensk, Bryansk, Kursk, Belgorod, Orel, Voronezh, and Volgograd, which typically have voted for the KPRF or its allied parties.[26] In-depth analysis of how these regions have fared in gaining shares of national resources is still needed to determine the nature of the overall center-periphery relationship. For the moment we turn to the "cities of federal significance."

Moscow and St. Petersburg

The Russian Federation's two largest cities are formally accorded a special status within the governing system due to their size, economic resources, and primacy as decision-making centers for the entire country. In the Soviet era the party leaders of both cities were the effective mayors of the respective cities and among the most powerful individuals in the CPSU hierarchy (Yeltsin was briefly First Secretary of the Moscow party committee). Under the 1993 constitution the "twin capitals" were designated "cities of federal significance" giving them a status independent of the oblast administrations which surround them.

The last decade has produced dramatic changes in both cities and their decision-making processes, in particular the strain on their resources caused by the size of their populations (in 1999 Moscow had an estimated 8.3 million people, St. Petersburg 4.6 million[27]). Soviet-era internal passports (*propiski*) controlled this to an extent; although the Russian courts formally did away with this practice in 1994 in favor of a system of individual registration beginning in 1995.[28] But the problems that the system supposedly addressed are endemic to large cities everywhere including housing shortages, job availability, inadequate infrastructure, and crime. Consequently, the *propiski* system remains in place today.

In the waning days of the Gorbachev era, strong mayor systems emerged for Moscow and St. Petersburg as the influence of the CPSU receded. In June 1992 Moscow's reform-oriented mayor, Gavril Popov, a major actor in the democratic movement, resigned and was replaced by his former deputy, Yuri Luzhkov. Luzhkov's tenure as mayor has been marked by his rise on the national political stage and subsequent accusations of corruption and continuing conflict with the federal authorities.[29] Despite having created many powerful political and economic enemies,[30] Luzhkov has cultivated an image among Muscovites of being a man of the people.[31] This proved to be a major factor in Luzhkov's overwhelming election victory in 1996 when he received eighty-nine percent of the vote, and in his consistent ranking as one of the most popular politicians in Russia.[32] Allying himself early on with powerful investment and banking sources, Luzhkov apparently accumulated great wealth and resources with very little accountability.[33] Subsequently, Luzhkov-supported candidates won twenty-seven of the thirty-five races in the 1997 city election, and thirty-three of thirty-five seats in 2001.[34] The upshot is that despite an electoral process that on paper is certainly democratic—in the December 1997 Moscow City Duma elections 357 candidates were registered to run for thirty-five seats representing the city's 128 municipal districts[35]—representative government in Moscow remains weak. The mayor's failed bid for the presidency in 2000, however, indicates that there are limits to what can be done behind the scenes, and Luzhkov might best be described as a "contained autocrat."

The federal government funds a substantial proportion of the Moscow city budget. In 1994 federal subsidies were reported to be as high as fifteen percent of the city's total budget. Moreover, Moscow—largely due to its core city status—gets a great deal of what it requests from central authorities,[36] although not the level of preferential treatment accorded it under socialism.[37] Luzhkov's administration embarked on numerous high-profile and high-cost projects such as the renovation of the Bolshoi Theater, the reconstruction of the Cathedral of Christ our Savior, and the extension of the Moscow Metro (subway) all of which required funding from the federal government. Moscow has gained substantially from such projects due to their importance to the tourist industry certainly, as well as for their potential in attracting foreign investors. But this also has implied the diminution of resources for other projects in other parts of the country in a period of restrictive federal aid. Given these circumstances governing officials in

Ekaterinburg, Novosibirsk, Irkutsk, or Vladivostok, for instance, might not be blamed for pursuing autonomous economic development despite the central government's wishes to the contrary.

St. Petersburg's politics bear a marked contrast to those of Moscow. Sometimes referred to as the "northern capital," St. Petersburg projects a uniqueness in its political and cultural character that more than makes up for its loss of capital city status in 1918. Its political culture is both more democratic and seemingly less encumbered with national-level political issues than is the case of its sometime rival to the southeast. The city's gubernatorial race of 1996, for instance, attracted national attention when six major candidates challenged the democratic-activist incumbent Anatolii Sobchak (who was subsequently defeated[38]) for his post.[39] Initially elected in August and October 1994, the city's Legislative Assembly consisted of fifty legislators representing various districts (raions) and parties in the city. A new city charter enacted in 1997 created 111 local neighborhood councils which appear to devolve power but have yet to prove their strength as focal points of authority in the city's divided political scene. St. Petersburg's governor (the title was changed from mayor in 1996 to indicate the city's importance) exercises considerable control over the Legislative Assembly due to his veto power, but this has diminished particularly as voters have become disenchanted by the process. This was no better evidenced than by the high profile assassination by criminal elements in St. Petersburg of noted Democratic Party leader **Galina Staravoitova** in 1998, an instance of political corruption that shocked not just the city, but the nation itself.

The politics of economic experimentation in both St. Petersburg and Moscow have often been described as so different from the rest of Russia as to make these cities appear to be separate countries. St. Petersburg has relied more on its own resources to revitalize itself than has Moscow where federal subsidies make up a sizeable portion of that city's budget. St. Petersburg's efforts to attract foreign investments (which are registered with the Mayor's Office Registration Chamber) have generally been more successful than those of Moscow.[40] Electoral contests have also found the two cities to be beyond the national norm. In the 1993 national parliamentary elections reformist parties captured in excess of sixty percent of the total votes in both Moscow and St. Petersburg, a factor some scholars attributed to the higher level of education of these urban populations.[41] By the 1995 elections these figures had been considerably reduced with approximately forty-one and forty-five percent of the vote respectively going to reformers in St. Petersburg and Moscow. At the local level, however, the story is less clear as the liberal Yabloko bloc fared poorly in the September 1997 and February 1998 St. Petersburg neighborhood elections, possibly due again to the electorate's general dissatisfaction with politics.

Siberia

Occupying two-thirds of the Russian land mass, Siberia is a world apart from historic Russia and its major cities. Long the land of Russian internal exile the outside world has known Siberia for centuries only through its bleak depiction by former prisoners, or through studies of its climactic distinctions and ecological wonders. Siberia today is a land destined for tremendous growth and development, of unparalleled natural differentiation, and as a potential experimental laboratory for political and economic change. Administratively it is composed of five republics, sixteen oblasts, one autonomous oblast, four krais, and eight autonomous okrugs. The far-flung positioning of the region's dominant cities such as Novosibirsk, Tomsk, Irkutsk, and Vladivostok prevents any one of them from being the primary focus for Siberia as a whole. And with a population as dispersed as is that of Siberia (approximately twenty-five to thirty million people), there is little possibility for the region to act cohesively. Instead, Siberia is often thought of in terms of geophysical traits such as the West Siberian lowlands, the Arctic lowlands, the Central Siberian plateau, the Lena Basin, and the Eastern Siberian highlands. With few highway or rail links connecting the Russian Federation from east to west—one hundred years after its inception the Tran-Siberian line remains the only east-west rail link for the country—Siberia has never posed a credible political challenge to Moscow.

Despite the severe limitations for political, economic, and socio-cultural development, Siberia's relationship with the western third of Russia is fundamentally intertwined. Russia's vast wealth of oil, natural gas, and other natural resources primarily lie within Siberia, and it is these commodities which have brought the country to the brink of economic greatness over the last two centuries. But Russia lacks much of the necessary technology for the effective extraction of this wealth—roads alone are in short supply—and the appropriate economic system needed to exploit them for the full benefit of the state. Were these prerequisites available, the Russian economic picture would be one of a much higher level of development as compared to today's standards.

On the whole Russia's policy toward Siberia has been that of exploitation of the area's natural resources and utilization of its vast spaces for military bases and defense industries. The relationship has been a one-way street with Siberia suffering from the lack of infrastructure, partially due to the inexperience of the region's political elites in negotiating with Moscow. One such effort to change this began in 1990 with the creation of **Siberian Agreement,** an association of regional leaders intent on recovering much of the wealth flowing out of the area. A compendium of presidents and governors and heads of legislative bodies, its economic mission took on political overtones by 1993 and earned the enmity of Yeltsin who emasculated the organization by replacing several of its key leaders.[42]

To date no distinct regional policy has been formulated and the central government has relied instead on cooptation of regional leaders when necessary by giving aid piecemeal to regions. Yeltsin utilized this approach in his 1996 reelection campaign as when he promised to pay off Defense Ministry debts to enterprises in Khabarovsk oblast.[43] Further promises of such assistance were effectively curtailed as Russia's economic crisis—especially the nonpayment of wages—deepened and became a protracted condition. Siberia thus continues to be what it has always been: a question mark in the plans of economic development and national integration.

The National Homelands

The Ethnic Republics

While federalism is compatible with many types of states, it seems to have particular resonance in ethnically diverse systems. The dispersal of power and decision making creates greater opportunities for cultural autonomy and self-government. The Russian Federation's principal non-Russian nationalities and their respective administrative territories are not all contiguous to one another, but instead dispersed throughout the country. Dating from tsarist times the concept of ethnic homelands has been used to placate non-Russian populations and to defuse supranationalist tendencies before they develop, particularly among Muslim peoples. All of the Russian Federation's twenty-one republics are ostensibly homelands of particular non-Russian ethnic groupings even though the titular nationality may not make up a majority of that republic's population. This has been taken to extremes in cases such as that of the Altai Republic where in 1989 the Altai people made up only 2.5 percent of the republic's population, and in the Karelian Republic which had an ethnic Karelian population of only ten percent. The Chechen, Chuvash, North Ossetian, and Tyvan republics are the only republics to actually have majorities of peoples which have achieved FNS. Balancing the interests of ethnic Russians to those of the local nationalities within these republics often seems to be the priority concern of Federation authorities thereby creating a very restrictive nationalities policy.[44]

In the last years of the Soviet system there were sixteen Autonomous Soviet Socialist Republics (ASSRs) within the Russian Federation, an administrative category just below that of the (then) union—now independent—republics. In July 1991 four ethnic territories of the Federation—Adygea (separated from the Krasnodar Krai), Altai (formerly the Altai Krai including the Gorno-Altai Autonomous Oblast), Karachay-Cherkessia (separated from the Stavropol Krai), and Khakassia (separated from the Krasnoyarsk Krai)—were raised to the status of republics.[45] In 1991 as well Tatarstan declared itself independent, while Chechnya not only proclaimed independence but separated itself from Ingushetia by reestablishing the border which had existed between them prior to 1934.[46] The Ingush for their part voted to continue their association with Russia on 30 November 1991 and the Russian Supreme Soviet formally accepted this in June 1992. Since that point only one other republican government—that of Bashkortostan (or Bashkiria)—has made any attempt to push the issue further.

In Tatarstan's case the 1994 decision of the Yeltsin administration to sign a treaty with this republic provoked criticism for the amount of attention that the central government paid to it. Coupled to Tatarstan's declarations of sovereignty (in 1990 and again in a popular referendum on 21 March 1994) Moscow's efforts to establish a balance with the independently minded republics appeared to be setting a dangerous precedent which others might follow. And yet there were good reasons for the central government to make a special consideration. The Tatars are the largest minority group in the Russian Federation with approximately 5.5 million people, or 3.8 percent of the total population (using 1989 census figures).[47] Of this figure about 1.76 million Tatars lived inside their namesake republic; two other groups, the Nogai and West Siberian Tatars form separate communities beyond these boundaries. Sizeable Tatar contingents also live in several of the surrounding ethnic republics, particularly Bashkortostan where the Tatars make up a slightly larger share of the local population than the Bashkirs (28.4 percent compared to 21.9 percent).[48] Within Tatarstan itself, however, the Tatars comprised less than half (48.5 percent) of the population, with Russians accounting for only slightly less (43.3 percent).[49] In both of the aforementioned cases it is not the size of the group alone that makes them significant to the Russian state, but rather their Muslim cultural identity.[50]

But there have long been significant differences between these two republics. The first of these included the identification with Islam itself. As pointed out by the Tatar leadership, particularly President **Mintimer Shaymiyev,** "centrism and pragmatism are our 'ideological' principles."[51] While trying to avoid the dangers associated with Chechnya's form of militant Islam, Shaymiyev was also implicitly recognizing the considerable differences within Islam itself and a very high level of secularization among the Tatar peoples.[52] This may be a decisive factor in the lack of support within Tatarstan for following the risky path of separatism espoused within Chechnya. Consequently, although Shaymiyev refused to sign the Federation Treaty he did negotiate a series of separate economic agreements with other parts of the Federation, and in February 1994 Tatarstan and the Russian Federation concluded the first power-sharing treaty. This document recognized the legitimacy of both the Federation's and the republic's respective constitutions but denied Tatarstan the condition of sovereignty claimed for the republic since 1991. Technically negotiated on the basis of *inter*-state rather than *intra*state relations the treaty nevertheless reduced Tatarstan to a co-equal status with the other parts of the Federation rather than making it co-equal to the Federation itself.[53] That Moscow had managed to manipulate and intimidate the Tatar leadership was apparent.[54] The more restrictive and pragmatic "Tatarstan model" was emulated in 1996 when the Republic of Tyva rescinded its constitutional provisions on maintaining its own armed forces and the right to secede.[55]

Leaderships of other republics have also negotiated their own versions of sovereignty or power-sharing, including Kalbardino-Balkaria, North Ossetia, Sakha-Yakutia, Buryatia, and Udmurtia. As one commentator noted, some regional leaders took Yeltsin's call for them to "gulp down" as much sovereignty as possible literally.[56] One example of this was shown in Bashkortostan, a region rich in natural resources vital for the Russian economy (and one of the few taxpaying regions of the country).[57] Unlike Tatarstan, Bashkortostan's political leaders signed the Federation Treaty and made no formal pronouncements of independence.

The treaty that was eventually signed with Moscow in August 1994 gained for republican authorities the ability to shape Bashkortostan's political institutions, to formalize the republic's territorial sovereignty, and to do all this with minimal interference from Moscow.[58] In particular, the treaty granted Bashkir authorities local sway over natural resources such as oil, and much of the petroleum processing industry, but conceded to Moscow the ailing defense industry and coal fields.[59] As well Bashkortostan's president **Murtaza Rakhimov** saw to it that local decision making extended to property concerns, the budget, taxes and even international activities,[60] all within the constructs of the Russian Federation's "common legal space."[61] The judicial and legal systems were to be within Ufa's (the capital) jurisdiction rather than that of Moscow.[62] In exchange for republican recognition of Moscow's overall dominance the intrigues of local politics were not questioned by Moscow, nor were the means of local elections. This, however, has begun to change under Putin's more careful scrutiny.[63]

A similar pattern of deference to Moscow in exchange for local freedom developed in the Republic of Kalmykia-Khalmg Tangc. In 1995 its legislature extended until the year 2000 the term of its president, **Kirsan Ilyumzhinov** (a native Kalmyk). Ilyumzhinov was, however, unsatisfied with this procedure and called instead for a formal election[64] (ITAR-TASS summed this up as a "queer decision"[65]) in which he ran unopposed and was therefore easily reelected. Moscow's reaction was to take no action since Ilyumzhinov, who had initially made overtures to Yeltsin's opposition, changed course and decided to back Yeltsin's concept of federalism.[66] What Moscow demanded was compliance by regional authorities with federal mandates and the constitutional system. In exchange, allegations of corruption, embezzlement, misuse of federal funds, harassment of the local media in Kalmykia,[67] and impoverishment of the local populations were all treated as local concerns.

The republic of Yakutia-Sakha, or as it is more commonly referred to, Sakha, demonstrated a different aspect of autonomous behavior. Sakha's vast size makes up eighteen percent of the total land mass of the Russian Federation, dwarfing the second largest republic—Komi—with its much smaller 160,600 square miles. Sakha's harsh climate (roughly one-third lies within the Arctic Circle), inaccessibility, and lack of population are offset by its vast natural resources, especially the gold and diamonds which make up the great bulk of Sakha's trade. The republic's leaders responded to the confusion of the waning years of Soviet power by passing a Declaration of State Sovereignty in September 1990. The republic's leadership, which was dominated by a majority of ethnic Yakuts (parliamentary representation of Yakuts in 1990 was in excess of fifty percent of total deputies even though they made up only thirty-three percent of the total population[68]), crafted a strong export-oriented economic policy in order to maximize its leverage with the central government.[69] Sakha's leaders called for a consultative council of republican and regional leaders (a forerunner to the current Federation Council),[70] under the authority of the Russian president, and created a new parliament (*Il Tumen*) which harbored distinctly nationalist sentiments.[71]

In 1995 the republican authorities in Sakha reorganized local self-government according to federal principles; organizational concepts long associated with the Soviet era (i.e., raions) were abandoned in favor of institutions with a local veneer (the "ulus").[72] The Sakha leadership had by this point sufficiently assuaged the fears of the Yeltsin administration that a treaty on delimitation of powers could be signed between the republic and the center in June 1995.[73] It was this sort of deal making which came to characterize the Yeltsin administration's regional policy.

The Autonomous Regions

Eleven other administrative districts are based on distinct ethnic populations; these are guaranteed control over their internal affairs and "local ethnic bodies of state authority and administration."[74] Ten of these are classified as **autonomous okrugs,** the lowest federal level of territorial administration. Most are located in remote regions of the federation such as in the Arctic (Nenetsk, Yamalo-Nenetsk, Taymyr, Evenk, Chukotsk), or in Siberia (Khanti-Mansiysk, Aga Buryat, Koryak, Ust-Orda Buryat). Only one is relatively close to the European cities of Russia: Komi-Permyak (west of the Ural Mountains). None have major urban centers within their administrative borders.

Most of the autonomous okrugs (A.O.s) are located in the northern-most sectors of the Federation. With but a few exceptions (the Aga Buryat A. O., the Ust-Orda Buryat A. O.) they are named for those small nations that Russian demographers refer to as **Peoples of the North** or what the constitution terms "numerically small indigenous peoples" (article 69). Twenty-six nations ranging in size from the relatively large Nen (35,000) to the tiny Orok and En (both about 200 people each!) make up this category.[75] The fact of their recognition as separate peoples by Moscow and their nominal political representation have not automatically translated into their economic betterment. Many of these peoples today live in considerable poverty in the midst of incredible natural resource wealth such as in the Khanty-Mansi and Yamal-Nenets A.O.s where lie as much as half of Russia's total oil and possibly as high as ninety percent of its natural gas reserves. The small nations, too, have found themselves overwhelmed by the migration to their regions of ethnic Russians who come to exploit the natural resource wealth. Increasingly, the populations of the autonomous regions find themselves tiny minorities in their own nominal lands and unable to determine their political fates. And with the dwindling of central governmental assistance comes the potential for increased social and political conflict.[76]

Russia's Trouble Spots

The North Caucasus

For Russians the Caucasus is a land of some mystery, its many peoples seemingly inhabitants from another world and time. In fact, the North Caucasus (the rest of the region is composed of the now independent states of Armenia, Azerbaijan, and Georgia) is a fascinating mix of peoples and cultures, administrative districts, regions, and republics. It is because of this very mix, however, that during the latter years of perestroika many of these peoples came into renewed conflict with one another, and sometimes with the Russians themselves. As a result the region is defined more by turmoil and disintegration of political entities than it is by integration into the new political and economic systems.

The North Caucasus includes three Russian-dominated regions—Krasnodar Krai, Stavropol Krai, and Rostov Oblast—and five ethnic republics—Chechnya, Dagestan, Ingushetia, Kabardino-Balkaria, and North Ossetia. It is an important region for Russia both in commercial terms and agricultural development, although the population is largely urban in character particularly in the Russian-dominated regions. These regions represent the furthest southern reaches of the Russian people and where they most immediately come into contact with the non-Slavic world. In 1989 Russians accounted for sixty-seven percent of the total population in the North Caucasus; this figure has declined as the ethnic homelands in the region have increasingly become hostile territory for ethnic Russians. At the same time elements of the Russian population have also appeared aggressive as with the various **Cossack** communities of the region (there are twelve Cossack "hosts" in Russia) which have experienced a revival since the fall of communism. Persecuted under communism as counterrevolutionary elements, today an estimated two million people claim Cossack lineage. In the Don, Terek, and Kuban regions of the North Caucasus they represent one of the more visible symbols of Russian nationalism claiming simultaneously the right to reassert Russian control in old imperial domains, and discrimination at the hands of the small non-Russian nations.[77]

For its own political purposes the Yeltsin administration in 1992 declared the Cossacks an ethnic group despite the fact that they are peoples descended from Russian and Ukrainian serfs who fled bondage. In 1996 Cossack units were again integrated into the Russian army as they had been in the tsarist period, grants of land were provided for them in their native districts,[78] and a special department for Cossack affairs was created within the presidential administration (the **Main Directorate on Cossack Units**).[79] Cossacks have been employed as mercenaries by Russia in Chechnya, Georgia, and Bosnia, for which they receive special treatment back in Russia. Inevitably this aggravates relations between the Russians and other groups of the Caucasus.

Related to all of this are the more pressing problems of territorial conflict and the subsequent overflow of refugees from these conflicts into neighboring areas. Since 1988 and the eruption of fighting between Armenia and Azerbaijan over Nagorno-Karabakh, the Caucasus has proven to be the most volatile region of the former Soviet Union. Ossetians and Ingush have fought one another, as have Russians and Chechens, and Muslims and Christians. The result has been a massive refugee problem for many of these regions which are often ill-equipped to deal with displaced persons. Housing and land are in short supply and each republic's/region's governing structures are largely left to deal with these problems with little help from Moscow.[80]

Cultural homogeneity is no guarantee that harmonious relations will exist within any given state structure, especially if the primary ethnic group has been responsible for repressing others. Five groups of peoples from the North Caucasus were deported in their entirety in 1944 for supposed collaboration with the Germans: the Balkars, Chechens, Ingush, Karachai, and Cherkess. Although these peoples were allowed to return beginning in 1956, issues of territorial boundaries and immigration have never been fully resolved.[81] At the time of the 1989 census Rostov Oblast had the highest percentage of Russians in the North Caucasus at eighty-nine percent of the population. Taking into account Ukrainians and Belarussians living within Rostov oblast, the Slavic population represented roughly ninety-five percent of the total.[82] Compare this to the most ethnically diverse part of the North Caucasus, the Republic of Dagestan (also one of the most economically depressed regions in the Federation[83]), where the largest group—the Avars—are only twenty-seven percent of the population, and at least ten other populations must exist side-by-side. The problems of peaceful

Russian troops on patrol in Grozny

Source: AP/Wide World Photos

integration of so many groups and equal treatment and representation within the political and economic systems are just as obvious.

Chechnya

For sheer intensity and potential impact on the stability of the political system the Chechen efforts at secession find almost no parallels in the Russian Federation's short history. The conflict has demonstrated the worst elements of ethnic and cultural relations in the Russian state, and the depths of despair that accompany the politics of extremity. The human toll especially has been high: between December 1994 and September 1996 as many as 40,000–80,000 were killed by the fighting,[84] and by 1996 there were upwards of half a million refugees and forced migrants in the Caucasus as a result of the war.[85] With the second war in 1999 the entire tragedy was revisited as thousands more died on the battlefields, and at least 200,000 people were again forced to flee for their lives.[86]

The wars in Chechnya have not been about an inevitable clash of cultures or peoples (the Chechens are overwhelmingly Muslim).[87] Forcibly annexed to Russia in the nineteenth century resistance to Russian imperialism was long and determined and the region was marginally pacified only in 1864. Matters did not improve under Soviet rule; as already recounted Stalin ordered the deportation of the Chechens, along with several other nationalities, to Siberia and Kazakstan. Among those deported, but eventually allowed to return was **Dzhokar Dudaev,** the future leader of the secessionist movement and president of the republic.[88] Dudaev became the personification of Chechen separatism in his native land. In the chaos of late 1991 Dudaev became president of Chechnya-Ingushetia and within a month successfully engineered a vote on the republic's secession from the Soviet Union.[89]

Relations spiraled downward from that point. Russian Interior Ministry troops were sent to the capital of Grozny in November 1991 to prevent secession and literally became captives at the airport until they agreed to leave. Over the next two years as Dudaev pushed the independence agenda and subsequently put himself at odds with other Chechen leaders, the Yeltsin administration played up rivals to Dudaev and fostered within the rest of the Russian Federation distrustful and suspicious attitudes toward the Chechen people.[90] At the time of the invasion in December 1994 a thinly veiled persecution of the Chechens as being a mafia-like, crime-oriented people was underway throughout Russia and particularly in Moscow (which government officials flatly denied).[91]

No one had more at stake politically than did Yeltsin who claimed that federal integrity had to be upheld, but also desired a sweeping victory to take the Russian electorate's minds off more intractable problems.[92] Hard-liners within the administration—the so-called "Party of War" rejected out of hand a plan for a negotiated settlement put forth by other members of the administration.[93] On 10 December 1994 a Russian expeditionary force (estimated at 23,800)[94] was sent in to crush the rebellion but met with remarkably fierce resistance, first in the capitol **Grozny** (the name, ironically enough, is Russian for "formidable"), and then in the countryside.[95] Despite Defense Minister Pavel Grachev's assertion that the whole campaign would succeed in hours the Grozny operation alone took over a month with thousands of Russian troop and civilian casualties. For the next twenty months Chechnya and Russia alike were wracked by the ferocity of the secessionist conflict as a disintegrating Russian military machine brutally slugged it out with a small, but committed Chechen resistance. Towns and villages were subjected to massive artillery assaults and aerial bombardments, and no one in the republic was safe from the carnage.

Popular sentiment toward the first war was never favorable, especially within the army.[96] Bad news of military defeats paralleled revelations of untrained and poorly equipped soldiers,[97] and by 31 March 1996, with his reelection prospects endangered Yeltsin ordered a unilateral cease-fire.[98] But the Chechen waters remained muddied by events. Feeling trapped by what Grachev described as a "no peace, no war state",[99] the army continued to fight and succeeded in killing Dudaev.[100]

For the Russian military the worst humiliation was yet to come. On 6 August 1996 Chechen fighters stormed and took Grozny leaving hundreds of Russian soldiers dead or hostage to the rebels. Yeltsin subsequently assigned his Security Council head, Alexandr Lebed, to find a solution and on 31 August the **Khasavyurt agreements** (named after the Dagestani village where the talks were held) were signed pulling Russian troops out of the republic and postponing the decision on independence for five years. But continued Chechen demands for independence, and an inability of leaders such as President **Aslan Maskhadov** to effectively reign in the local warlords, or to develop a functioning economy prevented the normalization of relations. After Islamic militants among the Chechens invaded neighboring Dagestan in August 1999 the fuse was lit once again. The Russian military, now directed by the more purposeful Prime Minister Putin, struck back at Chechnya itself, and although the new assault produced carnage on a scale equal to the first the Russian public was now overwhelmingly in support of the war.[101]

At the time of this writing Chechnya is nominally in Russian hands once again, and some Russian troops have even been withdrawn. But terrorism, assassinations, and the Russian policy of *bespredel* (no limits) regarding prisoners,[102] all point to a situation with only scant prospects for normalization. And so, too, Russia's regional policies lie on the brink of disintegration, for if Chechnya is not representative of Russia's regions, or the Federation's numerous problems, it does reflect the worst examples of a state lying somewhere between consolidated democracy and reconfigured authoritarianism. And as the late democratic activist and expert on ethnicity, Galina Starovoitova stated, "the peaceful achievement of national self-determination in posttotalitarian countries is possible only under the institutions of democratic rule."[103]

Key Terms

oblast	federalism
power-sharing arrangements	Yuri Luzhkov
Khasavyurt agreements	national homelands
Peoples of the North	Dzhokar Dudaev

Questions for Consideration

1. Given the tendencies in Russian politics toward centralized power is the idea of federalism a realistic organizing concept for the country?

2. Is the condition of *favored nation status* an indication that the republics have real power, or is this a hangover from the Soviet period?

3. Putin's drive to bring the regions into line with the federal constitution poses what sort of challenges for regional autonomy?

4. Can the problems of Russia's regions be resolved by individual political leaders such as the governors or republican presidents, or must reform come from Moscow?

5. Are the problems that led to the two wars in Chechnya resolvable? Is there a peaceful future for the Caucasus if these wars continue?

Suggested Readings

Jeff Chinn and Robert Kaiser, *Russians as the New Minority: Ethnicity and Nationalism in the Soviet Successor States* (Boulder, CO: Westview Press, 1996).

Geoff Eley and Ronald Grigor Suny, eds., *Becoming National: A Reader* (New York: Oxford University Press, 1996).

Anatol Lieven, *Chechnya, Tombstone of Russian Power* (New Haven, CT: Yale University Press, 1998).

Walter Morris-Hale, *Conflict and Harmony in Multi-Ethnic Societies* (New York: Peter Lang, 1996).

Fen Montaigne, *Reeling in Russia* (New York: St. Martin's Press, 1998).

Alexander J. Motyl, ed., *Thinking Theoretically About Soviet Nationalities* (New York: Columbia University Press, 1995).

Vladimir Shlapentokh, Roman Levita, and Mikhail Loiberg, *From Submission to Rebellion: The Provinces Versus the Center in Russia* (Boulder, CO: Westview Press, 1997).

James Warhola, *Politicized Ethnicity in the Russian Federation: Dilemmas of State Formation* (Lewiston, NY: Edwin Mellen Press, 1996).

Hans Westlund, Alexander Granberg, and Folke Snickars, *Regional Development in Russia* (Northampton, MA: Edward Elgar, 2000).

Useful Websites

Allnews.ru
   http://www.lenta.ru

Chechnya Information Channel
   http://www.ichkeria.org

Chechen Republic Online
   http://www.amina.com

"Delovoi Petersburg"
   http://www.dp.ru

Goskomstat (State Statistics Committee)
http://www.gks.ru/

Kirsan Ilumzhinov—the President of the Republic of Kalmuckia
http://www.dol.ru/users/kirsan/engl/home1.htm

National News Service-Russia
http://www.nns.ru/index.html

Norwegian Institute of International Relations
http://www.nupi.no/russland/russland.htm

Endnotes

1. For a brief sample of what the Russian public was able to read about the first war see *Moscow News,* "Nation's Tears, General's Shame," 19 January 1996, and "Ministerial Cynicism," 2 May 1996.
2. *Ekonomika i Zhizn,* no. 8 1997, cited at RIA-Novosti website, 11 March 1997 [http://www.ria-novosti.com/products/dr].
3. *Constitution (Fundamental Law) of the Union of Soviet Socialist Republics* (Moscow: Novosti Press Agency, 1977), p. 56.
4. See Mikhail Gorbachev, "Report on Nationality Policy to the CPSU Central Committee," TASS, 19 September 1989 in *Reprints From the Soviet Press,* 49 (30 November 1989): p. 9.
5. *Moscow News,* 7 March 1996.
6. *Rossiiskiye vesti,* 24 October 1996, RIA-Novosti website, 28 October 1996.
7. For the text of the treaty see TASS International Service, 14 March 1992; FBIS-SOV, 16 March 1992, pp. 67–70.
8. Elizabeth Teague, "North-South Divide: Yeltsin and Russia's Provincial Leaders," *RFE/RL Research Report,* 2 (26 November 1993): pp. 7–23.
9. *Krasnaya zvezda,* 30 October 1993, translated in FBIS-SOV, 2 November 1993, p. 54.
10. ITAR-TASS, 16 September 1993.
11. *Krasnaya zvezda,* 14 September 1993, translated in FBIS-SOV, 16 September 1993; also, ITAR-TASS, 10 February 1994.
12. *Kommersant-Daily,* 29 October 1993, translated in FBIS-SOV, 2 November 1993, pp. 53–54. For the presidential edict granting the federal government these powers see *Rossiyskaya gazeta,* 6 November 1993, translated in FBIS-SOV, 9 November 1993, pp. 39–40.
13. See ITAR-TASS for 7 and 10 February 1994; also Mayak Radio Network, 10 February 1994, FBIS-SOV, 10 February 1994, pp. 39–40.
14. "Russian and Baltic Economies, The Week in Review," no. 52 (29 December 2000), Bank of Finland, Institute for Economies in Transition (BOFIT).
15. See, for instance, the article by Andrew Wilson, "The Post-Soviet States and the Nationalities Question" in ed. Graham Smith, *The Nationalities Question in the Post-Soviet States,* 2nd ed. (London: Longman, 1996), p. 39.
16. Vilen Ivanov, "Overhauling Russia's Administrative-Territorial System," *Executive and Legislative Newsletter,* no. 24 (1997), RIA-Novosti website, 16 June 1997 [http://www.ria-novosti.ru].
17. ITAR-TASS, 9 December 1995.
18. ITAR-TASS, 13 May 2000, cited in *RFE/RL Newsline,* 15 May 2000.
19. ITAR-TASS, 1 June 2000, cited in *RFE/RL Newsline,* 1 June 2000.

20. A comparative framework on ethnic-based separatism is found in Daniel S. Treisman, "Russia's 'Ethnic Revival': The Separatist Activism of Regional Leaders in a Postcommunist Order", *World Politics,* 49 (January 1997), pp. 212–249.

21. For an illustration of the philosophy behind this strategy see M. Strongina, "Local Self-Government and the Development of Territories" ("Mestnoe samoupravlenie I razvitie territorii"), *Voprosy ekonomiki,* no. 5 (1994), reprinted in *Russian Social Science Review,* 36 (July-August 1995): pp. 16–27.

22. *OMRI Daily Digest,* 12 January 1996.

23. Elena Chinayeva, "Boris Nemtsov, A Rising Star of the Russian Provinces," *Transition,* 2 (23 February 1996): pp. 26–28.

24. *Moscow News,* 9 February 1996.

25. "Profiles of Russian Cities: Nizhniy Novgorod," *Russian Defense Business Directory,* (Washington, DC: Bureau of Export Administration, United States Department of Commerce, 27 January 1994).

26. See the Central Intelligence Agency's publication "Russia: Regional Voting Patterns in the April 1993 Referendum," (Washington, DC: National Technical Information Service, 1993).

27. Statistics are from the Russian Federation State Committee on Statistics, Global Statistics website [http://www.xist.org].

28. See the editorial in *Moscow News,* 26 January 1996.

29. See Interfax, 3 June 1997.

30. For instance, see the statement by Korzhakov on problems in Moscow in *Argumenty i fakty* 18 January 1995, cited in *OMRI Daily Digest,* 18 January 1995.

31. For Luzhkov's electoral platform see *Moscow News,* 4 April 1996.

32. As an example see the poll in *Segodnya,* 30 January 1997, RIA-Novosti, 31 January 1997.

33. *Novaya yezhednevnaya,* 15 June 1994, FBIS-SOV, 20 June 1994, pp. 36–40. Also, ITAR-TASS, 9 February 1994.

34. For the 1997 elections see Interfax, 15 December 1997 and *Moskovskiy komsomolets,* 16 December 1997, both translated in FBIS-SOV, 22 December 1997. For 2001 see *Vremya novosti,* 18 December 2001, cited in *RFE/RL Newsline,* 19 December 2001.

35. ITAR-TASS, 14 December 1997.

36. *Kommersant-Daily,* 16 March 1995, translated in FBIS-SOV, 30 March 1995, p. 24.

37. See Elena Chinayeva, "Yurii Luzhkov—The Man Who Runs Moscow," *Transition,* 2 (23 February 1996): pp. 30–33.

38. *RFE/RL Newsline,* 3 June 1996.

39. *St. Petersburg Times,* 5–11 May 1996.

40. *St. Petersburg Times,* 2–8 April 1996.

41. Darrell Slider, Vladimir Gimpel'son, and Sergei Chugrov, "Political Tendencies in Russia's Regions: Evidence From the 1993 Parliamentary Elections," *Slavic Review,* 53 (Fall 1994): pp. 711–732.

42. See James Hughes, "Regionalism in Russia: The Rise and Fall of Siberian Agreement," *Europe-Asia Studies,* 46 (1994): pp. 1133–1161.

43. *OMRI Daily Digest,* 25 April 1996.

44. See the comments of Vyacheslav Mikhailov, Minister for Nationalities, "Russia's Nationalities Policy Today and Tomorrow," *Executive and Legislative Newsletter,* no. 43 (1996), RIA-Novosti website [http://www.russia/net/ria/dr/dg29101.htm].

45. *Izvestiya,* 22 July 1991, translated in FBIS-SOV, 26 July 1991, pp. 62–63.

46. TASS, 8 January 1992.

47. *First Demographic Portraits of Russia, 1951–1990* (Shadyside, MD: New World Demographics, L.C., 1993), p. 38.
48. Ibid, p. 55.
49. Ibid, p. 115.
50. Ron Wixman points out that assimilation amongst the Tatars was largely a condition of accepting the Islamic faith rather than a question of ethnicity. See "The Middle Volga: Ethnic Archipelago in a Russian Sea," in eds. Ian Bremmer and Ray Taras, *Nations and Politics in the Soviet Successor States,* (New York: Cambridge University Press, 1993), pp. 422–423.
51. *Rossiyskaya gazeta,* 15 February 1995, translated in FBIS-SOV, 16 February 1995, p. 31; also see the interview with Shaymiyev in Interfaks-AiF, translated in FBIS-SOV, 8–14 December 1997.
52. Susan Goodrich Lehmann, "Islam and Ethnicity in the Republics of Russia," *Post-Soviet Affairs,* 13 (1997), pp. 78–103.
53. An assessment of the treaty a year after the fact can be found in *Nezavisimaya gazeta,* 18 February 1995, translated in FBIS-SOV, 8 March 1995, p. 32. See also Elizabeth Teague, "Russia and Tatarstan Sign a Power-Sharing Treaty," *RFE/RL Research Report,* 3 (8 April, 1994): p. 20.
54. Marie Bennigsen Broxup, "Tatarstan and the Tatars" in Smith, *The Nationalities Question,* pp. 85–86.
55. ITAR-TASS cited in *OMRI Russian Regional Report,* 1 (2 October 1996), part II.
56. Oksana Gaman, "Regional Elites in Post-Soviet Russia," ("Regional'nye elity v postsovetskoi Rossii"), *Rossiyskaya Federatsiia,* no. 10 (1995), reprinted in *Russian Politics and Law,* 34 (May–June 1996): p. 30.
57. Interfax, 29 October 1996.
58. *Nezavisimaya gazeta,* 4 August 1994, translated in FBIS-SOV, 4 August 1994, pp. 26–27.
59. *Segodnya,* 7 February 1995, translated in FBIS-SOV, 23 February 1995, p. 58.
60. *Izvestiya Tatarstana,* 30 August 1995, translated in FBIS-SOV, 8 August 1995, p. 39.
61. *Nezavisimaya gazeta,* 4 August 1994, translated in FBIS-SOV, 4 August 1994, p. 26.
62. ITAR-TASS, 3 August 1994.
63. "Prickly Putin Moves Swiftly on Regions, Press, Say Analysts," 15 May 2000, Agence France Presse, reprinted in RussiaToday website [http://www.russiatoday.com].
64. *Selskaya zhizn,* 19 August 1995, translated in FBIS-SOV, 22 August 1995: p. 37.
65. ITAR-TASS, 16 October 1995.
66. *Trud,* 14 November 1996, RIA-Novosti, 15 November 1996.
67. See Vladimir Yemelyanenko, "No Ordinary Murder in Kalmykia," *Moscow News* (25 June–1 July 1998): p. 4.
68. Valerii Tishkov, "Ethnicity and Power in the Republics of the USSR," *Journal of Soviet Nationalities,* 1 (Fall 1990): pp. 41–42.
69. Interfax, 1 November 1993.
70. ITAR-TASS, 17 September 1993.
71. Marjorie Mandelstam Balzer and Uliana Alekseevna Vinokurova, "Nationalism, Interethnic Relations and Federalism: The Case of the Sakha Republic (Yakutia)," *Europe-Asia Studies,* 48 (1996): p. 106.
72. *Respublika Sakha,* 25 January 1995 and 27 January 1995, translated in FBIS-SOV, 2 March 1995, pp. 26–27.
73. *Rossiyskiye vesti,* 16 June 1995, translated in FBIS-SOV, 20 June 1995, pp. 50–51; *OMRI Daily Digest,* 30 June 1995.

74. *Peoples of the Soviet Union* (Moscow: Novosti Press Agency Publishing House, 1989), pp. 14–15.

75. U.S. Bureau of the Census, *USA/USSR: Facts and Figures,* U.S. Government Printing Office, Washington, DC, 1991, pp. 1–4, 1–5.

76. Ilya Maksakov, "Daghestan: Explosion-Prone Republic?", *Nezavisimaya gazeta,* 12 October 1996.

77. Interfax, 6 January 1997; also *Rossiyskaya gazeta,* 22 January 1997, RIA-Novosti website, 22 January 1997.

78. *Moscow News,* 2 May 1996.

79. ITAR-TASS, 18 December 1996.

80. See, for instance, the article "Kabardino-Balkaria Demographics 'Alarming'," *Kabardino-Balkarskaya pravda,* 4 July 1995, translated in FBIS-SOV, 10 July 1995, p. 48.

81. Jane Ormrod, "North Caucasus: Fragmentation or Federation?", in Bremmer and Taras, *Nations and Politics,* p. 452.

82. *First Book of Demographics of the Soviet Union, 1951–1990* (Shadyside, MD: New World Demographics, L.C., 1992), p. D-5.

83. *Rabochaya tribuna* cited in *OMRI Daily Digest,* 13 February 1996.

84. ITAR-TASS, cited in *OMRI Daily Digest,* 4 September 1996.

85. See "The Commonwealth of Independent States: Refugees and Internally Displaced Persons in Armenia, Azerbaijan, Georgia, the Russian Federation, and Tajikistan," *Human Rights Watch/Helsinki Report,* 8 (May 1996): pp. 22–24.

86. "Annual Report 2000, Russian Federation," 25 November 2000, Amnesty International website [http://www.web.amnesty.org/web/ar2000web.nsf/europe].

87. For a brief background on the Chechens themselves see Johanna Nichols, "Who are the Chechen?", *Central Asian Survey,* 14 (1995): pp. 573–577.

88. TASS, 6 September 1994.

89. John Colarusso, "Chechnya: The War Without Winners," *Current History,* (October 1995): pp. 330–331.

90. See the report concerning the right-wing National Republican Party of Russia in *OMRI Daily Digest,* 30 June 1995.

91. See the interview with Minister of Nationalities Nikolai Yegorov in *Rossiyskaya gazeta,* 29 March 1995, translated in FBIS-SOV, 5 April 1995, p. 25.

92. Michael McFaul, "Eurasia Letter: Russian Politics After Chechnya," *Foreign Affairs* (Summer 1995): pp. 149–156.

93. Interfax, 7 February 1995, cited in *OMRI Daily Digest,* 7 February 1995.

94. See Pavel Baev, *The Russian Army in a Time of Troubles* (London: Sage Publications, 1996), p. 143.

95. Two detailed accounts of the politics and preparations leading up to the 1994 invasion include Stasys Knezys and Romanas Sedlickas, *The War in Chechnya* (College Station, TX: Texas A & M Press, 1999), Chapters Three and Four; and Pontus Siren, "The Battle for Grozny: The Russian Invasion of Chechnia, December 1994-December 1996," in ed. Ben Fowkes, *Russia and Chechnia: The Permanent Crisis* (New York: St. Martin's Press, 1998), Chapter Four.

96. For instance, see the *Literaturnaya gazeta* interview with Duma deputy Vladimir Bauer reprinted in *Russian Politics and Law,* 33 (September–October 1995): pp. 90–93.

97. See *Moscow News,* 2 May 1996.

98. For a partial transcript of the decree see *Moscow News,* 4 April 1996.

99. *Moscow News,* 25 April 1996.

100. ITAR–TASS, 23 April 1996; also, CNN Interactive World News, 24 April 1996.

101. For instance, see question 6B of the VCIOM survey conducted 30 June–4 July 2000 which asks "How do you assess the actions of Russian forces in Chechnya: are they severe and decisive enough, not severe and decisive enough, or too severe and hurried?" Seventy-four percent of respondents replied that military actions are severe enough, or not severe enough. Center for the Study of Public Policy, University of Strathclyde website [http://wwwRussiaVotes.org/Mood/int/cur.htm].

102. Maura Reynolds, "War has no rules for Russian forces fighting in Chechnya", 17 September 2000, *Los Angeles Times* website [http://www.latimes.com/news/nation/20000917/5000087877].

103. Galina Starovoitova, *Sovereignty after Empire, Self-Determination Movements in the Former Soviet Union*, Peaceworks #19 (1997), Internet edition, United States Institute of Peace website [http://www.usip.org/pubs/pworks/pwks19/pwks19.html], Chapter Two.

Chapter 8

The Economy: From Central Planning to Market Dynamics

N o element of Russia's transition has proven as potentially destabilizing as that of the transformation of the economy. Altering the economy's character from central planning and management to free market ideals involves a rejection of the core ideology that governed the socialist system. The Russian government today plays a substantially reduced role in the national economy and coexists (albeit uneasily) with market dynamics. Moreover, the changes being weathered within the economy have had tremendous spillover effects on Russia's neighbors thereby providing a greater significance to the direction, pace, and intensity of change in Russia.

Determining exactly where the Russian economy is headed is problematic. One effective way to describe the collection of financial, fiscal, budgetary, and entrepreneurial changes occurring is to call it an *economy in transition,* that is, one somewhere in between the **centrally planned economy** (CPE) of old and the free-market economy familiar in the United States and western Europe. Certain conditions can be reliably agreed upon. First, the economic changes are long-term, whichever direction they might take. Second, the immensity of the transformation has, and will continue to result in large-scale social and economic dislocations including unemployment where little had existed before, and the enrichment/impoverishment of a great many people. Third, these changes have nominally determined much that now characterizes the political structures of Russia and the Eurasian countries. And finally, the changes require an extremely high level of participation from the population, both in terms of support and creative development if they are to succeed. It is this last point that may be the biggest determinant of the success or failure of government reforms.

The transition also implies much more than the transferring of wealth and the means of production from state control to a private sector. International, especially western, demands to privatize the economy are often at odds with Russia's real world economic needs and the economic culture of its peoples. A tremendous amount of change must yet occur before Russia becomes a full-fledged market economy, a goal that may not be in Russia's best economic interests! From Gorbachev's time to the present the resolution of this question has not been adequately addressed, thereby severely limiting that which Russia could become.

The Role of the State

The State as the Director/Guardian of Change

The Soviet economic system was founded on the idea that the state should be the guardian of the economic revolution.[1] The means of production which had been in the hands of a small elite of private individuals, families or corporations were expropriated by the Bolsheviks after the socialist revolution in 1917 in the interests of society in general, and the working class in particular. As the system came to be organized, the Communist Party diagnosed the problems confronting Russian society, prescribed the antidotes, and then utilized various state mechanisms to cure or correct the ailments associated with capitalism. Through scientific planning and bureaucratic management (as the Communist Party saw it) the socialist state replaced the supply and demand sides of the economic system and theoretically eliminated the class-oriented factor of personal enrichment.

The Soviet planning system took decades to fully evolve, but under the direction of Stalin its realization was the highest priority. Planning was both economic in content and political in purpose, designed to push the economic development of the Soviet Union ahead of the capitalist world.[2] The communist party's leadership set the guidelines to be attained, and then commanded state planning organs (originally the Supreme Council of National Economy, or VSNKh, and after 1931 the **State Planning Committee, or Gosplan**) to organize the specifics. The most visible aspect of the planning process was the five-year plan (first introduced in 1928), the general directions of which were announced in conjunction with the Communist Party's congresses. In these plans could be found the emphasis to be placed on a particular mode of production and the amount of investment allocated for major sectors of the economy. The plan was much more than a governmental blueprint for where the economy needed to go; instead, the plan was a *command* that the economy be moved in a given direction. The plan *was* the market!

To make these plans work the party's elite needed mechanisms to operate an economy of enormous size; the development of such instruments was a continual process. From Lenin's time to that of Gorbachev the Soviet state repeatedly organized and reorganized the numerous ministries, committees, and other bodies dealing with industry, agriculture, consumer goods, and the allocation and distribution of resources. In some respects, however, this was no different than the shifting structure of governments in any other political system. Governmental organs such as Gossnab (the State Committee for Material and Technical Supply) and Gostroi (the State Committee for Construction) carried out the distribution of resources, while Goskomtsen (the State Committee for Prices), Gosstandart (the State Committee for Standards), and **Gosbank** (the State Bank) provided the framework within which the economy functioned. The size of the governing apparatus grew in tandem with the sophistication of the economy. Occasionally Soviet leaders attempted to restructure components of the bureaucratic apparatus for the sake of efficiency, such as with Khrushchev's "economics over politics" reform in 1962,[3] or Gorbachev's 1986 creation of Gosagroprom (the State Agro-Industrial Committee), that saw the merger of five ministries and one state committee into a supraministerial organ.[4] Both innovations met with considerable resistance within the CPSU and were fated to abandonment in a short time.

Only toward the end of Gorbachev's *perestroika* program did the Soviet state attempt to come to grips with the changes confronting society. Loosening the reins of state control was a political battle pitting those who saw economic reform as a necessity for system survival against orthodox ideological elements within the party. Initially the strategy of change took the form of Gorbachev and others promoting the tandem concepts of *uskorenie,* or acceleration, and *intensifikatsiya,* or intensification, of the economy.[5] Even as reform-minded Soviet economists recognized that the economic growth rate had become flat,[6] the whole party still needed to be convinced. Any changes required justification within the guidelines of Marxist-Leninist ideology and the struggle to build socialism.[7] This strategy was employed to preempt resistance from those who had a stake in the economic status quo.[8]

The effectiveness of the centrally planned economy will always be a subject of intense debate. Certain points need to be emphasized for a clear understanding, in particular the immensity of the task of managing what became the second largest economy in the world, and the enormous and oftentimes draconian costs of implementing such far ranging economic change. The USSR's accomplishments were startling in their contexts, its failures monumental as well, but its characteristics definitely unique. So, too, were the components of the state's monopoly of ownership and production.

The State as Owner/Employer

The most significant characteristic of the Soviet economy was the principle of state ownership of the means of production. This was taken by both Marxists and outside observers as literally an article of faith. The concept of nationalization, substantiated in the writings of Marx, Engels, Lenin, and others, literally became fused with the concept of communism. This association was so powerful that in ensuing years other states which used nationalization as a policy tool such as those in the developing world were regarded by capitalist economies as being at the very least potentially socialist.

Getting the CPSU to accept private ownership in any sector, or even a reduced state role, implied that unemployment might have to be tolerated and political determinism lost. Since the state guaranteed everybody employment both

Soviet industry and agriculture were burdened with workforces far larger than that needed to produce effectively. From the standpoint of modern western capitalism the Soviet workforce was in need of downsizing; those who kept their jobs, it was hypothesized, would work more efficiently if they had no guarantee of employment. Gorbachev era reformers such as **Abel Aganbegyan** rejected this approach especially in light of the changing demographics of the Soviet work force, which was both decreasing in size and growing older.[9] But the movement away from strict central planning required that individuals be encouraged to take chances by leaving their jobs and starting out on their own. Thus incentives tied to productivity such as raises and bonuses were necessary so the workforce would produce more efficiently and have a greater sense of involvement in the economy. Inevitably, though, this would lead to greater income inequalities. Nevertheless, *perestroika* had at least presented the possibility of altering the economic aspect of the political culture equation. The failure of the Soviet political structure to accommodate such changes doomed that stage of reform, and set the foundation for a political structure which continues to define economics in Russia today.

The Emerging Market

Privatization: The State Sells off Its Assets

As with any other economic system, no matter the extent of government involvement, the state must generate revenues to pay for its programs. In the Soviet era the state had removed the "middle man" of the market. The citizen and the enterprises paid taxes to the state, and the state provided the investments (wages, operating expenses) necessary to move the economy. In the stripped down version of political economy that the Russian Federation has become, the process has been made to resemble the oversimplified revenues-and-expenditures equation common to western government budgetary debates. As discussed in the previous chapter a large proportion of the central government's revenue is lost by the regions' inabilities or unwillingness to pay required taxes.[10] But since 1992 another important source of revenue has been the policy of **privatization** which, theoretically at least, should have brought in trillions of rubles (billions of dollars) of extra revenue, although in reality much of this has simply been written off.[11]

The genesis of the privatization program may be traced to several sources, one of the most important being the 1990 attempt at reform known as the **500-day Plan** of Stanislav Shatalin (coauthored with the economist and later cofounder of Yabloko, Grigorii Yavlinskii). The program was largely stillborn due to the increasingly cautious attitudes of Gorbachev and his prime minister Nikolai Ryzhkov. Nevertheless, practical privatization of the Soviet economy had begun by 1991 with the passage of laws governing the housing sector and a general law on privatization. These represented tentative efforts by the Soviet state and CPSU to remain in the driver's seat as the economic environment changed. This roundabout effort at reform would be, as one source put it, "not so much on property as on decentralization and the introduction of rudimentary market institutions."[12]

Some of the more visible signs of change were that the enterprises and their managers were putting distance between themselves and the central authorities,[13] and that formal mechanisms of privatization were being established such as **Goskomimushchestvo** (GKI), the State Committee on Managing State Property (since 1997 this has been known as the Ministry of State Property, or MGI).[14] This, however, had to be in tandem with "the freeing of new economic activity and the provision of a relatively undistorted economic environment."[15] Privatization had barely been instituted by the end of the Soviet period and was largely left up to the successor Russian state to implement. With Yeltsin setting the policy agenda through presidential decrees, his team of liberal market reformers headed by acting Prime Minister Yegor Gaidar and directed by the Minister of Privatization Anatolii Chubais enacted a wave of reform beginning in late 1991. By 1992 the reformers were in the ascendency but not without opposition from the Congress of People's Deputies and the revived Communist Party. The extensive political opposition at a time when systemic reform was only in its infancy resulted in what has been called "suboptimal solutions"[16], much less than what the reformers intended.

Yeltsin's focus initially was on the rapid dismantling of some of the most obvious vestiges of the Soviet economy including reducing the size and influence of the bureaucracy, liberalizing prices, and balancing the budget.[17] Yeltsin made clear his intent to reduce both the size of government and the scope of state ownership. After a fitful start in the first half of 1992 a massive portion of the economy's production capabilities—an estimated 25,000 large and medium-size enterprises, which "had constituted the very fabric of the Russian economy"[18]— were targeted to be sold. In the second stage of privatization in early 1995 the government announced another massive rendering of some 7000 enterprises to be sold on the auction block,[19] and by June 1996 the State Statistics Committee was claiming 124,200 businesses and facilities had been privatized nationwide.[20] Entire components of the national economy including industries such as engineering, construction, automobile, and aircraft manufacturing were given over to public auction.[21] At this point as well the small business sector was largely in public hands and employing in excess of 14 million people.[22] In 1994 the administration earmarked approximately sixty percent of all defense-related industry for some degree of privatization,[23] and in 1995 developed a list of some 3000 "strategic" enterprises that were to remain state property.[24] But the state's need for revenue along with reformers' desires to reduce even further state ownership saw this latter number cut to less than 700 in 1998.[25]

Several problems consistently confronted the policy, including the need to find new investment capital, deciding who should benefit from privatization, and the nagging issue of corruption. Removing the state from much of its previous role of capital financing freed scarce resources for other sectors of the economy. This generally meant that unprofitable enterprises would fail, particularly those whose managers lacked effective business experience. As well, management had to learn on its own how to acquire funding and attract foreign capital.

Miners Block the Trans-Siberian Railway in a 1998 Labor Dispute

Source: © TASS/Sovfoto

Bureaucratic resistance to decentralized authority was great and caused no end to administration frustrations,[26] but was not enough to scuttle the program by itself. Even still, the old *nomenklatura* did manage to sap the process of badly needed momentum.

Who would benefit from privatization was as much of a political and social problem as an economic concern. The first phase of large-scale privatization required that the state determine quickly who the principal beneficiaries of its sell offs were to be: workers inside the enterprise, the general citizenry outside of it, or the enterprise managers and bureaucrats responsible for sectors of the economy. The government initially approved a general distribution of state assets, and in August 1992 a presidential decree initiated a **voucher system** whereby each citizen of the Russian Federation was given a coupon or voucher worth approximately 10,000 rubles (as valued at that time).[27] The citizen then had the choice of keeping the voucher in hopes of it appreciating in value, selling or transferring it to someone else, or investing it in a particular enterprise, firm, or business. Eventually almost all vouchers were redeemed by citizens (148 million were issued). Public opinion data subsequently showed that three-quarters of all Russians used or intended to use their vouchers for something tangible and were willing to trade them in for immediate gain.[28] The selling off of vouchers continued an already developing concentration of wealth in the hands of an elite few and the subsequent enlargement of a new class of entrepreneurs stitched together from members of the old *nomenklatura,* enterprise directors, risk takers, and the shadow economy.

From its beginning the process was fraught with massive logistical problems. Among these was the opening of the system to foreign investment and political intrusion such as that by the International Monetary Fund (IMF), foreign governments and banks, and multinational corporations. There was no easy way for any of this to proceed; indeed, the Russian Federation had before it several models of privatization, none of which provided the Russian public with a sense of economic security. The most destabilizing was the Polish variant known to the world as *shock therapy,* involving a rapid transition from the command economy as the state quickly sold off its assets and closed unprofitable enterprises. High levels of unemployment and inflation followed but once the shock had been absorbed, it was assumed there would be no turning back to the command economy. A more measured transformation was that favored by Czechoslovakia and its successor states, and overall the effects upon these economies was less destabilizing than the Polish variant. The goal was the same: transform the social and economic bases of the socialist market into a vibrant market-oriented economy.

The potential for political instability as a result of rapidly escalating prices and massive unemployment was an issue that the entire Russian leadership—both the administration and its supporters, as well as the opposition—saw as revolutionary. If the change proceeded in a relatively smooth fashion the prospects of returning to the centrally planned economy would be seriously diminished. If it failed outright, or produced just enough chaos, then the reformers would be turned out either through elections or by legislative pressure on the president. Thus, economic transformation was an issue of the highest political importance and of direct relevance to the average citizen's interests.

Throughout 1993 the position of the reformers weakened in favor of more conservative figures concerned with political and social stability.[29] A pattern emerged which was to be repeated in both 1996 and again on two separate occasions in 1998. By 1994 the first stage of privatization had ended having failed to achieve one of its primary objectives: generating sufficient capital for reinvestment through the voucher system. With well over half of the economy still owned by the state the government considered it essential to step up the pace by a public auctioning of assets. As such the privatization program entered its second stage in 1994.

The new stage of privatization, which came to be known as **money privatization,** proved to be as controversial as the first. After a protracted and losing battle in the State Duma to get a new version of privatization approved, Yeltsin instead issued a decree in July 1994 supporting Chubais' program to sell state properties directly for cash.[30] This new stage provided greater options to enterprises, banks, and foreign investors to buy shares in government holdings. The administration's stated goal was to gain new capital by offering enterprises at less than face value. Nevertheless, by early 1995 with government indebtedness mounting and being in need of quick fixes to this dilemma the government began dumping holdings at dramatically reduced prices. Even as Chubais issued favorable assessments of the program,[31] critics of privatization contended that state property was being drastically undervalued in favor of a new elite of robber barons who gained incredible bargains through personal connections, or political support for the Yeltsin administration.

All of this lead in March 1995 to a shift within the money privatization stage, in what became known as the **loans for shares** program. A consortium of Russian banks offered to make loans to the government in exchange for shares of privatized firms.[32] Some of Russia's largest and most valuable enterprises from the oil and gas, mining, defense, and other sectors were auctioned by the government and, again, at sharply reduced prices. Each of these sectors promised enormous profits for the government but always under difficult circumstances. In all three of the aforementioned categories the problem was the same: Who could provide the necessary capital for new investments? Oil and gas companies could raise revenue by selling shares directly to the public or to other large corporations. But the defense and natural resource sectors required substantial outlays of capital just to stay afloat and only the unlikely avenue of direct foreign investment could provide an offset to this problem.

The privatization of the defense industry sector begun in 1992 was especially important to the design of the Russian market economy. But the government was overly cautious in implementing this part of the program and adequate oversight was only established in 1996 with the formation of the Federal Commission on Defense Plant Privatization. The military-industrial complex had played a large role in the collapse of the Soviet economy since a huge amount of precious resources had been devoted to fueling the Soviet military machine. Defense conversion—that is, taking plants that produced weapons systems and converting them to the production of nonmilitary export-oriented goods—also involved the peril of the loss of hundreds of thousands of Russian workers' jobs. As the Russian government saw things the problem lay in "the use of the high technology capabilities of the defense complex to produce output capable of competing on the foreign market."[33]

As with the defense industry, the oil and gas industries have also encountered systemic changes. Unlike the defense industry the oil and gas sectors offer commodities vital for domestic consumption, and are capable of reinvesting significant amounts of capital. As such, this sector has become one of the most powerful of a select group of interest-associations in the new Russian economy.[34] As with the defense sector, privatization of oil and gas enterprises began in 1992 although a reorganization of the industry had already begun during the late Soviet period. But even with the world's largest known reserves of oil and natural gas both the Soviet and Russian states have restricted foreign companies' access to these commodities.

Coordinating the process proved to be just as important of a challenge as appropriate laws and rules were consistently lacking. As Stefan Hedlund has phrased it, "a potentially successful policy would have had to incorporate 'getting the institutions right.'"[35] GKI, for instance, the body charged with overseeing the sales of state assets, often seemed to have no idea of how to manage the process, or who was involved in purchases. Moreover, there was little coordination between GKI and other bodies such as the State Committee for Anti-Monopoly Policy,[36] which logically had a role to play. And as citizens perceived privatization to mean the selling off of the best elements of the economy to a combination of **nomenklatura capitalists** (a term coined by Aleksandr Lebed to mean elite members of the bureaucracy who were profiting from inside information), oligarchs, organized crime, and foreign investors at nominal value public confidence in the overall reform process sharply declined.[37] The corruption was not just perceived either; both opposition and proreform elements of the press reported in detail on the profiteering and manipulation occurring at state expense.[38]

In between the 1995 parliamentary and 1996 presidential elections Yeltsin made what seemed to be a sharp turn away from the reformist path. With the opposition belittling Yeltsin's efforts at change at every turn,[39] and his popularity sliding into single digit public approval ratings Yeltsin began to back away from reform. As Yeltsin's opponents effectively portrayed the president as responsible for the public's woes his closest advisors claimed that Yeltsin had been misled on reform and his orders perverted (a "spin" technique strongly reminiscent of strategies employed by the tsars). At no time, however, was privatization abandoned; instead a political decision was made to downplay the policy so as to deny the opposition less of a moving target to hit.

The outcome of the presidential race brought about a new phase of privatization whereby firms were individually sold off rather than *en masse,* and any firm in which the government retained twenty-five percent ownership could not be dissolved.[40] Dramatic structural changes were now things of the recent past since so much state property had already been transferred to private hands (128,500 enterprises had been privatized by January 1998).[41] Instead, key enterprises were individually targeted such as the sale of half of the government's stake in the state insurance company, **Rosgosstrakh.**[42] Similarly forty-nine percent of **Svyazinvest,** the state's principal telecommunications company was auctioned with half of these shares being offered to foreign investors,[43] and fifty-one percent of the state oil company Rosneft was also offered (unsuccessfully) for bids.[44] By putting ever larger amounts of the economy into the hands of an emerging entrepreneurial class—the so-called **New Russians**—the administration hoped to ensure that the gains made in the past several years were not lost. As economist Paul R. Gregory explained the strategy, "The New Russians have changed Russia. They have property to defend and cannot afford a reversal of privatization . . . In one sense they rule modern Russia as much or more than elected representatives and government officials."[45] Even still, in 1997 the Duma finally asserted itself by passing a law "On the Privatization of State Property and on the Basis for the Privatization of Municipal Property in the Russian Federation," the first full revision of privatization since 1991. This law, largely a reaction against the corruption and sweetheart deals that had come to characterize privatization, required the State Property Committee to present an annual plan to be approved by the Duma along with the budget. Unable to overturn the process the Duma instead sought to at least regulate the way it worked. In so doing the Duma, including the left opposition within it, committed itself to a rule-of-law form of governance and implicitly recognized the new system.

Building the Capitalist Infrastructure

For the capital and finance-oriented economic system to function there was an immediate need for new institutions, particularly banks and a securities market. In the earliest stages of the Bolshevik Revolution (27 December 1917) all banks had been nationalized; thereafter the state maintained a strict monopoly over the entire banking process.[46] At the center stood the Soviet State Bank, or Gosbank, which was responsible for first of all what was termed *current control,* that is issuing credits (cash or noncash) so that elements of the plan could be fulfilled, and, second, *auditing* to ensure that money or credits were spent as intended.[47] To carry through on these functions Gosbank operated a network of more than 70,000 savings bank branches,[48] and maintained nominal authority over other national-level banking institutions. Gorbachev's reforms divided banking functions between five structures: the Industrial Investment Bank, the Bank for Foreign Economic Relations, the Bank for the Agro-Industrial Complex, the Bank for Housing, and the Municipal Services and Social Development Savings Bank.[49] Citizens generally only had contact with the banking system insofar as they used the various savings branches, but as the Soviet era came to a close these banks were increasingly important as repositories of expendable income, particularly as there was so little on which to spend money.[50]

The dissolution of the Soviet Union led to the state's assets being nominally divided among the newly independent states. With this also came great opportunities for the expansion of capital resources and entrepreneurial activity; banks were a necessary outgrowth of these changes particularly in terms of the need to gain capital for investment. Laws regulating the banking sector lagged behind the rest of the economy. If the Soviet banking system served only as "an administrative means of channeling money to state enterprises and financing government debt,"[51] then the transitional economy needed to be altered to favor the banks as a source of renewable capital.

Private banks proliferated rapidly to the point where by the beginning of 1996 there were a total of 2295 licensed by the **Central Bank of Russia (TsB).** Saturated as the sector had become, Russian banking began to contract from this point. Under-capitalization in particular caused many banks to lose their registration and by the time of the financial crisis which struck the economy in August 1998 there remained only 1556.[52] That crisis, in fact, had been instigated by the increasing illiquidity of both the banks and the government which had been selling bonds to the banking sector at inflated rates of interest. When it all came due, the economy found itself in another of the all-too-frequent shakeouts that had plagued it during the transitional stage. One year later seven of the country's twenty-five largest banks had had their licenses rescinded by the TsB.[53] The government's response was cautious and studied: first, it called for a restructuring of the entire banking system and closing almost half of the country's remaining banks; and second, the government developed with the TsB an **Agency for Restructuring of Credit Organizations** (ARCO) to assist troubled banks in restructuring their debts, finding new investors, and giving them financial assistance.[54]

To cope with the volatility in banking the TsB has variously frozen accounts of troubled institutions, directly taken control of others, conducted comprehensive audits, closed insolvent banks outright (a total of 922 between 1994 and 1997),[55] renationalized at least one (the former Agroprombank),[56] and retained partial ownership in the largest banks (for instance **Sberbank,** the state savings bank, remains fifty-five percent state-owned). Despite an obvious need for stricter banking laws, the weaknesses of the system became even more transparent when the government announced a ninety-day moratorium on foreign debt repayments in August 1998.[57] No more than a tourniquet solution, this action provided no means for the banks to pay off their debts once the moratorium was lifted.

All of this has played out as high political drama as the president and the State Duma vied for control over economic policy. The president is charged by the constitution (art. 83, sec. d) with submitting to the State Duma candidates for chairman of the TsB, but the president also must seek Duma approval should he wish to dismiss the chairman. Opposition to Yeltsin in the State Duma impeded the selection of a bank chair throughout much of 1994 and 1995 until both sides agreed upon Sergei Dubinin. The unraveling of the economic program in 1998 again brought the Duma to exert pressure, this time upon a substantially weakened president, to attain the reappointment of former chairman **Viktor Geraschenko** who had a reputation for expanding the money supply to pay off state debts. In 2002 under pressure from Putin Geraschenko resigned and was succeeded by **Sergei Ignatiev,** a more pliant choice in the president's efforts to assert control over the bank.

The transitional process has also created another need: the development of stock/securities markets. As in the banking sector there has been tremendous fluctuation in the development of stock exchanges; as might be expected after rapid expansion these have begun to contract in number. From 1991 to 1994 there were approximately 1000 stock exchanges and city bourses; by 1994 this figure declined to approximately sixty. The consolidation of the stock exchanges has been attributed to the connections that exchanges had maintained with government agencies (all are licensed by the Ministry of Finance), bureaucrats, or members of the government itself.[58] That the securities, commodities, and stock exchanges are subjected to political pressure or manipulation should come as no surprise: The potential for economic gains have been enormous giving private citizens, legislators, and government officials alike considerable opportunities to amass wealth with few consequences for their actions.

Responsibility for most of the rules of operation of the various exchanges belongs to the **Federal Securities Market Commission** (roughly comparable to the United States' Securities and Exchange Commission). This commission consists of six members who can call upon the expertise of both an advisory council and an expert council in making decisions.[59] Like the market itself, the commission's authority was initially uncertain and in need of clarification by presidential involvement. Hence, in October 1996 Yeltsin issued a decree aimed at shaping a securities market. As the decree succinctly stated it, "the government fulfills the system-forming function which will constantly change in accordance with the tasks of ensuring national interests, with which it is confronted."[60]

The Individual and the Economy

Just as important as the macrolevel changes to the Russian economy have been the impacts experienced by the average citizen. To say the least the Russian citizen has borne the brunt of the changes in the economy especially in seeing his or her standard of living decline at a near calamitous rate. Inflation ran at breakneck speed throughout much of the early transition period and the ruble's value and earning power were slashed. Rising unemployment also provided an ominous sign that the market economy had truly arrived. Moreover, protection against the harsh realities of old age and ill health such as pensions and free medical care had largely disintegrated making life even more difficult for an already beleaguered population. In fact, the standard of living had deteriorated such that by 1998 the UN's Annual Human Development Report index (see Chapter One) placed Russia a dismal seventy-first of 174 countries surveyed.[61]

The four factors of inflation, ruble valuation, unemployment, and pensions— provide the most visible aspects of the economy's impact on the individual. The first of these, inflation, poses a constant struggle for any government. It also has the single greatest impact on the citizen as it applies to everybody and not just those who may be laid off or retired. Unaccustomed to inflation after decades of price controls and income supports, the Russian population was not prepared for what came in the first year of the post-Soviet era. In 1992 while government officials were forecasting that under good conditions inflation could be held to five percent per month, or sixty percent for the year,[62] the consumer price index (CPI) instead skyrocketed to 2539 percent for the year![63] Wages were growing at phenomenal rates as well, but this growth could not keep pace with the constant price hikes and consequently individuals' savings evaporated. The painful alterations were far from over: in the first quarter of 1994 the CPI averaged 140 percent;[64] and for the first half of 1995 the CPI averaged 179 percent![65]

Remarkably, with all of these obstacles before it the government's adherence to a tight monetary policy (required to assure the country of International Monetary Fund loans) was showing signs of working and inflation seemed at last manageable. In the first six months of 1996 it registered forty-eight percent, and in August it fell to zero.[66] The inflation rate for 1997 was trimmed back substantially to fourteen percent overall, and has consistently hovered since then around eighteen percent annually. Even though the government issued a 500,000 ruble note in February 1997,[67] confidence that the war against inflation had been won prompted the Yeltsin administration to announce it would eliminate three ze-roes from all ruble notes.[68]

For much of the Russian Federation's early existence currency stability proved elusive. As the centrally planned system collapsed the state was forced to float the ruble on international currency markets. Thereafter the ruble tumbled, sometimes precipitously (in one two-week period in 1994 it fell from approxi-mately 2896 to the dollar to slightly less than 4000 before the TsB stepped in to buy rubles and halt its slide). While economists saw devaluation as necessary, av-erage citizens saw their standard of living mercilessly kicked around. The ruble's continuing decline over the next three years also led to the disappearance from circulation of coins. What, after all, was the point of a kopeck (100 made up a sin-gle ruble) which was worth only .000167 dollars (July 1997 exchange rate of 6001 to the dollar)? Here, too, though, a turnaround was in the making. On 1 June 1996 the government announced the ruble would be a fully convertible curren-cy to be traded on the world market (the French franc, German mark, and American dollar were all being traded on the Moscow Interbank Currency Ex-change by December 1994).[69] And as already mentioned the government decid-ed that as of January 1998 it would eliminate three zeroes from all ruble notes and set the exchange rate at six rubles to one dollar. This time the government introduced the reform with plenty of advance warning so as to prevent panic (the kopeck was allowed to make a comeback as well).[70]

And yet, as the economy was poised to finally stage a recovery in 1998 the global economic downturn hit. The August 1998 crisis demonstrates the overall pressure facing a transitional economy, in particular one of Russia's size and complexity. General economic conditions had been favorable throughout much of 1998 with growth occurring in the trade, service, and construction sectors and a potential for total output growth by the end of that year.[71] Less visible but equally significant problems were surfacing, however, including the impact of Asia's economic depression upon the Russian stock market. Despite government denials of a pending devaluation,[72] the fixed ruble exchange rate was again sus-pended. In the next two months the ruble's value plummeted from six to the dollar to sixteen with obvious negative consequences for all classes but particu-larly the lower and middle classes.

The most personal factor of the transition has been that of unemployment. As Table 8.1 demonstrates, unemployment became a chronic problem through-out much of the 1990s even as the Gross Domestic Product (GDP) evidenced a dramatic comeback from its postindependence malaise. Even so, as the Russian Ministry for Labor and Social Development has acknowledged, real unemploy-ment is frequently several times greater than registered unemployment leaving millions of workers without economic protection of any sort.[73] In both the Soviet period and in today's Russia many workers are *under*-employed in that their skills are not being fully used, or their employers have temporarily furloughed them due to a lack of orders. As the reform process has developed the small business sector (firms employing up to 200 workers) has taken up some of the slack in the labor market. In 1996 fourteen million individuals were estimated to be em-ployed in nearly 900,000 small businesses, primarily in the trading and service

TABLE 8.1   Unemployment and Gross Domestic Product in the Russian Economy, 1992–2001 (in Percentages)

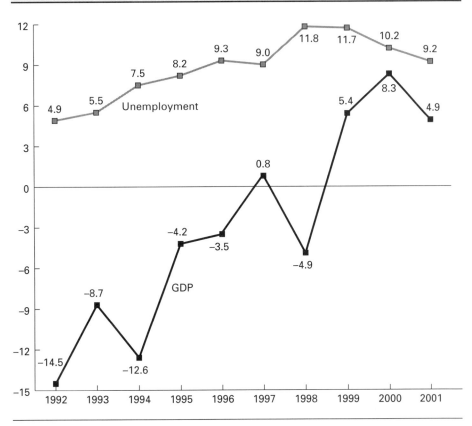

As of 1st quarter, 2001

Source: "Russian Economy, The Month in Review" 6 (2001), Bank of Finland Institute for Economies in Transition

sectors of the economy;[74] five years later the number of small businesses had fallen but even more people were involved in their operations.[75] Some assistance has been directed toward this sector through the **State Committee for Support and Development of Small Businesses,** but hostility toward small businesses remains strong within the State Duma and numerous obstacles to reforming this sector have blunted its potential for now.

Finally, there are the explosive issues of wages and pensions. The tendency of the government and enterprises to delay wages or not pay workers for months on end reached epidemic proportions by the middle of the 1990s. Trillions of rubles were owed to workers in key sectors of the economy such as education, mining, and defense, a situation that eventually government officials themselves recognized as "close to disastrous,"[76] and prompted nearly three-quarters of a million workers to strike in the first five months of 1997 alone.[77]

The TsB estimated in mid-1998 that one-third of budget expenditures were devoted to debt servicing,[78] thereby giving impetus to the strategy of paying debts owed to those who posed the greatest threat to social instability. The military in particular represents a potential flashpoint as most soldiers and officers go for months at a time with no pay. Illustrating the gap in expectations was the Defense Ministry's 1996 request for approximately 260 trillion rubles while the government promised 101 trillion rubles,[79] and actually spent only 83 trillion. The problem reached its peak in 1998 when, by the Russian government's measurements, total wage arrears accounted for two percent of GDP; between then and 2000 as the ruble continued to devalue and state revenues recovered, the government succeeded in cutting this figure to approximately 0.4 percent, thereby alleviating tremendous pressures.[80]

The plight of Russia's pensioners is certainly more tragic than that of workers or the military. The deterioration of the living standards of senior citizens and the disabled has had a great deal to do with the unprecedented decline in life span of the average citizen (as already discussed in Chapter 2). In 1994 nearly thirty million people were living below the poverty level;[81] at the end of the following year the figure was thirty-seven million,[82] and twenty percent of all pensioners found themselves in this condition. Even still the worst had not yet come as by September 1998 forty-four million people were poverty-stricken.[83] These conditions have been recognized by virtually all major political actors as needing immediate attention, especially given pensioners' support for the KPRF in State Duma elections. In January 1995 Yeltsin signed a decree to compensate pensioners for inflationary conditions,[84] and the next year gained Duma approval to increase the minimum pension by ten percent to 69,575 rubles a month (or about fourteen dollars).[85] For his part, Putin followed Yeltsin's lead in 2001 by signing into law a hike in the *average* monthly pension to approximately thirty-five million dollars.[86] Well-intentioned though these actions may have been, pensions like wages, have often gone unpaid for years, and by 1997 cumulative pension arrears had reached 10.5 trillion rubles ($1.8 billion).[87] Russia's economic recovery between 1999–2001 did not significantly alleviate this debt burden even as oil and natural gas revenues put the government in the unique position of achieving a budgetary surplus. Whether the government moves to address this issue in the short term will depend on the political elites' perceptions that the economic stability corner has finally been turned and it's time to pay those who supported the effort with the greatest sacrifices.

Dilemmas of the New Path

Crime and the Economy

No brief or extensive description of an economy's nature and status may be taken without an accounting of the extent of illegal economic activities, or what is commonly referred to as the **shadow economy,** or the "black market." The shadow economy, as described by the Russian economist Svetlana Glinkina, refers to "the totality of economic activity not covered in official statistics and not included in the gross national product."[88] Estimates as to how much of GDP is made up by illegal activities vary widely, but the Russian government itself has claimed anywhere from twenty to fifty percent of the total,[89] for a value (in 1996) of nearly seventy trillion rubles.[90]

For the transitional economy there is an important distinction between criminal activities and illegal activities. The latter can be taken to mean areas of the economy not yet adequately addressed by governmental action, or not formally legalized. Many of the laws necessary for setting the parameters of the new economy have taken years to pass (the land code comes to mind), and as such there have been considerable opportunities for "illegal" activities. It is a misnomer, then, to automatically apply what is easily the most misused term concerning the Russian economy, that of *mafiosi* (which implies someone in organized crime), to everybody doing something that is technically extra-legal. Otherwise not just members of criminal gangs but also those who use loopholes in the law for personal economic gain are part of the mafia. And since the Russian government did not revise the Soviet-era civil and criminal codes until November 1994 and June 1996 respectively, considerable confusion prevailed over what was or was not criminal.

Crime always had a role to play in the Soviet system and it did not spring from nothingness to its present state; it was, however, a controlled phenomenon. With the lifting of the strict authoritarianism of that period, crime seeped into the lives of almost every level of Russian society. It would have been unthinkable during the Soviet era for contract murders to be carried out against high-ranking political figures, and yet this has become an occurrence not infrequent over the last decade.[91] Crime reporters, too, pursuing dangerous leads have often been targets of the very people they seek to expose.[92] One of the most visible, and notorious, examples of the reach of criminal gangs occurred in November 1998 when popular Duma deputy Galina Starovoitova was killed outside her St. Petersburg home. Moscow alone had over 100 explosions that police linked to crime in 1995.[93] By 1996 the Interior Ministry estimated there to be 5000 separate criminal gangs nationwide with a probable total of 32,000 members;[94] the following year these figures were drastically revised upwards to 9000 gangs with probably 100,000 participants.[95] The high incidence of rapes, murders, and general mayhem in the capital prompted Yeltsin to sign a decree in July 1996 putting thousands of Interior Ministry troops on the streets of the city and suspending certain constitutional protections for those suspected of crime. Whatever the actual statistics on crime, it is a danger that does not bode well for the development of democracy, or promoting business and tourism.

The explosion of economic crimes over the last several years has brought into sharper focus the issue of corruption. Like crime in general, corruption was a fact of life in the Soviet state despite the Communist Party's protests to the contrary. Under socialism, the key terms for understanding how to get things done were **blat** (influence or pull) and **nalevo** (literally, on the left, or, on the side); together these implied knowing how to get things done by circumventing the bureaucracy and the rules of the game. The lack of property ownership fueled this need to bribe officials who otherwise had no incentive to speed up the workings of the government or the economy. And as already noted in Chapter Three there were many high profile incidents of corruption within the governing elite especially during the Brezhnev years.

As one might expect the police are frequently accused of fostering a climate of corruption; with this in mind the MVD has launched numerous internal probes of illicit police activities such as 1995's "Clean Hands" campaign. Within two years the Interior Ministry was claiming that 21,000 officials had been fired for misconduct of one sort or another, but how much this has effected the climate of corruption is not certain. Faced with low wages, lack of resources, the inexperience of officers, and competition for the most qualified individuals from private security firms, the war against crime has been a conflict the authorities are hard-pressed to win.[96] And as a result, the citizen is that much less protected from the worst aspects of the economic transition.

Agriculture in Turmoil

Long the bane of Soviet-era policy makers the agricultural sector continues its problematic development. For example, the 1997 harvest measured over eighty-eight million metric tons, an increase of twenty percent over the previous year.[97] This figure plummeted in 1998 to only 51.5 million tons,[98] the second lowest harvest on record. At root are several questions: 1) what relationship would exist between old farms and new? 2) to what extent would land be privatized and would privatization involve ownership? and 3) will levels of agricultural production require the importation of grain to feed Russia? Only in relation to the last of these has there been any answer to perennially poor harvests which have to be compensated by imports of many agricultural products.

The issue of land ownership remains the most politically ticklish of all economic reform issues. At the end of the Soviet era the state remained overwhelmingly in charge of the means of production. Altering this character in the post-Soviet era has proven to be a very slow process despite enormous pressures to do so. The transfer of ownership was provided for in several presidential decrees and federal laws, albeit with conditions.[99] The debate was taken up anew in March 1996 when Yeltsin issued another decree allowing owners to sell their land, give it away, lease it, or mortgage it if this was for agricultural purposes.[100] Yeltsin took this a step further in 1997 with a more specific decree allowing certain local governments to sell land to citizens for construction or leasing.[101] Duma opponents responded by claiming that the president had infringed upon the legislature's constitutional prerogatives, since Article 36 of the constitution states that "the conditions and procedure for the use of land are defined on the basis of federal law." Even though the term "federal law" seems to imply the legislature's ability to make laws, presidential edicts have the force of law and so long as they do not contravene the constitution are considered legally binding (Article 90).

Farming Near St. Petersburg
Source: © TASS/Sovfoto

Property, and especially land ownership, have remained hot-button issues at the beginning of the twenty-first century with opposition to the sale of land generated by the KPRF, the Agrarian Party, and other leftist political forces. Even the concentration of political authority in the executive branch has not proven to be sufficient to overcome the combination of tradition, deeply ingrained rural prejudices against reform,[102] and political opposition which have time and again inhibited the free marketing of land. The position of the Agrarian Party in the Duma after December 1993 was grounded in rural support for collective agriculture and opposition to individual ownership.[103] With the Agrarians in the lead, the Duma in 1996 passed a long-stalled **Land Code** which rejected the ability to buy, sell, or mortgage farmland. As with the President's edict the Land Code provided for "lifelong inheritable possession," but land not used for farming purposes reverted to state control.[104] Initially the Federation Council rejected this bill, but unanimously passed a revised version in July 1997. The lack of provisions for the purchase and sale of land gave Yeltsin reason to veto the bill but the Duma now had the strength to override, an action taken in September 1997.

For all intents and purposes the debate remained deadlocked until Putin, feeling secure in his own term of office, put considerable influence behind its revision in 2001. Putin's commitment to the cause comes, most likely not from ideology, but rather from the desire to move Russia ahead economically. This technocratic approach might have fit comfortably within the Soviet-era re-forms of Mikhail Gorbachev, but not as a part of the Soviet system in general. As a direct result, in the most highly publicized battle regarding the ownership of land to date, in June and July 2001 the Duma tackled the revision of the Land Code, but only after the Russian Orthodox Patriarch Aleksii II had pub-licly called for restricting foreigners in the purchase of land,[105] the KPRF and Agrarian deputies had stormed out of the Duma in the middle of the debate, and the Land Code was modified to include only the sale of urban land. Agri-culture's problems will not be solved by this new version, but by the same token, agriculture's problems will most likely not derail Russia's transforma-tion into a market economy, only delay its arrival toward some version of this sought-after goal.

Theoretically the problems of the Russian agricultural sector specifically, and the economy in general can all be fixed, and whether or not this occurs at the same time isn't really important. For many the reforms appear to have stalled, resulting in, as one commentator has put it, "the destruction of the na-tion's human and industrial potential instead of the formation of a basis for eco-nomic revitalization and growth."[106] Others have argued that the reforms have been in place for too short of a period to be effectively evaluated, or that the Putin administration has given them new vitality. But the game of politics does not pay as much attention to long-term policy preferences as it does to the de-mands of the population. Should public support for reform decline markedly, conservative forces will certainly use this to their advantage and push for their re-versal. If the population can bear the strains placed upon them, then the reforms will have opportunities to prove their worth. Stronger systems than the Russian economy have been swept away by the rising tide of a disaffected people.

Key Terms

Ministry of State Property
command economy
shock therapy
shadow economy
Unified Energy Systems (EES)

Five Year Plan
privatization
Central Bank of Russia
nomenklatura capitalists
Gazprom

Questions for Consideration

1. Has privatization been successful in Russia in your opinion?

2. What steps in the economic reform process are still lacking?

3. Is the opposition to private ownership of land in Russia something to be overcome, or is it a cultural condition suited to Russia's development?

4. What effect have Russia's oligarchs had on the stability of Russian politics? Can the oligarchs be held responsible for the lack of legitimacy of the economic system?

5. Has the legacy of economic reform been damaged beyond repair due to the pain and suffering that the average citizen has encountered in the process?

Suggested Readings

Anders Aslund, *How Russia Became a Market Economy* (Washington, DC: The Brookings Institute, 1995).

Matthew Brzezinski, *Casino Moscow, A Tale of Greed and Adventure on Capitalism's Wildest Frontier* (New York: The Free Press, 2001).

Michael Ellman and Vladimir Kontorovich, eds., *The Destruction of the Soviet Economic System: An Insiders' History* (Armonk, NY: M. E. Sharpe, 1998).

Lynn D. Nelson and Irina Y. Kuzes, *Radical Reform in Yeltsin's Russia: Political, Economic, and Social Dimensions* (Armonk, NY: M. E. Sharpe, 1995).

Alec Nove, *An Economic History of the U.S.S.R.* (New York: Pelican Books, 1982).

Victor M. Sergeyev, *The Wild East: Crime and Lawlessness in Post-Communist Russia* (Armonk, NY: M. E. Sharpe, 1997).

Useful Websites

Bank of Finland
 http://www.bof.fi/bofit
Central Bank of Russia
 http://www.cbr.ru/eng
Centre for Economic and Financial Research
 http://www.cefir.org
Interfax
 http://www.interfax-news.com/
Interstate Statistical Committee of the Commonwealth of Independent States
 http://www.cisstat.com/
Russian Federation and the IMF
 http://www.imf.org/external/country/RUS/index.htm
United Nations Development Programme
 http://www.undp.org

Endnotes

1. A good, brief overview of differing approaches to the political-economic relations in Russia may be found in Vadim Radaev, "Russia's Economic System Through the Prism of Ideological Systems," reprinted in *Russian Social Science Review*, 37 (March–April 1996): pp. 3–16.
2. For a brief chronicle of how the plans evolved see Alec Nove, *An Economic History of the U.S.S.R.* (Harmondsworth, Middlesex, England: Penguin Books, 1969), pp. 142–148.
3. See Carl A. Linden, *Khrushchev and the Soviet Leadership, 1957–1964* (Baltimore, MD: Johns Hopkins University Press, 1966), Chapter 8.

4. For the structure of this body see Ed A. Hewett, *Reforming the Soviet Economy* (Washington, DC: Brookings Institution, 1988), pp. 337–338.
5. Nikolai Ryzhkov, *Guidelines for the Economic and Social Development of the USSR for 1986–1990 and for the Period Ending in 2000* (Moscow: Novosti Press Agency, 1986).
6. For instance, see Abel Aganbegyan, *The Economic Challenge of Perestroika* (Bloomington, IN: Indiana University Press, 1988), pp. 1–3.
7. As an example see Leonid Abalkin, *The Strategy of Economic Development in the USSR* (Moscow: Progress Publishers, 1987).
8. Leonid Morozov, *Government Regulation of the Private Sector in the USSR* (Moscow: Progress Publishers, 1989).
9. Abel Aganbegyan, *Inside Perestroika* (New York: Harper & Row, 1989), pp. 61–63.
10. See G. Semenov, "Establishing More Rational Relations Between Federal and Regional Budgets," reprinted in *Russian Social Science Review,* 36 (September–October 1995): pp. 3–21.
11. For instance, see an assessment of the 1997 totals in Interfax, 8 January 1998.
12. Roman Frydman, Andrzej Rapaczynski, John S. Earle, et. al., *The Privatization Process in Russia, Ukraine and the Baltic States* (Budapest: Central European University Press, 1993), p. 59.
13. Ludmila V. Oborotova and Alexander Y. Tsapin, *The Privatization Process in Russia: An Optimistic Color in the Picture of Reform* (Columbus, OH: Mershon Center, Ohio State University, 1993), p. 6.
14. Darrell Slider, "Privatization in Russia's Regions," *Post-Soviet Affairs,* 10 (1994): pp. 368–369.
15. Jim Leitzel, *Russian Economic Reform* (London: Routledge, 1995), p. 91.
16. Andrei Zagorski, "Strategic Dilemmas of Russian Reform Policies," Economic Developments in Cooperation Partner Countries, NATO Economic Colloqium [http://www.nato.int/].
17. Anders Aslund, *How Russia Became a Market Economy* (Washington, DC: Brookings Institution, 1995), p. 66.
18. Ibid, p. 252.
19. ITAR-TASS, 13 April 1995.
20. Interfax, 3 August 1996.
21. *Russian Business News,* 16 October 1995.
22. *Izvestiya,* 23 February 1996.
23. Interfax cited in *RFE/RL Daily Report,* 15 November 1994.
24. ITAR-TASS, 24 September 1995.
25. ITAR-TASS, 23 July 1998.
26. See, for instance, Lynn Nelson and Irina Kuzes, "Coordinating the Russian Privatization Program," *RFE/RL Research Report,* 3 (20 May 1994): p. 23.
27. Aslund, pp. 235–236.
28. Richard Rose, "The Russian Response to Privatization," *RFE/RL Research Report,* 2 (26 November 1993): p. 55.
29. Aslund, pp. 238–239; also *RFE/RL Newsline,* 24 January 1996.
30. ITAR-TASS, 22 July 1994.
31. For instance see Interfax, 30 March 1995; also *Pravda,* 4 May 1995, translated in FBIS-SOV, 10 May 1995, pp. 56–57.
32. ITAR-TASS, 30 March 1995, cited in FBIS-SOV, 30 March 1995, p. 37.
33. See "Information on Russian Federation Laws" (Chapter Six), Russian Defense Business Directory, United States Department of Commerce, Bureau of Export Administration, Washington, DC (1994).

34. See the categorizations of Russia's primary interest groups in Igor Khripunov and Mary M. Matthews, "Russia's Oil and Gas Interest Group and its Foreign Policy Agenda," *Problems of Post-Communism*, 43 (May–June 1996): pp. 38–48).

35. Stefan Hedlund, "Property Without Rights: Dimensions of Russian Privatisation," *Europe-Asia Studies*, 53 (2001), p. 232.

36. *Moscow News*, 14 March 1996.

37. See, for instance, *Rossiyskaya gazeta*, 16 August 1995, translated in FBIS-SOV, 28 August 1995, pp. 29–30.

38. *Sovetskaya Rossiya*, 13 July 1995, translated in FBIS-SOV, 28 July 1995, pp. 34–37.

39. For instance, see *Moscow News*, 9 February 1996, and *RFE/RL Newsline*, 6 February 1996.

40. ITAR-TASS cited in *OMRI Daily Digest*, 19 June 1996.

41. Interfax, 8 January 1998.

42. *RFE/RL Newsline*, 14 April 1997.

43. Interfax, 28 April 1997.

44. Interfax, 29 July 1997.

45. Paul R. Gregory, "Sketches of New Russians," *Problems of Post-Communism*, 43 (September–October 1996): p. 60.

46. Alec Nove, *An Economic History of the U.S.S.R.* (Harmondsworth, England: Penguin Books, 1972), p. 50.

47. I. D. Zlobin, ed. *Soviet Finance: Principles, Operation* (Moscow: Progress Publishers, 1975), pp. 237–238.

48. Paul R. Gregory and Robert C. Stuart, *Soviet Economic Structure and Performance*, 3rd ed. (New York: Harper & Row, 1986), pp. 191–192.

49. Gertrude E. Schroeder, "Anatomy of Gorbachev's Economic Reform", in eds. Ed A. Hewitt and Victor H. Winston, *Milestones in Glasnost and Perestroyka: The Economy* (Washington, DC: Brookings Institution, 1991), p. 213.

50. Ed W. Hewett with Clifford G. Gaddy, *Open for Business* (Washington, DC: Brookings Institution, 1992), p. 101.

51. Juliet Johnson, "Banking in Russia: Shadows of the Past," *Problems of Post-Communism*, 43 (May–June 1996): p. 50.

52. The Central Bank of Russia cited in "Russian and Baltic Economies, the Week in Review, no. 42" (16 October 1998), Bank of Finland, Institute for Economies in Transition (BOFIT).

53. Interfax, 16 August 1999.

54. "Russian and Baltic Economies, the Week in Review, no. 49" (4 December 1998).

55. ITAR-TASS cited in *RFE/RL Newsline*, 28 April 1998.

56. *Kommersant-Daily*, 23 July 1996, cited in *OMRI Daily Digest*, 23 July 1996.

57. Reuters, 17 August 1998.

58. Andrei Yakovlev, "Commodity Exchanges and the Russian Government," *RFE/RL Research Report*, 2 (12 November 1993): p. 25.

59. *St. Petersburg Times*, 14–21 July 1996.

60. Decree of the President of the Russian Federation, no. 1008, "On the Approval of the Concept for the Development of the Securities Market in the Russian Federation," *Privatisation in Russia*, 9 (October 1996), RIA-Novosti website [http://www.ria-novosti.com/ria/privat.html].

61. "Russian and Baltic Economies, the Week in Review," no. 30 (30 July 1999).

62. *Moskovskiye novosti*, 5 January 1992, translated in FBIS-SOV, 9 January 1992, p. 42.

63. *Rossiyskaya gazeta*, 23 January 1993, translated in FBIS-SOV, 26 January 1996, p. 31.

64. *Rossiyskaya gazeta*, 27 April 1994, translated in FBIS-SOV, 28 April 1994, p. 43.

65. *Rossiyskaya gazeta*, 14 July 1995, translated in FBIS-SOV, 17 July 1995, p. 54.

66. ITAR-TASS, 4 September 1996; also AFP, 3 September 1996, cited in *OMRI Daily Digest,* 3 September 1996.
67. Interfax-FIA, 28 February 1997.
68. Interfax, 4 August 1997.
69. *Izvestiya,* 15 December 1994, translated in FBIS-SOV, 15 December 1994, p. 26.
70. Interfax-FIA, 4 August 1997.
71. "Russia and the Baltic Economies, The Week in Review," no. 31 (31 July 1998).
72. See Yeltsin's comments, ITAR-TASS, cited in *RFE/RL Newsline,* 14 August, 1998.
73. In 1997, the Ministry reported that there were 2.5 million registered unemployed, but possibly as many as 6.8 million total unemployed. Interfax, 9 February 1997.
74. *Izvestiya,* 23 February, translated in FBIS-SOV, 23 February 1996, p. 42; also see ITAR-TASS, 6 June 1996.
75. Interfax-AFI, cited in *RFE/RL Newsline,* 17 April 2001.
76. Interfax, 30 November 1996.
77. *Izvestiya,* cited in *RFE/RL Newsline,* 5 June 1997.
78. ITAR-TASS cited in *RFE/RL Newsline,* 18 June 1998.
79. AFP, 23 August 1996, cited in *OMRI Daily Digest,* 26 August 1996.
80. "State Arrears Diminish", *Russian Economy, The Month in Review,* 1–2001, Bank of Finland Institute for Economies in Transition.
81. *Sovetskaya Rossiya,* 13 September 1994, translated in FBIS-SOV, 14 September 1994, p. 30.
82. Associated Press, 4 February 1996.
83. Central Statistical Office cited in "Russia and the Baltic Economies, The Week in Review," no. 44 (30 October 1998).
84. ITAR-TASS, 30 January 1995, cited in FBIS-SOV, 31 January 1995, p. 11.
85. ITAR-TASS cited in *OMRI Daily Digest,* 18 April 1996.
86. "Russian and Baltic Economies, The Week in Review," no. 16, (20 April 2001).
87. ITAR-TASS, 26 June 1997, cited in *RFE/RL Newsline,* 26 June 1997.
88. Svetlana Glinkina, "The Shadow Economy in Contemporary Russia," *Svobodnaia mysl,* 3 (1995); reprinted in *Russian Politics and Law,* 34 (March–April 1996): p. 46.
89. See Interfax, 29 November 1996; and RIA-Novosti, 8 February 2001, cited in *RFE/RL Newsline,* 9 February 2001.
90. Interfax, 26 March 1996.
91. For instance, the Deputy Minister of Internal Affairs in the Udmurt Republic, and his family, were slain in October 1994. See *RFE/RL Daily Digest,* 18 October 1994.
92. *OMRI Daily Digest,* 14 May 1996.
93. *OMRI Daily Digest,* 28 December 1995.
94. ITAR-TASS cited in *OMRI Daily Digest,* 22 May 1996.
95. *RFE/RL Newsline,* 16 June 1997.
96. See Penny Morvant, "Corruption Hampers War on Crime in Russia," *Transition,* 2 (8 March 1996): pp. 23–27.
97. dpa and ITAR-TASS cited in *RFE/RL Newsline,* 8 January 1998.
98. "Russian and Baltic Economies, The Week in Review," no. 46, (13 November 1998).
99. For a discussion of the early decrees see Stephen K. Wegren, "Farm Privatization in Nizhnii Novgorod: A Model for Russia?", *RFE/RL Research Report,* 3 (27 May 1994): pp. 17–18.
100. Interfax, 7 March 1996; see also *Moscow News,* 21 March 1996.
101. Decree of the President of the Russian Federation, no. 1263, "On Sale to Citizens and Legal Entities of Plots of Land Meant for Construction on Them and Situated

on the Territories of Urban and Rural Settlements, or of the Right to Lease Them," 26 November 1997, RIA-Novosti website [http://www.ria-novosti.com/products/dr/1997/11/28-001.htm].

102. Stephen K. Wegren, "State Withdrawal and the Impact of Marketization on Rural Russia," *Policy Studies Journal*, 28 (2000): pp. 57–61.
103. For instance, see ITAR-TASS, 17 October 1995.
104. *Moscow News*, 2 May 1996.
105. ITAR-TASS, 13 July 2001.
106. Iurii Sukhotin, "Stabilization of the Economy and Social Contrasts," reprinted in *Russian Social Science Review*, 36 (March–April 1995): p. 39.

Chapter 9

The Baltics: A Case Study of Latvia

F ive years into the Republic of Latvia's newfound independence the issue of sovereignty was still burning bright. On 22 August 1996 the Latvian parliament—or **Saeima**—approved a "Declaration of Russian Occupation" which attempted to assess the period of Soviet control from the standpoint of a conquered people, and called on the world community to recognize the economic consequences of this occupation.[1] For the Latvian parliament the effort to set straight the historical record about the Soviet era seemed more important than currying favor with their immensely powerful neighbor. Predictably, the Russian government labeled the legislation an "unfriendly act" and used it to portray the Latvian side as the real impediment to normalization of relations between the two countries (see the following chapter for a Georgian version of the same action).[2] Despite the seeming irrationality of taunting the proverbial 900-pound gorilla (or, to use the Russia analogy, a grizzly bear) it is relatively easy to view the Latvians' actions not so much in terms of provoking a powerful foe, but as part of a quest for reviving and revitalizing the national identity.

Despite these states' historic connections to Russia, their diminutive size, and the overwhelming preponderance of power that Russia exhibits in relation to them, the Baltic states cannot today be considered clients bound to the Russian patron. All three states have successfully asserted themselves as independent entities in their regional environment. The limits on the Baltic states' quests for secure independence have not been fully tested as of yet, and much of what has occurred since 1991 has involved a search to determine how solid or porous these nation-states' boundaries may be. By looking at Latvia, the state which seems to be the best example of all three's problems and prospects, we can get an idea of politics in the Baltic context.

Breaking Out of the Soviet/Russian Sphere

The Baltics in Profile

In many respects the Baltic states have more in common with other countries bordering on the Baltic Sea including Denmark, Finland, Poland, Sweden, and

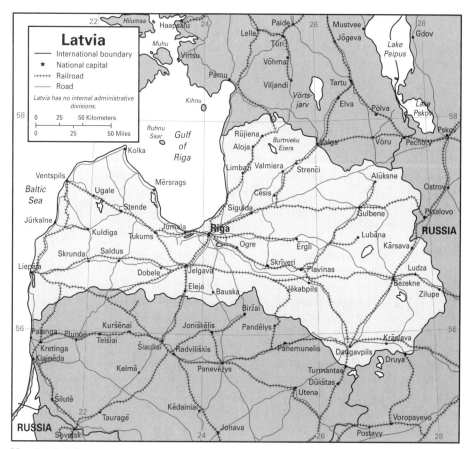

Map 9.1 Latvia

Germany than they do with Russia and the Eurasian states. Most notable is their size, both demographic and geographic. Latvia's *total* population of approximately 2.366 million people (2001)[3] is less than that of either Los Angeles or Chicago. In geophysical terms the total land area of Latvia is only four-tenths of a percent the size of the Russian Federation, and was an even smaller component of the Soviet Union. By themselves these figures make the Baltics' quests for independence, and their subsequent struggles to maintain their viability, that much more of an impressive challenge. And while these small nations reclaimed their independence after a four-year long campaign (1988–1991), the quest had actually been a condition of existence that smoldered throughout the long period of Soviet control. It can be argued that the quest began when the Red Army occupied them in June 1940.[4] It lasted throughout the terror of the Second World War, the forced deportations of the postwar period, and the prolonged resistance of partisan units hiding out in the forests (in Latvia some units conducted operations until their elimination by the KGB in 1957). As part of the Soviet pacification program as many as 119,000 Latvians were sent into exile in other parts of the Soviet Union and many more fled to safe havens in the West. To prevent the fading of these memories the 14th of June—the day when Soviet troops took control of the Baltic states—is officially designated "Commemoration Day" in all three Baltic states to honor those who fell victims to communist rule.[5]

Regionalism, too, is a feature of this small environment. Latvia, for instance, consists of the regions of Vidzeme in the north, Zemgale in the south, Kurzeme to the west, and in the east Latgale. Administratively the country is divided into twenty-six counties (formerly raions). Its capital of Riga is the largest city in the Baltic states with a population in 2000 of 764,328 people[6] (Tallinn, Estonia had 411,594 in 1998,[7] and Vilnius, Lithuania had 581,200 as of 1999[8]). State borders are stable but several disputes do exist, the most contentious of these being with Russia. Upon independence Latvia had laid claim to a 1,402 square kilometer area in the northeastern Abrene district, which the Soviet Union incorporated

Freedom Monument Riga, Latvia

Source: © M. Szepietowski/Sovfoto

into the Russian Federation in 1944 in violation of the 1920 Latvian-Soviet Russian Peace Treaty (the **"Riga Treaty"**).[9] All three Baltic states have expressed their willingness to renounce border claims against Russia as the Latvian government reluctantly did in October 1997.[10] This goodwill gesture has done little to alleviate Russian pressures upon Latvia, and the relationship between these states remains a tenuous one.

Independence has had the positive effect of facilitating the return of parts of the Baltic diasporas. As small nations the Baltic states have come to rely on the capital and skills of peoples of Baltic descent living abroad. To encourage ethnic Estonians, Latvians, or Lithuanians to come back to the Baltics these states' governments have included in their citizenship laws the **right of return.** Article two of the 1994 "Law on Citizenship of the Republic of Latvia" effectively embraces the entire Latvian diaspora by simply declaring as citizens those "persons who were citizens of Latvia on June 17, 1940 and their descendants who have registered according to the procedures established by law."[11] This policy's payoff can be partly measured by the high (eighteen) number of expatriate Latvians who were deputies to the Fifth (1993–1995) Saeima.[12] The most prominent example is that of **Vaira Vike-Freiberga,** a native Latvian who became a refugee following the Second World War and eventually went on to become a

Vaira Vike-Freiberga, President of Latvia since 1999

Source: © TASS/Sovfoto

distinguished academician in Canada. Within the space of a year of her return to Latvia she would be elected president of the country on 17 June 1999. As much as anything else this speaks to the strong sense of identity held by the peoples of the region.

Reasserting the "Baltic" Identity

Latvia, Estonia, and Lithuania largely draw their identities from their proximity to the Baltic Sea and their long (in the case of the Latvians and Estonians, five thousand years) association with it. None of these three are ethnically linked to one another, nor are any of them Slavic by definition. The Latvian (technically termed *Lettish*) and Lithuanian languages are part of the Baltic language group, which is unrelated to the primary Slavic languages of the region (Russian and Polish). Estonian is a **Finno-Ugric** language related to the larger Finnish and Hungarian language groups, but also to the obscure Livonian language, which in 1996 was spoken by only ten native speakers in Latvia.[13] Ethnic divisions especially lead to the conclusion that these are still fragmented political cultures which are on the way toward becoming dominant political cultures. These cultural distinctions may yet assist in the formation of collective state identities in the Baltics but to this point in Latvia national or ethnic divisions run deep and lead to the conclusion that Latvia is a fragmented political culture.

If by the term "Latvian" we mean all those people who reside inside the Latvian state, then classification is simple (see Table 9.1). However, when the term is more narrowly defined to mean only those of Latvian ethnicity, this group makes

TABLE 9.1   Ethnicity in the Baltic States

Estonia*	%	Latvia**	%	Lithuania***	%
Estonian	65.2	Latvian	57.6	Lithuanian	81.4
Russian	28.0	Russian	29.6	Russian	8.3
Ukrainian	2.5	Belarusian	4.1	Polish	7.0
Belarusian	1.4	Ukrainian	2.7	Belarusian	1.5
Finnish	0.9	Polish	2.5	Ukrainian	0.9
Tatar	0.22	Lithuanian	1.4	Jewish	0.4
Latvian	0.18	Jewish	.4	Others	0.1
Jewish	0.16	Gypsy	.3		
Polish	0.16	German	.15		
Lithuanian	0.15	Estonian	.12		
German	0.08	Libietis	.01		
Others	0.82				

Sources: *Data for 1999, Statistical Office of Estonia, home page [http://www.stat.ee/wwwstat/content/].
     **Data for 2000, Central Statistical Bureau home page [http://www.csb.lv/Satr/atsk2.htm].
     ***Data for 1999, Statistics Department of the Government of Lithuania home page [http://www.std.lt/].

up fifty-seven percent of the total population.[14] Among the Baltic states Latvia has the smallest titular nationality in relation to its entire population (ethnic Estonians make up sixty-one percent of Estonia's peoples, while Lithuanians represent eighty-one percent in their system). The remainder of Latvia's population is a polyglot collection consisting of Slavic peoples and in particular Russians who comprise slightly less than thirty percent of the national total (in fact, a contested figure). Fragmented ethnic identity is therefore typical in the Baltic states and is also the root of many of Latvia's (and Estonia's) problems in its efforts to build an independent state and a civic culture.

In cultural terms, too, the Baltic peoples are distinct from their Slavic neighbors. Influenced as they were over the centuries by the political domination of the Poles, Lithuanians, Swedes, and Germans, the Baltic peoples' cultural orientation became decidedly western in emphasis. For instance, the religions of the region, which often serve as cultural compasses, largely point these societies toward the West. As mentioned in Chapter Two the majority of the ethnic Estonian religious faithful are Evangelical Lutheran while the Lithuanians are overwhelmingly Roman Catholic. The Latvian population represents something of a religious fault line within the Baltic region as the majority of ethnic Latvians profess Lutheranism with a substantial minority of Roman Catholics who primarily reside in the Latgale region. The ethnic Russian population most often associates itself with Russian Orthodoxy, and there is even a religion unique to the Latvian people, **Dievturu.** In reaction to the repression of religious beliefs of the Soviet period Latvia adopted a law in 1995 governing the practice and organization of religions which even permits religious instruction in public schools.[15]

The most significant social statistics for the Baltic states are those of population growth and life expectancy. Population figures for Latvia declined by 5.6 percent between 1993 and 1998.[16] As one source so colloquially put it, "in 1996 some 538 babies were born per every 1000 persons who went on to the better world."[17] For Estonia the problem is even worse as its overall population fell by 12,200 in 1996 leaving the country with 1,464,100 people. The demographic situation has political implications as well reflecting shifts in the internal ethnic balance between Latvians and Russians. Ethnic Latvians do not represent a majority in any of the country's seven largest cities. Approximately forty-three percent of the population of Riga is, in fact, ethnically Russian, while in Daugavpils—Latvia's second largest city and close to the Russian border—the figure is officially reported to be 55.8 percent, almost definitely an underestimation.

Life expectancy in the Baltic states is also higher than in Russia; the average citizen/resident of Latvia now lives to be 69.65 years of age; in Estonia the figure is slightly higher at 70.17; and in Lithuania it is 71.37. A gap of roughly ten years exists between Baltic men and women with men suffering much earlier deaths, most often due to stress, alcoholism, and poor health care. Children have been affected, too: in 1998 one source estimated that seventy percent of all Latvian adolescents suffered from malnutrition or poor diets.[18] In general, quality of life indices remain below the norms for northern and western Europe.

The Struggle for Independence

The Gorbachev reforms and the general tumult of that period led to what came to be known as the **singing revolutions,** that is, protests begun through cultural festivals where nationalist songs gave vent to long-repressed sentiments especially the desire for political independence.[19] Popular Front movements in support of reforms were created in all three republics in 1988.[20] While the formation of the **Latvian People's Front** was organized after those of Lithuania and Estonia (most likely due to the size of Latvia's Russian minority[21]), by the end of 1988 it had become the principal organization in Latvia agitating for independence.[22] As the forces of change gained momentum Soviet authorities succumbed to the use of force when in January 1991 four people were killed in Riga by Soviet OMON troops, as were another eleven in Vilnius. This tragedy only served to fuel the determination of citizens of all ethnic backgrounds in the Latvian Republic to recreate the independent Latvian state.

By March 1991 Gorbachev and his advisors had effectively given up on the prospects for keeping the Baltic states within the Soviet Union. The subsequent "Nine plus One" formula for a new union treaty reflected the expectation among republican leaders that a rump Soviet federal state was all that could be expected. The August coup—just a day before the treaty's signing—was primarily a response by reactionary forces in the Soviet leadership to these demands for independence. The outcome of the coup provided the Baltics with the opportunity to seize the moment. Within days Yeltsin had pressured Gorbachev to allow the independence of all three republics.[23] On 6 September 1991 following recognition of Baltic independence by dozens of foreign nations, the Soviet leadership in the form of a briefly lived State Council acceded to the long-held demands.[24] Fifty-one years of emotional and traumatic Soviet rule had at last come to an end, and all that remained was the removal of Russian troops. From this point on the process of state-building had to take priority.

Citizenship as a Political Tool

The place of ethnic Russians in society is certainly the most sensitive issue facing Latvia today. As we have seen in other states, the tools most often used by the government for carrying out the policy of reestablishing national identity have been those of language laws, alien or residency laws, and the constitutions themselves. While Russian government accusations of "apartheid,"[25] and a **velvet deportation**[26] (that is, creating a climate where ethnic Russians leave these countries without actually being forced to do so) are difficult to prove.[27] Many ethnic Russians felt uncomfortable enough that 20,029 left in 1993 and another 16,874 in 1994.[28] Russian residents of the Baltic states are not entirely disenfranchised, however, and ethnic Russian deputies have been elected in each of the Baltic parliaments. But ethnic Russians have found it difficult to acquire citizenship; in Latvia by the end of 1996 only 1.29 million of the country's people were citizens, or roughly fifty-two percent.[29] Of the remainder most resident, noncitizens do not vote, hold jobs as civil servants, policemen, firemen, or make decisions about policy. Under the law they are considered "stateless persons" and issued special noncitizen passports which also serve as means of identification for Latvian authorities.[30] The extent of this problem was made apparent by a demonstration for higher living standards in March 1998 by ethnic Russians in Riga which was broken up by Latvian police wielding batons. This lead to an exchange of diplomatic accusations by the Russian and Latvian governments over the rights of ethnic Russians living in Latvia,[31] and eventually a reform by the Latvian parliament of the long-delayed citizenship law. The overall resolution of this issue, however, has only been postponed, not resolved.

The greatest obstacle to attaining full citizenship is that of language. All three Baltic states have incorporated language provisions in their citizenship requirements. Latvia's citizenship laws tend to be more accommodating than those of either of the other Baltic states. For instance, in Latvia's "Law on the Rights and Obligations of a Citizen and a Person" language is only mentioned in the context of guaranteeing "the right to establish educational institutions of various levels with any language of instruction;"[32] for that matter Latvian is the exclusive language of instruction only at the university level. Latvia's **Law on Citizenship** provides the vague condition that citizenship will be granted to those "who have a command of the Latvian language,"[33] while the language law requires sufficient proficiency for state employees to do their jobs. The testing of this knowledge is quite rigorous with candidates being required "to communicate on everyday topics" in the Latvian language.[34] This assertiveness of the Baltics' languages is at the same time both a rational and an emotional response to the long pattern of russification of the Baltic cultures. However, the Baltics' goals of joining European structures (the European Union, NATO) and continuing pressures from Russia require societal integration, not preclusion of the Russian populations. Toward this end in May 2002 the Saeima voted to amend the Election Law by removing the stipulation that candidates for the parliament needed to have fluency in the Latvian language, a move applauded throughout Europe.

But another condition also prevails, that is, Russian residents' failures to learn the local languages even after decades amongst the Baltic populations, and very favorable government assistance to learn the language. Now that the Russians are no longer in positions of power many claim they are being singled out and oppressed, even though human rights reports indicate that biased laws have not been effectively enforced,[35] and that in general the human rights climate has improved in the Baltic states.[36] Regardless of who is right concerning the language debate, language requirements affect who is to have access to certain jobs or housing. Land ownership, too, is restricted to citizens of the state for the purpose of preventing foreigners from buying up, and controlling, property. Such provisions preclude noncitizens, especially retired Soviet military officers, from permanently establishing themselves in the country. Overall, such laws foster a climate of distrust and suspicion about, as well as among, Russians.

The Parliamentary Model

Constitutionalism and the Rule of Law

Of all the former Soviet republics only a few had the option, and only Latvia made the choice, to reactivate its pre-Soviet (1922) constitution (Georgia's 1995 constitution refers to its 1921 version). The constitution (**Satversme** in Latvian) was readopted on 6 July 1993; in its original form it was almost exclusively concerned with the institutions and procedures of government. Civil rights and liberties were only briefly mentioned and these in the context of voting (articles 78–80), and protection before courts of law (articles 82, 85, and 86). The political repressions of the Soviet period required more than this, though, and in 1991 the parliament passed the aforementioned "Law on the Rights and Obligations of a Citizen and a Person."[37] The law's forty-four articles were superceded when parliament ratified a series of amendments to the constitution in October 1998. The twenty-eight articles in this section (Chapter VIII, "Fundamental Human Rights") combine civil liberties and economic guarantees (i.e., the right to freely choose form and location of employment, article 106). As an indication of the difficulties inherent in this issue article 114 only briefly addresses minority rights in stating that ethnic groups have "the right to preserve and develop their language and their ethnic and cultural identity." In the context of the government's ongoing struggle to preserve the Latvian identity and language, adequately protecting minority rights is one of the state's greatest challenges.

The constitution is remarkable for its brevity, its focus on creating a form of government where the legislature dominates, and in clearly limiting how government performs its tasks. The constitution was revived to strengthen the claim of post-Soviet Latvia to its previous experience as an independent state with a distinctive indigenous culture. This also involved a conscious effort to link Latvia to western Europe while divorcing it from the Russian experience. Even still, written guarantees about what democracy should be have their limitations and did not prevent the interwar Latvian regime from degenerating into authoritarianism with the assertion of power by former prime minister **Karlis Ulmanis** in 1934 (the great-uncle of modern day president **Guntis Ulmanis**). Nor was Latvia alone in losing sight of its ideals: Lithuania became a dictatorship in 1926 and Estonia followed suit in 1934, both prior to their absorption by the Soviet Union.

A key feature of the new Latvian system are its efforts to establish governmental accountability. The repressions of the Nazi and Soviet periods from 1940 until 1991 made the issue of holding governing officials accountable crucial for the survival of the Baltic states. During these trying years with so much of the population lost to deportations, external exile, or executions, the public came to long for guarantees that such repressions would not happen again. Accountability has since been addressed through regular national and local elections, a presidency answerable to the parliament, and a relatively easy mechanism for recalling the government.

Pluralism and the Multiparty System

Latvia and its political elites have opted for creating a pluralist—some would say hyperpluralist—system, particularly one that is measured in terms of political parties and parliamentary involvement. With over forty parties, movements, or other political organizations all vying for power the Latvian system presents much the same sort of confusion to voters as that of both the Russian and Ukrainian cases; still, this does not automatically lead to the conclusion that the system is unstable. For instance, the fall of a government through a vote of no-confidence, or the resignation of key ministers due to scandal sometimes allows a governing process to prove itself under pressure, or to revitalize itself. In parliamentary systems coalition and minority governments are normal conditions and elections provide the citizen with the chance to reshuffle the players without sacrificing the value of diversity. If the large number of political parties is any indication, diversity seems to be something Baltic electorates are not willing to surrender.

While government stability has been fleeting in Latvia (measured here by the number of prime ministers who have held office since 1991) elite change has been no greater than in Estonia, Lithuania, or for that matter, Ukraine (see Chapter Ten). Between 1991 and 2001 seven individuals served as prime minister of Latvia: **Ivars Godmanis** (1990–1993), **Valdis Birkavs** (1993–1994), **Maris Gailis** (1994–1995), **Andris Skele** (1995–1997; 1999–2000), **Guntar Krasts** (1997–1998), **Vilis Kristopans** (1998–1999), and **Andris Berzins** (2000–). Four of these—Godmanis, Birkavs, Skele, and Kristopans—gained their positions by means of elections, while Gailis, Krasts, and Berzins came to the office as a result of the previous governing coalition breaking down.[38] Skele initially resigned his position in January 1997 due to an inquiry concerning the abilities of one of his ministers, but was reappointed by the president as the best choice acceptable to the Saeima.[39] He again stepped down in July of that year when a law prohibiting officials from holding nongovernmental jobs called into question the integrity of several more of his ministers.[40] He returned to the prime minister's office in 1999, this time as the leader of the **People's Party** in conjunction with a three-party coalition after the previous government had failed.[41] As much as anything else these shifts in Latvian politics reflect both the flexibility of the process as well as the weaknesses inherent in the system.

The prime minister's ability to act is affected by the large number of political parties represented in the parliament: in the Sixth Saeima elected in 1995, nine parties and a number of independent deputies divided the 100 seats amongst themselves with the largest of these—the **Democratic Party "Saimnieks"** ("Master" in Latvian; hereafter DPS) receiving only eighteen.[42] In the Seventh Saeima the number of parties was reduced to six but the most successful of these—the People's Party—still gained only 21.19 percent of the votes for a total of twenty-four seats.[43] As with the previous government the new cabinet was wholly reliant upon coalition partners although not as many as in the preceding government.

Close to half of all parties/movements appearing on the 1993 ballot were by 1998 either no longer in existence, had joined together with other parties, or transformed themselves to better match policy issues (see Table 9.2). Voters had twenty-three parties, blocs, or movements to choose from in 1993, nineteen in 1995, and twenty-one in 1998. As in the other Baltic states, Russia, and Ukraine, virtually every shade of politics has found a place on the Latvian ballot. In the last several years this was largely the result of parties only needing 200 members to be officially registered, but in 1999 the Saeima increased this figure to 1000.[44] As of yet there is no definite correlation between large membership and electoral success, as was shown by the decline of the **National Independence Movement of Latvia/Latvian National Conservative Movement,** or LNNK (see below) in the 1995 elections, and the DPS in 1998. The enthusiasm surrounding a new party's formation, such as with the National Progress Party's creation in early 1997 with 300 members,[45] or the Peoples' Party which was founded in mid-1998 with around 1200 members,[46] is always a hopeful moment but unless this can be translated into votes its significance is minor. Reformist, nationalist, regionalist, and other groupings are all options available to the Latvian voter. None of this guarantees that either the parliament or the government will be balanced once formed.

Those parties which have achieved representation in the Saeima usually have strong ideological identification, if not great staying power. The DPS, for instance, a left-of-center, moderately progressive party concerned with social welfare issues was, for a brief period after the 1995 election, the most successful party of its kind. The DPS's decision in early 1998 to leave the government for what seemed political rather than principled reasons may have triggered a voter backlash against it. In the elections that fall the DPS polled a mere 1.61 percent of the vote as its followers abandoned it for more decidedly leftist parties. The DPS's political fate indicates that it was not the left that was discredited but rather the actions of political leaders.

Since its founding in 1993, **Latvia's Way** has been the country's principal centrist party and the only party to consistently be a member of the government. Its political goals are basically those of support for free-market economics with rapid integration into the world economy. Party leaders have focused little on the needs of workers, and are thus sometimes categorized not as centrist, but conservative. The 1993 elections saw this party gain thirty-six seats in the Saeima and form a solid working coalition with the **Farmer's Union,** which had won twelve seats. In a minority government of this sort the leading party has to promise to support the interests of coalition partners as Latvia's Way did in 1993 when it agreed to back Ulmanis, the Farmer's Union's candidate for president. Again in both 1998 and 1999 Latvia's Way entered into coalitions with its electoral opponents. These events demonstrate that consensus in Latvian politics is fleeting and governments are frequently under stress due to the internal contradictions of these governing coalitions.

In the first years of Latvia's renewed independence the political right has experienced only modest successes. The LNNK, which placed second in the 1993 elections, fared poorly in the 1995 elections and was forced to merge two years later with the conservative/nationalist **For Fatherland and Freedom** party.[47] This

TABLE 9.2 Political Party Representation and Change in the Latvian Parliament, 1993–1998

Party	Seats in 1993	Party	Seats in 1995	Party	Seats in 1998
Latvia's Way	36	Democratic Party Saimnieks	18	People's Party	24
National Independence Movement	15	Latvia's Way	17	Latvia's Way	21
Concord for Latvia—Rebirth of the Economy	13	People's Movement for Latvia (Siegerist Party)	16	For Fatherland and Freedom/LNNK	17
Farmer's Union	12	Union for Fatherland and Freedom	14	Popular Concord Party	16
Equal Rights	7	Latvian Unity Party	8	Latvian Social Democratic Alliance	14
For Fatherland and Freedom	6	United List: Latvian Farmer's Union, Christian Democrat Union, Latgale Democratic Party	8	New Party	8
Christian Democratic Union	6	Latvian National Conservative Party/Latvian Green Party	8		
Democratic Center Party	5	Popular Concord Party	6		
		Latvian Socialist Party	5		

Source: Saeima Home Page [http://www.saeima.lanet.lv/]

resulted in 1998 in this bloc placing third in the elections for a total of seventeen seats. Its position has been challenged since the creation in 1998 of Skele's People's Party, a free-market oriented party representing moderately conservative values prevalent in Latvian society. While much of this party's strength is found in Skele's personality, it seems equally likely that it will not be a personalistic party on the order of Russia's LDPR.

Parties representing the ethnic Russian community can expect only limited electoral success without a broad-based appeal. As an example, the **Party of Russian Citizens of Latvia** gained only slightly more than one percent of the total votes in 1995 and subsequently exercised almost no influence. Two other left-oriented coalitions have given some voice to the ethnic Russian community. The first of these, the Popular Concord Party (TSP), merged with the **Latvian Socialist Party** (LPS), the principal successor to the banned Latvian Communist Party). Together they scored 11.2 percent of the vote in 1995 and 14.6 percent three years later. Less attached to the communist past the **Latvian Social Democratic Workers' Party** (LSDSP) has also done well (12.8 percent of the vote in 1998) by staking out social democratic positions. All-in-all, while it is difficult to determine the extent to which the ethnic Russian community is attracted to these parties, it is apparent that they have rejected the political right and assisted in the reemergence of the left.

As hypothesized in Chapter Four, for the political system to be legitimately pluralist there must be available a free and competitive means of disseminating information. No other part of the former Soviet Union has embraced this concept as readily as the Baltic states where leaders and citizens alike have realized that independence is heavily contingent upon international attention. Due to their physical proximity to western Europe during the Soviet period the Baltic states experienced a greater flow of information than any other part of the USSR. In the first few years of independence many Baltic media outlets were quickly privatized, although news services more slowly. Parallel to Interfax's creation in Russia, an independent news agency, the **Baltic News Service** (BNS), was formed in Estonia in 1990. Today BNS is a multi-media communications enterprise with branches in the other two Baltic states providing thorough coverage of regional events,[48] which it does in conjunction with the state-owned **Estonian Telegraph Agency** (ETA).[49]

Latvia also maintains its own media sources including the state-owned **Latvian Telegraph Agency** (LETA), which reports primarily on domestic events. The existence of so many news producers points to redundant efforts by small states which don't want to rely on foreign sources of information. Still, along with the **Lithuanian Telegraph Agency** (ELTA, a privately-held company) LETA gives the public different perspectives on the news in marked contrast to the monopolization of information maintained under the Soviet system. If the Baltic information markets can sustain these numerous media sources their existence will certainly be justified by the knowledge they provide.

The Saeima: The Source of Authority

Latvia's political culture and its national elections have produced governments which are essentially moderate, whether center-right or center-left. The public has not been inclined toward extremist politics, but the fourteen percent of the vote won in the 1995 elections by the right-wing, nationalist **Popular Movement for Latvia** (or Siegerist Party, named for its founder and Latvian expatriate **Joachim Siegerist**) did register public dissatisfaction with the norm of politics.[50] The political moderation of the government may be viewed as a reaction against the hyperpluralist tendencies of Latvia's parties. For instance, in both the 1995 and 1998 postelection periods Saeima factions labored to find workable combinations of parties.[51] Deals were cut and coalitions built and then abandoned in the face of ever-changing political realities. What emerged in both cases was a consensus not to lean too far toward either extreme for fear of upsetting precarious arrangements.

In parliament-dominant systems such as those found in Latvia and Estonia, governmental responsiveness is achieved through two means: the electoral process itself and parliament's ability to vote no-confidence in the government. In the first case, all deputies to the Saeima are chosen based on proportional representation: no candidates are chosen through single-member mandates. All three Baltic parliaments are unicameral institutions with the Saeima having one hundred deputies and Estonia's **Riigikogu** 101. The Lithuanian **Seimas** is different in that of its 141 deputies seventy-one are elected from single-mandate districts and seventy on the basis of proportionality. In Latvia the citizen votes only for one party, although voters may indicate on their ballots the specific candidates from the party list that they favor or reject. Regular elections and referenda have guaranteed the voters a voice in approving governmental policy. In the three sets of national elections held in Latvia since independence (the Saeima was elected to three-year terms until the 1998 elections; terms are now four years) participation has been remarkably high with a 71.9 percent turnout in 1995 and 72.67 percent in 1998, but down from the more euphoric figure of 89.9 percent in 1993.[52]

The Saeima's internal operations and organization are the responsibility of the parliament itself. Bills are given as many as three "readings" to be either approved or rejected. A bill is considered adopted if it musters a simple majority vote of the total number of parliamentary deputies (article 24). Constitutional amendments are more stringently arrived at: two-thirds of the total number of deputies must be present during consideration with two-thirds of this number approving the changes (article 76). The president then signs the bill (article 70), but should he choose to send it back to the parliament for further action, the Saeima has the option to disregard the president's requests (article 71). This is truly legislative assertiveness!

Membership in the Saeima is not remarkable for its diversity. Gender is the most obvious distinction with women holding seventeen seats in the Seventh (1998–) Saeima, up from eight in the Sixth (1995–1998) Saeima. Two women— **Ilga Kreituse** in the Sixth Saeima,[53] and **Kristiana Libane** in the Seventh Saeima,[54] have been included in that body's leadership. Prior to the election of President Vaira Vike-Freiberga two other women—both from Lithuania—have been included in leadership positions: Kazimiera Prunskiene, now the leader of Lithuania's Women's Party, and Irena Degutiene, Lithuanian Social Security

Minister, both of whom served in the prime minister's role (Degutiene was an interim acting prime minister). In general, women have not been noticeably more involved than in other democratic systems. Ethnic Russians, too, are under-represented. In the Seventh Saeima only about a dozen deputies were Russians, virtually all from the left-wing Popular Concord Party. This low representation is symptomatic of the disenfranchisement of ethnic Russians in Latvia and will re-main a problem until citizenship rights are broadened.

Organizing the government is the single-most important activity of either a new or sitting parliament. The formation of the cabinet is governed by the 1993 Law on the Cabinet of Ministers. Members of the cabinet are drawn from the ma-jority party, from coalition member-parties, or from nongovernmental sources acceptable to coalition members. The government is divided into several levels of authority. First, there are the government ministers, or those responsible for overarching policy issues and their respective bureaucracies. Typically there are between thirteen and fifteen senior cabinet ministers including two special tasks ministers who deal with particular issues of domestic or foreign policy. Second, there are the state ministers, whose areas of authority lie within certain bureau-cracies (such as the State Minister for the Environment of the Agriculture Min-istry, or the State Minister for Health within the Welfare Ministry). These latter positions are roughly comparable to the junior ministers of the British political system in that second tier cabinet ministers may vote in cabinet meetings only on those issues that are directly relevant to their areas of concern.

Unlike the Russian system where governmental powers originate under con-stitutional authority the Latvian government's powers are supplemented by the Saeima in order for it to carry out its functions. The cabinet draws up a docu-ment indicating the direction it wishes policy to take.[55] This can be an almost strenuously detailed accounting of the policy to be followed, but a useful tool in forming a multi-party governing coalition. The cabinet's methods for creating policy are subject to change at the direction of the prime minister. Typically this has involved establishing a committee structure which compartmentalizes the policy agenda. Prior to January 1997 there were three of these committees: state and social affairs; foreign and security affairs; economics and finance. These were reduced in number to only one at that point and it remains to be seen if committee governance will continue to hold an important role.[56]

While some autonomy of action is accorded local government in Latvia the Saeima has more than a passing interest in what occurs. For instance, the legis-lature extended the term of local government councils in 1996 from three to four years.[57] The following year the Saeima further defined the distinctions be-tween local governments by declaring that cities and towns would elect their of-ficials while the country's regions would be represented by these same officials as delegates to the regions.[58] The extent of authority available to local govern-ment continues to be defined by the national government which is a key quali-fier in identifying the Latvian system as unitary in character.

Just as the American constitution empowers the legislature to establish courts and appoint judges, the Latvian constitution provides the same principle (article 84). In 1992 the Saeima passed the "Law on the Judicial Power" and in 1995 it began the process of laying a legal foundation consisting of district or local courts (with provisions for trial by jury), regional courts for the hearing of appeals, and a Supreme Court to oversee this part of the system. Also in 1995 a Judicial Training Center for jurists and court officials was created with financial and instructional assistance from western countries and the United Nations. In these respects Latvia moved critically closer to its goal of achieving a rule of law system.[59]

Separate from the criminal and civil aspects of the courts is the **Constitutional Court** which is responsible for determining the guidelines of constitutional actions. The development of this important institution has not been without problems. The Constitutional Court was only given form by the Saeima in June 1996 and when its seven members were finally selected by the legislature in October 1996 they had no building to work in, nor had a budget been approved for their work.[60] Gradually, though, Constitutional Courts have been deferred to by rule-making elites in all of the Baltic republics; thus, in Lithuania in early 1998 when that country's Constitutional Court declared that a sitting government must submit to a vote of confidence by parliament after a new president is elected virtually all political factions accepted the opinion.[61] But opposition to judicial reform remains as former Latvian Prime Minister Krasts admitted when he contended that powerful banking interests in particular remained an obstacle to judicial decisions and change.[62] To date little research has been conducted on the operations of the new courts, their effectiveness, or the quality of justice they dispense and our conclusions have to reflect these limitations.

The Presidency: Symbolic Power

Of all the post-Soviet states the Baltic states have gone the farthest in subordinating the executive branch to the power of the legislature. In both Latvia and Estonia executive power is distinctly de-emphasized and the legislature given the most important decision-making powers; in Lithuania the executive is accorded a certain amount of strength, but not enough to make them truly independent. Undoubtedly the best barometer of the Latvian presidency's lack of constituted authority is that it is a position chosen from within the Saeima. Until 1997 this was for a term of three years but was expanded to four years when the parliament extended its own term (see Figure 5.1).[63] It had been argued in the parliament that three years was too limited of a period for the advancement of legislative initiatives.[64] But since the Latvian president is not primarily involved in the development of legislation the presidential term extension seems more a matter of legislative housekeeping and order. The constitution's article 48 grants the president the ability to dissolve the parliament, but also requires that a referendum be held to affirm the decision. Article 50 provides the catch: If the public votes against the Saeima's dissolution it is the president who must resign, and the Saeima then votes for a new president to complete the unfinished term. In addition, when the prime minister resigns the president cannot reject the resignation, although he may decide to reappoint the same person.

As in virtually all of the Russian and Eurasian republics, the parliament possesses the power of impeachment (article 51). But a more peculiar option is that contained in article 52 which allows the president of the Saeima to assume presidential responsibilities should the president of the state be out of the country or somehow incapacitated. As a precaution against a strong chief executive, article 53 relieves the president of responsibility for policy outcomes, and demands that all presidential decrees be countersigned by either the prime minister or another minister who has authority for the legislation under question. All of these are restrictions which prevent the chief executive from establishing a duality of power and conflict over lines of authority.

As for presidential requirements the constitution only says that the president must be forty years of age (article 37). He or she must also be a citizen of Latvia and cannot hold dual citizenship; thus, President Vike-Freiberga, who had lived abroad from the age of seven until returning to Latvia in 1998, had to relinquish her Canadian citizenship. Statutory law also prohibits anyone imprisoned from being a presidential candidate, as well as former employees of Soviet or other foreign security organizations, and members of the Latvian Communist Party. This provision was specifically aimed at **Alfreds Rubiks,** the former First Secretary of the Latvian Communist Party who was tried and convicted for attempting to overthrow the Latvian Republic (a questionable charge as he was indicted by a retroactive law). Candidates must also have an excellent command of the Latvian language, a proviso which would restrict many candidates of the Russian ethnic community,[65] but again benefitted Vike-Freiberga.

In its current form the Latvian presidency has only existed since 1993 when the 1922 constitution was reactivated. The office of the presidency is largely a symbolic institution representative of all Latvian peoples; consequently, the president must relinquish any affiliation with political parties. The Saeima elects the president through a process of factional maneuvering and political deal making. The result is that neither Ulmanis nor Vike-Freiberga were favorites to win the post and both required numerous ballots to win (both won with just fifty-three of one hundred total votes).[66] Still, the president has not become subservient to the factions which elect him or her and is thus perceived as a servant of the general public.

Quite unlike the Russian, Ukrainian, or Uzbek cases, the Latvian presidency has few policy-making powers beyond the poorly defined "right of legislative initiative" (article 47).[67] The constitution instead places emphasis on foreign policy powers and especially the president's ability to "represent the State in an international capacity" (article 41), serve as chief of the armed forces (article 42), and "take steps indispensable to the military defense of the country" (article 44). The only other significant structural power held by the president is that of choosing the prime minister to head the cabinet (article 56).[68] The gist of the matter is that in Latvia (as well as the other Baltic states) the presidency is not meant to be as strong as parliament, and the parliament is unwilling to endorse any substantial changes in the constitutional order.

The Politics of Survival

The Latvian Economy

During the years of Soviet control Latvia had one of the most developed of all the post-Soviet economies. The work force was well-trained and literate, the economy diversified and had significant export potential, as well as access to Baltic shipping. Despite these advantages Latvia's economic transformation has not been an easy one. Trade diversification has largely been successful, although the Russian Federation remains one of its largest trade partners, especially in terms of shipping Russian goods through Latvian ports. The Baltic states' economies were damaged by the Russian economic crisis of 1998 as evidenced by sharp declines in their industrial and agricultural outputs (see Table 9.3).[69] The Latvian economy recovered substantially by 2000 when its GDP grew 6.6 percent;[70] nevertheless, this only puts Latvia at approximately twenty-nine percent of the European

TABLE 9.3   Gross Domestic Product and Industrial Output in the Latvian Economy, 1996–2000 (in Percentages)

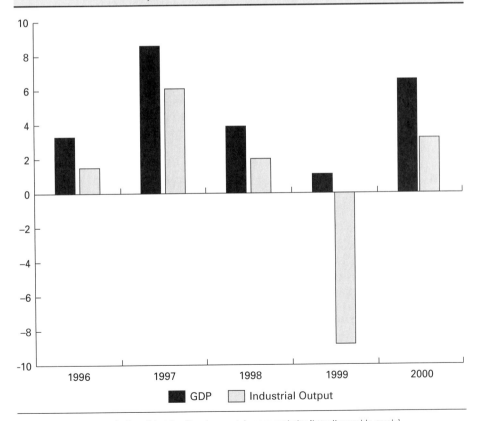

Source: "Macroeconomic Data," Latvian Development Agency website [http://www.lda.gov.lv].

Union average and estimates are that it will take Latvia thirty years to catch up with growth rates of seven to eight percent a year.[71] The issue of corruption has continually plagued Latvia which is usually considered to be much more subject to this problem than either Estonia or Lithuania.[72] For that matter the United Nation's Human Development Index has shown marked improvement in Latvia's standard of living which in 1999 was ranked seventy-fourth out of 174 countries,[73] but had climbed substantially to fiftieth of 162 by 2001.[74]

Balancing out these heavy costs have been the successes of the transition. The government introduced a new currency—the lat—in 1993. Foreign direct investments (FDI) in Latvia have grown although not as quickly as for either Estonia or Lithuania.[75] Latvia embarked on privatization more slowly than did either Lithuania (which began the process in February 1991 even before independence[76]) or Estonia, but certainly quicker than most other Eurasian states. To carry through on privatization the government set up two state bodies, the **Privatization Agency** and the **State Property Fund;** along with the political decisions of the Saeima and the prime minister, these bodies were given the principal responsibility for determining what was to be auctioned. Latvia chose the voucher system as the best approach to privatization, allowing both citizens and residents alike to trade for shares in enterprises being sold by the state. The crippling influence of inflation, which reached 960 percent in 1992, was quickly reduced due to the Bank of Latvia's currency board setting the exchange rate for the lat and thereby restricting monetary growth.[77] By 1999 inflation was registering only three percent[78] and remained roughly at that level in 2001.[79]

All three states have also established their own stock exchanges, all of which did well enough until the global economic crisis of 1998 hit home and all sustained heavy losses of seventy-five to eighty percent of their collective values.[80] Banking has also experienced mixed results. By 1995 Latvia had fifty commercial banks, but bank stability quickly became a paramount issue for economic policy. In May of that year the failure of the country's largest commercial bank, Banka Baltija,[81] and the government's suspension of three others precipitated a national financial crisis.[82] The concentration of most private deposits in a very few Latvian banks led the government to guarantee depositors' investments while also promising the Bank of Latvia that the government would produce a balanced budget for the next fiscal year.[83] The crisis showed how closely interrelated and fragile the economy of such a small country really is, but also demonstrated that the public was willing to accept relatively high costs to achieve a market economy.[84]

The Prospects for Democratization

Were you to bet on the Baltics' long-term abilities to sustain their transition to democracy odds would most likely be in your favor. To date the Baltic states have successfully maintained the pace of reform and for the most part have attempted to deal directly with the very issues which are most troubling for them: guaranteeing minority rights in the pursuit of national self-identity. The results have not always been satisfactory, but one might argue that due to the complexities of small states in unfavorable geographic circumstances the Baltic states have no choice except to deal with the issues. Expressing the pragmatism which may help the Latvian state survive former President Ulmanis cautioned the nation to deal with Russia based on current needs rather than memories of the past.[85] For the Baltic states this will always be a matter for some nervousness and a key determinant in deciding their collective fates.

Key Terms

the right of return
Finno-Ugric languages
Baltic News Service
citizen laws

Singing revolutions
Satversme
Saeima
Vaira Vike-Freiberga

Questions for Consideration

1. Are the Baltic states really Eurasian or European?

2. Can Latvia and Estonia exist as multicultural societies, or is integration of the Russian populations an impossibility?

3. Why the emphasis in the Baltic states on parliamentary systems as compared to mixed or strong presidential systems?

4. Is Latvia's multiparty system conducive to the country's development? What are the prospects for the consolidation of Latvia's party system?

5. What economic niche will Latvia fill in its position between Western and Eastern Europe?

Suggested Readings

David Arter, *Parties and Democracy in the Post-Soviet Republics: The Case of Estonia* (Brookfield, VT: Dartmouth Publishing, 1996).

Juris Dreifelds, *Latvia in Transition* (Cambridge: Cambridge University Press, 1996).

Ole Norgaard, *The Baltic States After Independence* (Brookfield, VT: Edward Elgar, 1996).

Janis J. Penikis, *Latvia: Independence Renewed* (Boulder, CO: Westview Press, 1993).

Andrejs Plakans, *The Latvians: A Short History* (Stanford, CA: Stanford University Press, 1995).

Rein Taagepera, *Estonia: Return to Independence* (Boulder, CO: Westview Press, 1993).

V. Stanley Vardys and Judith B. Sedaitis, *Lithuania: The Rebel Nation* (Boulder, CO: Westview, 1997).

Useful Websites

Baltic News Service
http://bnsnews.bns.lv

Cabinet of Ministers
http://www.mk.gov.lv/eng/

Central Statistical Bureau
http://www.csb.lv

Citizen and Migration Issues Board
http://www.pid.gov.lv

Government of Latvia data communication network
http://www.gov.lv/

Resources for regions of Latvia
http://latvia.vernet.lv/www/map.html

Saeima (Parliament)
http://www.saeima.lanet.lv/

Endnotes

1. Baltic News Service (BNS), 23 August 1996; also, Latvian Telegraph Agency (LETA), 23 August 1996.
2. *Panorama,* no. 45, RIA-Novosti, *14* November 1996.
3. Central Statistical Bureau of Latvia website [http://www.csb.lv/basic/pop.htm].
4. See, for instance, Alfred Bilmanis, *A History of Latvia,* (Princeton, NJ: Princeton University Press, 1951), Chapter Nineteen.
5. BNS, 14 June 1996.
6. Central Statistical Bureau of Latvia website [http://www.csb.lv/basic/pop.htm].
7. Statistical Office of Estonia [http://www.stat.ee].
8. Ministry of Foreign Affairs of the Republic of Lithuania website, "Basic Facts About Lithuania" [http://www.urm.lt/about].
9. For a brief account of these events see Dzintra Bungs, "Seeking Solutions to Baltic-Russian Border Issues," *RFE/RL Research Report,* 3 (1 April 1994): pp. 25–32.
10. BNS, 30 October 1997.
11. "Law on Citizenship of the Republic of Latvia", 22 July 1994, translation provided by the Embassy of the Republic of Latvia, Washington, DC.
12. See Dzintra Bungs, "Moderates Win Parliamentary Elections in Latvia," *RFE/RL Research Report,* 2 (9 July 1993): p. 5.
13. LETA, 5 August 1996.
14. Central Statistical Bureau of Latvia website [http://www.csb.lv/basic/pop.htm].
15. LETA, 8 September 1995.
16. Central Statistical Bureau of Latvia website [http://www.csb.lv/].
17. BNS, 30 January 1997.
18. BNS, 4 March 1998.
19. Walter C. Clemens, Jr., *Baltic Independence and Russian Empire* (New York: St. Martin's Press, 1991), Chapter Eight.
20. For a detailed accounting of these movements see Anatol Lieven, *The Baltic Revolution: Estonia, Latvia, Lithuania and the Path to Independence* (New Haven: Yale University Press, 1993), Chapter Eight.
21. John Hiden and Patrick Salmon, *The Baltic Nations and Europe* (New York: Longman, 1991), pp. 150–151.
22. Juris Dreifelds, "Latvian National Rebirth", *Problems of Communism,* 38 (July–August 1989): pp. 84–86.
23. Associated Press (AP), 3 September 1991.
24. AP, 6 September 1991.

25. Reuters, 11 March 1994 cited in *RFE/RL Daily Report,* 14 March 1994.
26. *Nezavisimaya gazeta,* 29 November 1996, RIA-Novosti, 29 November 1996.
27. An example of the Russian protests and Estonian responses can be found in BNS, 30 January 1997.
28. *Statistical Yearbook of Latvia, 1995* (Riga: 1996), pp. 78–80.
29. *Diena,* 9 December 1996.
30. BNS, 22 January 1997.
31. BNS, 5 March 1998.
32. Article 40, "Constitutional Law: The Rights and Obligations of a Citizen and a Person," Republic of Latvia; International Constitutional Law website [http://www.law.cornell.edu/law/lg02001_htm].
33. Article 12.1.2, "Law on Citizenship of the Republic of Latvia," translation provided by Embassy of the Republic of Latvia, Washington, DC.
34. "Regulations for testing the knowledge of persons applying for Latvian citizenship in the naturalization procedure," Regulation no. 29, section III, 22.4, Republic of Latvia Cabinet of Ministers, 7 February 1995.
35. As one example see *Human Rights and Democratization in Estonia* (Washington, DC: Commission on Security and Cooperation in Europe, September 1993), p. 2.
36. For comments on the U.S. Department of State report on Latvia see BNS, 31 January 1997; for comments on the Council of Europe report on Estonia see BNS, 31 January 1997.
37. "Constitutional Law: The Rights and Obligations of a Citizen and a Person."
38. Dzintra Bungs, "Latvian Government Resigns," *RFE/RL Research Report,* 3 (29 July 1994): pp. 8–10.
39. BNS, 29 January 1997.
40. BNS, 18 July 1997.
41. See "Republic of Latvia Prime Minister Andris Skele," Ministry of Foreign Affairs website [http://www.mfa.bkc.lv/mfa.htm].
42. "Elections of the 6th Saeima of the Republic of Latvia" (Riga, 1995), Saeima of the Republic of Latvia website [http://www.saeima.lanet.lv/].
43. BNS, 23 October 1998.
44. BNS, 21 October 1999 cited in *RFE/RL Newsline,* 22 October 1999.
45. LETA, 14 January 1997.
46. See the website for the People's Party [http://www.tautaspartija.lv/english.htm].
47. BNS, 21 June 1997.
48. BNS owns the Latvian newspaper *Diena.* See Baltic News Service website, [http://www.bns.ee/bns.htm].
49. BNS, 8 August 1996.
50. ITAR-TASS, 3 October 1995.
51. See, for instance, ITAR-TASS, 5 October 1995.
52. *RFE/RL Newsline,* 5 October 1998.
53. LETA, 8 November 1995.
54. See the "Coalition Agreement of the Factions of the 7th Saeima Forming the Government of the Republic of Latvia" [http://www.mk.gov.lv/eng/cabinetofministers/], 15 July 1999.
55. See the "Declaration of the Intended Activities of the Cabinet of Ministers," Ministry of Foreign Affairs of the Republic of Latvia website [http://www.mfa.gov.lv/mfa/pub/declar.htm].
56. BNS, 29 January 1997.

57. *Diena*, 1 November 1996.
58. BNS, 13 November 1997.
59. "Issues in Human Rights in the Republic of Latvia 1994–1997" (June 1997), Ministry of Foreign Affairs website [http://www.mfa.gov.lv/mfa/pub/HUM/issueng.htm].
60. *Diena*, 31 October 1996.
61. BNS, 10 January 1998.
62. BNS, 14 November 1997.
63. BNS, 4 December 1997.
64. BNS, 23 October 1996.
65. BNS, 13 June 1996.
66. On Ulmanis's election see BNS, 18 June 1996; on Vike-Freiberga's election see *RFE/RL Newsline*, 17 June 1999.
67. "Constitution of the Republic of Latvia," Saeima home page [http://www.saeima.lanet.lv/].
68. For instance, in 1995 Ulmanis charged the LNNK with forming a new government because the nationalist aspirations of that party were "popular in Latvia". See "Latvian President Motivates his Choice as to New Government Formation," BNS, 22 July 1995.
69. "Russian and Baltic Economies, the Week in Review," no. 33, (13 August 1999) Bank of Finland Institute for Economies in Transition (BOFIT).
70. "Increase in GDP in 2000—6.6 percent," LETA, 28 March 2001.
71. "Latvia will reach EU average level in 30 years if most optimal national development scenario is implemented," LETA, 30 July 2001.
72. Transparency International ranked Latvia as the fifty-ninth least corrupt state, Lithuania thirty-eighth, and Estonia twenty-eighth on its annual list in 2001. See BNS, 27 June 2001, cited in *RFE/RL Newsline*, 28 June 2001.
73. United Nations Development Report cited in "Russian and Baltic Economies, the Week in Review," no. 31 (30 July 1999).
74. "Latvia ranks 50th in UNDP Human Development Report," LETA, 10 July 2001.
75. "International Investment in Latvia in the 2nd Quarter of 1999", Central Statistical Bureau of Latvia website [http://www.csb.lv/ajaunumi.htm].
76. See "Republic of Lithuania Law on the Initial Privatization of State Property," [http://www.tm.lt/ENGLISH/Documents/94.HTM].
77. Iikka Korhonen, "Currency Boards in the Baltic Countries: What Have We Learned?", Bank of Finland Institute for Economies in Transition Discussion Papers, no. 6 (1999): pp. 12–13.
78. "Russian and Baltic Economies, the Week in Review," no. 40 (1 October 1999).
79. "Russian and Baltic Economies, the Week in Review," no. 2 (11 January 2002).
80. "Russian and Baltic Economies, The Week in Review," no. 45 (6 November 1998).
81. "Latvian Financial Crisis hits Major Banks, Government" and "Latvian Government to Control Largest Commercial Bank," *Baltic Business Weekly*, 18 (15–21 May 1995).
82. "Banking Crisis Hits other Latvian Banks," Ibid.
83. BNS, 25 May 1995.
84. See William Hallagan, "The Evolution of the Latvian Banking Market," *Journal of Baltic Studies*, 28 (Spring 1997): pp. 65–76.
85. BNS, 14 June 1996.

Chapter 10

The Western States:
A Case Study of Ukraine

U nlike the Baltic countries Ukraine emerged from the chaos of the Soviet breakup as the most reluctant of independent states. A land of immense potential, rich in agricultural prospects and industrial infrastructure, natural resources, and human gifts, it was completely unprepared for the cold and harsh realities of governing itself. In both the political and economic realms Ukraine has experienced considerable difficulties determining which direction to turn, whether toward democratic, free-market policies, the state-centric political and economic operations of old, or toward something as yet undefined in between. Collectively Ukraine's leaders have failed to indelibly set a course for the country, nor have its peoples found the means to craft a civil society commensurate to their needs. In this sense Ukraine is a set of anomalies in search of valid explanations.

But if Ukraine operates under considerable handicaps, pushing and pulling against the opportunities which lie before it, the up side is what the state may become. If any of the countries of the former Soviet space could literally explode onto the world stage as a political or economic powerhouse it is Ukraine. At the very least Ukraine could dominate its regional environment and prove to be a focal point not just for Russia and the Eurasian states, but for the transitional state systems of eastern and central Europe as well. Ukraine's success in avoiding violence in its ethnic and regional issues, and its relatively peaceful process of systemic change serve as examples of what states might achieve when motivated. But has this been enough to sustain the state in its early and crucial years of identity formation? The implications of the answer to this question will provide valuable lessons for all states' post-Soviet experiences.

A Reluctant Independence

The Western States in Profile

Of all the regions examined in this book, none is as artificial as that applied to Ukraine, Belarus, and Moldova, or the "western states." Realistically the term

Map 10.1 Ukraine

describes a grouping rather than a region since the latter term implies a bond between states based on a number of factors common to them all. In contrast, a grouping implies a collection of peoples, objects, or issues based on a loose association. Aside from geographic proximity there is no categorization binding these three states. The political environment does have an impact, however, in that Russia plays an important role in defining each of their political systems. Ukraine's large Russian community, for example, does not feel entirely comfortable beyond Russia's control; consequently, both Ukrainians and ethnic Russians are aware of their common Slavic identity largely as it relates to the Russian Federation.

In the two largest of the western states titular populations conflict or coexist with minority groups largely within the same racial groupings (see Table 10.1). In Belarus the combined Belarussian, Russian, Polish, and Ukrainian populations in 1996 registered approximately ninety-eight percent of the total population with Jews (1.4 percent) making up almost all of the remainder. Ukraine's Slavic totals were nearly the same (96.4 percent), although, as we will see the proportions of these groups are quite different and the Russian segment has often been at odds with the numerically dominant Ukrainians. The exception to the norm is Moldova, the smallest of the fifteen former republics and also the most densely populated. Ethnic Moldovans speak the Romanian language and are not Slavic. The ethnic Russian portion of Moldova is primarily concentrated in the eastern-most part of the country beyond the Dniester River and have waged a separatist struggle that has kept the government in Chisinau from establishing control in that part of the country.

These countries are all distinguished for the high proportion of their economies devoted to agriculture. Ukraine has long been known as the breadbasket of Russia due to its rich soil and the products of its peasants' labors. This position as a vital agricultural producer did not protect it from the brutality of Soviet collectivization, which resulted in the deliberately manufactured famine of 1932–1933 and possibly as many as eight million deaths.[1] But neither the terror of the famine, nor the heavy industrialization of the Ukrainian economy has caused Ukrainian society to entirely lose its unique attachment to the soil and much of its sense of national identity.

Ukraine was the birthplace of the first significant eastern Slavic state, **Kyivan Rus** (using the Ukrainian spelling). As already discussed in Chapter Two, Orthodox Christianity was introduced to the eastern Slavs with the baptism of the Kyivan Rus prince **Volodymyr** (Vladimir in Russian) who then declared Christianity the state religion in the year 988. As much as any other single factor, the Orthodox faith has shaped the Ukrainian, Russian, and Belarusian cultures. Today the majority of religious Ukrainians are Orthodox while a significant minority of **Greek Catholics (Uniates)** predominate in the west; as in Russia Protestant and Evangelical Christians supported by foreign missionary activities challenge the Orthodox Church's dominance. But as surely as Orthodoxy leant itself to the support of the state, the political system attempted to control the Orthodox Church.[2] Those religions which operated beyond the reach of the state incurred the suspicion and sometimes hostility of the governing structures. In 1946 Stalin forced the incorporation of the Uniates into the Orthodox Church. This demonstrated just how vulnerable the religious authorities were in relation to the secular world.

Ukraine's independence in 1991 found the various religious communities reasserting themselves from Moscow's control. This newfound freedom also resulted in the 1992–1993 splintering of the Orthodox Church into three competing factions.[3] Religious revivalism has been as much affected by politics as theological concerns.[4] At the same time faced with competition from dozens of foreign religious organizations seeking new converts, Ukraine's traditional faiths found protection in the Ukrainian parliament's 1993 revision of the 1991 **Law on Freedom of Conscience and Religion.** The revisions prohibited foreign religions from proselytizing without governmental permission, or outside of local congregations. But such advantages for Orthodoxy have not been enough to prevent its influence over or identification with Ukrainian society from diminishing.[5]

At 48.86 million people Ukraine's population is the sixth largest in Europe.[6] It is a diversified population not only in terms of ethnicity, but also as measured by occupational categories: In the mid–1990s industry and construction accounted for thirty-three percent of all jobs and agriculture and forestry another twenty-one percent.[7] The shift in population from rural to urban domains in the Twentieth Century was clearly dramatic. At the time of the 1926 Soviet census only 10.5 percent of all ethnic Ukrainians lived in urban areas.[8] The rapid pace of industrialization, coupled to the terrible death rate from famine, collectivization, and war produced a phenomenal shift to Ukraine's major cities; by 1995 seventy percent of the population lived in cities (the figure for Belarus was seventy-one percent; for Moldova it was fifty-two percent).[9]

Population and life expectancy figures for Ukraine have also undergone considerable change declining consistently since 1991.[10] In 1993 there were 10.7 live births per thousand people while the number of deaths was 14.2;[11] within the space of five years (1999) the infant mortality rate had increased to nineteen per thousand while the population growth rate for the period 1995–2000 was estimated to be –0.38 percent.[12] Life expectancy had also fallen from roughly 70 years of age in the Soviet period to 66.8 years. Males now lived only 63.8 years on the average while females had much better expectations at 73.7 years.[13] According to the World Health Organization (WHO) these and similar conditions for the Eurasian states were partly explainable by the effects of "high alcohol consumption, a sedentary lifestyle, unhealthy nutrition and high stress levels, all contribut(ing) to the high prevalence of cardiovascular diseases, cancer, and other chronic conditions in the (Newly Independent States). The addition to these factors of poor nutrition and increased drug abuse creates a deadly pattern."[14] Given these conditions Ukraine could be assessed as experiencing a major and lingering health crisis.

As a result of its population shifts Ukraine has major cities in every region of the country. Kyiv, the capital, had approximately 2.6 people in 1997, followed by four other cities with populations in excess of one million. Most of the country's large cities lie in the eastern or central parts of the country where the concentration of ethnic Russians is greatest. To the west lie L'viv and Vinnytsia where higher percentages of ethnic Ukrainians result in stronger expressions of Ukrainian nationalism. In the Crimean (hereafter Krym) peninsula the population is largely Russian and it is the only region in Ukraine with a majority population of ethnic Russians. Over the last two hundred years ethnic Russians steadily displaced the local population, or **Krym Tatars** (more on them later). Both Simferopol (the region's capital) and Sevastopol (the Black Sea Fleet's home port) have been hotbeds of Russian separatist ambitions since 1991 as Ukraine and Russia argued over territorial rights. Finally, there is the cosmopolitan city of Odesa along the western sea coast. Long considered the Black Sea's version of Marseille, Odesa is home to perhaps the greatest blend of Ukrainian society outside of Kyiv.

Kyiv is bisected by the Dniepr River and this division stands as a metaphor for the cleavage that runs through modern-day Ukrainian society. The capital is a modern metropolis which seems to be continually trying to bring the past into the present. As the focal point of a great trading empire Kyiv became prominent in the reign of Volodymyr in the late tenth century who, as has already been seen, baptized his people and implanted a strong Byzantine influence into his flourishing capital.[15] In the thirteenth century Kyivan Rus was eclipsed by the rising star of Muscovy and slowly the birthplace of eastern Slavic culture faded to the status of a second and later third-rank city. Controlled over the centuries by Mongols, Poles, Russians, and others Kyiv, like the rest of Ukraine, is rediscovering its unique identity. Today a slowly revitalizing Kyiv presents to the visitor the striking golden cupolas of the **Lavra Monastery** (also known as the Monastery of the Caves due to its catacombs) and **St. Sophia Cathedral,** which rival the gilded splendor of Moscow's monuments. The beauty of its churches, palaces, and public buildings—all tributes to Ukraine's sense of nationhood—has been badly dimmed by the ages, the neglect of its own rulers, the horrific destruction of the Nazi occupation, and the Soviet disdain for the past. At the beginning of the new century Kyiv is a city of mixed visions: great tree-lined boulevards and distinctive architecture from days gone by are offset by the heavy-handed dullness of Stalinist/Soviet-era architecture and tributes to socialist realism. In spite of this Kyiv remains a city with a capital's significance and is no longer dependent on Russia for cultural development.

Ukraine is Europe's second largest country (603,700 square kilometers), forty-three percent larger than Germany but still only 3.5 percent the size of the entire Russian Federation. It is a state largely unmarked by natural borders with neighbors; thus, rivers and mountains do little to separate Ukraine from Russia, Belarus, Poland, Moldova, or Romania, although the mountains of the Krym peninsula and the Carpathian mountains in the southwest do break up the overall monotony. When this lack of defendable boundaries is taken into account along with the country's natural resource wealth, it is easy to see why Russian, Mongol, Tatar, Polish, Lithuanian, Cossack, Hapsburg, Ottoman, and German conquerors have readily moved across the country's surface. It's all the more amazing that with so few protections Ukraine could emerge from the Soviet period with recognizable and largely uncontested boundaries, with the exceptions of the Krym (see below) and the province of Bukovina, which formerly had belonged to Romania.

Ukraine is divided into twenty-four oblasts, the Autonomous Republic of Krym, and the cities of Kyiv and Sevastopol which have special legal status. These administrative divisions approximate the historical as well as ideological divisions of the country. The western-most oblasts, including the region of

Galicia, tend toward strong Ukrainian nationalism while the eastern oblasts, especially the Donbas, tend to be pro-Russian. These affinities have been quite apparent in the country's elections, but it is important to keep in mind that these administrative divisions represent long-established tsarist and Soviet-era provincial boundaries. Thus, some of the population's sense of attachment to the land derives from political considerations stretching back through their long history.

The Ukrainian Identity

Ukraine has defied the odds since independence by maintaining a positive, balanced relationship between its primary ethnic groups. Ethnic tolerance has been one of the major achievements of Ukrainian statehood even as states all around it have failed to build collective national identities.[16] Some of this is attributable to Ukrainian society's culture of acceptance, that is, a prevailing attitude among different ethnic groups to get along. Too, the culture has been assisted by governmental action, especially the Law on National Minorities passed in 1991. As a result, incidents of ethnic intolerance, although serious, are few in number and largely confined to those areas where nationalism is most strident (western Ukraine, Krym).[17] Potentially the gravest problem facing the new state—that of hostility between ethnic Ukrainians and Russians—has not emerged to the extent found in other states such as Moldova, the Baltics, or Kazakstan.

Citizenship in Ukraine is based on either the place of birth or place of residence at the time of independence. This is, of course, considerably at odds with the situations in Latvia and Estonia. But the establishment of national identity for a people long-subordinated to the political control of others requires more than this. Identity is often a matter of a "common historical tradition,"[18] such as in the efforts by the post-independence Ukrainian leadership to link the new state with its Kyivan Rus past.[19] Although in the last century the Ukrainian intelligentsia identified quite readily with their Russian neighbors, both the urban masses and the peasantry had their own worldviews quite apart from the Russian experience. By 1989 latent nationalism had risen to the surface encouraging many Ukrainians to distance themselves from the Soviet-imposed cultural and political integration. Having endured failed self-governance movements after World War I, and again during the Second World War, Ukrainian citizens at independence were not entirely convinced of their claim to statehood, or at least of their association with one another.[20] In contrast, the existence of a visible worldwide Ukrainian diaspora numbering more than nine million (over four million live in Russia, one and a half million in Poland, 600,000 in Moldova, 300,000 in Argentina, and a sizeable number in Canada) shows a nation that recognizes its identity. Calls by Ukrainians living in Russia for Russian Federation support of Ukrainian culture demonstrates an important cohesiveness within the Ukrainian diaspora.[21]

The policy of russification carried out under the tsars and then the communists deliberately created a sense of inferiority amongst the Ukrainian population. In the early days of the communist system national differences were thought to be resolvable issues based on the urban-rural divide of the population. But the influx of ethnic Russians as part of the industrialization drive both during and after World War II caused greater division, not less. Despite the increase in the total number of Ukrainians moving to the cities during the first decade of Soviet control, they also left the cities in substantial numbers during times of economic crisis thereby perpetuating Ukraine's ethnic divide.[22] Many ethnic Ukrainians tended to identify themselves in censuses as Russian, a pattern that persisted until independence when an increasing number of citizens began claiming joint Ukrainian-Russian ancestry.[23] Prejudices against the use of the Ukrainian language have persisted, however, and many citizens in the country's eastern and central regions continue to favor Russian over Ukrainian.

According to the Ukrainian constitution, Ukrainian is the state language while Russian is to be developed and protected as a minority language; ethnic Russians are a minority within Ukraine but their language has much greater usage amongst the population than Ukrainian.[24] The constitution did not affirm any special status for the Russian language which in itself may have prompted the Krym legislature to pass a law in October 1997 making Russian the official language (the Ukrainian president declared this action illegal). The real challenge for the state is not just that of language, however, but rather how to successfully integrate the whole population behind a common identity that recognizes what is meant by being a Ukrainian.

Even still the issue of separating the Russian populated regions and attaching them to Russia proper (that is, irredentism) is not widely accepted. The often expressed idea of reformulating the USSR, a position taken by the more radical elements of the left spectrum of Ukrainian politics, doesn't find much support within the general public. Since the radical left has not received strong electoral mandates from the voters, it can be concluded that there is not much desire for separatism. And with Russia having recognized the borders of the Ukrainian state despite the protestations of nationalists in the Russian State Duma, Ukraine's territorial integrity and sovereignty seem secure. That is, until we look to the Krym case.

Krym and the Limits of Autonomy

As in neighboring Moldova and Georgia (see Chapter Eleven), Ukraine has its areas where separatist sentiments are strong. This is especially true in the Autonomous Republic of Krym, the only region in Ukraine where ethnic Russians are in the majority. As a unitary state the central government in Kyiv sets the standards by which the entire country is governed. The Krym Peninsula is home to both Russian and Tatar nationalist movements. Conflictual and potentially dangerous, Russian and Tatar aspirations have caused the Ukrainian government to deal cautiously with the peninsula rather than forcefully impose control on it from Kyiv. Krym became the administrative concern of Kyiv only in 1954; after 1991 the fate of the peninsula again appeared as a major issue for nationalists on both sides. In May 1992 the Krym parliament passed a declaration of independence prompting Kyiv to immediately deliver an ultimatum to the republican authorities in Simferopol to back off, which they did. For that moment the secessionist issue cooled down and attention shifted to the division of the Black Sea Fleet.

The division of the Soviet Union's **Black Sea Fleet** between Ukraine and Russia has done as much as any other issue in diverting Ukraine's attention from more pressing problems. Thus, President **Leonid Kuchma** (see page 213) expended considerable effort in negotiating a settlement of the issue with Moscow which resulted in the mid–1997 Ukrainian-Russian agreement splitting up the resources of the fleet and determining long-term lease arrangements for Russian use of Sevastopol. For its part Russia agreed to long-term leasing of ports and facilities while Ukraine was to be restricted in its own use of harbors.[25] While none of this entirely satisfied irredentist elements within the Russian State Duma, and especially Moscow mayor Yurii Luzhkov,[26] it did prove to be a necessity for the long-awaited normalization of relations between Kyiv and Moscow.[27]

The need for normalization was apparent. During the 1993 presidential election in Krym there were numerous assassinations, bombings, and attacks on candidates. The eventual winner (two rounds were required) was **Yurii Meshkov,** the leader of the separatist and pro-Russian Republican Party and "Russia" bloc, who took 72.9 percent of the vote thereby causing consternation in Kyiv.[28] And yet with the subsequent change of administrations in Kyiv and the coming to power of Leonid Kuchma in mid–1994 there was room for cautious optimism that the Kyiv-Simferopol relationship might be workable. Meshkov himself saw Kuchma's election as an indication of the downplaying of Ukrainian nationalism in the new administration as Kuchma was thought to be more pro-Russian than his predecessor Leonid Kravchuk.[29] While this did prove correct, Meshkov and those around him seemed to misinterpret Kyiv's approaches to the dual concepts of nationalism and national independence.

Kyiv's determination to ensure the territorial integrity of the country had been affixed in the Ukrainian constitution, which devotes an entire chapter (Chapter Eleven, articles 134–139) to the delimitation of Krym's authority. The constitution explicitly states that the peninsula is "an inseparable integral part of Ukraine" which operates within the confines of Ukrainian laws (article 134). Under Meshkov a consolidation of power began to take place, which Kyiv saw as supplanting both its own authority and that of democratically elected institutions in the autonomous republic. Throughout 1994 and early 1995 tensions were again on the rise as Meshkov engaged in a power struggle with the regional legislature, the Supreme Council of Krym. The crisis reached a head in early 1995 as the Krym parliament attempted to depose Meshkov, who in turn responded by locking the parliament out of its own building. In February Kuchma took advantage of the divisions within the separatists' ranks when he pronounced invalid a series of edicts that had been issued by Meshkov.[30] Three weeks later the Ukrainian parliament suspended Krym's constitution,[31] abolished the republic's presidency, and called on the general prosecutor of Ukraine to file charges against Meshkov for abuse of power.[32]

The problems didn't stop there, however. January 1997 brought about a renewed challenge to Kyiv's authority when the Krym parliament voted for the fifth time in three years to dismiss the government headed by pro-Kyiv premier Arkadii Demidenko. Kuchma suspended the parliament's actions almost immediately and in April vetoed Demidenko's ouster on the grounds that it contravened the Ukrainian president's constitutional right to be consulted in the matter (article 136). By 1999 political positions within the parliament had been reversed as supporters of new Krym premier Serhiy Kunitsyn voted to oust presidium chairman and Krym Communist Party leader **Leonid Hrach**.[33] Kyiv's role this time was limited to counseling compromise and waiting to see whether Kuchma would benefit by this high-stakes regional conflict.

A related aspect of the Krym problem is that of the Krym Tatars. Unlike the ethnic tensions that mark the Baltic states, the Tatar question stems from the fact that these Turkic peoples, expelled from their homes on Stalin's orders in 1944 (along with the Chechens and other Caucasus peoples, see Chapter Seven), have few hopes of returning to former homes or lands. Moreover, there is little understanding by either Kyiv or Simferopol of the extent of Tatar problems.[34] Few social services, little political representation, or police protection are available to the Tatars.[35] What the Tatars have to their credit is a strong sense of ethnic identity and a nationalist movement to match. How many more Tatars will return to Krym is uncertain (see Table 10.1), but the issue will not go away any more than will that of the rights of the Russian segment of the population.

The Structure of Power

Constitutional Prerogatives

Despite its great potential and obvious political importance Ukraine was the last of the Eurasian republics to adopt its first post-Soviet constitution. Several versions were drafted,[36] including a procommunist readaptation of the last Soviet-era fundamental law.[37] But the debate over which would prevail was dragged out for

TABLE 10.1   The Changing Face of Crimea: Ethnic Change on the Peninsula (% of the region's total population)

	1926*	1989**	1997
Ethnic Group			
Russian	42	67.0	68.4
Ukrainian	n.a.	25.8	25.6
Tatar	25	.4	8.0

Sources: *1926 Census of the Soviet Union in Frank Lorimer, *The Population of the Soviet Union: History and Prospects* (Geneva: League of Nations, 1946).

**First Book of Demographics of the Former Soviet Union* (Shadyside, MD: New World Demographics, L.C., 1993), p. D–6.

the better part of four years even as pressure mounted from foreign sources such as the Council of Europe (which Ukraine was trying to join) for a resolution to the issue.[38] Behind the scenes Ukraine struggled with its newly rediscovered, yet unresolved independence. What was striking about this debate was that among the entire political elite only those fringe elements among the communists who wanted to rebuild the Soviet Union seemed to be able to clearly express the direction they wanted Ukraine to take.

Keeping the state running until the constitutional issues were resolved required that the president and parliament at least temporarily come to terms on how power was to be shared. In May 1995 the two sides reached a deal which eventually became the basis for the new fundamental law of Ukraine.[39] The parliament opposed the president's version due to its emphasis on creating a strong presidential system, the formal adoption of Ukrainian as the state language (article 10), and the use of state symbols with decidedly nationalist overtones (article 20). A grudging acceptance of the draft was only achieved after Kuchma threatened the parliament with the prospect of calling a national referendum on the subject. While Kuchma's authority to call a referendum was questionable (a point he admitted),[40] the parliament conceded after having sensed the public's support of Kuchma. Thus, on 28 June 1996 the Ukrainian constitution was finally promulgated.

The Presidency and Government

On 10 July 1994 Leonid Kuchma, a russified Ukrainian (he spoke Ukrainian only haltingly) from the eastern city of Dnipropetrovs'k, a former manager of the Soviet Union's largest missile factory, and later a prime minister under President **Leonid Kravchuk,** defeated Kravchuk himself to become Ukraine's second president. Kravchuk's loss can be taken as a strong indication that Ukraine was making a transition toward pluralism and possibly democracy especially as this was the first peaceful presidential transition in any of the former Soviet republics. In the main it was a referendum on moving Ukraine beyond the old party elite's complacency and corruption. Kuchma's reelection in 1999 unfortunately also presented many of the same issues to the electorate, only this time it was Kuchma who was accused of corruption as well as authoritarian tendencies. Kuchma prevailed over a wide number of challengers representing every corner of Ukraine's political world. In the final round held on 14 November 1999 Kuchma bested **Petro Symonenko** of the **Communist Party of Ukraine** (KPU) by fifty-six to thirty-seven percent. Far from ending the turbulent politics that have characterized Ukraine's post-Soviet experience, it instead set the stage for a renewed presidential challenge to the parliament's opposition to reform.

By 1997 Kuchma had managed to successfully deal with several of the country's most pressing problems including the already mentioned Black Sea Fleet's division and the adoption of the new constitution. As in many other systems the political resolve to deal with an issue is a major determinant of policy adoption and issue resolution. This has been no less so in Ukraine, but the scope of presidential and legislative powers are also crucial. In Ukraine the president's powers are definitely not on a par with those of the Russian president; nevertheless, Kuchma, like Georgia's president (see Chapter Eleven), has steadily accumulated power largely at the legislature's expense. It seems almost natural that with the host of problems which have beset the Ukrainian state that the president would push for a strong say in establishing the policy agenda. Kravchuk had done just that in 1992 when he convinced the parliament to give him the authority to structure the cabinet.[41] This authority was extended by Kuchma in the 1995 compromise,[42] and again with the acceptance in 1996 of the constitution.

Probably most significant, however, was Kuchma's campaign begun immediately upon his reelection in January 2000 to subject the parliament to a popular referendum. Kuchma's goal was to gain greater responsiveness from the Rada by turning the legislature into a bicameral body. This proved to be a test of the Ukrainian political process at its most fundamental level especially after the formation of a propresidential majority (240 deputies) in January 2000. Walking out of the new legislative session these deputies proceeded to establish a rival parliament and elect their own speaker.[43]

Leonid Kuchma, President of Ukraine since 1995

Source: AP/Wide World Photos

As in Russia, the Ukrainian president accomplishes much of his work through the presidential administration. A relatively compact organization, the Ukrainian presidential administration was estimated in 1996 to have 315 people working for it.[44] This figure can only be expected to expand due to both the number of positions in the administration and the scope of its duties. The head of administration is the president's right-hand man, clearly answerable to the president. Restructured in 1996 the position is responsible for political analysis and planning as well as humanitarian and social policy issues. Perhaps more important, however, the reorganization gave the presidential administration a sense of purpose as it coordinated activities with the cabinet and developed cooperation with the parliament.[45]

While all of this might indicate the maturation of the executive authority in the Ukrainian political system, remnants of the authoritarian political culture and its disdain toward legal norms and political controls showed itself tragically with the murder of the Internet newsletter *Pravda Ukrayiny* editor **Hryhoriy Gongadze** in September 2000. In a rapid series of conspiratorially oriented events, suspicion about the murder was laid directly on Kuchma's doorstep after revelations of secretly taped conversations that seemed to link the president to a cover-up. For the next several months all eyes were on the widening scandal, and valuable time for political or economic change squandered. Kuchma proved able to ride out the worst of the storm (the murder had yet to be solved), but was substantially weakened and forced to turn increasingly to Russian President Putin for support, thus possibly compromising something of Ukraine's sovereignty.

Presidential powers are largely contained in article 106 of the constitution. Thirty-one powers are mentioned there, the most important of these being the appointment of the prime minister and the cabinet, as well as the heads of local state administrations (article 136 also allows him to approve the appointment of the Krym prime minister).[46] All of this is done with parliamentary approval, but the president is not required to solicit parliamentary opinions in dismissing cabinet members. The president also has the ability to call for referenda on either constitutional amendments or "on popular initiative". As already mentioned Kuchma tried to utilize this authority before he was actually granted the power in September 1996, but then exercised it in his dispute with the legislature in early 2000. The president also has the authority to override actions taken by both the Cabinet of Ministers of Ukraine and of Krym; his reasons for doing so apparently do not have to be explained (article 106, section 16).

The president's legislative powers are not as comprehensive as those of his Russian counterpart. The ability to initiate legislation, a key component in any chief executive's arsenal, is located under the constitutional chapter dealing with the legislature which seems to indicate a limited capability (Chapter Four, article 93). Both offices are roughly equal in their command of national defense and protecting the territorial sovereignty of the state (Kuchma used his decree-making authority in 1995 to take control over the National Guard, at that time a force of 40,000 troops[47]). Again the placement of these provisions in the constitution is important. Foreign policy powers are mentioned at the outset of Chapter Five of the constitution (dealing with the presidency) indicating a stronger foreign than domestic policy role may have been originally intended. The president's decree-making powers (article 106, paragraph 3), however, leave little doubt that the president is to be a major player issuing the equivalent of executive orders to implement the law. In this sense the executive has a powerful tool at his disposal and may use it to get around the parliament.

The Ukrainian presidency does not have the strong oversight capabilities of either the Russian or French executives; this is largely the responsibility of the Ukrainian parliament. As in the French system the Ukrainian president appoints the cabinet which then formulates policy based on the direction given to it by the president. Kuchma also decreed in December 1996 that the government's **power ministries** (Defense, Interior, Foreign Affairs), and the Ministry of Information be directly subordinate to him, much as Yeltsin did in Russia after 1993. This action caused some friction with the parliamentary opposition, but there was little they could do given the constraints of the constitution.[48] When the president resigns, so does the cabinet (article 115) thereby further tying these institutions together.

The prime minister is subject to parliamentary approval and rejection of candidates is always a possibility as when the Rada turned down Kuchma's renomination of his prime minister Valery Pustovoytenko shortly after Kuchma won reelection. Most likely this was the opposition's way of asserting itself given its inabilities to impeach the president the previous January, or stem the tide of Kuchma's increasing power. Most presidential decrees which deal with the cabinet, and those relating to civil, military, and governmental appointments, must be co-signed by the prime minister. The extent of consultation between these two officials would seem to depend on the strength of personality of both, as well as their personal relationship. Kravchuk, for instance, saw one of his prime ministers—Kuchma—resign after only eleven months in office due to policy disagreements and Kuchma's desire to eventually run for the presidency himself. For his part Kuchma also experienced difficulties with his prime ministers as the president found several of them either hostile toward reform, indifferent about corruption, or involved in it themselves. In general terms, Ukrainian prime ministers have not remained in office long and between 1990 and 2002 eleven persons held this office including three as acting prime ministers.

As the constitution states it, the cabinet is "the highest body within the system of bodies of executive power" (article 113). Unlike many of its neighbors the Ukrainian cabinet is charged with implementation of the law rather than its actual creation. Most important the cabinet drafts the state budget (article 116, section 6) but then must present it to the Verkhovna Rada for approval or amendment (article 85, section 4). Thus an adversarial relationship between branches is the norm for the budgetary process and inevitably it takes longer to reach an agreement on the budget than if it were solely the responsibility of the legislature.

The president may take account of the political makeup of the parliament and appoint to the cabinet members of other parties (again, as has occasionally happened in Russia). In Kuchma's case since he had no true party organization of his own in the parliament at the time of his election (see page 213) he was relatively unrestrained in his choices for ministers, although not free from party demands. Since 1995 the cabinet has included members from a number of parties and parliamentary caucuses, which theoretically should broaden its appeal. This also gives ministers the flexibility to move between factions with no penalties for their actions. Finally, the president can also move political allies into either the first deputy prime minister or the deputy prime minister positions so as to counter difficulties that may arise with the prime minister.

As called for by the constitution the court system in Ukraine is appended to the more powerful executive and legislative branches. The judicial system is further weakened by political interference and the lack of institutional structuring needed to make the courts work. For instance, the eighteen members of the **Constitutional Court,** the country's highest court, are appointed equally by the president, the legislature, and a congress of Ukrainian judges, all of this possibly leading to divided loyalties for the justices. This court's ability to act was severely limited by the president's and parliament's joint failure in finalizing the appointment of justices to the court: When the court began functioning in January 1997 two justices still had not been appointed.

Directly below the Constitutional Court is the system of "courts of general jurisdiction" (civil and criminal courts), consisting of the **Supreme Court** and specialized courts, appellate courts, and local courts. As a law reforming the court system has yet to be passed by the Rada the Soviet-era court system remains in place with twenty-seven regional and 742 district/city courts operating below the Supreme Court. Beyond the Constitutional Court, all judges are appointed by the president for an initial five-year term without the Rada's confirmation (article 128). Upon successful completion of a five-year term incumbents may be reappointed by the Rada with lifetime tenure (or until they reach sixty-five, article 126.2). However, without more definite laws governing legal structures and responsibilities the Ukrainian court system will remain hampered in its abilities to carry out justice.

The Legislature

The **Verkhovna Rada,** or Supreme Council, has been characterized since its inception by extreme polarization and hyperpluralism. Social conflict is acted out both on the streets of Ukraine as well as in the halls and chambers of the legislature. The Rada has changed little from its predecessor's—the Supreme Soviet—design; unlike several of its contemporary Eurasian institutions it did not legislate itself out of existence in agreeing to the new constitution but instead had that document conform to the legislature's political reality.

Internal operations of the Rada are directed by its chairman, or **speaker,** who is elected from amongst the deputies. The parliament's list of responsibilities is longer than the president's, comprising thirty-seven duties, the most important being adopting laws and approving the state budget (article 85, sections 3 and 4), conducting oversight of the prime minister and the government (article 85, section 13), approving a list of what is not to be privatized (article 85, section 36), and approving resolutions on confidence in the government (article 87). The Ukrainian parliament is an institution of moderate strength and more powerful than its Russian counterpart. But as illustrated by the formation of a rival body from within its own ranks in early 2000 it has not been capable of defining Ukraine's political agenda and can barely govern itself.

The first multiparty elections for the Rada were held in March 1990 and heralded the emergence of a younger political generation, albeit still largely communist in orientation. However, this did not make them particularly re-form-minded but rather more interested in becoming a new "party in(of) power."[49] From 1991 through 1994 the Rada battled with the presidency over the direction and pace of reform, the protection of the *nomenklatura's* privileges, the distribution of land and other forms of wealth in society, and of course, the distribution of political power. Despite the dominance of leftist groups the Rada acquiesced in the declaration of state independence and the breakup of the Soviet Union primarily because of the sense that this would happen anyway. Within the much smaller world of the independent Ukrainian state the parliament remained as conservative as it had been under the Soviet regime, but was also more fractious due to a competitive party system. In fact, the Rada has consistently had the largest number of unaffiliated deputies of any parliament amongst the Eurasian states with 227 in 1995, 114 in 1998, and ninety-five in 2002 (in contrast in 1997 there were no unaffiliated deputies in the parliaments of Estonia, Latvia, Moldova, Turkmenistan, or Uzbekistan). By the first session of any new parliament, autonomy is cast aside in favor of the security offered by whichever party has the greatest power. In 2002 this proved to be the propresidential United Ukraine thoroughly manipulated behind the scenes by Kuchma.

Since 1993 electoral contests have been characterized by the continual re-shaping of the electoral laws themselves. The first passed in that year provided for all deputies to be elected in single-member districts.[50] Unsatisfactory for those who saw their strength primarily in what the party stood for rather than individual allegiances or ideologies (especially the KPU), the law recast the Rada in December 1997 in imitation of the Russian State Duma whereby there would be 225 deputies from party lists and 225 from single-member districts, all elected for five-year terms.[51] Effectively erasing the uncertain results of the 1994 elections which had been drawn out well into 1995, the 1998 Rada was in strong opposition to President Kuchma. The drama played itself out again in 2001 when the legislature passed several new versions which were vetoed by Kuchma and only at the end of the year with new elections looming did the president acquiesce.

Again, as in Russia, the left has maintained a strong presence in the legislature (see Table 10.2). The left's—and particularly the KPU's—abilities in building its strength results from three factors: 1) strong organization (the KPU was one of only two parties in the 1998 elections to field a full party list of 225 candidates and accomplished this again in 2002; 2) regionalism; and 3) voter dissatisfaction with reform. Consequently, in every electoral cycle the public has

TABLE 10.2 Political Party Representation and Change in the Verkhovna Rada, 1995–2002

Party	Seats in 1995	Party	Seats in 1998**	Party	Seats in 2002***
Unaffiliated*	227	Communist Party of Ukraine (KPU)	119	Viktor Yushchenko Bloc Our Ukraine	112
Communist Party of Ukraine (KPU)	95	Popular Democratic Party of Ukraine (NDPU)	84	For United Ukraine (ZYU)	102
Rukh	22	Rukh	47	Unaffiliated	95
Peasant Party (PZU)	18	Hromada	39	Communist Party of Ukraine (KPU)	66
Socialist Party (SPU)	15	Bloc of the Socialist Party and Peasant Party (SPU/SelPU)	35	Socialist Party of Ukraine (SPU)	24
Ukrainian Republican Party (URP)	11	Unaffiliated	31	Social-Democratic Party of Ukraine (United)	24
Congress of Ukrainian Nationalists	5	Social Democratic Party of Ukraine (SDPU(o))	24	Yulia Tymoshenko Election Bloc	21
Labour Party of Ukraine (PTU)	5	Green Party (PZU)	24	Unity	4

(continued)

TABLE 10.2 Political Party Representation and Change in the Verkhovna Rada, 1995–2002

Party	Seats in 1995	Party	Seats in 1998**	Party	Seats in 2002***
Party of Democratic Rebirth of Ukraine (PDVU)	4	Reforms and Order Party	21	Democratic Party of Ukraine/Democratic Union	4
Democratic Party of Ukraine (DPU)	2	Progressive Socialist Party (PSP)	17		
Civic Congress of Ukraine (GKU)	2	Agrarian Party of Ukraine (APU)	10		
Social Democratic Party of Ukraine (SDPU)	1				
Ukrainian Conservative Republican Party (UKRP)	1				
Party of the Economic Revival of the Crimea (PEVK)	1				

Sources: 1995: *Political Handbook of the World;* 1998 and 2002, Central Electoral Commission of Ukraine, Elections Around the World website [http://www.electionworld.org].

*Number of unaffiliated deputies at time of election only. Most deputies declare themselves to be members of already existing factions shortly after parliament convenes.

**As of 14 May 1998

***As of 14 April 2002

facilitated a battleground attitude by approving simultaneously of presidential goals alongside large blocs of leftist deputies.

Banned between 1991 and 1993, today the KPU's membership ranges as high as 160,000, a respectable figure given the commitment of older voters (pensioners) and the disaffected in Ukrainian society. Like the KPRF in Russia, the KPU has had a difficult time attracting younger voters and many of its qualified candidates for elected office have quit to found their own parties. Under Petro Symonenko's leadership, the KPU committed itself to an antireformist stance and the abolition of the presidency which Symomenko himself sought in 1999. As well the KPU embraces much of the symbolism associated with the Soviet state and presses consistently for a revivalism of that state's structures and functions.

Other successors to the communist legacy have included the **Socialist Party of Ukraine** (SPU) lead by **Oleksandr Moroz** who was the Rada's chairman from 1995 to 1998, the Peasant Party of Ukraine (SelPU), and the Progressive Socialist Party (PSP). The PSP proved particularly adept in 1998 in tapping into social discontent, especially in areas closest to the Russian border.[52] But by 2001 with many other parties forming electoral coalitions for the upcoming year the PSP reformed itself as the **Nataliya Vitrenko Bloc** (the PSP leader) and found itself without a meaningful basis of support (it won only 3.2 percent and no parliamentary seats). For its part the SPU has promoted state regulation of the economy, the reassertion of the rights of ethnic Russians, and opposition to privatization. As its positions were nearly indistinguishable from those of the KPU it won only fifteen seats in the 1995 Rada; an electoral alliance with the Peasant Party in 1998 brought a total of thirty-five seats, all from single-member districts, but in 2002 the SPU made its best showing ever gaining twenty-four seats.

Stepping out of the crowded electoral field after 1998 were several parties of either centrist or center-left orientations. Probably the most significant of these is the **Viktor Yushchenko Bloc Our Ukraine** formed by the ex-prime minister out of ten small parties and groups. With its reformist orientation it managed to capture the single largest share of votes and 112 deputies. But Yushchenko was not able to prevent his former boss from gaining control of the Rada through the propresidential **For a United Ukraine** (ZYU) fronted by Kuchma's head of administration **Volodymyr Lytvyn.** With 102 seats of its own ZYU brought under its control many of the unaffiliated deputies for a total of 177. In conjunction with the oligarch dominated **Social-Democratic Party of Ukraine (United),** or SDPU(o)[53] and several other small parties ZYU was able to accomplish the election of Lytvyn as Rada chairman as well as the first and second deputies to the chairman. Kuchma's efforts have stymied the proreform and anticorruption drives of his opponents, at least for the present. In the process he may have also compromised the integrity of the electoral system and threatened the foundation of a democratic society.

On the center-right side of the Ukrainian party system are clustered a number of organizations known as **national democrats.** These groups favor progressive economic reform, a strong unitary state, advancement of the Ukrainian language and culture, and a rejection of integration with Russia.[54] As a rule the national democrats disavow the ethnic intolerance and Russo-phobia associated with right-wing nationalists such as the Ukrainian National Assembly and the Congress of Ukrainian Nationalists; for the most part, however, national democrats tend to be anticommunist. The strongest among these center-right organizations is the **Popular Movement of Ukraine,** or **Rukh.** Founded in the western city of L'viv in 1989 by **Vyacheslav Chornovil,** a prominent Soviet-era dissident, Rukh's support has been concentrated in nationalist strongholds of the western oblasts, especially L'viv, Ivano-Frankivs'k, Ternopil', and Rivne where the Ukrainian language is most widely spoken. Fighting within the organization between Chornovil (who died in a traffic accident in 1999) and other members of the party, as well as Kuchma's efforts to sow dissent within a rival and highly critical organization, caused it to split prior to the 1999 presidential contest. Recognizing the erosion to their positions the two factions agreed to reconcile prior to the 2002 parliamentary contest and submerged themselves within the Viktor Yushchenko Bloc. Always tenuous, Rukh's position as an alternative to Kuchma, the KPU, or even other national democrats has largely evaporated.

The presence of such radically divergent parties in the legislature ensures a volatile mix for policy making. As in the Russian case, disagreements on policy rooted in the fundamental differences between parties has occasionally resulted in fights,[55] but this is rare. One way to control this is to put limits on who may form a political party and on what basis. The Ukrainian constitution briefly addresses this issue (articles 36 and 37) although formal guidelines only came in 1997 when the Rada drafted a bill requiring prospective parties to have at least 2500 members and prohibiting most nonelected public officials from joining parties.[56]

The Reform Imperative

The Status of Reform: Too Little, Too Late?

The irony of Ukraine's economic woes is that it is such a diversified and developed system. Under Soviet rule Ukraine's economy included the already mentioned resource extraction and agricultural production, and also massive industrial output generated by its heavy industry sector. But this declined dramatically and by 1998 the industrial sector accounted for only twenty-six percent of GDP while agriculture made up twelve percent, and services sixty-two percent.[57] What had been Ukraine's strengths are now its weaknesses as aging and inefficient industry consume valuable, limited resources. Throughout much of the 1990s Ukraine's economy was in a state of depression. The GDP growth rate remained in negative figures for much of this period, and only achieved positive growth in 2000. Hyperinflation reached record levels (10,156 percent in 1993) before being brought down to manageable levels (approximately twenty-five percent in 2000). By January 1996 seventy-two percent of the population were estimated as living below the official poverty level.[58] (See Table 10.3).

TABLE 10.3   Key Economic Sector Performance in Ukraine, 1995–2000
(in percentages)

GDP   Industrial Production   Agricultural Production

Source: "Main Macroeconomic Indicators of Ukraine," Commonwealth of Independent States website [http://www.cisstat.com/eng/ukr.htm].

Unfortunately, the litany of economic difficulties does not stop there. Energy needs have long been a vexing problem for the economy even though Ukraine exports coal and electricity. Ukraine still finds it necessary to import natural gas and oil from Russia and has even attempted to pay for these commodities by barter arrangements, such as in Ukraine's 1996 agreement to give Russia twenty-five bombers and several hundred cruise missiles in exchange for partially offsetting Ukraine's energy debt (this later fell through).[59] Perhaps a more telling example lay in the coal sector. Despite a 1996 World Bank credit, Ukraine did not have the funds necessary to close a number of its coal pits that were losing money. Ironically, as one government official put it, "if this trend continues, there will be no closures."[60]

Privatization has been a volatile political issue for Ukraine. As in other Eurasian states privatization is considered a core element in Ukraine's transition to a market economy. Kuchma came to value it within the overall reform process

and promote it to the population despite his own initial opposition to it (he originally favored a program of stabilization and moderate governmental control
over the economy). Following his reelection in late 1999 Kuchma tried to reinvigorate the process by appointing a new proreform prime minister, and by approving a decree targeting over 2000 firms for sale,[61] but this was met with
skepticism and opposition within the Rada.

Ukraine's economy today includes a state-governed sector of major enterprises that will remain in place until large capital private investors are found to shore
up the economic infrastructure. This is true for both agriculture as well as industry. In contrast there is the burgeoning small business sector which has proven
only marginally competitive with the state sector.[62] As one observer has phrased it,
Ukraine's economy resembles a "state-capitalist model of development" involving
the rejection of "rigid monetarism."[63] Indeed, what Kuchma initially sought was a
slow pace of reform that would still guarantee Ukraine international financing
from the IMF and other lenders. This was useful for a (then) new president in
dealing with a reluctant parliament, resulting in a political accommodation in
1995 between Kuchma and the Rada. Since then Kuchma has pursued a progres-
sively more assertive reform strategy of political and social stability while taking
measured economic risks.[64] This cautious approach to reform has not been well-
received by the international lending community (especially the IMF and World
Bank) which are reluctant to strategically assist an economy that has resisted programs due to political concerns (seemingly indifferent to the need to calculate
political concerns as well).[65] It is doubtful that Ukraine's economic recovery can
succeed without the promise of such aid, or negotiations on debt forgiveness, but
economic reform clearly entails massive political risks.

As with the other Eurasian states Ukraine has been beset by a tremendous increase in crime; the shadow economy's share of GDP has been estimated at a
staggering fifty-five percent![66] Some of this is caused by the economic hardships
which have gripped the country since independence, but much is also attributable to the corruption and influence-peddling that exists within the government.[67] The competition for economic spoils between the regional elites of
Donetsk and Dnipropetrovs'k was most likely behind the assassination attempt
against Prime Minister Pavlo Lazarenko, and the murder of Rada legislator
Yevgeny Shcherban,[68] both in 1996. As the economy goes through its metamor-
phosis the competition for the spoils of resource allocation will continue to be
fierce until the boundaries of the new system are made more certain. New laws
and guidelines are now emerging but there is little political will to prevent excesses until the transformation is complete. Thus transitional societies seem
acutely vulnerable to the worst side effects of capitalist development because of
the very fact that they *are* in transition!

Foreign investment interest in the country has also suffered due to ambigu-
ous laws, overregulation, and in general a negative investment climate.[69] On the
plus side the government has made conscious efforts to reduce the trade deficit
and seek out new trade partners beyond the confines of the CIS. Hyperinflation
had been overcome and the inflation-ridden temporary currency, the *karbovanets*

(also known as kuponi), was finally replaced by a permanent currency, the *hryvna* in September 1996. Agriculture, too, seems on the upswing as in 2000 this sector registered its first growth since independence. But Ukraine must still prove that it can keep its own population at home and interested in working for the expansion and development of the economy before complete confidence in the system will be restored.

Chornobyl and Ecological Devastation

No single factor has touched the Ukrainian economy quite like that which occurred at the **Chornobyl** nuclear power plant near the Belarussian border on 26 April 1986. The damage imposed on the country by the explosion and fire in the unit housing Chornobyl's number four reactor has gone far beyond the immediate consequences of the disaster.[70] Just prior to the accident the plant's five reactors were providing the USSR with ten percent of its total electricity production and was also exporting energy abroad.[71] The immediate effects of the explosion and fire were the deaths of thirty-one individuals, serious injuries to hundreds more, and the evacuation of almost the entire surrounding countryside. Beyond this the Chornobyl accident spread nuclear radiation throughout eastern Europe and Scandinavia, damaged extensive tracts of farmland in both Ukraine and Belarus, and caused first Soviet, and then independent Ukraine to drastically revise their heavy reliance on nuclear power.[72] Over the long-term the human toll has been tremendous with possibly 8000 having died since 1986 due to radioactive exposure, and Ukraine devoting nearly five percent and Belarus a whopping twenty percent of their respective budgets to dealing with the results of the accident.[73]

In an economy supported by centrally allocated resources such that the Soviet Union was, Ukraine might have been able to deal with shutting down the reactors. But in the cash-strapped independent economy Chornobyl has proven to be a serious drain on the national budget. Kyiv has been forced to seek from foreign lenders including the Group of Seven (G-7), the European Bank for Reconstruction and Development (EBRD), the U.S. government, and others billions of dollars in aid to close the plant. Shutting down Chornobyl entirely has been a stated goal of the government for much of the past decade but frequently delayed as Ukraine struggles with the question of what will replace this crucial resource. The Chornobyl disaster remains an analogy for all that Ukraine has become, has undertaken, or abandoned. The economic effects, like the social impacts, are as much a part of the Ukrainian political, social, and economic dynamic as any cancer attacking the human anatomy. But if Ukraine can overcome this crisis then it can probably stand as one of the true survivors of the post-Soviet period.

Key Terms

Leonid Kuchma	Verkhovna Rada
Rukh	hryvna
Petro Symonenko	national democrats
Chornobyl	Russian irredentism

Questions for Consideration

1. Why has Ukraine not been able to move beyond its Soviet experiences and institute effective reforms?

2. Is the integration of ethnic Russians into Ukrainian society reducible to the language issue, or are there other elements which must be defined as well?

3. Are the Crimean Tatars the "wild card" of Ukrainian politics that could disturb the status quo between ethnic Ukrainians and ethnic Russians?

4. What sort of effect have the allegations of corruption surrounding the Kuchma administration had on Ukraine's ability to define itself as a stable political system?

5. Why has Ukraine remained so dependent on the Russian Federation?

Suggested Readings

Taras Kuzio, *Ukraine Under Kuchma: Political Reform, Economic Transformation, and Security Policy in Independent Ukraine* (New York: St. Martin's Press, 1997).

Taras Kuzio and Andrew Wilson, *Ukraine: Perestroika to Independence* (New York: St. Martin's Press, 1994).

Zhores Medvedev, *The Legacy of Chernobyl* (New York: W. W. Norton, 1992).

Alexander J. Motyl, *Dilemmas of Independence: Ukraine after Totalitarianism* (New York: Council on Foreign Relations Press, 1993).

Andrew Wilson, *Ukrainian Nationalism in the 1990s: A Minority Faith* (New York: Cambridge University Press, 1996).

Useful Websites

Cabinet of Ministers of Ukraine
   http://www.kmu.gov.ua/

DINAU, State Information Agency of Ukraine
   http://news.dinau.com.ua/

Institute of Statehood and Democracy-Rukh
   http://freelunch.freenet.kiev.ua/ISD/ISD-HOME.HTM

"Kyiv Post"
   http://www.kpnews.com

Verkhovna Rada homepage
   http://www.rada.kiev.ua/welcome.html

Ukrainian home page
   http://www.ukraine.org/

United Nations site about Ukraine
   http://www.un.kiev.ua/

Endnotes

1. As just a sample of the sources on the famine see Robert Conquest, *The Harvest of Sorrow* (New York: Oxford University Press, 1986); Miron Dolot, *Execution by Hunger* (New York: W. W. Norton, 1985); and Malcolm Muggeridge's historical novel, *Winter in Moscow* (Grand Rapids, MI: William B. Eerdmans Publishing Company, 1987).

2. Anatoly Kolodny, "Church and State in Ukraine Past and Present," *Ukrainian Review*, 42 (Winter 1995): p. 33.

3. Jaroslaw Martyniuk, "The State of the Orthodox Church in Ukraine," *RFE/RL Research Report*, 3 (18 February 1994): pp. 34–41.

4. Chrystyna Lapychak, "Rifts Among Ukraine's Orthodox Churches Inflame Public Passions," *Transition*, 2 (5 April 1996): pp. 6–10; also, Oleh W. Gerus, "Church Politics in Contemporary Ukraine," *Ukrainian Quarterly*, 52 (Spring 1996): pp. 28–46.

5. Kolodny, p. 35.

6. "Census counts 48.86 million people in Ukraine," Associated Press, 27 December 2001.

7. *CIA World Factbook, 2001,* Central Intelligence Agency web site [http://www.odci.gov/cia].

8. Frank Lorimer, *The Population of the Soviet Union: History and Prospects* (Geneva: League of Nations, 1946), p. 50.

9. *World Development Report, 1997* (New York: Oxford University Press, 1997), pp. 230–231.

10. *Post-Postup* (Kyiv), 26 January–3 February 1996, translated in FBIS-SOV, 23 February 1996, pp. 34–35.

11. *Population and Vital Statistics Report*, 48 (1 January 1996): pp. 14–15.

12. "Indicators on population," United Nations Statistics Division web site [http://www.un.org/Depts/unsd/social/population.htm].

13. "Indicators on health," United Nations Statistics Division web site [http://www.un.org/Depts/unsd/social/health.htm].

14. Arun Nanda, Anatoly Nossikov, Remigijus Prokhorskas, and Mirvet H. Abou Shabanah, "Health in the Central and Eastern Countries of the WHO European Region: An Overview," *World Health Statistics Quarterly*, 46 (1993): p. 4.

15. Clarence A. Manning, *The Story of Ukraine* (New York: Philosophical Library, 1947), pp. 33–35.

16. Paula J. Dobriansky, "Nationalism and Democracy in Ukraine," *Ukrainian Quarterly*, 51 (Spring 1995): pp. 35–44.

17. See *1995 State Department Report on Human Rights in Ukraine,* (Washington, DC: United States Department of State, 6 March 1996), pp. 7, 10.

18. John A. Armstrong, *Ukrainian Nationalism,* 3rd ed. (Englewood, CO: Ukrainian Academic Press, 1990), pp. 3–4.

19. For a more critical view of this historical association see Alexander J. Motyl, *Dilemmas of Independence: Ukraine After Totalitarianism* (New York: Council on Foreign Relations Press, 1993), pp. 87–89.

20. Victor Stepanenko, "The Social Construction of Identities in Ukraine," *Ukrainian Review,* 2 (Summer 1995): pp. 14–15. The author makes a case for how different segments of Ukrainian society perceive themselves but presents no data to back it up.

21. *Kiyevskiye vedomosti,* 27 October 1997, translated in World News Connection [http://wnc.fedworld.gov].

22. George O. Liber, *Soviet Nationality Policy, Urban Growth, and Identity Change in the Ukrainian SSR, 1923–1934* (Cambridge: Cambridge University Press, 1992), pp. 52–53.

23. See Stephen Rapawy, "Ethnic Reidentification in Ukraine," International Programs Center Staff Paper No. 90 (Washington, DC: United States Bureau of the Census, 1997): pp. 2–10.

24. Article 10, Constitution of the Republic of Ukraine, BRAMA, Gateway Ukraine web site [http://www.brama.com/ua-gov/conste.html].

25. *Delovoi mir,* 29 May 1997, reprinted at RIA-Novosti website, 29 May 1997 [http://www.russia.net/ria/ria_main.html].

26. See, for instance, *Segodnya,* 6 December 1996, reprinted at RIA-Novosti website, 6 December 1996 [http://www.russia.net/ria/dr/dc06122.htm].

27. See the "Treaty of Friendship, Cooperation and Partnership Between the Russian Federation and Ukraine," *Rossiyskaya gazeta,* 5 June 1997, reprinted at RIA-Novosti website, 6 June 1997 [http://www.ria-novosti.com/products/dr/1997/06/16-3-1.htm].

28. Andrew Wilson, "The Elections in Crimea," *RFE/RL Research Report,* 3 (24 June 1994): p. 7.

29. Interfax, 19 July 1994 and UNIAR, 20 July 1994, translated at FBIS-SOV 20 July 1994, p. 40.

30. *Uryadovyy kuryer,* 25 February, 1995, translated in FBIS-SOV, 30 March 1995, p. 47.

31. ITAR-TASS, 17 March 1995.

32. *Infobank,* 21 March 1995, translated in FBIS-SOV, 21 March 1995, p. 53.

33. Interfax, 16 December 1999 cited in *RFE/RL Newsline,* 20 December 1999.

34. M. N. Guboglo and S. M. Chervonnaia, "The Crimean Tatar Question and the Present Ethnopolitical Situation in Crimea," reprinted in *Russian Politics and Law,* 33 (November–December 1995): pp. 31–60.

35. Ian Bremmer, "Ethnic Issues in Crimea," *RFE/RL Research Report,* 2 (18 April 1993): pp. 24–28.

36. Constitution of Ukraine (Draft), submitted by the Constitutional Commission of the Parliament of Ukraine, 27 May 1993, Embassy of Ukraine in the United States, Washington, DC.

37. Marta Kolomayets, "Communists Propose own Version of New Constitution for Ukraine," *Ukrainian Weekly,* 31 March 1996.

38. Interfax, 16 October 1995; RFE/RL, 23 April 1996.

39. See the "Constitutional Agreement Between the Supreme Rada of Ukraine and the President of Ukraine on Basic Principles of the Organization and Functioning of the State Power and Local Self-Government in Ukraine Pending the Adoption of the New Constitution of Ukraine." [http://www.std.com:80/sabre/UFPWWW_Etc/Law/ULF/const.agreement/ca_intro.htm].

40. Ustina Markus, "Rivals Compromise on Constitution," *Transition,* 2 (26 July 1996): pp. 36–37.

41. Ibid.

42. *Rukh Insider,* 8 June 1995.

43. *RFE/RL Newsline,* 24 January 2000; ITAR-TASS, 31 January 2000, cited in FBIS-SOV, 1 February 2000; *RFE/RL Newsline,* 2 February 2000.

44. Interfax, 19 December 1996.

45. Interfax, 18 December 1996.

46. See, for instance, UNIAN, 26 February 1996, translated in FBIS-SOV, 27 February 1996, p. 46.

47. ITAR-TASS, 8 and 9 October 1995.

48. ITAR-TASS, 19 December 1996, World News Connection.

49. V. V. Fesenko, "The Political Elite of Ukraine: Contradictions in Its Formation and Development," *Polis,* no. 6 (1995), reprinted in *Russian Politics and Law,* 35 (January–February 1997): pp. 54–68.

50. For an assessment of the law see Myron Wasylyk, "Ukraine Prepares for Parliamentary Elections," *RFE/RL Research Report,* 3 (4 February 1994): pp. 12–14.

51. "Law of Ukraine on Elections of People's Deputies of Ukraine, 1997" [http://www2.essex.uk/elect/electip/ukr_el97.htm].

52. *Kyiv Post,* 3 April 1998.

53. For a profile of the party see *Vysokyy zamok,* 26 November 1996, translated in World News Connection, 26 November 1996.
54. Dominique Arel and Andrew Wilson, "The Ukrainian Parliamentary Elections," *RFE/RL Research Report,* 3 (1 July 1994): p. 8.
55. *Rukh Insider,* 27 November 1995.
56. Intelnews (Kyiv), 3 February 1997.
57. *CIA World Factbook, 2001,* CIA web site [http://www.cia.gov/cia/publications/factbook/index.html].
58. *Donbass,* 30 January 1996, translated in FBIS-SOV 23 February 1996, p. 55.
59. Interfax, 30 November 1996.
60. Interfax-Ukraine, 7 January 1997.
61. Interfax, 29 December 1999, cited in *RFE/RL Newsline,* 30 December 1999.
62. Taras Kuzio, "After the Shock, the Therapy," *Transition,* 1 (28 July 1996): p. 39.
63. Serhiy Tolstov, "Ukraine at the Economic Crossroads: Hopes and Opportunities," *Ukrainian Review,* 42 (Winter 1995): pp. 9–10.
64. Alexander J. Motyl, *Dilemmas of Independence: Ukraine After Totalitarianism* (New York: Council on Foreign Relations Press, 1993), p. 126.
65. *RFE/RL Newsline,* 11 July 1997.
66. *Kyyivska pravda,* 5 December 1996, translated in World News Connection.
67. Heiko Pleines, "Ukraine's Organized Crime is an Enduring Soviet Legacy," *Transition,* 2 (8 March 1996): pp. 11–13.
68. Interfax-Ukraine, 4 November 1996.
69. World Bank officials cited in *RFE/RL Newsline,* 3 December 1999.
70. An excellent description of the disaster is to be found in David R. Marples, *Chernobyl and Nuclear Power in the USSR,* (New York: St. Martin's Press, 1986).
71. Ibid, p. 116.
72. For an assessment of the cumulative effects of the disaster on the Soviet Union see Zhores Medvedev, *The Legacy of Chernobyl* (New York: W. W. Norton, 1990), pp. 303–307.
73. Chrystyna Lapychak, "The Chornobyl Fallout Persists," *Transition,* 1 (17 November 1995): p. 23.

Chapter 11

The Caucasus States: A Case Study of Georgia

Issues of territorial integrity always raise the volume of a country's political debate. In no part of the former Soviet space is the matter as volatile as in the Caucasus, and especially in Georgia where turmoil has characterized the political system rather than been an exception to the norm. Civil war, secessionist movements, armed militias run by local warlords, and a foreign military presence have all contributed to Georgia's inability to establish a stable governing order. In particular the separatist crisis in **Abkhazia,** in the northwest part of the country, has bubbled and frothed to the extent that Georgia's political agenda has become consumed with its resolution. So it was on 3 April 1997 that the Georgian parliament passed a conception (resolution) that equated "steady social development" with Georgia reasserting its authority over both Abkhazia and the region of South Ossetia.[1]

All of this points to the need to establish national identity, a condition which we have just seen as being a major facet of Latvia's political culture. It is not, however, the only major obstacle to Georgia (or Armenia and Azerbaijan) in its quest for national development. Economic growth in particular is closely tied to the resolution of the military conflicts. Leadership development and succession also remain intangibles in other parts of the Caucasus as evidenced by the assassination of the Armenian prime minister in 1999. The penchant to resolve political issues by resorting to violence has seemed almost too easy of a choice for many Georgians to make. These problems are compounded by the state's lack of a clear direction for its future. Phrased another way, Georgia doesn't know what it wants to be when it grows up.

Lands of Conflict and Instability

The Caucasus in Profile

As the wars in Chechnya have vividly demonstrated the Caucasus is a region of beliefs passionately held and independence fiercely guarded, all of this largely due to the incredible mix of peoples and cultures. Creating an integrated political

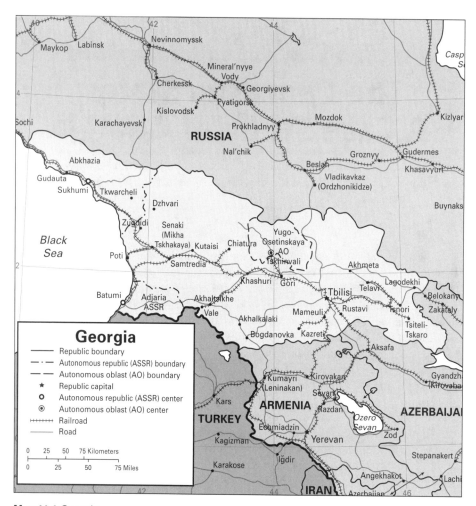

Map 11.1 Georgia

culture has proven to be a difficult enough task in the North Caucasus, which is part of the Russian Federation. The Southern Caucasus, which includes the post-Soviet states of Georgia, Armenia, and Azerbaijan, has been ravaged by violence and political instability in recent years beginning with the Nagorno-Karabakh conflict in 1988. Since then the Caucasus has been the setting for numerous political coups d'etat, civil war, separatism, terrorism, contested elections, pogroms, and ethnic cleansing. Coupled to natural disasters such as the 1988 earthquake in Armenia which killed 25,000 people, and an economic downslide which seems perpetual, it would be easy to dismiss the Caucasus as a backward region with the lowest prospects for political or economic development. This litany of troubles has generally remained out of the views of western publics since the region is decidedly off the beaten track of international politics and economics. The notoriety of larger and sometimes overbearing neighbors such as Russia, Turkey, Iraq, and Iran have instead captivated world audiences while the small states of the Caucasus are squeezed between them.

More so than in any of the regions examined in this book the Caucasus personifies the concept of *fragmented political cultures*. This is not to say that the societies themselves are fragmented (although in some respects this may be the case), but instead that their political systems are challenged by the most serious assortment of problems that states can face. One commentator, for instance, described Georgia in terms of being "Westernized enough for the model of a democratic nation-state to dominate its political agenda, but not Westernized enough to implement this model."[2] A troubling indicator of this fragmentation is the resultant hyperpluralism of parties which in 1997 reached a total of sixty-five prior to declining to fifty-six in 1999.[3] For a state with approximately 5.23 million people (2000 estimate)[4] this can spell out a weak party system dominated by special interests and personalism.

The collective hopes for harmony and growth in the Caucasus states rest upon their ancient senses of ethnic identity, and their abilities to see beyond the limitations of ethnicity. As with other states national identity in the Caucasus is founded upon religion and language. The Armenian and Georgian peoples were converted to Christianity in the fourth century, with the Armenian Apostolic Orthodox Church being established in the year A.D. 314 and the Georgian church later that century (Georgian legend holds that the death of Jesus Christ was known at that time to the Georgian tribes). Both churches are branches of the Orthodox faith and have their own hierarchies, the heads of which are referred to as the *Catholicos*, or supreme patriarch. The close association between these religions and their peoples' ethnic identities has done much to shape each nation (article 9 of the Georgian constitution specifically mentions this).

The rugged terrain of the region permitted both the Georgians and Armenians to create and sustain their own states. Over the centuries Mongols, Seljuks, and Persians all sought to overwhelm and occasionally convert these mountain kingdoms; Georgia (or **Sakartvelo,** the Georgians' own name for their land) maintained its independence the longest. In the nineteenth century the threat to Georgia's sovereignty came from another direction, that of the Russian empire to the north, which steadily intruded into the Caucasus. Despite a renewed, brief period of independence from 1918–1921, very nearly the entire Caucasus came under Soviet domain by 1921. Thereafter Georgia's fate became closely linked to that of its most infamous native son, Stalin, who along with fellow countrymen such as **Sergo Ordzhonikidze** and **Lavrenty Beria** brutally weeded out separatist sentiments. Ironically, Stalin is still revered by many in Georgia today.

Each of the Caucasus states are formally defined as republics. Armenia and Azerbaijan are unitary systems, while Georgia's constitutional status has not been finally determined due to its unresolved separatist conflicts. The capitals of all three states are large core cities (Tbilisi had 1.23 million people in 1999; Baku had 1.7 million people in 1997; and Yerevan had 1.2 million in 1999) that dominate both the national and regional political environments. A system where regionalism prevails, Georgia is composed of thirteen districts (including Abkhazia, Adjaria, South Ossetia, and Tbilisi) representing a highly divisive (fragmented) political culture.

Each of the Caucasus states has a distinct titular ethnic group which enjoys favored nation status (see Table 11.1). Ethnic Georgians account for seventy percent of the country's population and a large mix of other nationalities make up the remainder. Ethnicity is a difficult concept to measure in the Caucasus since it is equally recognizable in terms of lineage, religious identification, or language. The Adjarians, for instance, are ethnically Georgian but primarily Muslim in religious identification. Other subgroups are found within the Georgian population such as the Meshketians, Mingrelians, Svan, and Laz peoples, all of whom speak languages related to, yet distinct from, Georgian. Beyond these subgroups the largest ethnic minority in Georgia is the Armenians who account for more than eight percent of Georgia's population (437,000) with nearly half of these living in the capital Tbilisi and large groups concentrated near the border with Armenia. A sizeable number of Azeris (307,600) also live within Georgia, again largely near the border. The relative proximity of these last two peoples has been a source of occasional friction due to the Nagorno-Karabakh conflict.

TABLE 11.1   Ethnicity in the Caucasus States

Armenia* (1989)	%	Azerbaijan* (2000)	%	Georgia** (1997)	%
Armenian	93.3	Azerbaijani	71.0	Georgian	70.13
Kurdish	1.7	Talish	11.0	Armenian	8.10
Russian	1.5	Russian	6.0	Russian	6.32
Assyrian, Greek, other	3.5	Lezgin	4.0	Azerbaijani	5.7
		Dagestani	3.0	Ossetian	3.04
		Kurdish	3.0	Greek	1.86
		Avar	2.0	Abkhazian	1.78
				Ukrainian	0.97
				Kurdish	0.62
				Jewish	0.46
				Others	1.05

Sources: *"TransCaucasus, A Chronology", IX (January 2000), Armenian National Committee of America website [http://www.http://www.anca.org/tcc.html].
**Data for 1997, Parliament of Georgia website [http://www.parliament.ge/GENERAL/popl/pp2.html]

Separatist sentiments have been frequently expressed by two of Georgia's regional peoples: the Abkhaz and the Ossetians. Neither of these are directly related to the Georgians, and although there may be some mixing of these peoples with the Georgians, the Abkhaz and Ossetians have not been well integrated into Georgian society. The **Abkhaz,** who are relatively few in number (95,000), live primarily in the autonomous republic of Abkhazia. The "south" or "Georgian" **Ossetians,** numbering about 164,000 at the time of the last Soviet census, are also native to the Caucasus but ethnically akin to Iranians. The Ossetians' religious preferences are split between Christianity and Islam, but the more important issue is their integration into Georgian society which has been limited by political conflict. Both may be considered to have FNS within their respective territories.

Russians make up the third largest ethnic group in Georgia (about 6.3 percent of the total) and, as we have seen in other states, their very presence complicates the local political scene. According to the 1989 Soviet census approximately 341,000 Russians lived in Georgia. Many ethnic Russians do not speak the Georgian language (which belongs to the South-Caucasic language group) making their inclusion into Georgian life difficult at best. Russia itself has no formal territorial claims against the Georgian state, but it has become entangled in the Abkhazian, Ossetian, and Adjarian regional disputes, and has drawn out its withdrawal from its four Soviet-era bases in Georgia.

Elections, Revolutions, and Violent Change

The irony of elections in any of the three Caucasus states is that they come so easy, but provoke such violent outbursts after the fact. Georgia's presidential and parliamentary elections have proven to be relatively peaceful affairs, but usually beset by charges of corruption and manipulation. Despite considerable wrangling in 1990 over how Georgia's democratic prospects would be achieved the initial results were quite hopeful. The elections of October 1990 were already multiparty since the Georgian Communist Party had been marginalized by events. The original conception of the parliament was that of a 250 seat, unicameral body elected both on a proportional basis (with a four percent threshold) and majoritarian districts.[5] **Zviad Gamsakhurdia,** a nationalist dissident given to uncompromising stands with opponents, was elected in November 1990 as the leader of a broad-based coalition called **Round Table/Free Georgia** to the Supreme Soviet.[6] In May of the following year he was confirmed as president by eighty-seven percent of the general electorate. And yet the tendency of Caucasian electoral contests is to degenerate into fratricidal conflict belying whatever accomplishments the state may have made. Gamsakhurdia's increasingly strident nationalist policies, and his unwillingness to condemn the August 1991 coup in Moscow crystallized opposition against the president. A bloody month-long battle (December 1991–January 1992) fought in the streets of Tbilisi and the siege of the president in the parliament building consequently spelled doom for Georgia's first effort at electoral change.

Formal and Informal Political Power

The Presidency and the Focus of Power

Of all the presidencies in the post-Soviet republics the Georgian institution was clearly the least planned. The presidencies of Gamsakhurdia and **Eduard Shevardnadze** were crafted in the context of strong parliamentary systems. The uprising against Gamsakhurdia brought about an effort to weaken the power of the executive, but the divisions which were by 1992 embedded in Georgian political society required an individual firmly in charge of the ship of state. This served to enhance personalistic rule as shown in the latter career of Shevardnadze. Under the internationally renowned former Soviet foreign minister those initial, difficult years of independence saw the development of what is termed a **"half-presidential model"** where the president is the dominant political figure but without certain significant powers. As the 1995 constitution states "the President of Georgia heads and exercises domestic and foreign policy of the state" (article 69, sec. 2). But compare this to the legislature's role of "determin(ing) the main direction of domestic and foreign policy" (article 48).

Shevardnadze's position as one of the chief architects of Gorbachev's *perestroika* program was a major factor facilitating Georgia's independence movement. In his native land Shevardnadze was variously remembered for his personal resistance against corruption, but also his harsh policies against dissidents that resulted in the arrests of thousands while he was Soviet Georgia's Interior Minister.[7] In the wake of the anti-Gamsakhurdia coup, Shevardnadze was viewed to be the only person capable of leading Georgia through its troublesome first years of independence causing him to return to Georgia in March 1992 at the request of the members of the **State Council** (originally the Military Council) to head that body. Later that year Shevardnadze was elected chairman of the parliament and then head of state, in effect reprising his earlier position when he served as First Secretary of the Georgian Communist Party.

At first Shevardnadze had to proceed cautiously while trying to build consensus.[8] On 5 November 1995 Shevardnadze gained popular confirmation as president when he amassed 74.9 percent of the vote in the first contested presidential election since independence. Shevardnadze's electoral success was attributed to his considerable popularity among both the general public and the former communist apparatus (many of whom became members of the president's party). It was dramatically helped, however, by the public's association of his opponent (**Dzhumber Patiashvili** of the Communist Party of Georgia) with the 1989 massacre of Georgian protesters by Soviet troops in Tbilisi, and public sympathy after an attempted assassination of Shevardnadze on 29 August 1995.[9] Unlike many of his Eurasian contemporaries Shevardnadze ran for his post as a member of a distinct political party, the **Union of Georgian Citizens** (SMK); nor does the constitution prohibit him from remaining a member of a political grouping while holding office (although he did resign as chairman of the party in September 2001).

Eduard Shevardnadze (President of Georgia)

Source: © Novosti/Sovfoto

The real issue of Georgian politics is who wields power, either formally or informally. Nonconstituted forms of leadership have long been endemic to the Caucasian political scene regardless of legal formalities. Thus the constitution's delegation of powers is only significant if the authority of that document is upheld. The Georgian constitution leaves few doubts about the balance of power. The president's constitutional term of office can extend through two full terms of five years each (article 70, sec. 1). The president appoints the government, although with parliamentary approval (article 73, sec. 1(b)), and the government is responsible to him alone (article 79, sec. 1). He submits the draft of the state budget after consultation with the appropriate committees within the parliament (article 73, sec. 1(e)). Pointedly, the constitution restates this authority as if to demonstrate where real power lies (article 93, sec. 1).

One important power denied to the Georgian president is that of suspending the parliament, thus serving as a check on executive power. In contrast, the parliament possesses the power of impeachment (articles 63 and 75) which only partially offsets its lack of budgetary authority. The Georgian president has the right of legislative initiative (article 67, sec. 1), a decree-making power (article 73, sec. 1(i)), and may call for a referendum provided the referendum doesn't limit personal liberties or overturn laws. Presidential succession falls to the Speaker (or chairman) of the Parliament who in such an eventuality retains most presidential authority, but would only serve for forty-five days prior to new elections (article 76, sec. 3).

The organization of the executive branch was laid out in the 1995 "Law on the Structure and Activity Regulations of the Executive Power" which lays out the composition of the cabinet and the internal workings of the ministries.[10] Unique to the Georgian governing system is its lack of a prime minister; the position was eliminated with the 1995 constitution and the office's powers divided between the president and his primary assistant, the **state minister.** Recognizing this as something of a mistake Shevardnadze proposed in 2001 to reconstitute the position of prime minister, although the parliament, then in the throes of governmental crisis, was not willing to pursue the matter. The state minister's principal responsibility, the **State Chancellery,** is a collective body of advisors including a national security advisor and an advisor on economic matters who work directly for the president. Overall the State Chancellery coordinates the work of the ministries, regional and local governing bodies, and the private sector in the implementation of reform.[11]

The president appoints and fires all cabinet ministers as well as their first deputy ministers (article 73, section 1[b and c], and article 79). Technically, the president is denied the ability to dismiss the *entire* government, and instead must rely on the state minister "suggesting" this action (as was the case in both July 1998 and November 2001). As in the Baltic states, Georgian cabinet members do not have to come from the parliament. Again, some of these appointments may be controversial. Shevardnadze's selection in April 1997 of the then twenty-six-year-old governor of Guria (Shevardnadze's home region) Mikhail Chkuaseli to head the Ministry of Finance was heavily criticized,[12] but the move indicated Shevardnadze's continuing balancing of the old *nomenklatura* against a new elite ostensibly committed to reform, and to the president. Beyond this, in consultation with the state minister and his top advisors, the president also appoints the heads of the bureaucracy's "main offices and inspections" and permanent commissions (those dealing with sectoral and topical concerns). In addition, in 1997 the parliament gave the president the authority to appoint mayors and their deputies for the country's seven largest cities.[13] Although Shevardnadze promised that this power would be returned to the local level in 2001,[14] this controversial move threatened to remove the impetus for democratic participation and concentrate power instead in the hands of the president.

The Legislative Process

In some respects the Georgian parliament (Sakartvelos Parlamenti) is structured and acts like a classical model of parliamentary government. In other respects, such as in 1997 when parliament was accused of passing laws without a quorum the body has seemed only superficially democratic.[15] Proper legislative procedure has taken some getting used to even though there have been four sets of parliamentary elections since October 1990. That first parliament was dissolved in January 1992 on the heels of the coup by the Military Council. New elections were held in October 1992 and again in 1995 and 1999. In Georgia the legislature's primary strength is law making and there is little direct interference with its work by the executive branch. The constitution gives the parliament "general control over the Cabinet of Ministers" (article 48) but the parliament has been unsuccessful in exercising this authority and making the government responsive.[16]

The constitution provides for a two-house assembly but to date only one chamber, the **Council of the Republic** with its 235 deputies, has met. As in both Ukraine and Russia deputies are elected through both proportional representation (150 seats) and single-mandate contests (85 seats) for four year terms. The upper chamber—the **Senate**—has yet to be configured pending the establishment of what the constitution refers to as "appropriate conditions and when self governing bodies have been created over the whole territory of Georgia" (article 4, sec. 1). The same constitutional provision goes on to state that the Senate "will consist of members elected from Abkhazia, Adjaria and other territorial units of Georgia as well as five members appointed by the President" (sec. 3). In other words, the Senate's form of representation will be territorial in nature. But until the Abkhazian and South Ossetian conflicts are resolved the formation of the Senate will have to wait.

Parliamentary elections since 1992 have reinforced the hyperpluralist ideological, economic, and regional choices available to Georgians. Voter turnout has been consistent at approximately sixty-eight percent of eligible voters.[17] Georgia's lack of control over Abkhazia and South Ossetia, as well as the refugees displaced by the civil conflicts must be considered extenuating circumstances in turnout. However, turnout ranks favorably with more developed democratic systems and one might expect that this figure may induce greater stability and negate some of the dangers brought on by the regional conflicts.

As with other parliamentary systems examined here no Georgian party or bloc has come close to acquiring an electoral majority although by 1999 Shevardnadze's party, the SMK had managed to gain 41.9 percent of the popular vote and a working majority (fifty-three percent for 121 seats) within the parliament. Two essential differences have shifted the political landscape. First, the threshold level for party/factional entrance to the parliament was raised effective for the 1999 elections from five to seven percent, thereby compressing the number of parties in the legislature. Second, what may be emerging is a two-four party system since only a small number of parties may be considered competitors with any measure of influence. Together these changes may yet produce stability for an otherwise chaotic political process, although it still appears too early to tell.

Given its electoral successes and the favoritism shown toward it by Shevardnadze, the SMK was considered Georgia's party of power from its foundation as a centrist party in November 1993. It has drawn its membership from an array of former communist party apparat members, as well as liberals and conservatives, but the internal tensions thus produced began to pull the party apart by 2001. Having campaigned on the themes of law and order, moderate paced economic reforms guaranteeing social protections, and minority rights and protections,[18] the SMK displayed an ineffectiveness in dealing with Georgia's protracted separatist conflicts, economic downturns, and corruption in government. The cohesion of the SMK was strained beyond retention with Shevardnadze's unsuccessful effort to promote his State Minister, Vazha Lortkipanidze, to succeed the SMK's leading reformer, **Zurab Zhvania,** as speaker of the parliament in November 2001. The end result was a most unlikely scenario: The election of a woman, **Nino Burdjanadze,** to the post in a political system with deeply rooted values of male dominance. Alternately a critic and supporter of Shevardnadze, Burdjanadze may provide the healing elements necessary for the parliament to do business.[19]

The SMK's closest competitor, and one that seems to be developing more than a regional following, is the **Aghordzineba** (All Georgian Revival Union, or simply Revival) movement. While polling 6.84 percent in 1995, by 1999 it had quadrupled this with a 25.7 percent showing of electoral support. This party is led by the mercurial chairman of the Supreme Soviet of Adjaria, **Aslan Abashidze.**[20] Largely regionalist in character Revival has been viewed as Abashidze's stalking horse for the Georgian presidency. The party explicitly supports the 1995 constitution, favors the reintegration of Abkhazia and South Ossetia into the Georgian state, the rebuilding of Georgia's national defense, development of the economy along free-market lines, and enhancing foreign investment.[21] More particularly, Abashidze has encouraged regionalist aspirations amongst the Adjarian population, and has been implicitly supported in this by the Russian government which maintains a military presence in the region. This is a potentially explosive approach within both regional and national politics as sentiment against Russian interference in Georgian politics runs very high.

The parliament's leadership is structured along party lines reflecting the electoral strength of the various factions.[22] Serving with the chairman are five deputy chairman, two of whom represent the parliamentary majority, one each for Adjaria and Abkhazia (article 55, sec. 1), and the last standing for the parliamentary minority.[23] The representation accorded Georgia's autonomous republics is only nominal, however, as the deputy chairman from Abkhazia is actually an ethnic Georgian, and not a member of the government in power in Sukhumi, the regional capital.

The Council of the Republic is responsible for territorial representation questions that eventually will fall under the Senate's authority. Regionalism has found expression through the small **Abkhazeti** ("Abkhazia-My Home") faction and the already mentioned Aghordzineba. Due to the dominance of parties and factions in the lower house minorities have been largely left out of the current system. To a large extent women have been too; prior to the 1999 elections there were sixteen women in parliament, or seven percent of the total deputies.[24] This overwhelming orientation toward males, though typical of the general political culture, is certainly not out of line in relation to the majority of post-Soviet states. The constitution does not specifically prohibit parties being formed on either ideological or racial/ethnic bases unless these are for the purposes of either overthrowing the state or causing unrest (article 26, sec. 3). "Citizens of foreign

countries and stateless persons" are prevented from founding political organizations and participating in politics (article 27), but to date this has not been a
major concern of the government.

Warlordism, Clan Leaders and Militias

The character of Georgia's political system has been shaped almost as much by
militia groups and warlords as by political parties. Conflict and warfare have long
been ways of life in many parts of the Caucasus, and probably nowhere more so
than in Georgia. A weak state caught between large and expansionist empires
Georgia's peoples have over the years turned to regional or militia leaders (warlords) for protection. While these tendencies were repressed during the Soviet
years, they reemerged as the communist state's power receded. Militias had already begun to form prior to the disintegration of the Soviet Union and several of
these were used as the foundation for Georgia's national defense forces. The
paramilitary organizations were primarily responsible for the overthrow of Gamsakhurdia, and the leaders of these groups went on to form the Military Council
which governed immediately following the coup. Generally speaking the warlords
were strongly nationalistic in outlook favoring efforts to protect Georgia's territorial integrity, but also securing for themselves graft and corruptive influence. The
separatist conflicts in Abkhazia and South Ossetia allowed the paramilitaries to
expand their influence even as they aggravated the conflicts in those regions.

   The existence of militias represented a duality of formal and informal power
centers, a condition generally considered untenable in stable political systems.
With little formal power or control over the military to back him up Shevardnadze threatened to resign his position as head of state in September 1993 unless
given emergency powers to rule by decree. While this effort did not entirely rein
in the militias Shevardnadze had set the ground rules for what constituted legitimacy in Georgia. An abortive coup effort by Gamsakhurdia in 1993 resulted in
the former president's exile and suicide which cleared the way for Shevardnadze
to deal with the warlords who had put him in power in the first place.

   Among the most important of the militias was the **National Guard.** Founded
in December 1990 as the core of an eventual national military force,[25] the guard
became the personal militia of one of the most powerful men in Georgia, **Tengiz
Kitovani.** The National Guard proved to be crucial in the struggle against Gamsakhurdia and then later in the efforts to suppress Abkhaz separatism. More dangerous to the stability of Georgia's newfound democracy, however, were the
activities of **Jaba Ioseliani.** As head of the paramilitary **Mkhedrioni** (Knights or
Horsemen), which he created in 1988 and eventually comprised as many as 5000
members,[26] Ioseliani was a key figure in the overthrow of Gamsakhurdia in
1991–1992. Along with Kitovani, Ioseliani formed the Military Council and then its
successor the State Council to rule in the wake of the deposed president. Recognizing the need to legitimize their regime they invited Shevardnadze to head the
new government with Ioseliani as Deputy Chairman, second only to Shevardnadze. At the same time Ioseliani continued his paramilitary operations which

resulted in repeated conflict between the Mkhedrioni and Zviadists (Gamasakhurdia loyalists) in western Georgia in 1992,[27] with numerous deaths and assassinations on both sides.[28] The Mkhedrioni were also one of the major forces involved in the Abkhazian conflict in 1992–1993, and again clashed with the Zviadists in 1993. In 1994 the Mkhedrioni was formally recognized as a "rescue corps" for its part in protecting the state.

Shevardnadze's efforts to ensure state control over the militias led him in 1995 to order the disarmament of the Mkhedrioni,[29] and in the wake of an attempt on his life on 29 August to subsequently disband them.[30] Arrested in 1996 initially on drug and weapons charges,[31] and later indicted for conspiracy to assassinate Shevardnadze,[32] Ioseliani was put on trial, imprisoned, and had all of his property confiscated[33] (he has since been released). For his part Kitovani and a number of his supporters also received prison terms for their paramilitary activities.[34] Gamsakhurdia's supporters were treated even more harshly and one of his lieutenants, Vakhtang Kobalia, was even given the death penalty.[35] Consolidation of political authority by the center seemed to have prevailed and the era of warlords and militias appeared to be at an end.

Political Pluralism and Tolerance

In between the warlords, adventurers, political parties, and the common people a pluralist political culture has emerged. As already noted political parties have flourished in Georgia with relatively minor restrictions. Even so a different kind of threat to pluralism lies in key opposition figures being arrested and police harassment of demonstrators rather than the banning of entire organizations.[36] Abuses of citizens' rights are even more egregious in Abkhazia where the Georgian government cannot protect its citizens from arbitrary political trials, assault, torture, and other crimes.[37]

Pluralism is also expressed through the existence of a competitive media. News agencies, newspapers, radio and television sources compete avidly with one another in expressing the viewpoints of the public and the political leadership. In 1996 there were approximately ten information agencies and thirty regularly published newspapers in Georgia; by 1999, however, the ability of the market to sustain so many outlets had contracted and only four information agencies remained.[38] As noted in earlier chapters government and private media outlets are underfunded both in terms of salaries and operational costs. Article 24, section 2 of the constitution guarantees a free and uncensored media and generally the Georgian government has resisted the temptation to directly harass media sources and outlets which disagree with administration policies. Still, in comparison to the Soviet period the availability of the news in Georgia today (and in the Caucasus in general) is light years apart.

Pluralism has evoked a price. Human rights have been frequent casualties in the pursuit of political development. Ultranationalists and regime opponents of different political backgrounds remain targets for arrest or detention by the Georgian government.[39] Accusations of torture, physical abuse, and even murder of citizens in police custody are fairly commonplace.[40] Georgia also retains much of the harsh prison regime (including psychiatric wards and penal colonies) that prevailed under the Soviet system. As but one example a Georgian human rights group estimated in 1999 that eighty percent of prisoners in Georgian jails suffered from tuberculosis.[41] Inflated or not the claim represents the serious nature of the problems confronting Georgia's social and legal transitions and the limitations posed by a lack of official concern and chronic underfunding.

The failure to protect human rights may be directly attributable to a lack of respect for a rule of law society. Several significant advancements were made in 1997 when parliament passed the "Law on the Courts," the "Law on the Procuracy," and a Criminal Procedures Code but these were not put into force until 1999.[42] The constitution does provide for a **Constitutional Court** and a system of "general courts" (article 83, sections 1 and 2). The long-delayed establishment of both the Constitutional Court (April 1996) and the general courts (May 1997) meant that Soviet norms and processes prevailed well after independence, but with United States financial assistance the courts have experienced extensive reform. Among other things the Constitutional Court now consists of nine members with three judges each appointed by the president and parliament; rather oddly, the remaining three jurists are appointed by the **Supreme Court,** a technically inferior court.[43] Georgia's legal transformation continues to be drawn out, however, due to the poor training of jurists, low pay, and corruption which reaches even the highest levels of the legal system.[44] All of these act as impediments to Georgia's acceptance into the European community of nations. Only in 1999 did the legislature ratify the European Human Rights Convention and join the Council of Europe;[45] the lateness of these efforts indicates a lack of leadership commitment to these important goals.

Threats to Georgia's Statehood

Russia's Interests in the Region

On 17 January 1996 the Georgian parliament finally ratified the treaty of friendship and cooperation which had been signed between Georgia and Russia in 1994. While the treaty was easily approved (the Russian legislature did not ratify it) opposition appeared to what many Georgians viewed as an effort to forge a military union between the two countries.[46] But the treaty reflected the political reality of internal instability which has so plagued the Georgian system. Recognizing early on that Georgia's territorial integrity could only be secured by agreements with the Russians Shevardnadze made several moves. First, he agreed that Russia would act as arbitrator in the Abkhazian conflict and eventually provide the peacekeeping force necessary to separate the two sides. Second, in October 1993 Shevardnadze was forced to go to Russia in search of military support at a time when, as he dramatically summed it up, "those who play with the forces of darkness in Moscow seem to be trying to drag Georgia back into medieval darkness."[47]

The price for Russian troop assistance has been high: Shevardnadze committed Georgia to joining the CIS in 1993, a decision grudgingly ratified by parliament in 1994.[48] Russia was allowed to retain its four military bases initially for two years, and to station there 20,000 of its troops (later reduced to two bases and 15,000 troops).[49] Russia's goals were simple: 1) reassert its presence in the Caucasus; and 2) preclude increasing Turkish influence. For Shevardnadze the agreement caused him to be vilified by his political opponents particularly after Russia brokered a new cease-fire in Abkhazia in April 1994.[50]

But the Georgian president was demonstrating the skills that had first brought him to the world's attention: In particular, Shevardnadze encouraged good relations with Turkey and Iran while simultaneously playing "the Russian card."[51] Moreover, Georgia has reiterated its desire for UN intervention in Abkhazia, membership in NATO,[52] and made it clear that Georgia would not be part of a recreated supranational state, or the CIS's version of economic integration.[53] In probably the most controversial move in 2002 Shevardnadze invited American troops to Georgia as part of an effort to curb "terrorism" in the border region with Chechnya/Russia (the Pankisi Gorge), a policy which provoked considerable protest among Russian policy makers.

The real danger for Georgia, however, has been the instability in Russia's southern Caucasus, in particular the Chechnya crises. The 1999 invasion saw increasing tensions between the Georgians and the Russians as the Russians tried to prevent Chechen militants from using Georgia as a safe haven. When Georgia rejected a Russian proposal for Russian troops to patrol the Georgian-Chechen border from within Georgia the Russian reaction seemed ominous.[54] Georgians traveling to Moscow were suddenly required to have visas, and rumors flew amongst Georgian officials that Russian special forces were being built up at a Russian base near Tbilisi.[55] Russian air attacks on Georgia's Pankisi Gorge near the Chechen border where both Chechen refugees and militants congregated further demonstrated how high a price Georgia would have to pay for sovereignty.[56] It seems that the tension in these two states' relations will be present regardless of Russia's military problems: conflict in Georgia's separatist-minded regions bears this out.

The Separatist Conflicts

The issue of separatism is at the same time about failed efforts to integrate disparate peoples, nationalism taken to extremes, and legitimate aspirations of self-governance. Both Abkhazia and South Ossetia are regions which have long been under Georgian control and the relationships that have developed between the Georgians and these region's titular populations have been uneasy at best and openly hostile at their worst.[57] Fueled by the fears of extreme Georgian nationalism the Abkhaz' pursuit of sovereignty was also fed by Russian desires to shape events in Georgia.[58] Toward this end the Abkhaz were assisted in their successful campaign against invading Georgian forces in 1992–1993 by Russian arms,[59] Cossacks, mercenaries, and members of the Confederation of Mountainous Peoples of the Caucasus (including Chechen militants[60]). In 1994 Abkhaz military units also received training from Russian separatists in the Transdniester region of Moldova.[61]

The weak and disorganized Georgian military and militias proved no match for the Abkhazian forces and by 1993 Georgia could no longer claim control over most of the region. Since that time, however, outbreaks of fighting have occurred periodically between Georgian guerillas and Abkhaz security forces including May 1998 when Abkhaz reprisals against the Georgian population in the Gali raion led to 40,000 ethnic Georgians fleeing to Georgia proper to join 200,000 others from 1992–1993 (approximately 45.7 percent of the region's total population in 1989; see Box 11.1). The comparatively small Abkhaz people thus had become the new "favored nation."

Hoping that diplomatic pressure would produce a breakthrough in 1996 Shevardnadze convinced the CIS (including Russia) to enact an economic boycott against Abkhazia that remains in force today despite being little observed, much to Abkhazia's benefit. He followed this soon after with an appeal to the UN Security Council to affirm Georgia's right to determine Abkhazia's political status.[62] In February 1997 the CIS recognized that Abkhazia was "an undeniable

---

BOX 11.1   Refugees: The Tragedy of the Caucasus

Each of the three Caucasus states has become home to a significant number of displaced persons, largely due to the ethnic cleansing that has accompanied the various regional conflicts. In the Armenian case these are refugees who fled across what was at the time internal boundaries of the Soviet Union. In both Georgia and Azerbaijan the largest number of refugees are internally displaced persons (IDPs) due to civil strife and separatism in distinct regions of the country. Azerbaijan also has a large number of refugees coming from Armenia, Georgia, and Central Asia. The creation of large refugee populations has had the effect of eliminating ages-old ethnic communities in both Armenia and Azerbaijan and creating more ethnically homogeneous societies.

	# of refugees	IDPs
Armenia	310,000	72,000
Azerbaijan	233,682	616,546
Georgia	20	277,000

Source: United Nations High Commission for Refugees, January 1999, [http://www.unhcr.ch/un&ref/numbers/numbers.htm]

part of Georgia," and not long thereafter Abkhaz officials declared that they had renounced independence in favor of finding either a federal or confederal relationship with Georgia.[63] Still, the deadlock remained and when hostilities intensified in May 1998 between Abkhaz forces and White Legion guerillas Shevardnadze explicitly admitted that his government was giving assistance to the guerillas.[64] The situation escalated again in September 2001 as a combined Georgian-Chechen force of irregulars invaded Abkhazia before being repelled by Abkhaz forces. Today Abkhazia remains an impediment to Georgia's political development and a diversion for Georgia's political elites from equally pressing problems.

The South Ossetian conflict has also involved spilled blood. Gamsakhurdia's stridently nationalist policies such as canceling the region's autonomous status, forced many Ossetians to leave the region.[65] Unlike the ethnic breakdown within Abkhazia, however, Ossetians make up a solid majority (66.2 percent, 1989) of the region's (called **Tskhinvali** by Georgians) total population (Georgians accounted for twenty-nine percent). Fighting consumed the area in 1991 and in December the region's government declared itself independent. Since the end of fighting in mid-1992 South Ossetia has treated Georgia as a foreign state due more to the fact that relations between the two had not been settled than for any other reason.[66]

Nevertheless, the South Ossetian conflict has not completely fallen victim to the impasse that has characterized Abkhaz-Georgian relations. Talks mediated by Moscow in May 1996 resulted in the two sides signing a peace "memorandum" as the first stage in settling the conflict,[67] and in March 1997 the South Ossetians (and implicitly Moscow) recognized Georgia's territorial integrity, while Georgia agreed to an unspecified level of "self-determination" for South Ossetia.[68] Shortly thereafter the South Ossetian leadership began encouraging its refugees to return to the region.[69] The South Ossetian government's decisions to hold elections prior to the complete reintegration of refugees has been condemned by Georgian authorities,[70] demonstrating that a considerable distance remains to be traveled on the road to normalized relations.

The Economics of Independence

The Georgian economy has operated under the most strenuous of circumstances since independence. An IMF estimate of the country's economic conditions in 1991 showed that Georgia's net material product (NMP) had declined by twenty-five percent, inflation increased from five percent to eighty percent in one year, agricultural output fell by eighteen percent and industrial production was down by twenty-five percent.[71] Against the backdrop of a country in the throes of civil war the trade deficit grew not just with foreign countries but with other former Soviet republics.[72] Georgia's leaders also exhibited considerable ineffectiveness in developing a market-oriented economy. The government failed to liberalize prices as other transitional economies had done leading in 1992 to nearly tenfold price increases in basic commodities (bread, milk).

The Georgian economy's primary exports are principally agricultural goods such as tea and citrus products; this leaves Georgia dependent on foreign trade for manufactured goods. Like many of the Eurasian states, Georgia has been a net importer of heavily subsidized energy products. With constant disruptions of energy supplies arriving through areas of military conflicts (for instance, Abkhazia cut electricity supplies to Georgia in April 1997 in retaliation for Georgia stopping telephone connections between Abkhazia and Russia[73]) Georgian production has suffered greatly. Much of Georgia's future economic growth is conditional upon the transhipment of oil and natural gas from Azerbaijan to Turkey through the Baku-Supsa and Baku-Ceyhan pipelines. Georgia has gained some outside assistance for improving its energy sector,[74] but the IMF and other international lenders are increasingly reluctant to assist an economy that is charitably characterized as being chronically corrupt.[75]

In general Georgia has pursued a market-oriented economy open to foreign and domestic investors. To realize this goal the constitution recognizes "the universal right of property" and agricultural land has largely been privatized.[76] Constitutional guarantees also exist for "acquisition, transfer and inheritance" (article 21, section 1), the right to freedom of movement and residence (article 22, section 1), and "the freedom of intellectual creativity and intellectual property rights" (article 23, section 1). And yet, as with the Russian and Ukrainian cases, there remains a substantial state-controlled sector.

A consensus does exist among political leaders that Georgia should function as a transit point for goods flowing between Europe and Asia. This is the underlying philosophy behind the development of oil export pipelines from Azerbaijan to Turkey, and a considerable source for revenue for the beleaguered economy. In addition, despite tensions with Russia, trade with that state has been revived particularly as Russia can provide Georgia with the natural gas it needs for its shaky production facilities. In both cases the continual political instability of the Caucasus will most likely be the deciding factor for the long-term success of these enterprises.

In macroeconomic terms Georgia's economy has begun to pick itself up out of the ashes. Despite near calamitous conditions (in 1994 GDP had plummeted to only twenty percent of its 1990 figure), 1995 saw a return to real growth rates.

By 1997 GDP was registering impressive gains and industrial production shot up by ten percent as the pace of industrial enterprise closings slackened.[77] Although delayed by the civil strife the introduction of the **lari** to replace the coupon system in September 1995 was still a full year earlier than Ukraine's currency transition.

As with the other Eurasian states 1998 proved to an unsettling year as both industrial and agricultural development plunged (see Table 11.2). The trade deficit ran at alarmingly high rates (it grew by 150 percent from 1996 to 1997) as at least eighty percent of production now originates outside of the country. As much as sixty-five percent of Georgia's entire population was living below the state's poverty level in 1997[78] and seventy percent of the population of the

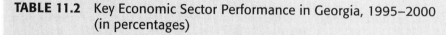

TABLE 11.2   Key Economic Sector Performance in Georgia, 1995–2000 (in percentages)

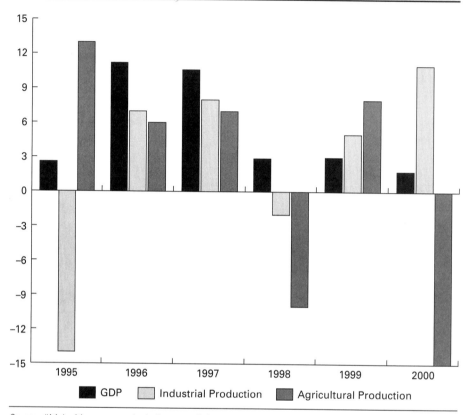

Source: "Main Macroeconomic Indicators of Georgia," Commonwealth of Independent States website [http://www.cisstat.com/eng/georg.htm].

capitol were as well two years later.[79] Estimates of the number of people out of work over the last several years have hovered at twenty to thirty-two percent of the entire work force.[80] In addition, as much as forty percent of productivity may be engaged in the shadow economy,[81] thereby limiting the state's potential for sustained development.

Certainly Georgia's peoples deserve a break from the unrelenting calamities that have befallen them. Much depends on the stability of the political system that has taken root under Shevardnadze's direction, but again there are clear warning signals. One man cannot impose his rule on a country and still expect that the system's foundation will be strong enough to outlive him. Moreover, the country's political elites have to resist their own tendencies toward hyperpluralism which so far have led to political and economic paralysis. Georgia's fate is only *affected* by the regional environment; its peoples are ultimately responsible for making their country a prosperous and attractive state. But in this respect, as we will see in the next chapter, they have much greater opportunities than those who live in Uzbekistan and Central Asia.

Key Terms

Abkhazia

Zviad Gamsakhurdia

warlords

Union of Citizens of Georgia

lari

Mkhedrioni

half-presidential model

state minister

Questions for Consideration

1. What is Georgia's hope for maintaining its territorial integrity?

2. If the Caucasus states' economies were to rebound, what would be the implications for their governments' stability?

3. What obstacles stand in the way of Georgia moving beyond the Shevardnadze era?

4. Is corruption endemic to a society like Georgia's, or is the problem the result of Georgia's style of governing?

5. What long-range strategies would you expect reformers in Georgia to employ in making their political and economic systems work?

Suggested Readings

Bruno Coppieters, ed. *Contested Borders in the Caucasus* (Brussels: VUBPress, 1996).

Revaz Gachechiladze, *The New Georgia: Space, Society, Politics* (London: UCL Press, 1995).

Ronald Grigor Suny, *The Making of the Georgian Nation,* 2nd ed.(Bloomington, IN: Indiana University Press, 1994).

Tadeusz Swietochowski, *Russia and Azerbaijan: A Borderland in Transition* (New York: Columbia University Press, 1995).

Useful Websites

Abkhazia information
  http://abkhazia.caucasus.net/

Central Eurasia Project-Georgian resources page
  http://www.soros.org/georgcep/georgia.html

Georgian information links
  http://www.sakartvelo.com/

Georgian Parliament
  http://www.parliament.ge/

Press Office of the President of Georgia
  http://www.presidpress.gov.ge/

Prime News Agency
http://www.prime-news.com.ge/

Sarke News Agency
http://www.sarke.com/

Endnotes

1. "Georgian parliament adopts territorial integrity restoration conception," BGI News Agency (Georgia), 3 April 1997.
2. Ghia Nodia, "Nationalism and the Crisis of Liberalism" in eds. Richard Caplan and John Feffer, *Europe's New Nationalism* (New York: Oxford University Press, 1996), p. 113.
3. Georgia Parliament home page, "List of Parties and Blocks in Georgia taking part in the Elections," 2 December 1997 [http://www.parliament.ge/GEORGIA/S_P/blpar.htm]. Also see "Parties and Blocs Participating in the Election of October 31, 1999." [http://www.parliament.ge/ABOUT/election_99/election_list.htm].
4. "Indicators on population", Population Division and Statistics Division of the United Nations Secretariat, United Nations Statistics Division [http://www.un.org/Depts/unsd/social/population.htm].
5. On the background to these elections see Darrell Slider, "Georgia" in ed. Glenn E. Curtis, *Armenia, Azerbaijan, and Georgia, Country Studies* (Washington, DC: Superintendent of Documents, 1995), pp. 208–12.
6. Reuters, 15 November 1990.
7. See Carolyn McGiffert Ekedahl and Melvin A. Goodman, *The Wars of Eduard Shevardnadze* (College Station, PA: Pennsylvania State University Press, 1997), Chapter One.
8. Stephen F. Jones, "Georgia's Power Structures," *RFE/RL Research Report,* 2 (1 October 1993): p. 5.
9. Jonathan Aves, *Georgia: From Chaos to Stability* (London: Royal Institute of International Affairs, 1996), pp. 11–13.
10. "Law of Georgia About the Structure and Rules of Activity of the Executive Power," Parliament of Georgia website [http://www.parliament.ge/PARLIAMENT/L_A/35-Is_e.htm].
11. Interview with Niko Lekishvili, *Svobodnaya Gruziya,* 12 June 1996, World News Connection [http://wnc.fedworld.gov/].
12. BGI, 1 May 1997.
13. *Resonance,* 16 October 1997.
14. *Akhali* Taoba, 18 November 1998.
15. BGI, 14 May 1997.
16. *DGHE,* 26 July–1 August 1996, cited in FBIS-SOV, 8 August 1996, p. 52.
17. "Parliamentary Elections in Georgia", *Parliament of Georgia Newsletter,* November 1999 [http://www.parliament.ge/NEWSLETTER/november_99.html].
18. Aves, p. 15.
19. "Speaker's Expectations of Serious Changes in Government Did Not Come True," Sarke Information Agency, 5 December 2001 [http://www.sarke.com/cgi/search/news.asp?Code=8971].
20. See Elizabeth Fuller, "Aslan Abashidze: Georgia's Next Leader?", *RFE/RL Research Report,* 2 (5 November 1993): pp. 23–26.
21. See the platform of the Parliamentary Faction of Georgia "Revival" ("Aghordzineba"), Parliament of Georgia website [http://www.parliament.ge/PARLIAMENT/agor-p.html].

22. This last position was added only in 1999 See "Parliament elected 4 vice speakers and decided to introduce the post of the 5th one," 25 November 1999, Sarke Information Agency Daily News: Politics [http://www.sarke.com/cgi/].
23. "Correlation of Men and Women in the Parliament of Georgia," Parliament of Georgia website [http://www.parliament.ge/PARLIAMENT/S_P/STAT/menwomen.htm].
24. See Elizabeth Fuller, "Paramilitary Forces Dominate Fighting in the Transcaucasus", *RFE/RL Research Report,* 2 (18 June 1993): p. 80.
25. Ibid.
26. *RFE/RL Daily Report,* 6 July 1992.
27. Russian TV, 18 June 1992, cited in RFE, 19 June 1992.
28. *RFE/RL Daily Report,* 2 August 1993.
29. AFP, 4 May 1995, cited in FBIS-SOV, 5 May 1995, p. 85.
30. ITAR-TASS, 6 October 1995.
31. *OMRI Daily Digest,* 16 November 1995.
32. Interfax, 14 December 1995.
33. *Akhali taoba,* 11 November 1998, cited in "Annotated Daily Headlines of the Georgian Press," Caucasian Institute for Peace and Development (CIPDD) [cipdd@access.sanet.ge].
34. Reuters, 9 October 1996.
35. *OMRI Daily Digest,* 20 November 1996.
36. BGI, 9 April 1997.
37. "Amnesty International Annual Report 2000: Georgia," Amnesty International website [http://www.amnesty.org/].
38. "Media in the CIS," Internews web site [http://www. internews.ras.ru/books/media/georgia_4.html].
39. See BGI, 18 April 1997.
40. "Georgia Country Report on Human Rights Practices for 1998," 26 February 1999, Bureau of Democracy, Human Rights, and Labor, United States Department of State website [http://www.state.gov]: pp. 1–2.
41. National Section of Georgia of the International Society for Human Rights (ISHR) [http://members.delphi.com/levur/index.html].
42. "Georgia Country Report on Human Rights Practices for 1998," pp. 6–7.
43. "The Law of Georgia About the Constitutional Court of Georgia" (unofficial version), Parliament of Georgia website [http://www.parliament.ge/PARLIAMENT/L_A/95-rs_e.htm].
44. See Eka Pirtskhalava, "The Constitutional Court Defeated Democracy Yesterday," *Sakartvelos gazeti,* 4 November 1998; also, *Droni,* 5 November 1998, p. 1, translated in FBIS-SOV, 5 November 1998.
45. ITAR-TASS, 20 May 1999.
46. Interfax cited in *OMRI Daily Digest,* 18 January 1996.
47. Simon Sebag Montefiore, "Eduard Shevardnadze," *New York Times Magazine,* 26 December 1993: p. 16.
48. Interfax, 1 March 1994, cited in *RFE/RL Daily Report,* 2 March 1994.
49. Pavel Baev, *Russia's Policies in the Caucasus,* (London: Royal Institute of International Affairs, 1997), p. 24.
50. For an assessment of this cease-fire from the Russian perspective see Emil Pain, "The Political Situation in Conflict Zones," Analysis Center, Office of the President of the Russian Federation, May 1994, translated by Robert R. Love, United States Army Foreign Military Studies Office, Fort Leavenworth, Kansas.
51. Radio Tbilisi, 7 July 1997, World News Connection, 8 July 1997.

52. Interfax, 29 April 1999; also, "Cooperation with NATO Parliamentary Assembly," 14 May 1999, *Parliament of Georgia Newsletter,* May 1999.
53. Interfax, 30 March 1997.
54. Caucasus Press, 7 October 1999 cited in *RFE/RL Newsline,* 10 October 1999.
55. Interfax, 12 November 1999.
56. Caucasus Press, 18 December 1999 cited in *RFE/RL Newsline,* 20 December 1999.
57. See Yuri Anchabadze, "Georgia and Abkhazia: The Hard Road to Agreement," *Caucasian Regional Studies,* 3 (1998): p. 2.
58. Vladimir Kyznechevsky, "Why Shevardnadze Wants to Distance Georgia from Russia and CIS," *Ekonomichesky soyuz,* no. 8, in *RIA-Novosti Daily Review,* 3 March 1998; also A. Zaitsev, "Russia and Transcaucasia," *International Affairs* (Moscow), no. 5 (1997): pp. 180–187.
59. For a Georgian perspective on this see *Resonance,* 9 July 1996, translated in FBIS-SOV, 17 July 1996, p. 52.
60. ITAR-TASS, 4 June 1996.
61. *Izvestiya,* 12 November 1994, cited in *RFE/RL Daily Report,* 15 November 1994.
62. ITAR-TASS, 9 July 1996 and Interfax, 13 July 1996.
63. BGI, 11 April 1997.
64. Georgian Radio monitored by the BBC, 25 May 1998.
65. Stephen F. Jones, "Georgia: A Failed Democratic Transition," in eds. Ian Bremmer and Ray Taras, *Nations and Politics in the Soviet Successor States* (Cambridge: Cambridge University Press, 1993), pp. 295–96.
66. BGI, 24 April 1997.
67. Interfax, 16 May 1996; the text of the memorandum may be found at the website of the United States Information Service [http://www.sanet.ge/usis/facto/osset1.txt]; see also the interview with South Ossetian leader Ludvig Chibirov in *Resonance,* 4 July 1996, translated in FBIS-SOV, 10 July 1996.
68. BGI cited in OMRI, 7 March 1997.
69. BGI, 11 April 1997.
70. ITAR-TASS, 12 May 1999.
71. *Economic Review: Georgia* (Washington, DC: International Monetary Fund, 1992), p. 3.
72. Ibid, Table 7, p. 38.
73. Interfax, 16 April 1997.
74. BGI, 7 April 1997.
75. See, for instance, Interfax, 3 November 1994 cited in *RFE/RL Daily Report,* 4 November 1994, and Caucasus Press, 8 December 1999 cited in *RFE/RL Newsline* 9 December 1999; also Institute for War and Peace Reporting, Caucasus Reporting Service, 17 December 1999 [http://www.iwpr.net].
76. "Decree of the Georgian parliament on the Implementation of the Law 'On the Ownership of Land for Agricultural Use'", *Svobodnaya Gruziya,* 15 May 1996, World News Connection [http://wnc.fedworld.gov].
77. Ministry of Economy of the Republic of Georgia, cited at the Embassy of Georgia in the United States website [http://www.steele.com/embgeorgia/econ/stat.htm].
78. BGI, 23 April 1997.
79. *Resonance,* 27 November 1999.
80. BGI, 24 April 1997 and *Dilis gazeti,* 26 August 1999 cited in Prime News Agency, 26 August 1999.
81. State Statistical Department figures reported in *Akhali taoba,* 27 December 1997.

Chapter 12

The Central Asian States: A Case Study of Uzbekistan

Prior to the breakup of the Soviet Union, Central Asia was one of the most consistently neglected and obscure regions of the world. During the Soviet era, studies of the Central Asian republics were largely focused on demographic factors concerned with corruption and environmental degradation, or the relationship of Islam and society.[1] Surprisingly, in the decade since 1991 things didn't change that much as global centers of power continued to look at the region in the primarily one-dimensional terms of economics (oil and natural gas production). An entirely new conceptualization of the region burst forth after the events of September 11th 2001 and the ensuing war led by the United States against the Afghanistan regime known as the Taliban. Almost overnight Central Asia became readily identifiable and policy makers and students alike learned of the geographic and cultural links of this region to pressing world events. No longer dismissively swept aside, Uzbekistan and its immediate neighbors are for the near future integral to the interplay of international politics.

The generally accepted explanation of Central Asia holds that these political systems remain authoritarian in a time of emergent democracy with few traditions of, or allowances for, political pluralism. Until recently that has meant precious little data has been gathered or comprehensive studies conducted of the functioning of these political systems. Studies of the structural aspects of Central Asian governments have only infrequently been emphasized and policy making and policy implementation in the region have been downplayed in deference to human rights issues. The importance of human rights as the basis for the establishment of participatory government is undeniable but it is not the entire story. Without a proper understanding of what motivates political actors in these systems it is difficult to legitimately assess their levels of political development or political futures. To an extent this is a condition of the lag time involved in collecting data, establishing contacts, and coming to grips

Map 12.1 Uzbekistan

with societies which are greatly at variance with even most of the other post-Soviet states. Central Asia has much more to offer than we generally realize.

Development and Culture

Central Asia in Profile

To enter into a discussion of Central Asia is to be as much at variance with Russia and the other Eurasian states as possible. The definition of the region and its general parameters are based on certain assumptions of commonality. First there are the facts of Russian political, economic, and cultural imperialism dating to the eighteenth and nineteenth centuries. Initially with the tsars, and followed by the communists, the authoritarian khanates and satrapies of the region were peripherally absorbed into a quasi-European system of development. Largely foreign political and economic institutions were grafted upon tribal and clan associations and barter and subsistence-oriented economies. The colonial legacy was a classic example of a patron-client relationship in which local elites were reliant upon St. Petersburg/Moscow for their positions and authority.

The second point of commonality is the role of Islam, arguably the single-most significant cultural determinant affecting Central Asia which is why it is treated in more depth further on. And finally there is the burgeoning nature of the population. At the end of the Soviet period the Central Asian states had the fastest growing segments of the population and accounted for slightly more than seventeen percent of the USSR's total. Today the size of the Central Asian populations is not an issue of security for the Russian Federation but nonetheless weighs heavily on those states where resources are already precariously stretched. All of these identifiers have the potential for making or breaking the individual states' efforts at development.

First impressions aside the Central Asian populations are strikingly diverse. The number of languages spoken in each state varies considerably with Tajikistan having ten, followed by Uzbekistan at seven, Kazakstan at six, and Turkmenistan and Kyrgyzstan each having two.[2] With the exception of the Tajiks who are a people of Persian origin, the Central Asians are Turkic peoples. The four Turkic states, and sometimes Azerbaijan, have long been referred to as **Turkestan** due to their common ethnic heritage and occasional association with the vision of creating a broader pan-Turkic federation of peoples as a solution to political divisiveness.[3] Other ethnic groups are generally not in positions to compete for cultural or political dominance. This does not mean that interethnic relations are unimportant factors, however. Kazakstan is an especially critical case in this regard due to the near equal size of its ethnic Kazak and Russian communities. The Russian population there was the single largest minority group in all of the Central Asian republics in 1989 with approximately 6.2 million persons, although by 1997 as many as one sixth of their total had left Kazakstan. Of the nearly 400,000 Russians living in Tajikistan prior to independence only between 80,000 and 150,000 remained by 1996.[4] Less visible but just as telling has been the emigration of the ethnic Germans communities (including the **Volga Germans** who were deported from their Russian homelands to Central Asia in the 1940s). Numbering nearly one million in 1989, ethnic Germans in Kazakstan (the third largest group in the population) had by 1995 declined to approximately 523,000,[5] and to around 300,000 in 1997 as many migrated to Germany. No community can easily sustain its sense of identity in such conditions of decline; nor for that matter can developing states suffer the loss to their economies of thousands of skilled and professional workers.

The status of the Russian language provides a symbolic measurement of the shifts in political power. The Russian language has been stripped of its official status in all of the Central Asian countries and is now mentioned only in the

Kazakstan constitution (article 7, sec. 2). The Kazak parliament passed a new language law in 1997 which called upon all citizens to learn the Kazak language as their "duty."[6] On the other hand also in 1997 Kyrgyzstan elevated Russian from the category of "official" to "state" language in an effort to keep ethnic Russians from leaving the republic.[7]

While each state has its share of unique features, Uzbekistan is given special attention in this chapter for several reasons. First, it has the region's largest population at 23.9 million people. Moreover, Uzbekistan's population is growing faster than is any of its neighbors (see Table 12.1). Sizeable Uzbek communities live in three of the other Central Asian states (the exception is Kazakstan) and approximately twenty-five percent of Tajikistan's population are ethnic Uzbeks. Second, Uzbekistan is the only state which borders on each of the other Central Asian republics (as well as Afghanistan) thereby giving it a truly central role in the region. Geographically, Uzbekistan's eastern-most regions of Andijan and Fergana twist deep into Kyrgyzstan, and with nearly half of Uzbekistan's population living in these regions or in the nearby **Toshkent** (Tashkent) area Uzbekistan has a particularly noticeable influence over Kyrgyz and Tajik affairs (Uzbekistan was deeply involved in Tajikistan's civil war throughout the 1990s). From this arises the third point, Uzbekistan's desire to position itself as the regional power broker.

Administratively, Uzbekistan is a unitary, centralized state consisting of twelve regions (**wiloyatlar**) generally named for the principal city governing that region; the Autonomous Republic of **Qoraqalpoghiston** (Karakalpakstan, named for the Karkalpak people, roughly the western third of Uzbekistan, and one of its poorest regions); and the capital of Toshkent. Below the regional level are the **khokimiyats,** or local administrative units. Toshkent is not the only city of significance in the country: Bukhoro (Bukhara) and Samarqand (Samarkand) have long histories as political and economic entities along the Silk Road, the historic trade route between China and the western world. The merger by the

---

TABLE 12.1   Population Growth in the Central Asian States (2001)*

	Total Population (millions)	Growth Rate % 2000–2005	Titular Group, % of Total Population**
Kazakstan	16.09	−0.37	46
Kyrgyzstan	4.99	1.16	52.4
Tajikistan	6.13	.69	64.9
Turkmenistan	4.84	1.88	77
Uzbekistan	25.26	1.39	80

Sources: *"Indicators on Population," United Nations Statistics Division, United Nations home page [http://www.un.org/Depts/unsd/social/population.html];

***CIA World Factbook, 2000* estimate, [http://www.odci.gov/cia/publications/factbook].

Soviets in 1924 of the ancient khanates of Khiva and Kokand with the emirate of Bukhoro resulted in the formation of Uzbekistan, and for the Soviets an extension of their control over Central Asia. Physically and administratively the new Uzbekistan was an enlargement of ancient Bukhoro,[8] but Toshkent remains the first city of the republic.

The State and Limited Nationhood

The Uzbek people's origins are shrouded in controversy as Arab, Mongol, and Timurid invasions of the region destroyed much of what might have been told of pre-Islamic civilization. Soviet and more recently Uzbek historians have attempted to establish the Uzbek people's emergence as predating, but attached nonetheless to the conquests of **Timur** (Tamerlane or Timurlane), the powerful Turkic-speaking ruler who conquered much of the Mongol domain and beyond in the late fourteenth century.[9] For modern Uzbekistan Timur's significance lies in the establishment of a distinct (although not national) state.[10] Consequently, as one commentator puts it, the current government's goal is to claim antiquity as "the regime strives to present the Uzbek nation as a constant in time. Eternity . . . belongs to Uzbeks and by extension to the champion of Uzbekness . . . i.e. the state."[11]

Although the independence movement was slow to develop in Uzbekistan, reactions against a century of russification did become apparent in the Gorbachev period. Analysts of Central Asia have concluded that when the newly founded Uzbek state faced its independence in 1991 it was with virtually none of the mechanisms of an independent state in place; instead, the government had focused its energies on crafting a national identity.[12] As in the Baltic states, the use of the Uzbek language became a symbol of popular national expression and a debate ensued over whether Uzbek would be given equal status with the Russian language.[13] Finally achieved in 1989 this proved to be only the beginning of a long process to reclaim the native Uzbek heritage. Nevertheless, the clamor for national identity at that time was largely the domain of the intelligentsia while remaining undeveloped among the average citizenry.

Religion and Political Culture

The role of Islam has been central to Uzbekistan's political life since the Muslim faith first penetrated the region in the late seventh century. Since independence religion has been outwardly defined by the 1992 constitution which stipulates that there shall be no discrimination based on religion (article 18), that "everyone shall have the right to profess or not to profess any religion," and that "any compulsory imposition of religion shall be impermissable" (article 31).[14] All religious traditions have not been treated equally by the law, however, and Christian faiths which have sought converts amongst secular Muslims have met with governmental prohibitions against proselytizing.[15] Constitutional prohibitions and protections aside the Uzbek national identity is strongly, if not exclusively, associated with Islam.

Central Asian Islam is primarily moderate in its political tones; today it represents an effort by a people to find themselves, to recreate their sense of national individuality. Even though Uzbekistan's variation of Islam is considered "the most religiously fervent" in the region,[16] this cannot be taken to mean the form of fundamentalism associated with either Iran (most Central Asians are Sunni Muslims), or the Taliban in Afghanistan. The Islamic factor alternately generates different reactions from Uzbek (and Central Asian) elites. On the one hand, as Martha Brill Olcott has noted, "strictly observed Islam is an inviting substitute for the deposed ideology of communism."[17] That is, the authorities keep the public's passions about political, social, and economic change under control by diverting attention away from politics and economics and toward religious observances. Turkmenistan's President **Saparmurad Niyazov,** for instance, spent over fifty million dollars to construct a mosque in Ashgabat while Uzbekistan's President **Islam Karimov's** government opened both an Islamic television channel,[18] and an Islamic university.[19] Both leaders, as well as Kazakstan's **Nursultan Nazarbaev,** have made the *hajj* (pilgrimage) to Mecca, to demonstrate their belonging to the Islamic community, or *umma.*

Uzbek authorities (and other regional elites) have taken the stance that Islamic fundamentalism poses a destablizing influence which could result in calls for an Islamic revolution at a crucial time in the state's reform process.[20] Karimov's administration has frequently portrayed religious fundamentalism as an ideology directed against, and therefore incompatible with, the secular nature of the state.[21] Using the government-controlled mufti's offices Uzbek authorities have fired or harassed prominent or popular Muslim clerics, or dissidents often accusing them of promoting radical doctrines such as wahhabism.[22] Toward this end the parliament passed in 1998 a revised version of the 1991 Law on Religion making it more difficult to register religious organizations.[23] The government has also been suspected in the deaths of religious leaders such as Imam Abduvali Kori Mirzaev of Andijon who vanished while in the security police's custody in 1995. Thus the Uzbek leadership's paradoxical attitude toward Islam is fostered as much by political concerns as it is by the desire for greater social integration.

The Structure of Power

Cultural Determinants and Power

The political systems of all five states of the region are paternalistic in character with only superficial trappings of western-style democracy, and all are heavily weighted toward presidential power. Regional leaders have crafted constitutional structures largely for external audiences while continuing to act according to authoritarian patterns of old. Moreover, although policy is typically formulated and implemented by the bureaucracy, it is through the clan structure—a loyalty based on kinship and regional origins—that most leaders have maintained their holds on power. Edward Allworth has stressed that from the nineteenth through the twentieth centuries Central Asia's political leadership "deified power and the mobilization of resources for selfish or ideological ends."[24] Gregory Gleason observes that "among the oases peoples (i.e., Uzbeks), it is considered gracious to obey, impolite to disagree, treacherous to oppose . . . in native Uzbek society, open political contestation is considered foreign."[25] Intrinsically western in their judgments and subject to changes brought on by modernity, urbanization, and technological development, these assessments do indicate that western-style values of governance are a long way from realization.

The Executive Authority

Social change in Uzbekistan is directed by the executive branch. President Karimov has been more successful than most of his regional contemporaries in striking a balance between what the outside world wants in economic and human rights terms, and what he and his coterie of supporters are willing to tolerate politically. The overriding goal thus far in Uzbekistan's politics has been the achievement of stability (in 1994 Karimov named it as the first of four "priority tasks" for the country).[26] Presidential elections have been showcased twice but were only marginally competitive and instead carried out only for the legitimating effects (no chief executive in Central Asia has yet to be replaced by this means). Moreover in both 1995 and 2001 Karimov held referenda to lengthen his terms of office and thus bypass the constitutional limitation of two consecutive terms (article 90).[27] Only Kyrgyzstan's **Askar Akaev** among Central Asian presidents has failed to justify his power in this manner.[28]

The constitution of Uzbekistan provides the president with the same basic functions held by most chief executives. The presidential power to "issue decrees, enactments, and ordinances binding on the entire territory of the Republic" (article 94) is shared—although by radically different degrees—by thirteen of the fifteen Russian and Eurasian presidents (see Table 5.1). The Uzbek president's ability to "suspend and repeal" any acts passed by either the **khokims** (the heads of regional governments or governors) or the bodies of state administration (article 93, section 13) strengthens his role dramatically. Through decrees the president has the authority to reshape the outlines of government such as in 1997 when Karimov abolished the Ministry of Communications and replaced it with a new Postal and Telecommunications Agency. Nor has Karimov been reluctant to use such powers especially when the bottom line has been his developmental policy or the goal of attracting foreign investment.[29]

President since March 1990, Karimov has held his post longer than any other post-Soviet Eurasian leader except Kazakstan's Nazarbaev (and only by a matter of weeks). Rising through the ranks of the Soviet system Karimov's keen survival instincts and political skills were the primary factors assuring him power. Earlier positions in the Ministry of Finance and as chairman of Uzbekistan's State Planning Committee provided him with valuable economic awareness. On 23 June 1989 in the wake of riots in the **Fergana Valley** between ethnic Uzbeks and Meskhetian Turks (several hundred of the latter were killed and more than 15,000 Meskhetians had to be evacuated to Russia) Karimov was promoted from

Islam Karimov, President of Uzbekistan since 1990

Source: © Reuter New Media Inc./CORBIS

First Secretary of the Kashka Darya oblast party committee to First Secretary of the Communist Party of Uzbekistan. Seemingly his selection was a compromise choice made by those who wanted someone with a weak base of power. Instead, Karimov created his own "clan" of supporters consisting of individuals from throughout the country who owed their fealty exclusively to him. While not formally fostering a cult of personality Karimov has permitted an almost slavish deference to his authority by low and mid-level officials; consequently none within the leadership have counted themselves as his rivals.

There are few restrictions on who may serve as president of Uzbekistan although the constitutions's article 91 does say that he "may not hold any other paid post." In June 1996 Karimov resigned his position as chairman of the **Chalk Democratik Partijasi** (CDP, Democratic People's Party), formerly the Communist Party of Uzbekistan.[30] He did, however, accept the superficially significant nomination of that party's successor, the **National-Democratic Party Fidokorlar** (Self-Sacrifice) in preparation for the January 2000 presidential elections.[31] Karimov subsequently won reelection with 91.9 percent of the vote and virtually no opposition.

Uzbekistan has no vice-presidency as the post was abolished in January 1992 when Karimov forced his former ally and potential rival **Shukhrullo Mirsaidov,** from the office. Not subject to removal except in cases of medical impairment, the president becomes a lifetime member of the Constitutional Court once his term ends (article 97); nowhere else in the former Soviet space is a chief executive elevated to another post like this. And since nothing is said to the contrary, it may be assumed this happens even should the president lose a reelection bid. Once on the high court the president is also granted immunity from prosecution as are the rest of the court's members. Thus as in Yeltsin's resignation guarantees in December 1999, so too has Karimov ensured that his retirement will be blissfully free from embarrassing investigations or political retribution.

As already demonstrated in the Russian and Ukrainian cases the appointment process gives the Uzbek president a tremendous range of authority over the government. In Uzbekistan the president may hire and fire any or all of the cabinet,[32] nominate the members of the republican-level courts, hire and fire all judges from the regional level down to the local level (article 93), and control the selection of the leadership of the Republic of Qoraqalpoghiston; thus in July 1997 Karimov had the republic's parliamentary speaker replaced due to accusations of incompetence.[33] In such matters there is no questioning of the president's motives or his ability to exercise such power. As with Yeltsin, Karimov has publicly chastised or dismissed subordinates for policy failures (particularly in regard to economic reform), or shifted them within the administration if they were thought to retain some utility in government service. Apparently this was the dynamic at work when Karimov removed Kobiljon Obidov, his first deputy prime minister, from the cabinet, but reappointed him to his previous position as khokim of Andijon province. Karimov explained it this way:

> "Even though Mr. Obidov works in Toshkent, his mind and thoughts are in Andijon. He is still interested in reforms in his province. He understands the problems and needs of Andijon. So we decided to bring him back to his home town."[34]

Despite this cushioning of the blow for the official it is apparent that Karimov had a substantial grip on power and there was not much to be profitted from resisting.

Under the direct authority of the president is the Cabinet of Ministers. The cabinet's function is that of "provid(ing) guidance for the economic, social and cultural development" of the country, and the execution of the laws as mandated by both president and legislature (article 98). The government's structure is reminiscent of those in neighboring Central Asian states and in particular of the Soviet bureaucratic system. At the top is the prime minister who presides over a first deputy prime minister and a number of deputy prime ministers each responsible for a specific area of policy. In addition there are approximately twenty-one ministries (the number fluctuates), ten state committees, the powerful **National Security Service** (the successor to the Uzbekistan KGB), and the heads of the National Bank of Uzbekistan and the National Bank for Foreign Economic Activity. This, then, is the heart of the bureaucracy, although there are numerous state-owned enterprises, committees, and departments which round out the governmental sector.

No other political leader in the region has articulated so well a plan for overall change as has Karimov. As the Uzbek president stated it in 1995 this involved an Eastern concept "based on the principle of collectivism, paternalism and preeminence of public opinion" instead of extolling western ideas of "individualism and excessive politicization of the masses."[35] Coupled to this is the philosophy that rights go hand-in-hand with obligations, or as one commentator put it, "it is common knowledge that where human rights are being violated, some people are necessarily disregarding their obligations."[36] Appealing on one level the argument is flawed if you consider India's success at blending eastern philosophical concepts and western democratic and free market norms. Moreover, it acts as a justification for political and human rights abuses if citizens don't comply with regime strictures, as is so often the case in Uzbekistan.

Controlling the Legislature

The difference between the theory and reality of the legislature's power in Uzbekistan is a wide one. According to the constitution—the **Oliy Majlis** (Supreme Assembly) is the "highest state representative body" of the country (article 76). At best a bland endorsement of legislative power the constitution reveals little of the actual distribution of power between the legislature and the president. The Oliy Majlis' primary responsibility is, of course, that of legislating, and on paper it also has the opportunity to forge the country's domestic and foreign policies (article 78, section 3) and to craft the guidelines of all governmental powers (section 4). The legislature does possess a limited impeachment power which applies only in cases of removing the president due to poor health; an interim president is then elected who serves for three months until the next general election (article 96). But it's unrealistic to expect that Karimov would let himself be removed in this fashion. In point of fact his domination of the legislature was substantially increased with the previously mentioned 2001 referendum which approved not just an extended presidency, but also a new bicameral legislature, albeit one which was not described to the voters despite their heavy approval of this move (ninety-three percent). Whatever emerges it will bear little resemblance to the independence-minded bodies of the Baltic states or even the Russian Federation.

Prior to the 1994–1995 legislative elections Uzbekistan's communist-era Supreme Soviet created the Oliy Majlis and then legislated itself out of existence.[37] The successor institution was unicameral consisting of 250 deputies, as compared to the 500 of its predecessor. Only eighty-three of the seats were filled by direct elections, and the remainder chosen by local councils throughout the country. Since the president appoints and dismisses all regional, district, and city heads of administration (article 92, sec. 12) this ensured that all other deputies would be highly dependent upon, and supportive of, the president.

Debate in the parliament has been strictly limited and follows an agenda prepared by its executive committee, the **Council of the Supreme Assembly.** Factions do contribute to parliamentary operations but primarily in a formalistic sense. Immediately following the 1995 elections (for which there was a Soviet-style turnout of 93.6 percent[38]) four such groups were formed, one for each of the three parties represented, and one composed of deputies elected by local bodies of power. Two new factions took shape after the 1999 elections although their existence did nothing to guarantee independent action within the legislature. What little power not held by the Council is thinly disbursed amongst the rank-and-file deputies who are prevented by law from serving on more than one committee or commission at a time.[39]

The Council directs the activity of the parliament particularly by means of drafting the parliamentary agenda and all laws coming before the parliament.[40] This is not to say that debate can't occur, but instead that there has been no willingness to buck the system and defy Karimov. Thus the speaker of the parliament, Erkin Khalilov noted in 1995 that in the legislature's third session that year major issues were unanimously passed,[41] indicating that the legislature does little more than rubber stamp presidential policies. Even more transparent was Khalilov's admission that even though the legislature passed the 1996 budget without access to the data relating to it, passage was justified since most deputies were not specialists on the budget and instead simply trusted in the government's experts.[42] Karimov has occasionally protested that he has no need for such sycophancy,[43] but his actions speak much louder than his words.

Why the quiescence? Olcott observed that Uzbekistan's citizens have not readily embraced dissident opinion or revolutionary thought because they fear a breakdown of public order and economic decline.[44] But there's more to it than this particularly given the region's historical association with authoritarian governance. The bottom line for any authoritarian system is its reliance on the use of force, in Uzbekistan's case the National Security Service and manipulation of the law to fulfill the regime's ends. The opposition politician **Mukhammed Solikh** pointed out that since the constitution prevents anyone from holding office who was convicted of a crime, the government went out of its way to try opposition figures prior to the 1994–1995 parliamentary elections.[45] Manipulating the law this way has let the regime keep the public from hearing other voices and intimidate them into accepting things as they are.

Uzbekistan's judicial branch is, at best, quasi-independent and structurally doesn't differ much from other former Soviet republics. The constitution lays out the guidelines for a four-tiered court system consisting of a **Constitutional Court, Supreme Court, Higher Economic Court,** and the regional and local courts (article 107). There is also a semiautonomous court system for the Republic of Qoraqalpoghiston which is subordinated to the republican courts. Curiously, the constitution described the leadership positions of the Constitutional Court but unlike the other Eurasian states left it to Parliament to determine the number of jurists. The Oliy Majlis finalized this process in August 1995 with the passage of a law providing for seven judges serving terms of five years (one of the shortest terms of office in any of the post-Soviet states).[46]

Pluralism, Parties, and Dissent

Pluralism in Uzbekistan is a contradictory thing. The republic owes a considerable debt to the development of interest/opposition groups like Birlik and Erk during the latter days of *perestroika*. With independence came a harsher reality, however, in the form of governmental crackdowns on those who challenged the old party elite's right to continue governing. The organs of state authority and the republic's intelligentsia struggled over who would define the principles for the new system. From the beginning it was an uneven contest and the suppression of dissent was tempered only by how the regime wanted to be seen by the outside world.

Unlike the case in the Baltic states Central Asian nationalist movements did not develop from the ground up to eventually encompass the leadership. Instead the Central Asian communist party leaders filled the power vacuum which had already begun to develop during Gorbachev's tenure. Independence or nationalist movements were unprepared to effectively challenge leaders such as Karimov who had been supportive of the August 1991 coup against Gorbachev and not desirous of independence. Confronted with the new political reality, Karimov quickly co-opted much of the nationalist program of the nascent Popular Front movement in Uzbekistan.[47] Even still, an opposition did develop beyond Karimov's concept of managed democracy. The **Birlik** (Unity) **Popular Front of Uzbekistan,** was founded in November 1988 by Uzbek intellectuals favoring pluralistic democracy, Islamic revivalism (but not fundamentalism), Pan-Turkism, and Uzbek nationalism.[48] Moderate though these goals were, they still were perceived as a challenge to Karimov's own efforts to restrict the volatile mix of politics and religion. At stake was the ability to set the policy agenda. Harassment of Birlik began shortly after its founding: members were charged with criminal activities and given high-profile public trials, and Birlik was suspended by the Supreme Court in January 1993. The movement was later prevented from registering as a political party under the terms of the Law on Public Organizations, although none of this prevented Birlik from continuing to actively speak out against Karimov's rule.

With the clampdown on Birlik, opposition energies were concentrated in the hands of the **Democratic Party Erk** (Will), the only remaining legally registered political opposition movement. Erk was formed in 1990, and with former Birlik cofounder Mukhammad Solikh as its head, the party contested both the 1990 republican Supreme Soviet elections (it won ten seats to the Communist Party's 450) and the 1991 presidential election (as his party's candidate Solikh scored only twelve percent of the vote to Karimov's eighty-six percent). These results could be interpreted either as Erk's failure to deliver a message appealing to the voters, or the party having faced insurmountable challenges. While the former explanation is partially correct, the government's harassment of dissidents and the banning of Birlik brings a substantial amount of weight down behind the second assumption.

Critics of Karimov's regime have contended that the president recreated much of the repression of the Soviet era by having opponents and dissidents alike tried and jailed for legal infractions.[49] Many of the country's leading dissidents have fled to Germany, Turkey, or the United States, or otherwise disappeared with no accounting for their whereabouts. Nor have Uzbek authorities been content to merely force their foes into exile. On several occasions the Uzbek police, or UVD

(Administration of Internal Affairs) have intruded into neighboring countries (Kyrgyzstan in 1993;[50] Kazakstan in 1994[51]) to assault, abduct or otherwise intimidate the opposition. Uzbek authorities have also gained the tacit support of the Russian Federation in dealing with vocal critics,[52] and in a controversial incident in November 2001, convinced Czech Republic authorities to detain Solikh as he arrived in Prague for an interview at Radio Free Europe.[53]

The Uzbek government's stance on dissent is marginally conditioned by its desire for greater assistance from international lending institutions.[54] In 1996 the government permitted the **Uzbek Human Rights Society** to hold a conference in Toshkent and for its leader Abdumanop Pulatov to attend. Pulatov's conclusion that "there is no *open* (emphasis added) persecution for human rights activities"[55] was less a statement of fact than a comment on what lay below the surface of Uzbek politics, that is, a policy of external image-building.[56] In November of that year the government renewed its harassment of former vice-president Mirsaidov by evicting him and nineteen family members from their homes,[57] and then in 1997 accusing him of money laundering and misuse of power while he was vice president.[58] It seems safe to say from these and other incidents that the Uzbek government remains a largely unbridled regime concerned only occasionally by external condemnations and even less frequently by internal opinions.

The political party system of Uzbekistan is a classic example of a mobilization model. Parties are heavily proscribed by the government and even some nominally opposition-oriented parties are little more than conveniences for foreign consumption rather than legitimate expressions of popular interests. Several are worth mentioning although not because of their legislative capabilities. The former Communist Party and presidential vehicle, the Democratic People's Party, (CDP) had as many as 400,000 members in 1994.[59] Clearly placing its support behind Karimov,[60] the party won sixty-nine seats in the 1994–1995 elections and forty-eight seats in the 1999 national elections. Technically no longer a communist party, the CDP has moved beyond strict Marxist dogma and publicly embraced a policy agenda of implementing a free-market economy including a program of privatization of selected state assets, law and order, and a foreign policy of moderate integration with the other states of the region. The party lost its presidential support, however, with the December 1998 founding of the aforementioned Fidokorlar in yet another move by Karimov to develop a national party in his own image.

The **Progress of the Fatherland Party** is not dramatically different from the NDPU in its approach to policy issues. Formed in May 1992 by Usman Azimov, Karimov's State Advisor on Problems of Youth, its principal areas of recruitment have been among the intelligentsia, scientists, urban youth, and entrepreneurial groups of society. With its membership largely concentrated in Toshkent and Samarqand it is difficult to classify it as a mass movement. The party's manifesto has proclaimed it to be in favor of a free-market, the enhancement of the people's material conditions, the development of a technological infrastructure, respect for different peoples and cultural traditions, and a mildly pan-Turkic-oriented foreign policy.[61] Finally, there is the **National Rebirth Party,** founded in June 1995 by

Uzbek artists to foster national self-consciousness. The party's support for the government's programs gained for it formal registration.[62]

Karimov's carefully controlled system-building has been aimed at precluding all spontaneous or autonomous political opposition. A 1996 law guarantees the rights of parties to participate in elections and generally take part in the country's political life, but also prohibits the formation of ethnic or religious based parties. Among other things this reaffirmed the 1992 ban on Islamic-based organizations such as the **Social Democrat Adolat** (Justice) **Party** and the **Islamic Renaissance Party** (IRP). Adolat presented a unique threat to the Uzbek president's vision of political development. Cofounded by former Vice-President Mirsaidov the party called for not only the democratization of Uzbek society, the election of state bodies, and market reforms with social protections, but for greater involvement in public life by the country's religious leaders.[63] None of this escaped the notice of the government, and restrictive actions continue to be the norm. Laws in Uzbekistan are designed, after all, to counter pluralism, not promote it.

Among the Eurasian states Uzbekistan has been one of the most restrictive of an independent media. Through the State Committee on the Press the government controls media registration, accreditation, and access to newsprint and printing presses.[64] As in all the other Eurasian states there is a government-run news agency, **UZTag,** which feeds information to media outlets. No independent media agency such as Interfax or BNS has been permitted to operate. Television is limited to two state-run channels and an independent channel which operates in Samarqand; although there have been licenses issued for other such ventures operating conditions have been difficult at best.[65] Both the electronic media and newspapers are confined in their political content to what the government wants to be seen or heard. Government-controlled papers such as *Narodnoye slovo* and *Khalk suzi* are the formal organs of the parliament responsible for publishing laws and decrees. As well, *Pravda vostoka* a formerly independent newspaper was taken over by the Council of Ministers in 1994 as the government's source for "maintaining close contact with the economic and state structures."[66] That has left very little for the public to consume which is not officially sanctioned, and as journalists are subject to legal punishment for "offending the honor and dignity of the president" critical assessments of government policy are highly unlikely.

Issues Facing Uzbekistan

Opening the Economy

Uzbekistan's transition beyond the central planning of the Soviet period has not been a clear goal of the Karimov government. The country remains as in Soviet times a very poor one. The condition of wages describes one dimension of this: In November 1996 the government announced that the *minimum* monthly wage was to be raised to about twelve dollars[67] (still higher than the official *average* monthly wage in Tajikistan for mid-1997 of eleven dollars[68]). Price controls on basic commodities such as flour and cooking oil have mitigated the poverty facing the average citizen as did the government's successful reduction of inflation which in 1993 ran as high as 1300 percent annually (estimated at forty percent annually in 2000[69]). In general, though, efforts to raise the standard of living have largely been subordinated to macroeconomic stabilization such as GDP growth where progress is more readily apparent (see Table 12.2).

Under Soviet direction each republic was assigned its role in the development of the socialist economy and for Uzbekistan this was the establishment of the cotton industry. Uzbekistan's lack of industrialization may have also been part of a deliberate attempt by Uzbek (and other Central Asian) leaders to deter ethnic Russians from settling in an economically unattractive area.[70] By Brezhnev's time the cotton culture had corrupted much of the new society and destroyed

TABLE 12.2   Key Economic Sector Performance in Uzbekistan, 1995–2000 (in percentages)

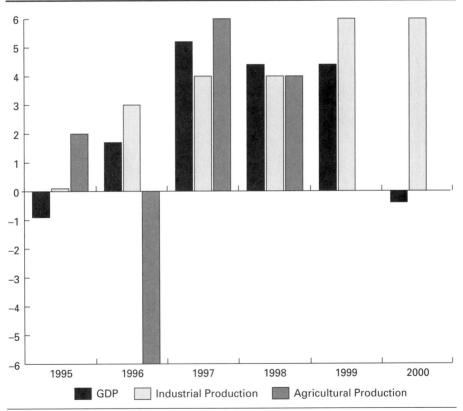

Source: "Main Macroeconomic Indicators of Uzbekistan," Commonwealth of Independent States website [http://www.cisstat.com/eng/uzb.htm].

Agricultural production figures for 1999–2000 not available.

large segments of the old as Moscow demanded increasingly higher quotas of the crop from the republican leadership. When Andropov assumed the CPSU leadership in 1982 the axe began to fall on those who were caught up in the "cotton" or "Uzbek" affair, with resulting purges of party leadership and rank-and-file. The limited efforts at reform, however, did little to halt the economic downslide and certainly it did nothing to put Uzbekistan on a successful path to economic independence once the opportunity arose. Instead with independence the government maintained the **monoculture of cotton,** that is, an overreliance on the cotton crop for export, jobs, and development despite declining harvests (in 1997 only 2.86 million tons were harvested instead of the projected four million tons[71]) and the tremendous environmental degradation to the country.

Karimov's economic approach has paralleled his political strategy; he has rejected out of hand "blindly copying various model(s)" and contended that special circumstances will always dictate how a state organizes itself.[72] The government was in no particular hurry to introduce its own currency, instead remaining a member of the ruble zone until Russian demands for hard currency payments caused Uzbekistan to leave in 1993. The som coupon was introduced on a temporary basis and in July 1994 the **som** took its place as the country's legal tender. Subsequently, the Uzbek Council of Ministers banned the Russian ruble as a means of exchange although other convertible currencies were permitted to circulate. To this point the som is still not a fully convertible currency and its stability remains questionable.

Privatization has been focused primarily in the small and medium-size business categories while large-scale industries, extraction, and farming remain in the hands of the state.[73] In 1995 Karimov announced a **Mass Privatization Program** (MPP) but the program lagged as the government avoided the adoption of a voucher system like Russia's; in 1996 at best only forty percent of GDP was a result of private production.[74] The state also continued to maintain price controls on basic commodities (flour, butter) which lead to new shortages and profiteering.[75]

Land reform has also been problematic. Land that was distributed to individual farmers or families was often of poor quality hindering the peasants in the production and marketing of their goods. In 1994 for the first time the government allowed farmers the opportunity to sell surplus cotton on foreign markets.[76] The government's general inclination overall has been to micromanage the economy, to establish more oversight commissions, and for Karimov to personally intervene in the replacement of incompetent economic elites.[77] None of this indicates a clear sense of direction or hope for true reform of the agricultural sector for the immediate future.

Foreign investment has perhaps been one area of success in Karimov's development scheme. Taking the view that a state's level of development is conditioned by its ability to sell certain commodities on international markets Karimov has initiated very liberal terms for foreign investment such as exempting foreign firms from profit taxes for seven years and granting joint ventures relatively low profit tax rates.[78] Major U.S., European, and Asian corporations have assisted in developing Uzbek infrastructure, or expanded trade,[79] thereby demonstrating that the government's learning curve on attracting capital has been at least as successful (if not more so) than the Russian case.

Limiting Outside Influences

Since independence Uzbekistan has kept a cautious distance between itself and its former Russian patron trying instead to shape the process to suit its own needs rather than those of its neighbors. It is no mistake that foreign policy is mentioned prominently in the beginning of the Uzbekistan constitution. Karimov's foreign policy initiatives have been highly successful. His priorities could best be summarized as follows: 1) make Uzbekistan the regional power within Central Asia; 2) reduce economic dependence on Russia, Iran, Turkey, and other states especially in the area of energy supplies; 3) prevent the reassertion of Russian hegemony within Central Asia; 4) control the resurgence of Islam in Uzbekistan; and 5) seek out development assistance from western states and lending agencies. While none of Uzbekistan's neighbors have agendas as ambitious as those of Uzbekistan there have been conflicts.

Consistently wary of Russian power Uzbekistan in the 1990s moved away from Russian calls for greater integration and by 1999 Toshkent had decided to withdraw from the CIS Collective Security Treaty.[80] Neither has Karimov warmed to the integrative philosophies promoted by Belarus, Kazakstan, or Kyrgyzstan partly due to those states weak economies. Since independence Karimov has perceived his state's economic growth prospects to be tied to cooperation with Europe and the United States. Keenly sensitive to those states' criticisms of Uzbekistan's human rights record Karimov nevertheless remained certain of western desires to foster a new clientelism in the region for investment and resource extraction purposes. Germany has been courted by Karimov as Uzbekistan's "priority trade partner in Europe"[81] and as a conduit to the European Union,[82] while the United States has also devoted energies to developing ties with Uzbekistan. Since the visit by U.S. Secretary of State James Baker to the region in early 1992 there has been a constant interchange of American and Uzbek officials to each others' respective capitals. In 1995 the two countries signed a memorandum on mutual understanding and cooperation in military matters with U.S. Defense Secretary William Perry praising Uzbekistan as a center of calm and stability in the region.[83] This, of course, was severely tested with the U.S. bombing campaign against Afghanistan in October 2001. More than any other state in the region, Uzbekistan acceded to American calls for basing privileges and other access and almost immediately allowed American troops to stage operations from Uzbek soil, an unthinkable proposition for much of the Twentieth Century.

All of this leads to the conclusion that Karimov's vision for his country is that of a regional hegemon, able to either determine the course of politics for neighboring states or influence the choices other states make. As with Russia's willingness to cut off the supply of oil and gas to debtor states, so too Uzbekistan has

occasionally held up natural gas supplies to Kyrgyzstan.[84] Uzbekistan's supplying
of troops to Tajikistan to prop up that country's government and its support of
warlords during Afghanistan's civil war have demonstrated an Uzbek willingness
toward interventionism (despite later financial problems in maintaining these
commitments). Still, the Uzbek leadership seems determined to have a say in
how political vacuums occurring within the region are filled.

Environmental Degradation

Nowhere in the former Soviet space have the lessons of environmental control
been as harsh as in the Central Asian republics. To put it mildly, the Soviet legacy to the area was catastrophic. Aggressive and reckless agricultural development poisoned both land and water due to the unchecked use of irrigation and
pesticides. The most visible disaster has been the drying up of the Aral Sea
brought on by the pollution and depletion of the Aral's fresh water supplies—
the Syr Darya and Amu Darya Rivers—for irrigation.[85] In general, the Central
Asian environmental picture is grim—for instance, the Syr Darya runs through
the Fergana Valley with its dense concentration of peoples posing massive
health risks for the region's inhabitants. Given the hard-pressed state of Uzbekistan's economic resources, it is doubtful the capital will be available to reverse
the pollution.

Environmental conditions prevalent in Central Asia have handicapped the
chances of these countries' successful political and economic development. But
in case it is forgotten these states have also been the beneficiaries of infrastructure development greatly superior to that of Afghanistan, Pakistan, Mongolia,
and western China. Uzbekistan's independence journey toward the twenty-first
century thus has the earmarks of either a descent into chaos or at least a jump on
some of the competition. It is not clear at this point which direction the country
will turn; at best we can say that the Uzbek model, based on its own distinct political culture, must go a route that would not be recommended for the Baltic
states or Ukraine, but may have limited appeal in other Eurasian states.

Key Terms

Islam Karimov	Oliy Majlis
Timur	Birlik
Council of the Supreme Assembly	khokhims
clan structure	monoculture of cotton

Questions for Consideration

1. Why has Central Asia been unable to move beyond authoritarian governance in the
   post-Soviet era? What does this mean for the prospect of reform?

2. Why does Karimov distrust representative institutions? Does his form of directed democracy hold a future for an active legislature?

3. What does the concept of limited nationhood mean for Uzbekistan's development?

4. How does the government of Uzbekistan rationalize its human rights record and in particular its suppression of rival political parties?

5. Can Islamic fundamentalism be co-opted by the authorities in Toshkent, or must Karimov's government resist it as a threat to the state?

Suggested Readings

Edward Allworth, *The Modern Uzbeks* (Stanford, CA: Hoover Press, 1990).

Annette Bohr, *Uzbekistan: Politics and Foreign Policy* (London: Royal Institute of International Affairs, 1998).

Peter Ferdinand, ed., *The New States of Central Asia and Their Neighbors* (New York: Council on Foreign Relations Press, 1994).

Gregory Gleason, *The Central Asian States: Discovering Independence* (Boulder, CO: Westview Press, 1997).

Shireen T. Hunter, *Central Asia Since Independence* (Westport, CT: Praeger, 1996).

Hafeez Malik, ed., *Central Asia* (New York: St. Martin's Press, 1994).

Michael Mandelbaum, ed., *Central Asia and the World* (New York: Council on Foreign Relations Press, 1994).

Martha Brill Olcott, *The Kazakhs* (Stanford, CA: Hoover Press, 1987).

Yaacov Ro'i, ed., *Muslim Eurasia: Conflicting Legacies* (London: Frank Cass, 1995).

Useful Websites

"Birlik" opposition party website
http://www.birlik.net/

Cyber Uzbekistan
http://www.cu-online.com/~k_a/uzbekistan/

Official Uzbekistan government
http://www.gov.uz

Uzbekistan resource page
http://www.soros.org/uzbkstan.html

Endnotes

1. On the Soviet press and Central Asia see Kathleen Watters, "Central Asia and the Central Press: A Study in News Coverage," *Journal of Soviet Nationalities*, 1 (Summer 1990): pp. 99–121.
2. See the segments on Central Asia in Barbara F. Grimes, ed., *Ethnologue*, 13th ed. (Dallas, TX: Summer Institute of Linguistics, 1996).
3. One observer's argument in favor of this may be found in Graham E. Fuller, "Central Asia: The Quest for Identity," *Current History*, 93 (April 1994): pp. 145–49.

4. "Russian Community in Tajikistan," *Bulletin,* no. 4 (June 1996), Asia-Plus News Agency web site (Tajikistan) [http://www.internews.ras.ru/ASIA-PLUS/index.html].

5. *Kazakhstanskaya pravda,* 8 July 1995, World News Connection, 8 July 1995 [http://wnc.fedworld.com].

6. ITAR-TASS, cited in *RFE/RL Newsline,* 16 July 1997.

7. Russian TV, 1 April 1997, cited in *RFE/RL Newsline,* 2 April 1997.

8. Donald S. Carlisle, "Uzbekistan and the Uzbeks," *Problems of Communism,* 40 (September–October 1991): p. 26.

9. Devendra Kaushik, *Central Asia in Modern Times* (Moscow: Progress Publishers, 1970), pp. 22–23; see also the comments of the historian Zeki Velidi Togan, "The Origins of the Kazaks and the Ozbeks" in ed. H. B. Paksoy, *Central Asia Reader: The Rediscovery of History* (Armonk, NY: M. E. Sharpe, 1994), pp. 27–37.

10. See, for instance, Kenneth Weisbrode, "Uzbekistan in the Shadow of Tamerlane," *World Policy Journal,* 14 (Spring 1997): pp. 53–60.

11. Shahram Akbarzadeh, "Nation-building in Uzbekistan," *Central Asian Survey,* 15 (1996): p. 30.

12. See Meryem Kirimli, "Uzbekistan in the New World Order," *Central Asian Survey,* 16 (1997): p. 53; also Sergey Kolchin, "Importance of Russian Interests in 'Near Abroad' Stressed," *Mirovaya ekonomika i mezhdunarodnoye otnosheniya,* (April 1995): pp. 47–48.

13. A summation of the controversy can be found in James Critchlow, *Nationalism in Uzbekistan* (Boulder, CO: Westview Press, 1991), pp. 99–108.

14. *Constitution of the Republic of Uzbekistan* (Tashkent: Uzbekistan Publishing, 1993).

15. "Fresh Concerns Arise Over Religious Liberty in the OSCE," *CSCE Digest,* 20 (June 1997): pp. 64, 66.

16. Mehrdad Haghayeghi, "Islamic Revival in the Central Asian Republics," *Central Asian Survey,* 13 (1994): p. 250.

17. Martha Brill Olcott, "Central Asia's Islamic Awakening," *Current History,* 93 (April 1994): p. 152.

18. *Kommersant-Daily,* 3 February 1996, translated in FBIS-SOV, 3 February 1996, pp. 61–62.

19. Interfax, 3 September 1999.

20. See the comments of Rafik Saifulin of the Uzbekistan Presidential Institute of Strategic Studies, "The Fergana Valley: A View From Uzbekistan," *Perspectives on Central Asia,* 1 (April 1996), Center for Political and Strategic Studies website [http://www.cpss.org/casianw/saif.txt].

21. ITAR-TASS, 23 February 1999, World News Connection, 23 February 1999 [http://wnc.fedworld.gov].

22. Interfax, 5 June 1998, World News Connection, 5 June 1998 [http://wnc.fedworld.gov].

23. Interfax, 1 May 1998.

24. Edward A. Allworth, *The Modern Uzbeks* (Stanford, CA: Hoover Institution Press, 1990), p. 5.

25. Gregory Gleason, *The Central Asian States: Discovering Independence* (Boulder, CO: Westview Press, 1997), pp. 117–118.

26. "Uzbekistan," *Central Asia Monitor,* no. 5 (1995): p. 14.

27. "Uzbekistan," *Central Asia Monitor,* no. 3 (1995): p. 11.

28. *RFE/RL Newsline,* 9 February 1996.

29. *Pravda vostoka* (Tashkent) 24 July 1997, World News Connection, 24 July 1997 [http://wnc.fedworld.gov].

30. Interfax, 21 June 1996.

31. Interfax, 22 September 1999.
32. See ITAR-TASS, 10 March 1998, World News Connection, 10 March 1998 [http://wnc. fedworld.gov].
33. Interfax, 17 July 1997, cited in *RFE/RL Newsline*, 21 July 1997.
34. *Current News From Uzbekistan* (United States Information Service), 6 May 1997.
35. *Narodnoye slovo* (Toshkent), 24 February 1995, World News Connection [http://wnc. fedworld.gov].
36. U. Tadzhikhanov, "Are There Rights Without Obligations?" *Pravda vostoka*, 25 April 1997 [http://wnc.fedworld.gov].
37. *Rossiyskaya gazeta*, 5 October 1994, translated in FBIS-SOV, 5 October 1994.
38. Tashkent Radio, 29 December 1994, World News Connection [http://wnc. fedworld.gov].
39. Ibid, article 18.
40. Ibid, article 17, sections 1 and 3.
41. Interfax, 31 August 1995.
42. *Novoye vremya*, April 1996, World News Connection [http://wnc.fedworld.gov].
43. Tashkent Radio Mashal, 24 February 1995, World News Connection [http://wnc. fedworld.gov].
44. Martha Brill Olcott, "Central Asia: The Calculus of Independence," *Current History*, 94 (October 1995): p. 341.
45. Muhammed Saleh, "Equality Under Lawlessness (Human Rights in Uzbekistan)," part 2, Voice of America, 14 October 1994.
46. Interfax, 12 September 1995.
47. This point is made by Gregory J. Moffitt in his "Diverging Paths: The Popular Front Movements in Uzbekistan and Azerbaijan," *Central Asia Monitor*, No. 3 (1993): pp. 24–27.
48. Ahmed Rashid, *The Resurgence of Central Asia: Islam or Nationalism?* (London: Zed Books, 1994), pp. 98–99.
49. Mukhammed-Babur M. Malikov, "Uzbekistan: A View From the Opposition," *Problems of Post-Communism*, 44 (March/April 1995): pp. 19–23.
50. For Pulatov's perspective see his article "Pursuing Dissidents in Exile: Illegal Activities of Central Asian Security Forces (Part I)," *Central Asia Monitor*, 2 (1995): pp. 31–36.
51. For an overview of this incident see *Novoye vremya*, June 1994, pp. 15–17, World News Connection [http://wnc.fedworld.gov]. Also, Interfax, 31 March 1995.
52. *Moskovskiye novosti*, 9–16 July 1995, World News Connection [http://wnc.fedworld.gov].
53. *RFE/RL Newsline*, 30 November 2001.
54. This is the conclusion of the report "Uzbekistan, Persistent Human Rights Violations and Prospects for Improvement," *Human Rights Watch/Helsinki*, 8 (May 1996).
55. Interfax, 7 September 1996.
56. More detailed comments from Pulatov can be found in his interview with Tashkent's Radio Mashal, 11 September 1996, World News Connection [http://wnc.fedworld.gov].
57. Human Rights Watch/Helsinki, 26 and 27 November 1996.
58. Current News from Uzbekistan, 11 March 1997.
59. Interfax, 18 September 1994.
60. Interfax, 22 February 1995.
61. *Narodnoye slovo*, 26 November 1994.
62. "Uzbekistan," *Central Asia Monitor*, no. 4 (1995): p. 13.
63. Interfax, 18 January 1995, FBIS-SOV, 19 January 1995, p. 48; also *Lidove Noviny* (Czech Republic), 16 March 1995, translated in FBIS-SOV, 22 March 1995, p. 68.

64. "Uzbekistan: Legal and regulatory framework for the media," Media in the CIS, Internews website [http://www.internews.ras.ru/].

65. Eric Johnson (with Martha Brill Olcott and Robert Horvitz), *The Media in Central Asia: Kazakhstan, Kyrgyzstan, Uzbekistan* (Washington, DC: Internews, 1994), p. 30.

66. *Pravda vostoka*, 27 September 1994, World News Connection [http://wnc.fedworld.gov].

67. Uzbekistan Radio, 26 November 1996, cited in *OMRI Daily Digest*, 2 December 1996.

68. ITAR-TASS, 3 August 1997 cited in *RFE/RL Newsline*, 4 August 1997.

69. *CIA World Factbook, 2001*, Central Intelligence Agency website [http://www.cia.gov].

70. This idea is attributed to Terese S. Zimmer in her Ph.D dissertation "The Politics of Regional Development in the USSR: A Case Study of Uzbekistan" (Johns Hopkins University, 1983); see Gregory Gleason, "Marketization and Migration: The Politics of Cotton in Central Asia," *Journal of Soviet Nationalities*, 1 (Summer 1990): pp. 85–86.

71. Reuters, cited in *RFE/RL Newsline*, 22 July 1997.

72. *Rossiyskaya gazeta*, 17 August 1996, translated in FBIS-SOV, 23 August 1996, p. 39.

73. Michael Kaser, "Economic Transition in Six Central Asian Economies," *Central Asian Survey*, 16 (1997): pp. 19–20.

74. "Uzbekistan: Economic Overview," 10 March 1997, Business Information Service for the Newly Independent States (BISNIS), U. S. Department of Commerce website [http://www.iep.doc.gov/bisnis/].

75. Uzbekistan Television, 29 July 1997, World News Connection [http://wnc.fedworld.gov].

76. Uzbekistan Television, 2 December 1994, World News Connection [http://wnc.fedworld.gov].

77. *Pravda vostoka*, 19 March 1997, World News Connection [http://wnc.fedworld.gov].

78. Interfax, 3 December 1996.

79. See, for instance, ITAR-TASS, 5 July 1999, World News Connection, 8 July 1999 [http://wnc.fedworld.gov].

80. "Karimov confirms Uzbek CIS Security Treaty Withdrawal," ITAR-TASS, 23 February 1999, World News Connection, 24 February 1999 [http://wnc.fedworld.gov].

81. Interfax, 30 May 1996, FBIS-SOV, 31 May 1996, p. 61.

82. Uzbekistan Television, 30 May 1996, World News Connection [http://wnc.fedworld.gov].

83. Uzbekistan Television, 18 October 1995, World News Connection [http://wnc.fedworld.gov].

84. Interfax, 3 December 1994 and 11 May 1996.

85. For a more involved description of these conditions see Keith Martin, "Central Asia's Forgotten Tragedy," *RFE/RL Research Report*, 3 (29 July 1994): pp. 35–48.

Chapter 13

Conclusions

Reexamining the Model for Analysis

What has been learned thus far adds up considerably, but what is its value, comparative or otherwise? Certainly politics in each of the countries examined are unique to the particular systems, and yet reminiscent of the ways that things are done in other regions of the world. The lessons of Russian and Eurasian politics are not that one type of government is superior in comparison to others but rather that each state practices the art of politics—that is, its political culture—unique to itself. And yet we can find the points of commonality between disparate systems as well as the dissimilarities among states which are alike.

The relationships between Russia and its neighbors remain vital, yet indeterminate. Moscow is no longer the focal point for all decision making or resource allocation. In some cases—notably those of Armenia, Belarus, Kazakstan, and Ukraine—Russia exercises influence and thus effects policy in these states, but does not control them as in the past. The Russian Federation also continues to express strategic interests toward the Baltic states and the Caucasus. And yet readily apparent cultural distinctions and governing styles makes it increasingly difficult to justify including such diverse political systems in the same analytical context. For the moment these distinctions and political dynamics are not so much at odds with the model presented in Chapter One that it should be rejected or even substantially altered.

The most obvious conclusion is that these fifteen political/economic systems are in a state of constant change, although not to the same degree that they were in the period immediately following independence. The Baltic states have made the transition toward new political and economic systems more completely than the other Eurasian states. In some other cases—notably Ukraine—the rate of change seems disturbingly slow as the dispute over Kuchma's role in the disappearance of the Ukrainian journalist Gongadze demonstrated. Continuing and escalating civil wars and Islamic insurgencies in Central Asia leave many among local publics longing for the surety of Soviet-era governance. In no case has the governing process been able to escape the reality of external pressures which exacerbate already fragile domestic environments.

273

In the case of Ukraine, Armenia, Georgia, and Moldova, change has become institutionalized. The occurrence of "sophomore" and even "junior" elections—that is, second and third sets of contests—indicates that differing governing concepts are seriously experimented with, if not wholly accepted. Authoritarian societies reliant upon population mobilization have gravitated toward choice-oriented, participatory societies. Not yet fully accepting of democratic governance models they are nevertheless refining as these systems become used to the procedures of competition and elite selection that might at some point lead to a consideration of democracy's other prerogatives. System transformation continues, of course, and there remain prospects for alteration in all of the Eurasian states. To this point as well the politics of "normalcy" are not yet in place since it still can't be determined what will happen when system-shaping political elites leave the scene. Boris Yeltsin presented the most notable case to date, a model of system stabilization which is encouraging for all Eurasian systems. The fates of all that Eduard Shevardnadze and Islam Karimov have built are much less certain, however, as social problems are barely contained beneath the surface of politics and economics. But if these systems manage to survive the passing of such elites, then the process has proven itself and gained a certain autonomy of its own.

Excepting the Baltic states, most of the Eurasian states have not attained the measure of stability that has already emerged in Russia. The strong-man republics of Central Asia and the Caucasus still are heavily reliant upon the personal visions of individual leaders (Aliev, Karimov, Nazarbaev, Niyazov) to transform their respective environments. Any of these systems could collapse in the midst of succession crises, civil war, national or economic disturbances. But simply guessing at this outcome without having first carefully examined the proper information is to stray from our analytical goals.

Related to this issue of stability is our recognition that scandals come and go in politics, but if the scandals occur within established political systems they have less of an impact than if the system was institutionally weak or built on a weak foundation. For instance, over the past decade a number of sensational political developments have occurred in Russia and the Eurasian states. The Russian presidential and parliamentary elections, the numerous government shake-ups, and the sustained economic crises are the most prominent but certainly not the only cases of their kinds in Russia. Georgia's problems seem legion in number, Ukraine's intransigent in nature, and Uzbekistan's problems just waiting to happen. Only in the Baltic states is there a semblance of certainty and direction about the rites of political passage that have permitted three countries to weather some very trying times, including financial mismanagement by officials, ministerial resignations, and the ever-present ethnic disputes. In all of these cases what has counted is that these problems are offset by resources such as highly qualified and committed elites, and close political contacts with Western Europe.

Here again we return to the theme of political culture. The norm of politics in each country differs largely as a result of culture or cultures (again, as in

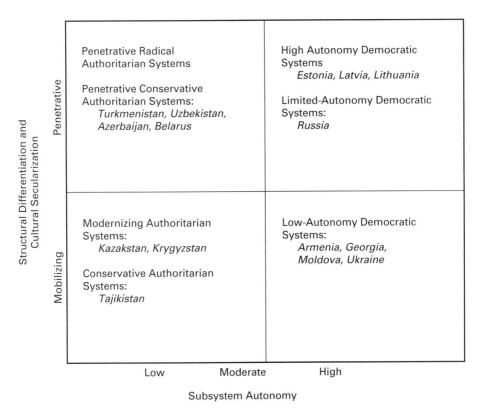

Figure 13.1 Political Organization and Cultural Development

Adopted from Gabriel A. Almond and G. Bingham Powell, *Comparative Politics: System Process, and Policy*, 2nd ed. (Boston: Little, Brown, 1978), p. 72.

the cases of fragmented, dichotomous, or even dominant political cultures). In the Baltic states the publics accept the goals of the political systems, particularly the advancement of democracy and joining of the European system of states. Consequently, issues such as elite change are expected rather than feared for their consequences. This hasn't prevented elites from trying to lead voters, but the potential for manipulation is greatly decreased due to the openness of the society and the public's awareness of political options and events. The upshot of all of this is a confluence of high levels of penetration among the public and subsystem autonomy of governing institutions justifying the placement of all three Baltic states in the upper-right quadrant of the model established in Chapter One.

In Russia these conditions are nowhere near as well-established, but the Russian Federation must still be considered as belonging within the same developmental context as the Baltics. Less pronounced structural differentiation and a less autonomous public situates Russia below the Baltics' conditions of political and economic development. It would seem that at any time Russia's internal conflicts—power sharing, the prospects of turning the clock back to the desired goals of an authoritarian elite—allow for the possibility that the Russian Federation be classified elsewhere. And yet, the Russian public displays a high level of political awareness, and a reluctance to roll over and play dead in the face of social (crime, nationalism), political (official corruption), or economic (declining standards of living) pressures. In this sense the Russian public finds itself somewhere between acquiescence on the one hand and a resolve to participate on the other. The Russian public's desire to participate has already once—in 1991—produced a dramatic alteration in political development. What is really important is not whether another chain of events such as that again takes place, but rather to what extent the public remains involved in determining leadership.

Again the point is not the degree of democracy attained by society. Some of the Eurasian systems have not moved substantially in either direction since independence in 1991. Of the five cases studied Uzbekistan is the state with the lowest civil participation and subsystem autonomy. All of the Central Asian states, due to their limitations on public penetration of the political process, and the lack of autonomous decision making by individuals, remain politically and economically undifferentiated. These states are only marginally outdone by Belarus which seemed since 1996, bent on returning to authoritarian governing patterns. Both the Belarusian president and public have been responsible for this course of events and it is uncertain if this system has either the desire or the energy to move much beyond its current status of development.

The most interesting questions remain those surrounding Armenia, Georgia, Moldova, and Ukraine all states with semblances of democratic and pluralistic procedures and yet not entirely free from authoritarian tendencies. What has been discerned in the case studies of Ukraine and Georgia is that political elites and the general public have not come to a consensus on national political and economic goals. Divisions in society are all too apparent in all four of these countries with political elites either too weak or unable to fully impose their wills upon the society. For their part, the citizens have not effectively responded to their new role of participation by calling their leaders to task. The designation of "fragmented political cultures" remains appropriate, much to the detriment of both governors and governed. These are systems with low-grade fevers unable to shake their viruses but not totally certain the sympathy they receive isn't worth the inconvenience.

Nothing in politics is static, even in the most controlling of societies. What can be seen to this point may change tomorrow and that should make even the most casual observer wary of hard and fast conclusions. Had our case studies been of Belarus, Azerbaijan, Lithuania, and Kyrgyzstan the results wouldn't be quite the same and yet not radically divergent from what has been depicted so far. The norm within each group of countries is what we sought and that apparently is what we got. What cannot be concluded is that the Baltic states will always remain democratic in form, that the western states are fated to be divided societies, that the Caucasus will be fraught with conflict, or that the Central Asian states are inclined towards authoritarian control. Each state goes its own way, but certainly within the constraints allowed by the regional and international environments.

Integration or Disintegration?

Given the differences that have emerged or reemerged between the fifteen successor states our justifications for discussing these states in the same contexts are no longer what they once were. The Baltic and Central Asian states in particular, while still being affected by their relations with the Russian Federation, can only marginally be described as part of the Russian political experience. The physical proximity of these states to Russia will always result in some need to accommodate that physical reality. For instance in the August 1998 economic crisis, Russian problems had very substantial impacts on the Baltic states, particularly Lithuania which saw its Russian and CIS markets accounting for forty-six percent of all of its exports dry up literally overnight.[1] But the inability of Russia to extend its power beyond its own borders—which is not the same thing as extending its *crises*—has altered the political equation. Equally important are the conditions which draw these states away from Russia, particularly cultural determinants. Again, the Baltic states have made the most conscious of efforts to redefine themselves as part of the general European culture. They will be limited in their endeavors for years to come by their geographic proximity to Russia, as well as by their largely differentiated ethnic Russian populations. Several Central Asian states, meanwhile, have found new interests in the Islamic *umma* (community of believers) and to some extent in a Pan-Turkic identity. In each case cultural forces pulling these states away from Russia are indeed strong, but economic conditions continue to draw them back together.

New groupings or associations of the Eurasian states are bound to develop in the not-too-distant future. At the time of independence there was only the CIS; since then a customs union has emerged within the CIS, as has the reintegration movement that finds support in Armenia, Belarus, and to some extent Russia. In 1997 another loose association called GUUAM—short for Georgia, Ukraine, Uzbekistan, Azerbaijan, and Moldova—took form in the region's headlines (Uzbekistan has since left it). Politics is not the first consideration in any of these organizations, although it may yet become so. Instead, economics has proven to be the most important area for discussions *among* states. In the twenty-first century we may reasonably expect even more variations of economic integration. And yet regional dissimilarities noted here threaten these nation-states with a continuation of the disintegration that began with the failure of the Soviet Union.

If anything can be counted upon as a means to disturb the status quo, it is nationalism, that over the last decade has proven to be more of a divisive factor within states than a unifier of peoples. And whereas the Russian Federation might take the opportunity to draw into its fold the twenty-five million or so Russians living in the Eurasian states, or what they refer to as the **Near Abroad,** it is also subject to separatism. Russian, Estonian, Georgian, Azerbaijani, and other national policy makers—and those of us analysts trying to square the Russian or Eurasian circles—would all be well-advised to examine carefully the dynamics at work in republics, regions, provinces, and districts. Whereas once there were excuses for avoiding any studies of what went on beneath the surface of Soviet politics (that is, studies of the fourteen former republics) due to a lack of information this can no longer be justified in the post-Soviet era.

And what of Russia? Again turning to the political culture/political economy model used here the Russian model can be categorized for the extent of transition it has experienced. In this sense, Russia is no different than any of the other states under consideration. Russia's population especially has remained largely detached from the political process and the factionalism represented within it. Whether manipulated by Yeltsin, Putin, Berezovskii, or Zyuganov, Russian politics is perceived cautiously by the average citizen most likely because they do perceive that manipulation is occurring. Russian politics may be taken too lightly if seen only in the context of political "saviors" such as Putin or Luzhkov, and although these types of elites may be part of a long-standing tradition in Russian history, it is not at all clear that this is what the public wants any longer. The extent of political pluralism demonstrated in just a few ways in Chapters Four and Five makes it clear that the political process is much more complex today than was the case during either the tsarist or communist periods. For that matter it would be a serious error to try to analyze Russian politics solely in bureaucratic terms; Chapter Six indicated the formalism of how the government works, but also stressed the dynamics of change that prevent us from making assessments based solely upon the bureaucratic factor. In this way again, it must be emphasized that Russia is a culturally differentiated political society that may or may not end up in a democratic construct. That in no way diminishes the facts of either system complexity, or that a rule of law society has emerged to some degree.

It would be very easy at this stage to leave you with some bland pronouncements about the future of politics in each of these states. Will the reform process continue with Putin in the Kremlin? Will the Duma become more conservative/revisionist based on the latest elections and the strength of the political left, or the Federation Council more complacent as Putin constricts that body's field of action? Russian politics are not much better defined when measured against former dependents as has been shown in Georgia and Ukraine. Shevardnadze's own passing from the political field leaves us with no greater number of answers especially in light of the culture of secessionism which has wracked that country since its inception (a factor Russia only barely has to accommodate). Is this the norm for Caucasus politics generally or might those states' publics demand another way? Azerbaijan's manipulated presidential election in late 1998, and the assassinations of half of the Armenian government in 1999 indicate a negative response, but little else about how these societies might develop. Politics and economics in Ukraine could be superceded by a sharp turn toward authoritarianism by the president, or the public might continue to take a middle course as it has in previous elections.

Compare these conditions to Uzbekistan where Karimov has estimated that personal strong-man rule is compatible to the dominant Central Asian political culture. But does this form of governance accommodate public demands, especially given the radicalization of politics with the exporting of Islamic fundamentalism from neighboring Afghanistan? This problem proved worrisome enough that the Uzbek political elite permitted their territory to be used in support of the American campaign against Osama bin Laden and Afghanistan's Taliban regime in 2001. This must be taken as a defense of Karimov's methods of governance and control, as well as his vision for Uzbekistan. In general, each of these systems poses puzzles that could well be solved within a short space of time or linger for years to come.

What is apparent is that each political society has characteristics—ethnic identity, economic growth or contraction, historic greatness or repression—which tell us something about potentials for change. Here is a brief check list of problems, conditions, and developments that may now be considered characteristic of Russian and Eurasian politics:

- In the five states examined here the undeniable fact of political life is the continuity of these countries' political cultures. Whether coming from a background of dependence or dominance all have managed to shape a general culture reflecting attitudes toward participation, governorship, and types of policy which have had profound impacts on the practice of politics, and from which they cannot divorce themselves.
- Russia is a pluralist society which now has to accept not just this point but the reality that differences among peoples are sometimes hard to take. Conflict is a constant companion to compromise as shown by the rise of Russian fascism, nationalism, and intolerance toward the diversity of Russian society.
- The Russian political system, and to varying degrees the Eurasian systems, have become accustomed to openness. This increasingly means the public demands explanation and accountability for political actions regardless of who is in power. But the road is a long and sometimes dangerous one for such types of participation in many of these states, and the expectation for immediate changes should be tempered by insight rather than simply expectation.
- The Russian political system is marked by diversity, but after a decade it is the presidency and less so the individual which has become important. Both Boris Yeltsin and Vladimir Putin have tried to articulate their visions for the institution (Yeltsin in three books, Putin in one) but actions speak louder than words. Thus the presidency's future hinges more on Yeltsin's choice of force instead of compromise in 1993, and Putin's harassment of the independent media rather than how well the constitution reads.
- For good or ill the Russian economy has been opened up to a waiting world. It will be difficult indeed to close it off again. The Russian public has encountered deprivation and despair in the last decade unlike anything

since the period of collectivization and industrialization of the 1920s–1930s. And yet, the often-observed capacity of the Russian public for enduring hardship is not a logical means for evaluating Russia's long-term political development. It is, in fact, too much of a stereotype to be taken seriously in analysis.

- The Baltic states remain linked to Russia. They want little from their mammoth neighbor beyond trade and respect for their sovereignty. Expecting more than most of the other Eurasian states they have eagerly plunged into the maelstrom of European politics for both physical security from Russia and for the specific intention of redefining their societies as European.

- Ukraine has tried to cast itself as a state in the middle of Europe and as a neutral actor, but Ukrainian politicians and public alike have let too many opportunities to achieve these goals slip by. Ukraine remains today a state with a poorly developed sense of national identity unwilling, or unable to sever its dependence upon Russia and wary of what awaits it as a state with both an independent and European identity.

- The most volatile of regions, the Caucasus and Georgia in particular, have not reconciled the concepts of nation with those of the state. Separatism continues to haunt the state, and Russian involvement for the purposes of reestablishing its regional power status promises years of instability and stunted development for Georgia. The political elites cannot see their way clear to a common consensus of the state's problems or needs and thereby further the cycle of conflict.

- Uzbekistan's political elite are in that country's driver's seat for as long as popular will is poorly expressed and can be tightly controlled. Outside investment and foreign appetites for oil and natural gas are most likely to keep the regime in power. The elite are, however, only poorly sheltered from underlying social forces and political reality may catch up to them in a messy fashion.

To those who will see the regions or physical boundaries used throughout this book as no longer useful to the study of Russia the original premise of this study should be remembered: Russia, studied in the context of comparison with its Eurasian counterparts validates more than confuses the picture. Russia and the Eurasian states will never again be exactly what they were. That old world is fading fast in memories while the new political and economic realms fairly cry out for new evaluations. Russia and Eurasia will always stir up a world of images; the peoples, however, are of real flesh and bone. It remains a complicated task to reconcile the tsars, khans, communist party leaders, demagogues and democrats, onion-domed churches, vast steppe lands, towering mountains, and arctic wastes within a common framework. As with the restoration of an ancient fresco, the smoke and grit of the Soviet era are even now being removed to reveal a mosaic of peoples, politics, and cultures of strikingly vibrant colors. Hopefully this book has enhanced these features and our general understanding of politics.

Questions for Consideration

1. Do Russia and the Eurasian states have a common future? Does it make any sense to try to "type" Russia and the Eurasian states within a similar framework?

2. Should the Russian Federation be evaluated according to standards that are representative of the Baltic and western states or those for Central Asia and the Caucasus?

3. Do the continuing prospects of political instability within some Eurasian states run the risk of damaging political stability in others?

4. What form of integrative strategies may emerge in the Eurasian space which might preclude a revival of the Soviet Union? Which states seem most inclined toward a closer relationship with the Russian Federation?

5. If political culture is the undeniable fact of political life in Russia and the Eurasian states, how might this sharpen or lessen political conflict in these states?

Endnotes

1. DPA cited in *RFE/RL Newsline*, 23 September 1998.

Index